What people are saying about

Meditations from the Classics

Each of the meditations contained in this book begins with a carefully selected passage from the ancient classical writers. These stories blend well with the author's musings and the scripture selections that accompany them. The closing words are sure to uplift the reader.
The Very Reverend Robert F. Coniglio, Rector Emmanuel Episcopal Church, Physician Associate, Eastern Shore Rural Health Systems

Anxiety taints every corner of people's lives today. It does not get any better than turning to the classical writers of the past to find genuine peace and contentment. David R. Denny has hit a home run with this devotional book that links the lives of ancient people with the Light of the Bible.
Gene Albert, curator of the Tennessee Bible Museum, founder of the Christian Heritage Museum in Hagerstown, Maryland, and expert and aficionado of ancient texts, peoples, and customs of the past

T0418247

Meditations from the Classics

Ancient Voices for Modern Listeners

Meditations from the Classics

Ancient Voices for Modern Listeners

David R. Denny

MANTRA
BOOKS

Winchester, UK
Washington, USA

JOHN HUNT PUBLISHING

First published by Mantra Books, 2023
Mantra Books is an imprint of John Hunt Publishing Ltd., No. 3 East Street, Alresford
Hampshire SO24 9EE, UK
office@jhpbooks.com
www.johnhuntpublishing.com
www.mantra-books.net

For distributor details and how to order please visit the 'Ordering' section on our website.

ISBN: 978 1 80341 297 9
978 1 80341 298 6 (ebook)
Library of Congress Control Number: 2022910822

A CIP catalogue record for this book is available from the British Library.

Design: Lapiz Digital Services

UK: Printed and bound by CPI Group (UK) Ltd, Croydon, CR0 4YY
Printed in North America by CPI GPS partners

We operate a distinctive and ethical publishing philosophy in
all areas of our business, from our global network of authors to
production and worldwide distribution.

Dedication
To Alice, the beloved voice

Introduction

It's faint, but I can still hear my grandma's voice mingling with the Georgia crickets. She often rocked on her rickety share cropper's porch at night, where she spun personal tales of hardship and joy. Surrounded by cornfields eight feet tall on a dirt road to Doles, a nowhere town with a single intersection, she sing-songed her way through the night hours, her words often the black keys.

But when the Georgia wind stops and the crickets sleep, I hear voices from before the Great Depression, melodies that tug at time's ancient skirt. I hear Horace rambling down the Sacred Way toward the Roman forum, pondering trifles and trying in vain to rid himself of a pest who won't leave him alone. I smile at Horace's satirical jabs at the stranger who ignores the hints.

As those notes fade, a politician rises timidly in the Roman senate. This newly almost-minted emperor, Tiberius, unused to power, unfurls his fake humility, practicing the art of humblebrag. "I could never replace Augustus," he shrieks.

Then, while musing on Tiberius' thin strategy, I hear, in a time long before Rome, the tinkling of a golden key crafted by Hephaestus dangling from Queen Hera's neck. Approaching her boudoir door made of Acacia wood, the lock submits, and heavy hinges creak. Sitting before a beveled mirror, she anoints her delicate skin with olive oil and ambrosia and mutters midnight schemes against Zeus.

Ah, the voices.

There is so much intrigue in the lives that preceded ours. Far from forgotten, they live again in these **Meditations from the Classics**, daily remembrances of a living continuum that binds us with them. So pause with your morning coffee, walk past grandma's porch to the classics' pulsing theater, and sip wisdom from an ancient fountain.

David R. Denny. Ph.D.

Day 1

***

Absence (AD 10)
Ovid, *Metamorphoses*, 11:452–480

***

King Ceyx stood forlornly before his wife, who trembled with fear. "I must go to Claros, my darling," he said. "The oracle's guidance will help me find my brother."

Alcyone objected, her face pale as boxwood. She couldn't stop weeping and tried three times to offer objections but could not speak. Finally, though sobbing, broken syllables tumbled forth. "Please don't cross the sea, my love. Go overland. I have read too many words on empty tombs and seen broken timbers on endless shorelines."

Ceyx, moved deeply, touched her tears. "I will return in two months, my love. I promise." They embraced, but all she could say was "farewell" before fainting.

The young rowers, eager to test the waves, churned the waters with strong strokes. Alcyone saw him wave to her high upon the distant, bobbing stern. She waved back, and the ship sailed on until she could see him no more. Still, she watched until the sail tip slowly vanished into the mist.

Turning homeward, she returned, ghostlike, to her lonely cottage and flung herself upon the couch, feeling the grip of his *absence*. Now he was gone, perhaps forever.

***

Farewells poison the soul, leaving us spiraling ever downward, questioning our existence. Alcyone's worst fears came true.

Her husband's ship sank in a midnight storm, making *absence* permanent.

After the Passover, as night shrouded the streets, Jesus strolled solemnly toward death, promising his absence would be temporary:

***

"If I go and prepare a place for you, I will come again and receive you to Myself, that where I am, there you may be also" (Jn. 14:3).

***

Tie your absence to God's promises and live.

***

"Absence is to love what wind is to fire;
it extinguishes the small, it enkindles the great."
Roger de Rabutin

Day 2

Accidents (AD 10)
Ovid, *Metamorphoses*, 10:183

***

Apollo and Hyacinthus faced off in a sporting contest beside the quiet Eurotas River, charting its pleasant course through the Spartan valley. The contestants, full of cheer, rubbed themselves down with oil, each claiming victory before even picking up the discus.

Apollo threw first, hurling the missile high into the clouds, urging it on until it began a distant descent. The young Hyacinthus, anxious to take his turn, ran to retrieve the falling discus. As it hit the earth, it bounced once and slammed into the face of the lad. Shuddering, he slumped to his knees and then, bleeding profusely, collapsed into a quivering huddle, his features pale and lifeless.

Aghast, Apollo desperately applied healing herbs to the wound, but to no avail. The lad lay in a deadly heap, the crimson gash beyond cure. Apollo grieved that day, accepting blame but knowing it was only an *accident*.

"I will never forget you, my friend," he cried sorrowfully. As Apollo trudged away, bright crimson flowers sprouted where puddles of blood had stained the ground.

***

Accidents are a part of life. Often difficult to accept, they weave themselves into our lives, often at inopportune times. The tears by the Eurotas River follow us to Troas, where Paul lingered for five days. A throng of disciples sat crammed in a synagogue listening to Paul preach. One boy, perched high on the third floor, fell asleep and hit the floor, dead. Such a tragic accident! Paul wept.

***

"But Paul went down and fell upon him, and after embracing him, he said, 'Do not be troubled, for his life is in him'" (Acts 20:10).

***

Turn your latest accident into praise today.

***

"Accident is the name of the greatest of all inventors."
Mark Twain

Day 3

***

Accountable (AD 24)
Tacitus, *The Annals of Imperial Rome*, 4:20

***

The charge against the Roman general Gaius Silius was stunning.

He had served valiantly for seven years fighting the Gauls and won many decisive battles. But the trumped-up charges claimed that while he fought Gauls, his wife, Sosia, had been out spending a fortune in the marketplaces.

"It wasn't her money," claimed the prosecutors. "Oh no. She stole money from local village tax collections. Your wife was out of control, and now you must pay!"

The official Roman decree, manufactured by senate sycophants, stated that all officials, however free they might be of guilt themselves, must be *accountable* for their wives' wrongdoing.

The general remained silent as the prosecutors smeared him before Tiberius. Finally, he stood and pointed the finger at his accusers. "It's all a lie!" he told the court emphatically. "None of it is true."

Sensing his demise, he strolled home in silent rage and killed himself that evening. The next day in court, undeterred, the prosecutors called for the banishment of his wife, Sosia Galla, leaving her children destitute.

***

Too bad St. Paul wasn't in court on that day. He would have urged everyone to take a break, breathe deeply, and find a way

5

to understand Sosia (Rom. 14:1). He would have stood and reminded everyone that, in the end, we must all be *accountable* before the judge.

***

"But why do you judge your brother? So then each of us will give an account of himself to God" (Rom. 14:12).

***

Quiet! God is summoning you to the throne.

***

"It's the one thing you can control. You are responsible for how people remember you—or don't. So don't take it lightly."
Kobe Bryant

Day 4

Accusations (138 BC)
Juvenal, *Satire*, 1:150–171

***

Accusations scorch the soul, that is, the guilty soul.

In Rome's first century, corruption was rampant. Juvenal mentioned a renowned criminal who had poisoned three uncles and then, with his newfound wealth, rode majestically about town in their gaily-decorated litters, swaying on the road like royalty.

"You better seal your lips," warned Juvenal. "Confront this criminal, and you won't live to regret it. You'll be a torch in a tunic smoldering and smoking like the other brave victims who dared to stand against evil. Shush! No confrontational *accusations* if you value your life."

Juvenal hated vulgar Rome and admired the ancient satirist Lucilius who once spoke against society with a fearless scowl. "When Lucilius made an accusation, the guilty sweated," smirked Juvenal. "I can almost hear his crackling words today as he tackled the vices of yesteryear. He courted confrontation and often drew his verbal sword, growling at guilty scoundrels. When Lucilius cornered a shifty politician, that man's face would shift into a crimson blush, his soul frozen under the satirist's pointed finger. The crook's brow would drip with sweat, and his sputtering lies would slither down his satin cloak."

***

Sometimes, a brave critic needs to step forward. Be careful, though. *Accusations* must rest upon truth's bedrock. Paul told Timothy to make sure he had at least a handful of reliable witnesses before making an accusation. But, if the case was solid and harm was polluting the congregation, then speak with authority:

***

"rebuke in the presence of all so that the rest also will be fearful of sinning" (1 Tim. 5:19–20).

***

Be the whistleblower if you feel the cause is just. But be careful.

***

"Guilt has very quick ears to an accusation."
Henry Fielding

Day 5

***

Admiration (1177 BC)
Virgil, *Aeneid*, 8:150–170

***

Aeneas' warships crawled along the winding Tiber, its surface smooth as glass until, beneath a blazing noonday sun, they saw the citadel. Perched high on Rome's peaks, it loomed above a few scattered huts with pitched roofs. Steering toward the bank, Aeneas disembarked and, with a small band of warriors, approached the settlement.

A grand festival honoring Hercules sparkled with merry villagers in a grove just outside the fortress walls. The notable citizens, burning incense to the gods, ceased worshipping and raced for their weapons. Aeneas extended an olive branch and declared his peaceful intention. "We're looking for Evander, the king of this realm."

After friendly greetings, Aeneas retold his woeful story. All the while, King Evander sat quietly studying the whole man as he talked, observing the details of his face, his eyes, hearing a familiar timbre in his voice.

"I remember your father so clearly," the king said. "When I was but a lad, I *admired* Anchises, who visited my homeland in Arcadia. I worshipped all the Trojan chiefs then, but none was taller than your father, who walked with such regal pride through our town's streets. How thrilled I was to take his hand and guide him through the village. When he left, he gave me a fine quiver of Lycian arrows and a gold-embroidered scarf."

***

Admiration's shadow often lingers through generations. It can lift a nation, inspire hope, and mold a generation of hero-worshippers. How far does your shadow cast?

Saul, like tall Anchises, inspired all who gazed upon his youthful promise.

***

"He had a son whose name was Saul, a choice and handsome man,... from his shoulders and up he was taller than any of the people" (1 Sam. 9:2).

***

Be admirable today. Inspire the world.

***

"We live by admiration, hope, and love."
William Wordsworth

Day 6

***

Adornment (1184 BC)
Homer, *Iliad*, 14:155–190

***

Hera of the golden throne prepared to set her trap. She would lure Zeus, her husband whom she loathed, to her bed and there, rock him to sleep, preventing his nefarious deeds against the Greek army.

Having set her mind, she glided softly over the palace floors and opened her boudoir with a secret key made only for her by Hephaestus, her son. Quickly locking the bolt behind her, she cleansed her skin from all impurities and then anointed herself with olive oil, scented with heaven's ambrosia. The fragrance, like a divine hymn, filled her suite with delicious melodies as she plaited her hair that flowed river-like in golden tresses past her waist.

Standing, she selected a wondrously embroidered robe made cleverly with intricate designs by Athene's hand. *Adorning* herself in the delicious frock, she fastened it about her bosom with golden clasps and then circled it all with a thousand-tasseled girdle. Glancing meticulously into the bronze mirror, she selected several glistening pendants reflecting lantern lights and fastened them to her ears. Sighing with satisfaction, she tossed a lovely new veil over her head, slipped her sandals on, and rose, whispering a prayer to Aphrodite.

***

This classic frieze of an ancient woman preparing for romantic battle confirms how little human behavior has changed for millennia. A beautiful princess will always need a secret key and a bottle of perfume. But Peter gives us a spiritual perspective on *adornment*:

***

"Your adornment must not be merely external—braiding the hair, and wearing gold jewelry or putting on dresses" (1 Pet. 3:3).

***

Your truest beauty lies within.

***

"Adornment is never anything except a reflection of the heart." *Coco Chanel*

Day 7

Affliction (550 BC)
Herodotus, *The Persian Wars*, 1:175

***

The priestess of Athene strolled nervously through the corridors of the Parthenon. Testing the spirits high atop the acropolis, she sensed trouble far away. Beautifully robed in her flowing garments, she felt dark clouds gathering on the distant village of Pedasa that hovered high above the Asian coastline overlooking the Adriatic. Starring off toward the East as twilight settled over Athens, she knew the little town atop the isolated peak would soon face the Persian army's wrath.

She touched her face and felt the stubble of a budding beard. Only thrice had this happened, and each time it had been a horrible portent of impending *affliction* to Pedasa and its close neighbors. Within a few days, with a thick beard wet with tears, she grieved for her friends far away.

Pedasa stubbornly resisted the Persian army and, in a short time, fell, slaughtered by the hand of Harpagus, the Persian general. But still, I see the fading shadows of the bearded priestess weeping alone in the distant Parthenon. It's an odd tale, but her empathy reminds me of another place centuries later.

***

Let us step quietly into the small village of Bethany high above the distant Jordan River valley. We notice that Jesus was mourning Lazarus' *affliction*. Visibly shaken by the cacophony

13

of wails and moans near the tomb, Jesus shared His grief openly. Overcome by sorrow, He wept as the tears trailed down His bearded cheeks.

***

"Jesus wept. So the Jews were saying 'See how He loved him!'" (Jn. 11:35–36).

***

Beard growing? That's a good sign!

***

"Could a greater miracle take place than for us to look through each other's eyes for an instant?"
Henry David Thoreau

Day 8

***

Alarms (1177 BC)
Virgil, *Aeneid*, 7:480–530

***

Allecto, stirring up rage against the Trojans, flew to the top of a steep-pitched shippon and gazed mischievously over the countryside. Her hair swarming with black vipers, she scanned the vales beyond as she lifted her crooked horn. Then, with a full demonic breath, she blew the *alarm* through the still evening air, a shrill cry ricocheting off distant mountain faces. The surreal Lake of Diana heard, as did the white Nar River and the springs of Velinus near Rome.

Hardened countrymen heard the summons and, quicker than thought, raced to snatch their weapons from dark sheds. Brandishing fire-hardened stakes or knotty shillelaghs, those wooden cudgels born by mountain men, an army swarmed the hills, racing toward the call.

Allecto, that hellish Fury, sneered, watching sinister forces rally to battle. Peaceful men and women, now drugged by the scent of violence, clamored to find the cause, racing down country lanes.

Battled-hardened Trojans, sensing trouble, scrambled to face this new foe. Perplexed Ascanius, the forbidden stag slung over his shoulder, greeted the frantic soldiers who formed a protective circle about him, preparing for the assault. Soon, the forest clashed with bristling swords, sending steel sparks heavenward.

***

With endless *alarms* sounding through the modern world, it is easy to disregard these clattering sounds. I once lived in a country parsonage beside a firehouse. Eventually, I got to where I never heard the screeching horn atop its building. But every spiritual pilgrim knows to listen for the final trumpet sound:

***

"For the Lord Himself will descend from heaven with a shout, with the voice of the archangel and with the trumpet of God, and the dead in Christ will rise first" (1 Thess. 4:16).

***

Listen with discernment. Some alarms are real.

***

"We live in the midst of alarms."
Abraham Lincoln

Day 9

***

Alliances (1177 BC)
Virgil, *Aeneid*, 10:125–200

***

Midnight pulled Aeneas' desperate ship northward through the chilly Tyrrhenian Sea. Tortured by necessities' temporary abandonment of his countrymen beside the Tiber, he paced the poop deck restless and praying. News of the imminent destruction of his battlements on Rome's hills plagued his every breath. He must find help, an alliance with some mighty king.

Hemmed in upon their burning ramparts, Aeneas' besieged forces fought on, awaiting news of their sea-bound commander and visionary. Fire now encircled the walls as Turnus's forces closed in for the massacre. Within the fortress, the Trojan men stood hopeless and dispirited as thinning forces manned the heights. Standing tall among them was Ascanius, Aeneas' son. He glowed among the destruction, his hair falling about his milk-white neck. Like an artist's hero painted in bold strokes, he fought for Troy's future, relishing his father's dreams for this new homeland.

At midnight, Aeneas' ship plowed into an Etruscan beach. Leaping into the surf, he ran toward distant campfires. There, he told King Tarchon of his plight and sought an *alliance*. "These same pillaging forces will come soon and destroy your Etruscan villages as well," he warned. The king agreed and within hours, the mighty bronze-beaked naval vessels set sail, guided by midnight stars, bringing deliverance.

***

Alliances among friends, those diamond-studded chains, lock hearts forever. Without them, we wander the dark nights alone, vulnerable. Such a bond fused David and Jonathan's souls through difficult times.

***

"So Jonathan made an *alliance* with the house of David ... because he loved him as he loved his own life" (1 Sam. 20:16–17).

***

Pledge *your* life to someone today.

***

"When a man makes alliance with the Almighty, giants look like grasshoppers."
Vance Havner

Day 10

***

Alphabet (AD 47)

Tacitus, *The Annals of Imperial Rome*, 11:14

***

Claudius, the Roman emperor, stared uneasily at the letters of the Latin *alphabet*. Something was missing. He wet his quill and began doodling on some old parchment paper, first drawing the letter C and attaching a backward C to its spine. The two Cs, back to back, looked strange but tantalizing. It would combine two sounds into one. After all, the Greeks did this with their letter psi. So why couldn't he?

Next, he flipped an F on its head and turned it backward. This would take the place of that awful W. It would be simply the U of W. He clapped his hands with glee. Making up letters that would shape history was exhilarating. The world would change forever with the power of these new letters.

Inspired, he added one more. He took the H and chopped off the right side. What was left was half an H, a mystical form to be sure, but it resonated with a powerful euphony that pleased him.

With these three new letters, he began using them at once on city boundary markers, followed by inscriptions on sacred temples and public buildings. After his death, however, they quickly became obsolete.

***

Jesus, too, doodled with the *alphabet*. The Pharisees dragged an adulterous woman into the temple and threw her at His feet.

"She's guilty," they cried, their fingers gripping stones. Jesus merely stooped and began to etch letters on the temple floor that whispered of grace and leniency.

His letters live today, while Claudius' letters sigh no more.

***

"But Jesus stooped down and with His finger wrote on the ground" (Jn 8:6).

***

What will your letters to a weary world say today?

***

"I knew the alphabet. Maybe I could be a writer."
Hubert Selby Jr.

Day 11

Ambition (424 BC)
Aristophanes, *Knights*, 140–200

***

Tired of sitting in that dark, powerless corner at work? Maybe you need a broader perspective, a little *ambition* booster. Go ahead and stand on your desk and claim the world about you.

This very opportunity tempted a poor, greasy sausage maker in ancient Athens. A few politically clever slaves surrounded him as he chopped away at a pile of sheep guts. They looked him over carefully and smiled. "He would make a great replacement to the king we have now," they said.

"Hey, you!" they shouted at him, "how would you like to be king of Athens someday?"

The bloody meat cutter looked utterly confused. "Who? Me?"

"Yes, you!" they screamed with enthusiasm demanding he stand on his sausage table and look around. "You see those islands out in the sea?"

"Yeah, I see them. So what?"

"You see the towns and the shipping ports and boats crowding the harbor?"

"Yeah."

"Do you see the marketplaces, the Pnyx, and the courts?"

"Yeah."

"It will soon all be yours. You will be the greatest man on earth!"

***

Be cautious with *ambition*. It's a powerful temptress that can, at times, lead us astray. Jesus also stood and looked at the kingdoms of the world.

***

"Again, the devil took Him to a very high mountain, and showed Him all the kingdoms of the world and their glory; and he said to Him, 'all these things will I give You, if You fall down and worship me.' Then Jesus said to him, 'Go, Satan!'" (Matt. 4:8–9).

***

Don't stand on the sausage table too long. You might fall off the edge.

***

"Ambition is believing in yourself, even when no one else in the world does."
Anonymous

Day 12

***

Anxieties (423 BC)
Aristophanes, *Clouds*, Act 1, Scene 1

***

An old moon drifted sleepily over the Athenian night sky. Everyone slept but the old man Strepsiades who tossed restlessly, listening to his son snore heavily in the room down the hall. Life used to be so simple for him when he was a bachelor living in the country. He tended to his sheep, ate blissful garden meals, and sipped Rapsani, a red wine from the gods. But then he married a city girl from Athens who encouraged her son to race horses and spend money—the old man's money.

The bills and creditors haunted Strepsiades night and day. He seemed to live at his little desk, pouring over the bank statements beneath a waxing moon, wondering how life got so screwed up. "All my son wants to do is wear his hair long and work on his chariot."

Pacing restlessly in the wee hours of the morning, his *anxiety* rising, he ordered his slave to bring him the ledger books one more time along with a lamp. "Let's see," he muttered, running his finger down the page, "what exactly do I owe now?"

***

Seventeen thousand theater fans sat laughing at Strepsiades' crumbling life. The theater, built in the shadow of the Dionysian Temple beneath the Acropolis, rocked with revelry as they followed the antics of Strepsiades sweating over his bills at night.

Jesus, several centuries later, stood in the bow of a small Galilean fishing boat. The shoreline gallery pressed in without laughing to hear these words on *anxiety* from the Master:

***

"The worries of the world will destroy your lives if you let them" (Matt. 13:22).

***

Anxieties will make your life a tragic comedy if you let them.

***

"Every moment is a fresh beginning."
T.S. Elliot

Day 13

***

Apology (1184 BC)
Homer, *Iliad*, 4:326–360

***

Far off, across bloodied plains near the Trojan walls, heated battle cries erupted, summoning all noble fighters. But Odysseus heard none of it. Loitering near the rear, he and his men, brave of heart, waited, pacing impatiently. It was there that King Agamemnon saw them from a distance, idling as if a coward's shadow shrouded their hearts.

The king, his chariot wheels spinning dust as he rallied the rear lines to charge, stopped before the warrior. His temper flaring, he spat vulgar abuses at Odysseus for lingering. "What are you doing back here, twiddling your thumbs? The battle cry has sounded!" The king paused, vitriol dripping, as he gazed impudently at the coward. "You were pretty happy to come to any feast I held when peace ruled the land. You loved to drink my wine and eat the roasted meats I provided."

Odysseus stiffened. "How dare you speak to me this way. I'm no coward. I wait here for the trumpet's sound." Picking up his spear and shield, he glared at the king.

Agamemnon blushed, sensing his error but glad to see this angry outburst. "Please forgive me and accept my humble *apology*, valiant heart. I see I misjudged you." Glancing heavenward, he continued. "I will make amends for my mistake."

***

Apologies are best served fresh. They tend to stale over the years, but even at life's end still serve a noble purpose. Such was the case with aged Jacob, who, on his death bed, offered Joseph a family apology.

***

"Please forgive, I beg you, the transgression of your brothers and their sin, for they did you wrong" (Gen. 50:17).

***

No more rehearsing. Apologize today.

***

"Love is one long apology."
Marilyn L. Rice

Day 14

***

Appearances (AD 60)
Petronius, *The Satyricon*, 5:38

***

Julius sat nervously in the special seat for freed slaves who had struck it rich. This dinner out with his prestigious friends was a big deal. Only he knew the forbidden secret: he was bankrupt!

It had taken some time to wriggle into this high society, but he had done it with his funeral business. Everyone got used to sending him grieving clients. "Just see Julius," they would say over their dinner martinis. "He'll fix you up." But business had turned sour on him, and he had to keep up *appearances*.

He glanced about at his neighbor's expansive dining room filled this evening with snoots who lived in mansions uptown. He had once hosted such a dinner where he served boars roasted whole with pheasants while chefs and pastry cooks all rushed about. But no more. He was done. No one knew.

Quietly desperate, he was selling off his furniture and possessions just to keep afloat. But he couldn't let anybody know, so he had a clever idea. "I'll post in the morning newspaper that I'm having an auction of my spare furniture. That will throw them off for a while."

***

Appearances matter in our modern times. How can you be seen driving that old clunker or wearing last year's dress? But living false lives takes its toll. Jesus just shook His head at it all. He had "nowhere to lay His head" (Lk. b 9:58). Jesus looks past our

27

failures and loneliness and bids us come to Him no matter our current lot in life.

***

"Come to Me, all who are weary and heavy-laden, and I will give you rest" (Matt. 11:28).

***

Somebody, please text Julius and tell him Jesus already knows.

***

"The greatest wisdom is seeing through appearances."
Buddha

Day 15

***

Applause (AD 65)

Tacitus, *Annals of Imperial Rome*, 16:3

***

Nero, having completed his poetic reading, stood center stage, waiting for the *applause* to end. The spectators, sycophants to the soul, demanded Nero display all his accomplishments. Without hesitation, he called for the lyre and tuned the strings meticulously as the restless crowd settled back, awaiting the symphony of one.

Once the pitch was perfect, the artist plucked a melody that fell from the heavenly deities' laps. Adhering to the rules of genuine harpists, he stood while strumming and used only his robe sleeve to wipe away perspiration, allowing no moisture from his mouth or nose to drip callously to the stage floor.

When finished, he awaited the verdict while resting on bended knee, pretending trepidation as if the ruling might be perilous to his reputation. Familiar with professional performances, the audience cheered wildly as Nero waited on the judges. The crowd applauded in a rhythmic cadence, urging the panel's highest award.

Tourists from the remote towns who didn't understand the game rose in disgust to leave, finding the entire spectacle outrageous. However, guardsmen cuffed their heads, forcing them to sit. Tacitus could only cover his face at this national disgrace.

***

In faraway Palestine on the Roman Empire's fringes, I hear the sweet strings of another lyre. Nothing duplicitous here, only the soft sounds of God's praise from David's melody. When finished, nature erupts spontaneously in genuine *applause*.

***

"Sing praises to the LORD with the lyre, with the lyre and the sound of melody.... Let the rivers clap their hands, let the mountains sing together for joy before the LORD" (Ps. 98:5–8).

***

The sycophant's symphony always ends in disgrace.

***

"You must be prepared to work always without applause."
Ernest Hemingway

Day 16

***

Ascensions (1177 BC)
Virgil, *Aeneid*, 9:630–660

***

Scarcely had the arrow left the young prince's bow and split the head of vulgar Numanus when Apollo thundered congratulations from heaven. "More power to you, Ascanius!" said the god. "Troy was never big enough for you." Then Apollo drifted down from glory's gates and assumed the shape of Butes, Ascanius' aged personal aid. He had the same voice, complexion, and white hair along with his battle-worn armor that boasted of past accomplishments.

"You've done well for yourself," he said to the lad. "Great Apollo commends your fighting spirit and this sweet first victory on the battlefield." But then Butes backed slowly away with a warning in his eyes. "But now, my prince, you must retreat from war's dangers. No more fighting. Seek your higher purpose."

Having uttered these mysteries, Apollo *ascended* as he spoke, his voice blending with the clouds until he vanished from sight. The commanders and field soldiers recognized Apollo, hearing the rattle of his quiver as he left. Taking the warning to heart, they deterred Ascanius from further battle, leaving the youngster yearning for war's exploits.

***

Ascensions change history, forcing us to reconsider our purpose in life. When Jesus vanished above the Mt. of Olives, He challenged His followers to receive the Spirit and revel in a revolutionary vision. No more petty battlefield jaunts; instead, each breath would be divinely inspired, each task heaven sent.

***

"but you will receive power when the Holy Spirit has come upon you; and you shall be My witnesses both in Jerusalem, and in all Judea and Samaria, and even to the remotest part of the earth" (Acts 1:8).

***

Find ascension's inspiration and change the world.

***

"There's always another level up. There's always another ascension."
Elizabeth Gilbert

Day 17

***

Assumptions (546 BC)
Herodotus, *The Persian Wars*, 1:91

***

Croesus, once king of Sardis, an Asian city renowned for wealth, now rose each morning shackled with a heavy chain. His humiliating loss to Cyrus, king of Persia, chained him forever to some critical false *assumptions* he once made about his life. One day he approached Cyrus with this humble request. "Your highness, may I make a wish?"

Having grown to respect the fallen king, the king granted it readily. "Ask me for anything, Croesus, and I will grant it."

Croesus thanked the potentate and made this petition: "May I send these shackles to Delphi where the Greek gods reside and ask them why they tricked me and cost me my kingdom?"

Cyrus granted the request, and after several weeks, the delegation dumped the shackles at Apollo's feet in the Delphian temple. The temple priestess gazed contemptuously at the pile of metal and made a quick retort:

"Apollo did not trick you. He told you this: 'If Croesus attacks the Persian king, he will destroy a great kingdom.'" The priestess paused, clucking. "But Croesus never asked which kingdom!'"

***

Ah, the *assumption*! Croesus never bothered to probe a little more about this cryptic reply. Instead, he assumed the empire to fall was Persia. But alas, it was his own!

Ancient mirrors of the Egyptians and Greeks were often polished bronze, yielding distorted images. Assumptions sometimes flicker in dark mirrors that are difficult to interpret. It's easy to get a false impression.

***

"For now we see in a mirror dimly, but then face to face; now I know in part, but then I will know fully just as I also have been fully known" (1 Cor. 13:12).

***

Put your shadowed mirror down and guard your assumptions.

***

"Assumptions are the termites of relationships."
Henry Winkler

Day 18

Astray (1184 BC)
Virgil, *Aeneid*, 2: 230–250

***

The sleek, wooden horse crept slowly toward the Scaean Gate, where joy swept the citizens into a religious delirium never before seen in Troy. The shrines, festooned with floral rainbows, watched as leading men aided in toppling portions of the impregnable walls, laying open the city's soul. Rollers were placed under the beast, and hemp hawsers around the creature's neck pulled it forward in methodic spurts.

Bit by bit, the mechanical horse, its belly filled with venom, jockeyed through the yawning walls and onto the inner streets. Boys and virgin girls escorted the horse forward, singing psalms, joyfully gripping the traces as it trundled toward the metropolis' center beneath the great shrine. Often, as it stopped and then jerked forward, its stomach jangled with menacing clangs. The discordant notes seemed but angelic melodies to those who persevered ever upward, madly led *astray* by a mirage fed by self-deception.

When the Trojan horse finally settled into its resting place before the temple, Casandra, the priestess, stepped forward. Silence fell over the multitude as she cried out warnings, ripping the rainbows from every happy face. But Casandra's pessimism drifted among the chuckling crowd. No one ever listened to Casandra.

***

I can hear now the priestess's shrill voice, echoing among the temple pillars, spilling down its marbled entrance to the milling audience. She bore Apollo's curse that though she could predict the future, no one would believe her. Isaiah, like Cassandra, roared, but all went *astray*.

***

"All of us like sheep have gone astray, each of us had turned to his own way" (Isa. 53:6).

***

Careful! You're starring with gullible glances at the horse.

***

"Every day people are straying away from the church and going back to God."
Lenny Bruce

Day 19

***

Atheist (423 BC)
Aristophanes, *Clouds*, 250–370

***

Strepsiades, aged, wracked, and ruined by debts, begged Socrates for help. "I need you to teach me eloquence, so I can defend myself in court. I swear by the gods I will pay whatever it costs."

Socrates, that veteran *atheist*, looked him over with a measure of disgust. "There aren't any gods here. Sit down on this pallet."

"Okay, I'm sitting. Now what?" The old man, eager for guidance, waited.

"Put this chaplet on your head and prepare yourself for the celestial ritual all beginners must pass through." Socrates poured meal over the initiate's head, the dust choking the air. "Now we can begin," he said.

"Bow your head as I pray for the Lady Clouds to appear." The old man, his eyes half-closed, wondered at it all.

Socrates lifted his hands and prayed: "O worshipful Clouds, present yourself. Gather from Mt. Olympus and the Ocean's glade and the River Nile. 'Tis you we all adore."

Slowly a heavenly murmur crept over the distant horizon as Socrates summoned the wistful clouds. "Can you hear them? They speak softly."

"I don't hear anything. No, wait. There are distant voices. But if only I could see them," whispered the old man.

As the graceful formless ladies appeared, Socrates stared at Strepsiades. "Just remember. There is no Zeus! Only clouds."

***

Clouds, like cumulus pearls strung across a blue sky, have their place. They delight, but they aren't God. Paul once strolled through Athens, Socrates' hometown, and paused at an *atheistic* altar etched with the words "To an Unknown God."

***

"What you worship in ignorance, this I proclaim to you..." (Acts 17:23).

***

Admire the clouds, but pray to the God who loves you.

***

"For a while, I thought of myself as an atheist until I realized it was a belief, too."
George Carlin

Day 20

***

Baggage (1177 BC)
Virgil, *Aeneid*, 9:350–400

***

Nisus and his beloved friend Euryalus slithered through the enemy camp beneath a silent moon. Stealthily, one by one, they slaughtered drowsy soldiers until Nisus, measuring the fourth watch, knew time was nearly empty. Soon the sun's rays would shine upon their deeds. They must go now. No spoils. Leave the glittering accouterments where they lay, blood-smeared and homeless.

But Euryalus could not resist the gold-studded baldric worn by Rhamnes, who lay gutted at his feet. Once a king's gift, this treasure must be salvaged, worn with pride, a tribute to Euryalus' courage.

"Let's go!" whispered Nisus. "No spoils! We must travel with the wind."

But Euryalus lingered, staring. Surely the helmet of Messapus with its gay plume must be saved. He quickly fitted it upon his head. Adjusting the baldric, he turned, stepping over the bodies of Rutulian soldiers who died wordless. Leaving the enemy camp, they raced for safety, unaware that 300 Rutuli were nearby on horseback, delivering a message to their general.

The helmet's glitter, reflecting moonbeams, betrayed the fleeing Euryalus lost in the woods, Nisus having gone ahead. A cavalryman shouted. But it was too late. Hampered by the weight of his *baggage*, Euryalus stood surrounded by hostile forces and was slain.

***

A shrill voice cries to us all from the letter to the Hebrews. "Put down your *baggage*! Travel lightly with a pure heart." The enemy is near. No spoils. Will you heed the call?

***

"Therefore, since we have so great a cloud of witnesses surrounding us, let us also lay aside every encumbrance and the sin which so easily entangles us..." (Heb. 12:1).

***

Cast aside the glittering helmet. Walk without entanglements.

***

"The journey is inevitable. Baggage—optional."
Tev Aliage

Day 21

***

Baptism (AD 10)
Ovid, *Metamorphoses*, 11:120–145

***

Granted his preeminent wish by Bacchus, Midas strolled merrily homeward with golden dreams. Testing the magic, he picked up a dusty stone and watched it turn chameleon-like into pale yellow. An apple plucked from an orchard glistened gold. Bathing his hands in the river's edge, he watched as little wavelets crested in amber.

It was not, however, until he sat for dinner that he sensed trouble. The bread, crusty with nuggets, had no flavor, and the wine trickled through his jaws like molten gold. Lifting his hands, he sought Heaven's pardon. "Forgive me, father! I have sinned. Have mercy upon me. My gain tortures me."

Bacchus, ever merciful, took back his gift and pointed toward a distant stream in the land of Sardis. "Follow the river into the Lydian hills until you find the river's source. There, beneath the fountain's foam, duck your head and plunge into the cleansing water. Wash your sins away and be healed."

Humbled, Midas hurried toward the fountain's cure, remembering the simple pleasures he had once possessed. Arriving at the water's source, he *baptized* himself in the cleansing water and sighed joyfully.

***

Wishes are often poison-tipped darts that spread disenchantment rather than joy. Be careful, for answered prayers can sometimes leave you panting, ever thirsty. The cure, should this happen, is to seek cleansing as Naaman once did. Plagued by leprosy, he sought *baptism* in a river.

***

"So he went down and dipped himself seven times in the Jordan, according to the word of the man of God; and his flesh was restored like the flesh of a little child and he was clean" (2 Kings 5:14).

***

Find your cleansing fountain today.

***

"It's painful, but we can't heal ourselves unless we cleanse the wounds."
Bill Cosby

Day 22

***

Barriers (1184 BC)
Homer, *Iliad*, 12: 1–90

***

The great Achaean wall squatted near the seacoast, awaiting a Trojan onslaught. But it had never been blessed by the immortals. Before this pagan *barrier*, Hector and his rabid warriors halted their chariots on the brink of a great trench.

Over and again, Hector had charged at the wall urging his men to follow his example. But each sally stopped beneath its frowning shadow as the horses lunged and twisted, refusing to plunge into the crevasse that fronted the stones.

Finally, Polydamas approached the general. "Hector, our horses will never conquer this obstacle embedded with sharp stakes. Let's try a new strategy."

Hector's long hair fluttered in the sea breeze, his face sweating from repeated charges. "What is your idea?"

"Let's abandon our chariots here at the trench's edge and charge on foot in full armor. If the gods approve, the Greeks will never stop us, and we will own the beaches and burn their ships."

Polydamas studied the commander's face and observed subtle signs of awakening. Suddenly, Hector leaped from his chariot as screaming warriors followed his lead.

***

Barriers like bullies love to sprout along life's journeys. Just when a golden vista opens before us, a stake-studded wall rises from the mists and blocks our progress. But there will always be a whispering voice. Paul heard it when he stood lock-kneed at this same spot in Troy.

***

"And after they came to Mysia, they were trying to go into Bithynia, and the Spirit of Jesus did not permit them; and passing by Mysia, they came down to Troas" (Acts 16:7–8).

***

Learn to listen and then conquer your barriers.

***

"What's within you is stronger than what's in the way."
Erik Weihenmayer

Day 23

Beginnings (AD 120)
Juvenal, *Satires*, 3: 20–40

***

Umbricius wanted out. Rome had worn him to a frazzle, stolen his dreams, and given him the finger. He couldn't live here any longer and retain his old-age dignity. His reputation as a simple man who lived by honest labor wasn't good enough for sophisticated Rome.

Umbricius needed a new *beginning*, somewhere he could start over, settle down in peace, with integrity. While sitting by his evening hearth warming his aching hands, he had a brilliant idea. "I think I'll head over to the land where Daedalus shed his wings—Sicily." As he savored the fragrances of this daring concept, he became more determined to make it happen.

First, he rattled off, in a dull monotone, an honest assessment of his life as it was in Rome. "My hair has just turned white, so I'm a young, old man. I can still walk without crutches, so there's time for one last adventure." He paused, feeling some of the old confidence returning. "I can do this," he thought. "You have to be a crook to live here, and that's just not me. But Sicily. Now that's the place for new beginnings."

***

Check your feet. Are they stuck in some deep ruts? Perhaps you should call Umbricius in for a little dream time. Or, better yet, chat a while with Saul. He, too, heard *beginning's* cry in a distant city, leaving crusty Jerusalem in his wake:

***

"Saul got up from the ground, and though his eyes were open, he could see nothing; and leading him by the hands, they brought him into Damascus" (Acts 9:8).

***

Find your Sicily today and then just go!

***

"Beginnings are always messy."
John Galsworthy

Day 24

***

Betrayal (401 BC)
Xenophon, *Anabasis*, 1:6

***

Cyrus the Younger was off on a visionary mission to seize the Persian throne from his brother. He marched with high hopes toward Babylon, gathering his army as he went. But one personal friend named Orontes *betrayed* him not once but three times.

The final act of treachery began with a midnight letter to a Persian confidant. "Take this urgent note to the Persian king and tell him Cyrus has pledged me a thousand skilled horsemen. Tell the king to join me quickly with his forces." Unfortunately, the supposed confidant gave the letter to Cyrus, who ordered an immediate trial in his tent.

Confronted with his handwritten letter, Orontes admitted his deceit. When the trial ended, the jury grabbed his waistband, a sign of the guilty verdict, and led him away. Orontas' closest friends bowed as the traitor passed by, knowing the judgment was death. From that day forward, no one ever saw him alive again. No grave was ever found.

***

Three times Orontes *betrayed* Cyrus. Each time it was a fresh dagger in the general's heart. Often, we say we will never abandon those we love; however, despite these protestations, we often do.

Peter pledged fealty to Jesus, his closest friend. He looked the Savior in the eye and declared that he would never forsake Him (Matt. 26:35). But before the night was over, the unthinkable deed was done:

***

"Immediately while he was still speaking, a rooster crowed. The Lord turned and looked at Peter. And Peter remembered the word of the Lord, how He had told him, 'Before a rooster crows today, you will deny Me three times'" (Lk. 22:60–61).

***

Burn the letter. Don't wait for the rooster.

***

"Betray a friend, and you'll often find you have ruined yourself."
Aesop

Day 25

Birth (AD 10)
Ovid, *Metamorphoses*, 9:283–322

By the seventh day, Alcmena wanted to die. She lay on the cottage bed, writhing in pain, her pitiful groans begging help from Lucina and her two goddess-midwives. But Lucina sat unmoved, her knees crossed, her laced hands playing with a breeze. Alcmena, sick and weary, raised her lifeless arms to heaven, crying for divine aid. But none came. Lucina remained unmoved by the hearth.

Alcmena pushed again faintly with little strength remaining. Her hair, wet driblets, dangled about her white face. Occasionally, she managed a thin scream that stirred sympathy in nearby garden stones who listened with dark musings.

Galanthis, a yellow-haired servant, continually dabbed her mistress's forehead with a cold rag, sensing something dreadful at play. "Surely," she thought, "Juno, goddess of childbirth, is working some mischief." In and out of the doorway, Galanthis came and went, her heart struggling, fetching water from the well, passing the grim-faced Lucina, killing time.

Then, suddenly, came an infant's cry, and Galanthis leaped up celebrating. Laughing, she chided Lucina. "Whoever you are, you ought to at least congratulate my lady!" But Lucina leaped up, loosened her hands, and yanked the servant's hair, turning her into a weasel, dreading the implications of Hercules' *birth*.

Jesus, sitting with his disciples on the Mt. of Olives, sadly surveyed the grandiose temple complex across the Kidron Valley. Soon, he told them, the *birth* pangs will fall, and there will not be one stone left upon another of Herod's masterpiece.

***

"For nation will rise against nation, and kingdom against kingdom, and in various places there will be famines and earthquakes. But all these things are merely the beginning of birth pangs" (Matt. 24:7–8).

***

Push through your pain today. Jehovah reigns.

***

"Babies are bits of star-dust blown from the hand of God."
Larry Barretto

Day 26

***

Bitterness (AD 120)
Juvenal, *Satires*, 3:61–120

***

Juvenal closed his eyes and remembered joyful boyhood days rambling over Rome's Aventine Hill. He used to lay, nibbling on Sabine olives and drawing figures in the sky. "It's all gone," he thought. "Greeks now own the place. They've taken over, wearing their outrageous dinner jackets cluttered with Greek metals for this and that, smelling like sweaty wrestlers."

Now an old man swaddled in *bitterness*, Juvenal looked at the foreigners as a vast army of termites scrambling over the sacred Roman hills. His city had become a circus of babbling tongues, dissonant harps, and timbrels. Such chaos. Or, as he put it, "It's the mud of the Orontes pouring into the pure Tiber."

Juvenal shrugged, his once bright eyes now clouded with virulent racism. "I ought to just get up and run for the hills, anything to escape these masqueraders in purple robes. Nothing but freeloaders. That's what they are. Here's my theory," he muttered sourly. "They got here as stowaways hiding like roaches in the plums and figs from Damascus. I feel like I have been excommunicated, and all my years of loving labor for Rome have come to nothing."

***

Has life tumbled you about and turned you into a Juvenal? Do you wake each morning mumbling about the Greeks? I see

51

this in the prodigal son's *bitter* brother. He refused to join the festivities when his brother returned, broken from life's realities.

***

"And he said to him, 'Your brother has come....' But he became angry and was not willing to go in; and his father came out and began pleading with him" (Lk. 15:28).

***

Bid bitterness and Juvenal goodbye.

***

"Bitterness is the coward's revenge on the world for having been hurt."
Zora Neale Hurston

Day 27

Blood (1184 BC)
Homer, *Iliad*, 5:320–345

***

A huge stone, hurled by Diomed, struck Aeneas' hip joint sending him crumbling to the Trojan plain. Dazed, he propped himself up desperately searching, but night flooded his eyes, and all became quiet within. Aphrodite, horrified, veiled her son with folds of her heavenly garment, sheltering the dying soldier from further woe. Then lifting him, she made for the haven of Olympus.

Diomed, with savage eyes, spotted her fleeing the battle. He leaped into his chariot and sent dust flying as he closed upon mother and son. Then, after a long chase, he gripped his spear and hurled it at her delicate hand, the very hand that gripped her dying son. The spear point, raging, pierced the white skin between her wrist and palm.

Immortal *blood*, the ichor of heaven's gods, flowed freely over her ambrosial robes, spattering on the chariot floor. Aphrodite screamed. Dazed and terrified, she dropped Aeneas, sending him tumbling to certain death, had not Apollo lifted the dying soldier and brought him to Pergamus, where Apollo's sacred temple shone.

Fleet Iris, faster than wind, lifted the blood-smeared goddess off to heaven where Dione, Aphrodite's mother, offered comfort and soothing words.

***

It's a novel spectacle, watching a god whimper at her mother's skirts. This bloodletting reveals a troublesome vulnerability we don't expect from heaven's finest. How different was the somber scene at Golgotha when a soldier of another time pierced Jesus' skin, spilling His *blood*, an event that blackened the sky, split the temple veil, and brought salvation to a dying world.

***

"But one of the soldiers pierced His side with a spear, and immediately blood and water came out" (Jn. 19:34).

***

Touch the blood of the cross today and live.

***

"This is my blood of the covenant, which is poured out for many."
Jesus

Day 28

Bluffing (AD 66)
Josephus, *The Life of Flavius Josephus*, 32–33

***

Josephus, the governor of Judea, faced a mob of angry villagers who lived in a seaside town called Tiberias by the Sea of Galilee. They had spotted a few Roman soldiers on horseback nearby and assumed the conquering Romans were coming. The Jewish traitors surrounded Josephus. "We are now loyal to Rome!" they shouted.

Josephus, who had sent his army home for the Sabbath day observances, only had seven armed men with him. Unable to challenge the agitators, he raced back to his parents' village several miles away on the sea's southern side. Fearful and panicked, Josephus, ever the strategist, concocted a brilliant game of *bluff*.

He gathered his loyal friends in Taricheae. "Friends," he said urgently, "I need you all to quickly gather all of your fishing boats and bring one friend with you." Soon the tiny port of Taricheae bobbed with 230 white sails. Josephus led this flotilla of makeshift warships to Tiberias' harbor. When the revolting townspeople saw the massive fleet, they surrendered immediately. They never realized that each boat had only two occupants.

***

Josephus pulled off a daring bluff, but it didn't work so well for the prophets of Baal. They claimed they could call down fire from heaven, but Elijah called their *bluff*. Bluff long enough, and someone will call your hand. Learn to live authentically with truth and transparency.

***

"It came about at noon, that Elijah mocked them and said, 'Call out with a loud voice, for he is a god ... perhaps he is asleep...'" (I Kings 18:27).

***

Toss the poker glasses. Let your eyes speak the truth.

***

"The cardinal sin in poker is becoming emotionally involved." *Katy Lederer*

Day 29

***

Boasting (AD 200)
Babrius, *Fables*, 5

***

The two combatants circled slowly, their eyes straining for a weakness. The rustic cottage hugging the valley's edge beneath Mt. Helicon's stern gaze encouraged bloodshed, its reputation for violence well known to locals. A wet Corinthian breeze blew through the mountain forests above the valley, stimulating the cocks' fighting spirit. Bred of the Tanagraean breed, both roosters knew the subtleties of combat and prepared to fight to the end.

Circling warily, the dominant bird struck first and sent feathers flying. In an eye's blink, the contest ended with the wounded cock limping away to a corner of the house, shamed. The winning bird strutted about the ring, clucking a victory chant, and then flew to the housetop where it crowed loudly, *boasting* to distant village challengers. Flapping powerful wings, he claimed the Boeotian streets and byways.

An eagle watching these events unfold from a nearby olive tree took offense and, bolting from the limb, darted toward the boaster and snatched it from the roof, soaring into the clouds. The bleeding rooster, still whimpering in the cottage's dark corner, clucked softly at this sudden change of fortune. Wiping his face, he strutted toward the cache of hens, his defeat now a strange victory.

***

Rooftop rants often end badly. Pride's echoing taunts stifle friendship and turn loving hearts away. Better to let others speak softly of your talents. Find the voice of Paul who despised a *boasting* heart.

***

"But may it never be that I would boast except in the cross of our Lord Jesus Christ, through which the world has been crucified to me, and I to the world" (Gal. 6:14).

***

Get off the roof. Boast only of others.

***

"Mules are always boasting that their ancestors were horses."
German Proverb

Day 30

***

Books (AD 25)
Tacitus, *The Annals of Imperial Rome*, 4:34

***

The trial began with Tiberius grimacing at the defendant, Cremutius, as he flailed forth a doomed defense. "I meant the emperor no harm, your honor, when I wrote my *book*. It was merely an academic matter to praise Brutus in my History. I can cite many writers who criticized Augustus when he lived, but *that* emperor merely endured them. Surely the honorable Tiberius will follow this precedent."

The prosecutors, scowling, were friends of Tiberius, so the case was doomed from the beginning. But, still, Cremutius droned on and on until, exhausted, he walked out of the court muttering. Within a few weeks, he had starved himself to death, and the city officials ordered all his books burnt.

"It is so stupid," said Tacitus, our authority on this incident, "that people think burning a book will destroy tomorrow's memories."

***

John, the Apostle, exhorted all Christians to write the chapters of their lives with care and caution. "There will come a time when God Himself will call you forward to the dais and open your *book*. It is a fantasy to think the black pages of your life will burn before God sees them. Therefore, write with care each day a diary that will stand the test of time."

***

"And I saw the dead, the great and the small, standing before the throne, and books were opened; and another book was opened, which is the book of life..." (Rev. 20:12).

***

Dear Diary, today I will live honorably.

***

"Books cannot be killed by fire. People die, but books never die. No man and no force can abolish memory."
Franklin D. Roosevelt

Day 31

Bottomless (20 BC)
Virgil, *Aeneid*, 6:550–630

***

Jonathan Edwards strode with solemnity toward his pulpit in Northampton, Massachusetts, on July 8, 1741, and lifted the lid off of hell's orgy. With devastating detail, he dragged his congregation to the fragile edge and forced them to gaze at the demons below who, like greedy lions, were on the hunt for souls. But Edwards was not the first to walk the fiery paths of hell. Virgil took his readers on the same tour several millennia earlier:

This ancient poet led his readers by the hand toward a great cliff that hovered over a castle barred by massive gates. "Stand by the rusty gates," he urged, "and listen to the groans, the sound of the savage lash, the clang of iron, and the dragging of chains. See how the gate's guardians whip and lash the guilty who roam beneath the cliff."

Virgil's terrified audience screamed as the infernal gates began to open with a harsh grating. Hydra, with her fifty black gaping throats, yawned behind the iron bars. Then the fiery glow of hell bubbled below the cliffs, twice as far down as Mt. Olympus is high. There, in the *bottomless* pit, Titan's kids writhed in an unescapable fate of misery.

***

John, the writer of Revelation, also glanced into hell's *bottomless* crater and fanned the smoke upward that we might all believe:

***

"He opened the bottomless pit, and smoke went up out of the pit, like the smoke of a great furnace; and the sun and the air were darkened by the smoke of the pit" (Rev. 9:2).

***

Seek the bottomless love of Christ our Savior.

***

"They have no idea what a bottomless pit of misery I am."
Elizabeth Wurtzel

Day 32

***

Boundaries (65 BC)
Lucretius, *On the Nature of Things*, 1:968

***

"I have a question for you all and an experiment," said Lucretius. "Are you ready? The question is this: Where is the ultimate *boundary*? How far out into otherness should we go to find it? Does it exist?

"Now, while are you thinking about this," he continued, "let me suggest an experiment. Pick up this winged javelin and start running. Run to the boundary you have selected."

(Lucretius pauses to see if you are doing it or just standing knee-locked, pondering.)

"C'mon, now," he urges. "Pick up the javelin and run!

"When you get to the ultimate boundary, stop, and with a mighty thrust, hurl your spear and tell me what happens. I suggest that it will just keep on going. For in truth, there are no boundaries. It's all just space above us, beneath us, everywhere. Even heaven's thunderbolts never find a resting place. They just pierce the darkness in endless pursuit. There are no boundaries. There is no end."

***

David, of old, wondering at this conundrum, raises his hand.

"I think you're on to something, but you're missing the main point. As I consider the distant horizons, I see God's endless love reaching beyond the heavens. And His forgiveness to us all passes all *boundaries* east and west."

63

Lucretius' theories leave me lost and depressed. I prefer David's buoyant outlook on life. God's grace extends forever, never outrunning my desperation.

***

"As far as the east is from the west, so far has he removed our transgressions from us" (Ps.103:12).

***

Toss your javelin today. It will find heaven's throne.

***

"Love, having no geography, knows no boundaries."
Truman Capote

Day 33

/

Boxing (1177 BC)
Virgil, *Aeneid*, 5:360–380

***

The rowdy crowd pressed in, forming a rippling circle eager for brutality. Aeneas motioned for silence before the *boxing* match began. "Now that the races are finished, who has the courage and skill to step into the ring? A gold-horned bullock will be first prize, and a battle-tested sword, along with a fine helmet, will soothe the loser." Turning slowly, he challenged the spectators to send forth two champions.

Finally, shoving his way through the gallery, Dares entered the ring to gasps from every observer. Dares had killed the powerful mountain man, Butes, in a match back in Bebryces near Troy in the Bithynian region. Butes' granite muscles, hardened in the Thracian mountain passes, didn't save him. Dares left him gurgling blood in the sand beside Hector's tomb.

Taking center stage in the grassy amphitheater, Dares flung off his woolen cloak. His massive rawhide gloves, tethered up his forearms, were warnings to anyone who sought death's kiss. He began shadowboxing with a brutish grin, moving his broad shoulders about as his fists caught wisps of air. Leading with his left and then with his right, he circled the ring, pulverizing previous victims' ghosts.

***

Bluff and hyperbole win few *boxing* matches on life's spiritual pathway. Cheap talk and a braggart's shadow punches make little impression on the dark enemies that haunt us and seek to cripple our faith. Paul knew that only a disciplined and purposeful gait would win the day:

***

"Therefore I run in such a way, as not without aim; I box in such a way, as not beating the air, but I discipline my body and make it my slave..." (1 Cor. 9:25–27).

***

No more pretending. Take up the gloves with purpose.

***

"I've seen George Foreman shadow boxing, and the shadow won."
Muhammad Ali

Day 34

***

Braggadocios (1177 BC)
Virgil, *Aeneid*, 9:590–630

***

Remulus, the giant Italian soldier who had married the commander's sister, strutted back and forth beneath the Trojan battlements. Aeneas' forces lined the parapet, their arrows ready in defense of the citadel, but Remulus cared nothing for this bravado. With his giant physique, he shouted vulgarities at the Trojan warriors behind the walls. "Who dragged you babes from Troy to our Italian land?"

A thin malaise creased the faces of those on the walls as Remulus, a head taller than anyone else, continued to mock. With a flurry of *braggadocios* words, he recounted the strict discipline of his upbringing. "In my land, we take our children to the river, cut the ice, and force them to swim, hardening their bodies, teaching them to bear pain. Our boys hunt all night, tame horses, master archery, and work the fields to exhaustion. We all live with steel in our hands."

Relentlessly he clopped back and forth beneath the battlements, screaming incendiary remarks, insulting the troops above, calling them Phrygian sissies with their flowing, gold-trimmed gowns.

Suddenly Ascanius, the Trojan commander's young son, stepped forward and aimed an arrow at the giant. With a prayer, he sent the shaft flying and split Romulus' head in two, who tumbled ingloriously to the ground.

***

The *braggart's* tongue is powerless against the grace of God. Young David, like Ascanius above, encountered a similar scene when Goliath cursed the Israelite army relentlessly:

***

"And David put his hand into his bag and took from it a stone and slung it, and struck the Philistine on his forehead..." (1 Sam. 17:49).

***

Pity the braggart; embrace your faith.

***

"There is that in the glance of a flower which may at times control the greatest of creation's braggart lords."
John Muir

Day 35

***

Branding (AD 60)
Petronius, *The Satyricon*,103

***

Encolpius screamed, desperate to get off the ship. Sailing on the Adriatic's rough seas beneath a full moon, the last place he wanted to go was Tarentum, a city of exile. He and a couple of friends on the run had snuck onto this boat, thinking they were sailing to a pleasant harbor nearby. Now, this! Tarentum. "Never!" moaned Encolpius.

Huddled beneath sacks of grain in the hull, he and his buddies concocted a plan of escape. Eumolpus, his fellow stowaway, would sneak with him to the ship's railing in the black of night. There, Eumolpus' slave, who just happened to be a barber by trade, would shave their heads, eyebrows, and all. No one would recognize them.

With ink and pen in Eumolpus' handbag, he would etch the mark of a runaway slave on Encolpius' forehead in huge, inky letters. "I'll pretend you are my slave that I have recaptured, and we will disembark at the nearest port. What do you think?"

Encolpius, always the skeptic, winked. "I like it. I think it might actually work." And so, with midnight bravado, bent over the bobbing ship's rail, the shaving commenced. Then, with an artist's touch, the letters FUG for fugitive were *branded* masterly on his forehead.

***

At this same fingerprint in time, St. Paul picked up his quill, wet with ink. Writing to his new friends at Galatia, he paused and stared at the bitter *brands* crisscrossing his arms and legs. Then with a heavy sigh, he concluded his letter in these words:

***

"From now on let no one cause trouble for me, for I bear on my body the brand-marks of Jesus" (Gal. 6:17).

***

Check your forehead. Wear your spiritual *FUG* proudly today.

***

"We cannot learn without pain."
Aristotle

Day 36

***

Bravado (162 BC)
Josephus, *The Jewish War*, 1:1

***

It was a desperate moment.

Fifty thousand delirious Greek combatants under Antiochus Epiphanes surged forward, screaming vulgarities against Judas Maccabeus and the Jewish army. Antiochus' fighters, along with 5000 equestrians and 80 African elephants, charged against Judas' men. As the dust mingled with certain doom, all seemed lost until Eleazar, the commander's brother, broke from the Jewish front and, with fanatical *bravado* raced toward the charging pachyderms.

Both sides watched in disbelief as the soldier fought his way through a barrage of missiles, running heroically toward the lead elephant. Thinking Antiochus to be on top of the beast, he clawed his way through the enemy's front lines.

Unable to scramble up to the fighters high on the animal's swaying back, he drew his sword and plunged it into the elephant's gut. Jerking its giant tusks about wildly, startled and bleeding, it tumbled to its knees crushing Eleazar beneath its weight. Eleazar's brothers in arms, shouting with outrage, leaped forward with shouts of victory and revenge.

***

Pause and look back through the mists of time to a distant valley called Elah, southwest of Jerusalem. Here two armies faced one another: the Philistines and Jewish fighters. Standing

71

in a violent rage fronting the Philistine army stood Goliath, an impossible foe. But *bravado* flowed in David's veins as he jingled five smooth stones in his bag still wet from the creek.

***

"He took his stick in his hand and chose for himself five smooth stones from the brook ... and approached the Philistine" (1 Sam. 17:40).

***

Heroism pulses in your heart today. Go! Slay a giant.

***

"It ain't how hard you can hit. It's how hard you can get hit and keep moving forward."
Rocky Balboa

Day 37

***

Breakthrough (1184 BC)
Homer, *Iliad*, 12: 440–470

***

Arrows and heavy stones rained down upon the bellicose Trojans at the foot of the Greek battlements. Unable to breach the mighty walls that guarded the Danaan fleet, the endless struggle was evenly balanced. Then with a burst of violent rage, Hector, the mighty Trojan warrior, flung himself at the stake-infested barriers and screamed for backup. "Come, Trojans, *break through* the wall of the Argives, and let's burn their ships to the waterline!"

Inspired, the warriors rushed as one body straight at the wall and scaled the battlements with spears gripped tightly. Hector spotted a jagged boulder bigger than a horse and, with a gritty scream, lifted it above his head. Straight toward the thick gate with its double doors encrusted into the impenetrable walls, he hurled the stone. Closed with two crossbars, the gate shuddered beneath the blow. Hector lowered his massive shoulders and pushed, grinding the jagged rock into the crossbars until the hinges cracked, and Hector and the stone tumbled inside upon Greek soil.

Hector rose like a midnight whirlwind, his face dark as night, his bronze breastplate gleaming. Turning toward his troops, he flashed his spears, and within seconds the army scaled the battlements while others surged through the broken gates.

***

Barred gates litter the path we trod daily. Progress at times seems impossible, the walls before us unscalable. But even in the darkest storm, there is a way forward. Paul's breakdown on a dusty Damascus road was, in reality, his *breakthrough*. They come when we least expect them:

***

"And immediately there fell from his eyes something like scales, and he regained his sight, and he got up and was baptized..." (Acts 9:18).

***

Stuck beneath some stubborn gate? Your breakthrough is near!

***

"Never say never, because limits, like fears, are often just an illusion."
Michael Jordan

Day 38

***

Bride (AD 64)
Tacitus, *Annals of Imperial Rome*, 15:37

***

Nero, corrupted by every lust, fluffed his scarlet wedding veil
before a group of hideous spectators. His eyes sneered beneath
soot-blackened eyebrows scented with saffron. Pink rouge
pressed from poppy petals mixed with Belgium red ochre
transformed his face into a night-walking prostitute. Drenched
in Capuan perfume, Nero celebrated the happy wedding by
summoning Pythagoras, one of the boys in a perverted street
gang, to stand beside him as husband.

The witnesses to this atrocity cooed softly, sycophants to
the core. Nero wore the *bridal* cord about his waist tied in the
traditional Herculean knot that only a loving husband could
untie. Fluttering his floor-length veil in the shadows of the
flickering wedding torches, he led his husband to the wedding
bed surrounded by riotous onlookers hooting for action.

Unknown to the wedding guests, across town at the Circus
Maximus, Rome's mammoth chariot stadium, flames lit the sky
and then raged across the city unchecked, the first response to
a wedding from hell.

***

Nero, the painted bride of a debauched wedding, makes me
wonder at this ancient Roman world. As Nero partied and the
Circus fire drifted slowly over Rome's troubled metropolis, I
see another *bride* stepping shyly out of the heavens. John, exiled

and forgotten, put down his pen and stared with wonder deep within the cave on Patmos. Speechless, he followed the new Jerusalem's descent from heaven's portal, veiled and scented with heaven's love.

***

"And I saw the holy city, new Jerusalem, coming down out of heaven from God, made ready as a bride adorned for her husband" (Rev. 21:2).

***

Pause today and search the heavens for your bride.

***

"Love is composed of a single soul inhabiting two bodies."
Aristotle

Day 39

Bully (1177 BC)
Virgil, *Aeneid*, 8:170–280

***

Evander, king of Latium, led Aeneas to a maple chair draped with a shaggy lion's pelt. The Trojan prince sat as young men scurried to put away cups and dishes from the morning sacrifices. Then the altar priest brought on a sumptuous feast celebrating Hercules' heroic feats. Roasted bull steaks were served with wine from fertile orchards. And when all was consumed, Evander retold the notorious tales of Cacus, the ogre.

Pointing to the crumbled scarp beneath a distant, looming cliff, he flung his arms frantically with an actor's fervency, demonstrating the beast's horrifying antics. "The monster's cave floor was always bubbling with human blood," he said, his eyes sallow, enraged. "Human heads hung above his insolent doorway, staring with putrid eyes into the dark."

Evander paused and drank from his chalice. Then a sparkle of revenge glistened in his pupils. "But one day, Hercules returned, driving his herds of bulls and heifers to the lush valleys. When Cacus saw them with *bullish* greed, he rustled four bulls and four fine heifers, dragging them by their tails backward into his lair, disguising their trail. But Hercules stormed the black-clouded cave, throttled the ogre, and dragged his grotesque carcass, hemorrhaging and bloated, into the sunlight."

***

Cacus lives. He thunders in school hallways and office complexes, hanging his trophies for all to see. Like all *bullies*, he consumes his victims, leaving destruction rampant. These truths make Jesus' Sermon on the Mount all the more poignant.

***

"But I say to you, do not resist an evil person; but whoever slaps you on your right cheek, turn the other to him also" (Matt. 5:39).

***

Bullies never win on Jesus' mountain.

***

"He's a bully. I love bullies. They have such big, shiny red buttons to push."
Carrie Vaughn

Day 40

***

Cap (AD 60)
Petronius, *The Satyricon*, 5:40

***

The banquet spilled into the evening, delighting the guests with sumptuous surprises. After a plethora of savory dishes, the servants rushed in to refresh the couches upon which the diners relaxed. The embroidered coverlets, covered with hunting scenes, created a fresh challenge for the visitors who sat stumped, trying to find the hidden meanings.

Suddenly, amid this pleasant puzzle, the kitchen doors blasted open, and several huge mastiffs came bounding around the dining table. Behind the chaotic dogs, a slave bore a tray upon which sat an enormous wild sow, all pickled and flowered. Perched on its head was the freedom *cap* that newly liberated slaves wore in token of their liberty. Dangling from her tusks were two baskets woven from palm leaves: one was filled with Egyptian dates, and the other held sweet Syrian dates.

"I can't figure it out," whispered a guest. "What does it mean?"

"That's easy, stupid. They brought this same sow in yesterday for dinner, but everybody was so stuffed, they couldn't eat her. So, she won her freedom."

***

These conical freedom *caps* were the prize of a lifetime for any miserable servant. With it, they lived their lives with a measure

79

of dignity as citizens of Rome. But we don't have to look far to see freedom crowns upon the saints of the early church.

***

"Blessed is a man who perseveres under trial; for once he has been approved, he will receive the crown of life which the Lord has promised to those who love Him" (Jas. 1:12).

***

Leaving for work? Don't forget your freedom cap.

***

"Your crown has been bought and paid for. Put it on your head and wear it."
Maya Angelou

Day 41

***

Captives (69 BC)

Suetonius, *Lives of the Caesars*, 1:4

***

The Aegean Sea's wintry waves slapped the bow of Julius Caesar's boat. What a sweet relief he felt as he escaped Rome's turbulent politics. Having lost a major court case against a powerful Roman politician, this escape to Rhodes provided the perfect calm for his inner storm. He would lay low for a while, take a class or two in rhetoric, and then return a new man.

The pirate ship emerged through a thick fog, its buccaneers shouting demands as they hauled Caesar's small craft to the nearby island of Pharmacussa, a little north of Rhodes. Thrilled at their catch of a newly minted Roman senator, they demanded 20 talents of silver for freedom. Caesar mocked them, assuring the privateers that he was worth at least 50 talents.

For forty days and nights, sequestered against his will, Caesar waited for the ransom to arrive. Never cowering to his *captives*, Caesar demanded silence when he slept and only played games that he approved.

When his slave Burgundus finally returned, bearing the required treasure, the pirates released their prisoner. Caesar immediately sailed to Miletus just up the coast, raised a small navy, captured the pirates, and had them all crucified as he had promised.

***

I can't help but compare Caesar's forty days of *captivity* with Jesus' forty days and nights in the wilderness. Though in the grips of the devil, He too refused to submit, outwitting Satan at every turn. Caesar eventually escaped his jailers and ruled as the world's dictator. Jesus left His wilderness unconquered and became the world's Savior.

***

"Then Jesus was led up by the Spirit into the wilderness to be tempted by the devil" (Matt. 4:1).

***

Who will you follow to freedom?

***

"We're all captives of a story."
Daniel Quinn

Day 42

***

Castaway (AD 33)

Tacitus, *The Annals of Imperial Rome*, 6:19

***

Sextus Marius lived the dream that few can ever hope to obtain. His wealth was beyond measure. Once, he visited a friend in the countryside who owned a charming villa with marble fountains and rambling gardens. While the friend was absent for a few days, Marius, on a whim, razed the estate, planting a new complex shimmering in gold. This was easy for the billionaire to accomplish since he owned multiple gold and copper mines from which Rome made their coins.

Everyone knew Marius was the richest man in Spain. Couple this with his ties to the Roman emperor, Tiberius, and the portrait of a megastar shines vividly on the ancient horizon.

Marius had a beautiful daughter. Fearing that Tiberius, during his Reign of Terror, might summon and ensnare the girl with his well-known sexual proclivities, Marius sent her to a safe house far away. But Tiberius, discovering the deed, spread lies that Marius had himself defiled his daughter.

For this illusory crime, soldiers dragged him to the top of the Tarpeian rock, an 80-foot cliff overlooking Rome's forum, and flung him over like chaff in the wind. Considered by Romans to be a peculiarly shameful death, the golden name of Marius crumbled like dust as Tiberius seized the *castaway's* mines.

***

Twenty years later, St. Paul sat at a small Ephesian window desk, contemplating *castaways*. Perhaps with Marius in mind or other fallen disciples in the church, he picked up his pen and wrote about the shame of departing a purposeful life.

***

"But I discipline my body and make it my slave, so that, after I have preached to others, I myself will not be a castaway" (1 Cor. 9:27).

***

Be careful today! The Tarpeian Rock awaits.

***

"Disgrace brings sorrow to the noble minded."
Chanakya

Day 43

***

Chalice (1177 BC)
Virgil, *Aeneid*, 8:270–290

***

Potitius, the priest of Hercules, led King Evander and his guest, Aeneas, toward the sacred grove beneath Rome's ancient shadows. Having finished his emotional sermon retelling the slaughter of Cacus, the ogre, the villagers and guests gathered round Hercules' great altar with festive hearts.

Potitius, with his cadre of acolytes, held their torches high over the altar. Robed in hides, their customary vestments, the clerics prepared a second banquet that the festival might carry the night. Evander, the king, his head entwined with a circlet of poplar leaves, rose to pray. Holding the consecrated *chalice* in his raised right hand, his prayer drifted heavenward, a sumptuous offer to the gods who leaned over heaven's precipice with joy.

While the priests piled high their holy dishes upon the altar, the Salii, a choir of leaping youths, rehearsed the feats of Hercules, their melodies mingling with embers that drifted above the great altar. As twilight tucked the worshippers in with its calming night arias, Aeneas drew strength from these newly-made friends, knowing that he had finally found home.

***

Everyone needs a *chalice*. This world is too dreary for any traveler to embark on daily journeys without this treasure of remembrances. When we hold the chalice high at dawn or sunset's final sigh, we draw nearer to the divine. The Christian's chalice, jewel-encrusted with sacred symbols of Christ's selfless life, inspires us to imitate.

***

"And when he taken a cup and given thanks, He gave it to them, saying, 'Drink from it, all of you; for this is My blood of the covenant, which is poured out for many for forgiveness of sins'" (Matt. 26:27–28).

***

Don't leave home without your chalice.

***

"Tis the summer prime, when the noiseless air in perfumed chalice lies."
Elizabeth Oakes Smith

Day 44

***

Challenges (1184 BC)
Homer, *Iliad*, 3:325–380

***

The chariots, empty and motionless on the edge of the battlefield, joined the spectators. Armies on both sides of the Trojan plains waited, wondering how it would end. Great Hector placed both warriors' names in his helmet, turned his head to the side, and shook the lots until one flew out, sailing perilously through time until it fell upon neutral ground between two hostile armies.

Paris took the *challenge* and greaved his legs, binding the silver ankle clasps. Next, he fitted the cuirass and slung a silver-studded sword of bronze about his shoulder, accompanied by a mighty shield. The noble helmet, adorned with a horsehair crest, glinted in the sun. Grasping his spear, perfectly balanced, he strode out between the armies facing Menelaus, whose wife he had stolen ten years earlier.

The rules had been declared, followed by altar rituals that left several lambs bleeding, soaked in wine, an acceptable gesture for the gods who watched from Mt. Olympus. The winner would settle this decade-long argument once and for all. And so the chariots trembled in silent anticipation as Paris threw the first spear, desperate to slay his opponent.

***

Some *challenges* can't be avoided. There are times when corners disappear, leaving no place to hide. Perhaps even now, you hear a taunting voice looming nearby, spear in hand. Sometimes, facing a challenge is the only way to move on with life.

***

"And David put his hand into his bag and took from it a stone and slung it and struck the Philistine on his forehead. And the stone sank into his forehead, so that he fell on his face to the ground" (1 Sam. 17:49).

***

Your name just spun out of the helmet. Go! Meet the challenge.

***

"Fall seven times and stand up eight."
Japanese Proverb

Day 45

***

Character (BC 226)
Plutarch, *Marcellus*, 2

***

United Airlines and Nordstrom, a company that excels in customer relations, both have rule books to guide their employees. United Airlines' personnel often feared making personal judgments, yielding instead to the manual. Nordstrom, on the other hand, has only two guiding lights: One, workers are to use their best judgment in all situations, and two, there are no more rules. This simple Nordstrom concept places *character* front and center.

The classics tell us of a young man commended highly for possessing character so valued in the ancient world. Marcus, the rising son of the illustrious general and consul, Marcellus, was famous for his handsome appearance and high moral standard.

An older Roman man named Capitolinus, a colleague of Marcellus, repeatedly tried and failed to seduce Marcus. Finally, the lad complained to his father, who, enraged, brought charges against Capitolinus and dragged him into court. However, with no witnesses, the case teetered, lacking evidence. As a last result, the senate decided to call the lad himself. Marcus came before the senate embarrassed. Here is how Plutarch described the moment:

"Marcus stood humbly before the august senators, blushing and weeping as he told the court what had happened. As he spoke, the lad's indignation shone through his tears, and the senators quickly understood. Capitoline was found guilty and fined for outrageous behavior."

***

It almost feels like the apostle Paul was in that courtroom supporting Marcus. Emphasizing *character's* importance, he said:

***

"Prove yourselves to be blameless and innocent, children of God above reproach in the midst of a crooked and perverse generation, among whom you appear as lights in the world" (Phil. 2:15).

***

Keep your rulebook simple. Live with character.

***

"Character is much easier kept than recovered."
Thomas Paine

Day 46

***

Charade (AD 62)
Tacitus, *Annals of Imperial Rome*, 14:50

***

The honorable Burrus lay dying with a tumor lodged in his throat. For many years, Burrus, Nero's most faithful tutor, was no longer wanted. Nero impatiently tolerated the old man's wheezing and choking. Night's endless debaucheries playfully called the emperor, and loyal confidants were nuisances on his playground.

One evening after drinking heavily, Nero summoned his medical team and made further inquiries about Burrus' health. Dissatisfied with the patient's lingering, he suggested his own treatment. "Go," he said to the doctor, "and propose a new treatment known to cure tumors. Offer to paint his throat with this elixir and wish the patient my best." With these instructions, the doctor rushed to the dying man's bedside.

Burrus, wise beyond the brightest saints, saw through the *charade* immediately. However, he accepted the poisonous feather shoved down his throat as life's inevitable fate.

Several days later, as the "treatment" inexorably closed the old man's throat, Nero paid a house call. Burrus turned his face away, refusing to look at the kid he had taught life's lessons for fourteen years. "How are you doing?" inquired Nero, feigning concern. The patient refused to turn toward his former student. Managing only a weak response, muffled through his pillow, he moaned, "I'm doing all right."

***

Love's *charade* is heartbreaking to witness. Burrus died hearing that shrill inquiry, "How are you, my friend?" Pilate did the same thing as Jesus stood dripping with blood before him. He pretended. He foisted a charade upon the Savior who silently knew.

***

"And he said, 'Why, what evil has he done?' But they kept shouting all the more, saying 'crucify him'" (Matt. 27:23).

***

Live without the stain of shallow pretensions.

***

"We are just pretenders, lost in this charade."
Pretenders, "Bad Religion"

Day 47

Charlatans (AD 55)
Petronius, *The Satyricon*, 125

***

The vagabonds hit the jackpot in Croton.

This ancient southern town nestled on Italy's Pizzuta slopes that tumble to the Ionian Sea had welcomed these shipwrecked fools. Thinking they were wealthy tourists, villagers flocked to pamper them with morning wine and sumptuous breakfasts. Encolpius and his shipwrecked buddy Eumolpus thought it all a dream compared to their previous lives of slavery and grinding poverty.

Encolpius knew well hunger's grind and deprivation. A steady stream of lies dangled here and there helped ingratiate them to the locals who had never seen royalty up close and personal. Now, the *charlatans* strolled lazily down picturesque streets where the lilacs bloomed in the Ionic sea breezes.

Still, Encolpius, the old gladiator, worried. "What if they find out? What if somebody digs a little and discovers their true worthless identities? This charade can't last forever," he muttered to a bundle of black grapes in his hand. "It would only take one of my servants dropping a few hints here and there in town, and this game would be over! It could all end in a heartbeat, and we'd be back stuck in our wearisome lives of grinding poverty." He shuddered. "Man, that was an awful life."

***

Jesus, sitting on Capernaum's alluring slopes, gazed at the throngs that pressed Him, desperate for a heaven-sent message. As the Sea of Galilee shimmered in the afternoon sun's glow, Jesus warned the people of *charlatans* among them. "People aren't always what they seem," He told them. "It takes a discerning spirit to see through disguises."

***

"Beware of the false prophets, who come to you in sheep's clothing but inwardly are ravenous wolves" (Matt. 7:15).

***

Burn your wolf suit today.

***

"Surely nobody would be a charlatan, who could afford to be sincere."
Ralph Waldo Emerson

Day 48

***

Choices (AD 9)
Cassius Dio, *Roman History*, 56:2–10

***

Caesar Augustus, now an old man in his early 70s, was angry at the young noblemen of his city. He summoned them all to appear in the Forum of Rome. Standing on the rostrum, in the shadow of the ancient Temple of Saturn, he stared down upon the gathering knights.

When all were present, with a wave of his tremulous hand, he separated them into two groups: married and unmarried, curious to see the disparities. He stared in disgust at the paucity of married noblemen. Enraged but maintaining decorum, he doted over those who had chosen to live the ideal of matrimony.

"Is there anything better than a loving wife who cares for her family and enjoys keeping house? In health, she makes you glad, and in sickness, she cares for you. She consoles you when misfortune strikes and shares your good fortune when blessings fall."

Augustus then turned to face the bachelors who merely wanted to live wild lives,

free from wives and responsibilities. "I'm giving you guys a *choice*: get your acts together or else!"

***

Barely a day goes by without some pesky *choice* buzzing about our souls, making demands. Gaze back in time and hear Joshua confront the noblemen in his day. Having lived 110 years, he saw life's curtain closing and placed this choice before his villagers:

***

"choose this day whom you will serve, whether the gods your fathers served in the region beyond the River, or the gods of the Amorites in whose land you dwell. But as for me and my house, we will serve the Lord" (Josh. 24:15).

***

Some choice will corner you today. Be ready! Think clearly.

***

"May your choices reflect your hopes, not your fears."
Nelson Mandela

Day 49

***

Chosen (AD 38)
Suetonius, *Lives of the Caesars*, 4:36

***

Caligula settled upon his banquet couch, fluffing a purple gown of Koen silk over his legs. With a clap, the servers bustled in carrying pheasants roasted to perfection and a coterie of supporting dishes. The guests, well-known married women in Rome, chatted nervously with their husbands, sipping wine and waiting.

The dreaded moment arrived when Caligula, with a hand wave, ordered the nobles' wives to line up slowly and pass before him. One by one, the tragedy unfolded in cinematic slow motion, each pausing discreetly at Caligula's couch, posing, pirouetting so the emperor could evaluate skin tone and moody eyes desperately silent. Occasionally, he would rise and lift a woman's chin whose head hung, lowered in modesty.

Finally, as if buying a slave on Roman backstreets, he *chose*. Leading his victim ceremoniously from the banquet room to a back bedroom, Caligula courted and abused the victim, forced to replicate her wedding night. When finally sated with sex, the couple returned to the hall where, with imperial delight, he replayed each delicious moment. Quickly criticizing the woman's sexual shortcomings, he sent her scurrying back to her humiliated husband, sitting before uneaten pheasant wings.

***

The debauchery of Caligula is well-documented. Suetonius almost trembles with rage as he recounts the emperor's lustful trolling for beautiful women in the city. But while Caligula *chose* an innocent bedroom victim, a sacred selection unfolded in towns across the empire.

***

"for you are a *chosen* people. You are royal priests, a holy nation, God's very own possession ... for he called you out of the darkness into his wonderful light" (1 Pet. 2:9).

***

Pass the Savior's couch with confidence. You are chosen.

***

"We may not have chosen the time, but the time has chosen us." *John Lewis*

Day 50

***

City (AD 56)

Tacitus, *The Annals of Imperial Rome*, 13:25

***

Nero waited impatiently for the midnight hour. Oppressed by the palace's summer doldrums, he gathered his sordid gang of local miscreants and prepared to slither unnoticed into the labyrinth of brothels and rowdy taverns typical of Rome's mischievous byways.

Pacing giddily before his favorite outlaws summoned to share his debauched revelry, he prepared for the night's ecstasy. He happily shed the imperial robe draped elegantly from his frame to the regal-colored shoes. He tossed his laurel wreath upon the fabrics of royal power, denigrating the prestige they brought him.

Then, with a sordid comedic routine, he quickly donned a slave's woolen tunic. To make it more believable, he had some tools used by working slaves slung over his shoulder. Everyone laughed as Nero mussed his hair, adding a wild countenance to the costume.

As the night settled in over the seven hills, Nero and this assortment of ruffians slinked beneath a charred moon into the night, vagrant warriors on a muckraking mission to spread mayhem. With an orgiastic fever, he attacked innocent wayfarers, looted stores, and drank heavily at every tavern he passed—his identity never suspected.

Once this routine became general news, gangs set out at night imitating the emperor, looting with impunity. And as Tacitus tells us, Rome, by night, came to resemble a conquered *city*.

***

While Rome burns with this putrid fever, pause and look upward. There in the clouds, you will see a descending *city* "made ready as a bride adorned for her husband" (Rev. 21:2). The streets are blissfully still, void of arrogant emperors and the moans of death or pain, for these have passed away.

***

Passport ready? Heaven is waiting.

***

"My home is in Heaven. I'm just traveling through this world."
Billy Graham

Day 51

***

Cleansing (550 BC)
Herodotus, *The Persian Wars*, 1:172

***

The ancient sea towns in southwestern Turkey bristled with activity. The time for the *cleansing* ceremony was at hand. The drinking bouts had ended, and the woozy-headed men huddled together by a flickering fire.

Muttering religious threats against all foreign and unwelcome gods, these village devotees struggled to put on their war armor. Each warrior screamed and howled to clear his head. Staring at the stars and mumbling with fierce determination to rid the town of evil presences, the men rose with singular solidarity.

One by one, they grasped their spears, and then in a spirited march, strutted off into the night. They smote the air about them as if enemy deities were near, expelling them from their land. "Such was the custom of the Caunians," said Herodotus.

***

Cleansing the land is tough work. Herodotus observed the Caunians leaving their drinking parties, donning warrior's garb, and chasing out the pernicious influences of their villages. Similar traditions were evident in the Old Testament as men in Ezekiel's day passed throughout the land, cleansing it of stray corpses (Ezekiel 39:14).

Perhaps this is a good day to rise and do some personal *cleansing*. It is the ongoing work of Christ, according to Paul, who tells us that the Savior is constantly cleansing the church.

Do your part by splashing the Word upon your heart each morning and evening.

***

"Husbands, love your wives, just as Christ loved the church and gave Himself up for her to sanctify her, cleansing her by the washing with water through the word" (Eph. 5:26).

***

A little daily soul cleaning will brighten any day.

***

"Cleanse your heart and purify your soul before you wash your face."
Redouane Moustaghit

Day 52

***

Collapse (AD 120)
Juvenal, *Satires*, 3:190–202

***

Juvenal stared appallingly at the rickety high rises along so many of Rome's streets. They seemed to sway in the breeze, ready to collapse at nature's slightest whims. "They built the whole damn city on matchsticks," he muttered to himself, wondering if he would escape this death sentence. "It's nothing like living in the noble suburbs with beautiful woodlands."

How many times had he fearfully drifted off to sleep when he lived in one of Rome's dingy apartments? Sure, the landlord swore to the gods that it was all safe. "I've just made many expensive repairs," he claimed. "Look at the fresh plaster on the walls." But when the terrified shouts of "fire!" echoed through the streets, Juvenal knew better.

He could still remember it so well: the fire alarms clanging in the night, neighbors screaming for water while the top-floor beams *collapsed*. The first-floor folks scrambled to safety with the clothes on their backs, some hesitating, grabbing any valuables they could reach. But the fifth-floor suckers all perished in the billowing smoke as they hit dead ends on the buckled stairs.

***

In some ways, all of us live on the edge of imminent *collapse*. We're fleeing from Covid-19 or pink slips from the boss. If you read the Psalmist's lines, you can hear the heavy breathing of one who fell like a Pompeian ghost into calamity's hot embers:

***

"My soul collapses in the dust; Revive me according to Your word.... My soul weeps because of grief; Strengthen me according to Your word" (Ps. 119:25–28).

***

Tumble today into God's hands and sleep well.

***

"I predict the internet will soon go spectacularly supernova and in 1996 catastrophically collapse."
Robert Metcalfe

Day 53

***

Community (1184 BC)
Homer, *Iliad*, 13: 123–135

***

Zeus, lord of all, turned his eyes from the raging battle on Troy's seacoast. Far more interesting to him were the horse-breeders of Thrace and the noble Hippemolgi, the celibate herders who live on milk and divine thoughts.

But King Poseidon was obsessed, leaning over heaven's edge, keenly aware of the bloodshed. Against Zeus' orders, he strode mightily down Ida's slopes and called for his chariot beneath the sea. Then, snapping the reins, his steeds, with their golden manes flowing, flew across the wave tips to the shores of Troy's coast. There he urged the Greeks to gather courage and fight.

One by one, they stepped from the shadows where they huddled, cringing in fear, and made a living fence. Spear to spear, shield to shield, buckler to buckler, and helmet to helmet, they locked arms, a *community* of resistance inspired by unity. As they moved with an elegant symmetry toward the hostile Trojans, their horsehair crests formed a wall of gleaming helmets. Their spears, interlaced with deadly brotherhood, defied fate. Step by step, a chorus of victory rose from the embattled ranks who had hearts set on battle, fearing nothing.

***

I feel the earth shake as these unified warriors lock arms and stride into battle. Solitary missions have their place, but a *community* of souls inspired by a common purpose is an undefeatable force. Likewise, Peter, tuned to heaven's secret, urges his disciples to unite and form the living house of God Almighty.

***

"You also, as living stones, are being built up as a spiritual house for a holy priesthood, to offer up spiritual sacrifices to God through Jesus Christ" (1 Pet. 2:5).

***

Lock arms today with a higher cause.

***

"Alone we can do so little; together we can do so much."
Helen Keller

Day 54

***

Compassion (1184 BC)
Homer, *Iliad*, 11:800–849

***

Patroclus, Achille's trusted friend and companion, raced along the Trojan seashore bearing dark news. Unless Achilles relented from his obstinate refusal to fight the Trojans, the Greeks were lost. He paused at the altars dedicated to the gods near Odysseus' fleet of ships. Before he could lift a brief prayer, Eurypylus met him limping from the battlefield. A blood-streaked arrow bobbed in his thigh as he dragged himself toward Patroclus. The black wound oozed blood mixed with sweat pouring from the warrior's shoulders.

Patroclus, with no time to spare, nonetheless paused, speaking *compassionately* to the officer. "Friend, is this wound fatal? You are so far from your family and friends to be so hurt." He paused and then asked the inevitable question: "Does the Greek army stand a chance, or will we all fall to Hector's rage?"

Patroclus, squinting with pain, answered. "There is no hope for the Greeks. Troy gains strength daily and will soon prevail." With panicked eyes, he asked for help. "Could you possibly take me to the ships and treat my wound?"

Patroclus noting the setting sun felt his mission's urgency. He lingered, though, and clasping the soldier's waist, led him into a tent. Laying the man full-length upon a bullock skin, he cut the arrow out, washed the black blood, and spread bitter herbs upon the wound.

***

Life seems to be an endless sprint from one deadline to another. But we can admire Patroclus for his *compassionate* delay. We see this in another man from the ancient world:

***

"But a Samaritan, who was on a journey, came upon him; and when he saw him, he felt compassion..." (Lk. 10:33).

***

If you see Eurypylus today, please treat his wounds.

***

"Until you have real compassion, you cannot recognize love." *Bob Thurman*

Day 55

Concern (AD 80)
Suetonius, *Lives of the Caesars*, 8.8

***

Standing on his Palatine balcony, Titus, emperor of Rome, moaned. Far off into the distance, the night burned with dripping embers dancing over the city's rooftops. The fire raged for three days and nights, leaving Titus exhausted and broken. Suetonius records Titus' heartbroken sigh: "This has ruined me."

But more than fires wrenched his soul apart. An eruption of horrific dimensions blasted Vesuvius off the map. As if these tragedies were not enough, an outbreak of plague swept through Rome's corridors, killing many.

Titus bore these *concerns* like a father whose deep love for his children prompted heroic action. Casting off his mourning cape, he established a board of top officials to survey the damage. Titus also set up a fund to rebuild the devastated region. Unsatisfied with these bureaucratic efforts, he slipped into his mansion and stripped the walls of its decorations, donating them to the damaged temples and public buildings.

Daily he consulted with city doctors seeking remedies for the plague. He often visited the temples, making emotional altar pleas to the gods. When he died a year later in his early forties, the common people went into mourning as if they had lost a family member.

***

In the final days of Jesus' life, He rode his humble donkey toward Jerusalem. Pausing at a distance, he scanned with *concern* the walls that cradled the metropolis before Him. The temple's gleaming Herodian stones prompted tears from the Savior's eyes, stunning his friends who didn't understand the imminent catastrophe *at Titus' hands*!

***

"When He approached Jerusalem, He saw the city and wept over it,..." (Lk. 19:41).

***

Let concern for others lead you today.

***

"The essence of love is concern."
Nirmala Srivastava

Day 56

***

Conduct (55 BC)
Catullus, *Poems*, 12

***

The cool summer Alpine breezes wafted over Lake Garda through Catullus' villa windows. His delightful dinner guests rambled on about Italian pleasantries as the evening sun said its farewells, drifting over distant limestone cliffs.

With pride, Catullus had decorated the sumptuous dinner table with his newest sentimental treasures, Saebatan napkins from Spain's east coast near Valencia. His dearest friends, Fabullus and Veranius, had sent them recently as tokens of their friendship, and now, carefully creased, they graced his home's table.

But as the dinner unfolded with laughter and wine, Aisnius stole them. With his thieving left hand, he had deftly snatched a few napkins, stuffing them into his pockets when no one was looking. This bestial *conduct*, however, did not escape Catullus' quick eye and rebuke:

"You must think this is so funny, Aisnius. Well, it's not. It reeks of coarseness and has ruined my evening. Even your brother Pollio is humiliated by your actions. Why can't you be more like him? He knows how to entertain with clever talk and polite manners. If you don't want a public scolding, you better give me back my napkins at once!"

***

It seems such a silly thing, napkin stealing. But there is truth in the notion that people observe the *conduct* of others and draw conclusions. This is why Paul exhorts all believers to be careful about such matters. Simple courtesies matter in daily discourse, as Paul emphasizes to his Colossian friends.

***

"Conduct yourselves with wisdom toward outsiders, making the most of the opportunity. Let your speech always be with grace, as though seasoned with salt..." (Col. 4:5).

***

Return those napkins and conduct yourself with wisdom.

***

"Laws control the lesser man.... Right conduct controls the greater one."
Mark Twain

Day 57

Conflicted (1184 BC)
Homer, *Iliad*, 11:370–420

***

Paris, prince of Troy, drew back his mighty bow as he leaned against the temple's pillar. In the shadow of Athene's sacred wooden image, he set his arrow and, with urgent prayer, sent it flying toward Diomed, a fierce Greek soldier beneath Troy's walls. The missile flew, fueled by vengeance, striking Diomed's right foot and fixing it to the bloodied ground.

Trojans rushed to finish him, speeding toward the lame warrior. Suddenly Odysseus, his ally, stood over his curved shield offering shelter. Quickly, the fallen comrade sat down and yanked the arrow from his flesh, suppressing the pain as the enemy taunted him. Calling for a chariot, Diomed hobbled aboard and shuttled off to the Greek camp.

Odysseus stood alone before the Trojan wolves salivating. "What will I do now?" he asked himself. "If I run, history will name me a coward, and a shadow of shame will cover my soul. But if I fight, the mongrels will take me prisoner and lead me in chains through Troy's ancient streets. Do I flee or fight?"

Conflicted within a closing death circle, he ended his soliloquy in disgust. "I cannot live with two minds. Let me fight and quit the field a hero."

***

Each of us often stands *conflicted*, encircled by doubts, trembling at choices we cannot fathom. Our inner debates grow heated,

113

without finality, until exhausted, we fall before a holy God and weep. Paul knew this battle all too well:

***

"For what I am doing, I do not understand; for I am not practicing what I would like to do, but I am doing the very thing I hate" (Rom. 7:15).

***

Cease your waffling and take God's hand.

***

"The harder the conflict, the more glorious the triumph."
Thomas Paine

Day 58

Confrontation (540 BC)
Herodotus, *The Persian Wars*, 1:189–190

***

Cyrus the Great, known by many as King of the World, sat raging astride his warhorse. His vast army, marching to conquer Babylon, faced the turbulent Gyndes River that had just dared to *confront* this unconquered monarch. Cyrus' favorite white horse, a majestic, sacred stallion spooked by the current, had bolted into the stream. Caught in the Gyndes' watery grip, it tumbled and bobbed downstream until it washed ashore dead on an isolated embankment.

Enraged by this impudence, Cyrus dismounted, weighing his options. Such defiance would not be tolerated. Calling his engineers, he began laying out a series of 360 lines, each scratch on the sand a portend of retaliation. The sandy fingers stretched outward from the Gyndes' banks, a spidery web destined to punish the defiant river.

When the engineers finally completed their tasks, Cyrus ordered the soldiers to dig canals along the lines. They dug in the summer's heat, day after day, until, at summer's end, the mighty river slithered ashamedly through the desert, a whispery token of its past glory.

Cyrus, his imperious head held high, then marched onward across the skeletal stream toward Babylon.

***

Some *confrontations* are necessary, peeling away embedded pride and hypocrisy. It's a weapon to be used with utmost caution. It can leave permanent whelps upon its intended. Jesus knocked tables over at the temple to restore its sacred traditions; Paul used it once on an old friend who had surrendered his ideals.

***

"But when Cephas came to Antioch, I opposed him to his face, because he stood condemned" (Gal. 2:11).

***

A defiant river rages before you today. Confrontation calls. Caution!

***

"I think confrontation is healthy, because it clears the air very quickly."
Bill Parcell

Day 59

***

Conquerors (69 BC)
Suetonius, *Lives of the Caesars*, 1:7

***

Julius Caesar stood impatiently sighing in the temple of Hercules. He gazed at the statue of Alexander the Great, who, at age 32, had *conquered* the world. Caesar, at the same age, had done nothing. As quaestor, appointed to travel a circuit in Further Spain, he spent his days presiding as judge over an assortment of boring cases. Yet here before him was a god-man whose hands, early in life, had touched heaven and earth. Here was a general to reckon with who had triumphantly ridden Bucephalus into countless battles.

Caesar paced back and forth before Alexander's rapacious eyes that questioned him, challenged him, mocked his idleness. "By now," he seemed to say from his elevated throne in the temple, "I had crossed the Granicus, fought victoriously at Issus and Guagamela. What have you done?"

Caesar made no reply. He merely moaned as fading sunlight shone through the temple's gold and marble pillars. Muttering as he left, he dreamed that night of attacking his mother, ghoulish images that dismayed him greatly. Soothsayers interpreted it more valiantly. This means you will one day conquer mother earth.

And so he did.

***

Paul knew both men. Raised in literature, he had heard their distant screams and chants of victory after bloody battles. Paul had read about these *conquering* generals of history but looked beyond their sandy accomplishments. These generals were nothing but empty echoes of the past. Addressing the saints at Rome, he reminded them that they were current conquerors.

***

"But in all these things we overwhelmingly conquer through Him who loved us" (Rom. 8:37).

***

Forget Caesar's statue. Kneel before the Throne.

***

"Only things the dreamers make live on. They are the eternal conquerors."
Herbert Kaufman

Day 60

***

Conscience (AD 32)

Tacitus, *The Annals of Imperial Rome*, 6:4

***

Tiberius, slumped over his elaborate writing desk, struggled.

His Capri palace, perched on the edge of lofty cliffs with breathtaking views, could not ease his mutilated soul, ground to dust by a life of putrid malevolence. He dabbed the quill in ink and hovered over the blank manuscript.

There was no escaping his past. The record stood for all to read. His life of cruelty and sexual perversion was etched into the seams of history, haunting him relentlessly.

Still, the senate awaited a letter. He must write. Duty demanded it.

His first words were faltering, a subtle confession he had not intended to make. "I can't seem to find my words, gentlemen of the senate. I feel heaven is about to plunge me into a worse ruin than I feel today." He paused, his pen trembling. Then he continued like he was in a sinner's booth. "And I know that tomorrow will bring deeper despair and the next day even more."

He paused, wondering how history, who looked deeply into the souls of despots, would view him. They would inspect his wasted years closely.

He put down his pen, his *conscience* trembling.

***

Paul, too, sat at his writing desk, lit by a sliver of light between the jail cell bars. The year was 62 AD, and the shadows of a death mask dabbled on his small desk. He picked up his quill, and, without hesitation, the ink flowed with joyous memories and a buoyant *conscience*:

***

"I thank my God in all my remembrance of you, always offering prayer with joy in my every prayer for you all..." (Phil. 1:3–4).

***

Write the next lines of your life today.

***

"When once the gate is opened to self-torture, the whole army of fiends files in."
Henry James

Day 61

***

Consent (1184 BC)
Homer, *Iliad*, 1:423–530

***

Achilles wept loudly on the shore, sobbing to his mother, Thetis, goddess of the sea. "The king has demanded that I give him my war prize, Briseis, who loves me dearly. Please, Mother," he begged, "go to Zeus on Mt. Olympus and tell him to stop this crime."

Thetis moaned, knowing how difficult it was to get Zeus' *consent* for anything. "Yes, son, I will go, but it will not be easy."

For twelve long days, she waited for Zeus to return home from a festival with the other gods. Finally, when the time had come, she rose from the sea depths and slipped down the corridor of heaven. Finding him sitting alone, high on a mountain ridge, she kneeled, seizing his knees. Her woeful story tumbled forth as Zeus sat unmoved, silently distant. But Thetis persisted. "Please grant this request and nod to me as you do when you agree to help."

Zeus finally looked at the grieving mother and complained. "You don't know how much trouble this will cause me at home. My wife hates it when I promise to help other gods. But I will worry about that later." Then, he solemnly nodded assent, his head's ambrosial locks swaying, the sacred sign of approval.

***

It is in times of trouble that we need a friend. Difficulties are best conquered when shared with a willing confidant. God, too, awaits our requests, more than ready to nod His *consent*.

***

"I love the LORD, because He hears my voice and supplications. Because He inclined His ear to me, therefore I shall call upon Him as long as I live" (Ps. 116:1–2).

***

Lift your weeping eyes and watch God nod.

***

"Prayer delights God's ear; it melts His heart."
Thomas Watson

Day 62

***

Consequences (AD 9)
Cassius Dio, *Roman History*, 56:11

***

The fortress's flanks dug deeply into the hillside summit. This Dalmatian town would never fall. Germanicus, the Roman commander, made multiple assaults upon the castle to no avail. His siege engines were useless. Morale plummeted among the restless soldiers. Something had to happen soon, but Germanicus had no solution.

Morning broke over the Adriatic below, shimmering with new hope for the town's plucky combatants who refused to surrender. Once again, Germanicus sat in his chair, staring at the embarrassing debacle before him. And at the same time, far above, a Dalmatian soldier leaned groggily upon the parapet-lined fortress rim.

Suddenly, a great commotion stirred below in the Roman camp. One lone soldier, a German horseman, frustrated over the previous strikes' impotence, picked up a huge rock and hurled it against the wall with profound *consequences*. An unexpected ripple raced up a fortress crack weakening the parapet, which crumbled, dragging the soldier on watch down the ravine.

Frantic alarms sent panicked castle combatants scrambling toward the upper citadel, abandoning the walls. Germanicus, astounded, ordered an immediate assault and captured the obstinate fortress.

***

It's fascinating to follow the *consequences* of that fateful horseman's actions.

What about Lydia? I doubt she suspected her early morning stroll to the river in Philippi would open heaven's door. She had gathered a few of her purple garments and slipped silently through the town gates to pray. There, beside the gurgling stream, the gospel, like the stone above, struck a weak spot in her heart, followed by tears and spiritual surrender.

***

"and the lord opened her heart to respond to the things spoken by Paul" (Acts 16:14–15).

***

Hurl a love stone today and wait.

***

"Sooner or later everyone sits down to a banquet of consequences."
Robert Louis Stevenson

Day 63

***

Contemplation (AD 110)
Juvenal, *Satires*, 13:80–110

***

Juvenal spent one morning *contemplating* the existence of God. It wasn't going well. As he peered behind the veil of eternity, all he saw was either nothingness or divine apathy.

Most people told him the gods didn't exist, while others saw them as distant, vengeful, and haphazard in their punishments. "Some of the folks I've met in villages tell me that they think there is no divine agenda. The sacred altars don't mean anything to them," they said. "They're just stones in the road, nothing more."

Juvenal heard other opinions as he strolled the village near his house. Some people believed in vengeful gods but figured they were too distracted ever to punish them. These folks felt liberated to cheat, steal, and lie. "After all, the wrath of the gods might be great," said a local farmer, "but heaven is so busy with its affairs, it will never catch up to me."

"Hey, Juvenal!" shouted the local butcher. "I'm going to keep these stolen coins. Let Isis do whatever she wants. She can shatter my body with her sistrum. I don't care. I'm still not giving back my loot. It wouldn't matter to me if she broke my leg, punctured my lung, or hit me with ulcers." The guy paused, smiling. "She won't do it! She's got better things to do with her time."

***

David spent one evening *contemplating* the existence of God. He strolled beneath heaven's canopy and marveled.

***

"When I consider Your heavens, the work of Your fingers, the moon and the stars, which You have ordained; What is man that You take thought of him..." (Ps. 8:3–4).

***

Who will you stroll with this morning? Juvenal or David?

***

"I took a walk in the woods and came out taller than the trees." *Henry David Thoreau*

Day 64

***

Courage (58 BC)
Caesar, *Gallic War*, 4:25

***

Caesar's legions bobbed in their warships off the British coast near Dover. Opposite him on the shore, fierce tribes waited to smother his attack in the beating surf. The natives observed the Roman fear and pranced boldly on horses trained in the surf. Livid with rage, the barbarians charged into the sea, tossing missiles and daring Caesar's troops to disembark.

The ship-bound soldiers feared the water with its unknown depth and swirling currents. Most hesitated, leering over the rails' edge at unknown perils. Each warrior had the added peril of carrying heavy weapons, making the leap into the brine more dangerous.

Suddenly, when all seemed lost, one noble-hearted Roman warrior who carried the tenth legion's eagle began to pray. Calling upon heaven's graces, with his hands extended skyward, he placed his life in Jupiter's hand.

A sacred silence swept the ship as the lone soldier screamed over the howling wind. "Now is the time," he shouted to his comrades. "As for me, I will never betray our country or this eagle!" With that, he scrambled atop the ship's rail and leaped into the frothy sea. Instantly, *courage* swept the legion, and they all, to a man, joined the lone combatant in the surf.

***

On a stormy Galilean sea, when confronted with a raging storm and howling winds, the Lord's disciples, likewise, trembled in fear. Then with *courage*, Peter leaped out of the vessel into the abyss.

***

"And He said, 'Come!' And Peter got out of the boat, and walked on the water and came toward Jesus" (Matt. 14:29).

***

Tear your eyes from the dangers and see the *Eagle*. Be courageous today!

***

"He who is not courageous enough to take risks will accomplish nothing in life."
Muhammad Ali

Day 65

Courtship (1178 BC)
Virgil, *Aeneid*, 4:127–140

***

Dido, the queen of Carthage, still mourned her late husband, Sychaeus. Her virtue unquestioned, she lived each day in his shadow, love's ambition buried forever in memory's sacred devotion. But since Aeneas' arrival with his desperate Trojan vagabonds, lost and searching for a homeland, things had changed. Her heart throbbed again as love's music strummed her soul, gently awakening a long-buried desire for *courtship*.

She defied, at first, the dreams that hovered in the midnight hours as she lay alone, sleepless. But denial was threadbare now, the flame already burning. Her sister had urged her to love again, to spin a web to delay Aeneas' departure for Italy's shores.

Daily she sought the gods' favor, visiting their shrines, especially Juno's, who made the marriage-bond her business. Dido, beautiful in love's pursuit, chalice in hand, would pour libations between the horns of a milk-white heifer, slowly pacing by the dripping altars, flirting with a forbidden future.

One morning, having invited Aeneas to join her on a morning hunt, she loitered in the palace as Massylian riders galloped restlessly behind their waiting hounds. Finally, she slipped through the great doors dressed in a Phoenician robe, her hair piped in brightly-colored braids. A golden quiver draped her back, and a brooch of gold fastened the waist of her gown.

***

Courtship's call, fairer than evening whippoorwills, summons us all, stopping time, stretching our emotions, pouring its sweet libations upon our seeking hearts. These treasured moments linger through time, never forgotten. Solomon himself stared in awe at his queen, jangling in gold from Ophir as stringed instruments struck chords of grace.

***

"At Your right hand stands the queen in gold from Ophir" (Ps. 45:9).

***

Courtship awaits you. Find love's release today.

***

"They dream in courtship, but in wedlock wake."
Alexander Pope

Day 66

***

Cowardice (1184 BC)
Homer, *Iliad*, 3:1–40

***

Advancing like screaming cranes driven by winter's rain, the Trojan army thundered toward their rendezvous with destiny. Opposite them came the silently marching Greek soldiers, their shuffling feet spinning up dust that spread a curtain of dread, like a death mist, over the plains. Instinctively, both sides stopped and awaited the two champion fighters.

Paris stepped forward for the Trojans, his bearing haughty, Priam's noble blood roiling within him. A panther's skin dangled off his shoulders along with his menacing sword and bow. Two bronze spears gripped with hostility dared a challenger to step forward.

Menelaus, whose eyes feasted on this gift of the gods, sprang from his chariot eager for revenge. He fought for Helen, his stolen wife, and for Greek pride. Like hungry lions feasting on a fresh kill, he strode to the centerline between the armies.

Paris suddenly shrank back in fear at the glistening suit of armor before him. Trembling as if a slithering serpent had suddenly bared its deadly fangs, Paris flung himself behind the Trojan combatants, terrified. His brother, Hector, known for courage in battle, scoffed at this *cowardice*, berating him before the troops. "I wish you had never been born, brother!"

***

Daily life in our turbulent world demands confidence. Whether it's a job interview, a medical procedure, or a first date, fleeing is not an option. Departure will only postpone your success. I see this so clearly in Gideon's *cowardice* question to his troops before battle.

***

"Now therefore come, proclaim in the hearing of the people, saying, 'Whoever is afraid and trembling, let him return and depart from Mount Gilead.' So 22,000 people returned...." (Judg. 7:3).

***

Hold your ground on Mt. Gilead! Let courage prevail.

***

"Cowardice in a race, as in an individual, is the unpardonable sin."
Theodore Roosevelt

Day 67

***

Cross (AD 55)
Petronius, *The Satyricon*, 111–113

***

The grief of the poor widow was stunning.

She had loved her husband with such noble intensity that all the residents of Ephesus, where she lived, marveled at her fidelity. When he died, she was inconsolable, beating her breasts and wailing unceasingly. People came from neighboring towns to witness her chaste grief.

Across town, the governor ordered several thieves crucified. A soldier was posted at the *cross*, near the tomb where the widow still mourned day and night.

One night, the soldier noticed the tomb light not far away. Investigating, he saw the beautiful widow in mourning and did his best to encourage her to eat. She refused, but eventually, he prevailed. Once her strength returned, she fell in love with her rescuer. Love-making and marriage soon followed as he slipped away from the cross nightly and visited the tomb.

One night, the thieves' parents noticed the guard missing at the cross, and so they stole their son's body away for burial. When the soldier realized this, he was horrified and drew his sword to kill himself. The widow persuaded him to place the body of her former husband on the cross. The following morning, the entire town marveled at the miracle.

***

Petronius tells us this was a local Ephesian joke drawing rowdy guffaws. Stroll casually by any ancient pub and hear the *cross* jokes. Crucifixions were merely comedy routines, nothing more.

But to Paul and the saints of the early church, the cross was much more.

***

"For the word of the cross is foolishness to those who are perishing, but to us who are being saved it is the power of God" (1 Cor. 1:18).

***

Today, kneel beneath the cross.

***

"From the cross God declares, 'I love you.'"
Billy Graham

Day 68

***

Crossings (49 BC)
Suetonius, *Lives of the Caesars*, 1.31–33

***

Caesar stood on the tiny Rubicon's shore, draped in midnight, clawing at options. Pointing to the bridge that led toward Rome, he said to his closest confidants, "There is still time to turn back, but once we cross, if we cross, struggle and warfare await us all."

Pondering the implications of marching on Rome, he suddenly saw a magnificent apparition playing a reed pipe. A gathering of shepherds, enthralled by the midnight melody, sat listening. As this dream unfolded, some of Caesar's soldiers joined the concert. As they did so, the ghost snatched a trumpet from one soldier and, after a thunderous blast, crossed the little bridge.

Caesar, seeing this unfold in his mind, suddenly awoke and shouted to his army. "It's a sign from the gods! Let's follow the trumpet's call and *cross* to our fate beyond the river. The die is cast."

Assembling his troops on the other side, he tearfully urged them to follow him into the unknown. Ripping open his tunic, exposing his chest, he begged for their support. Pointing to the ring on his left hand, he declared that he would gladly bestow this equestrian ring to those who followed him.

***

Rubicons litter the landscape and cannot be avoided. Perhaps today, this very day, you stand on its edge, pondering a *crossing*. Be bold. There is no other way. Such was a day in Joshua's life on the edge of a desert.

***

"Then Joshua rose early in the morning; and he and all the sons of Israel set out from Shittim and came to the Jordan, and they lodged there before they crossed" (Josh. 3:1).

***

Celebrate your crossing today!

***

"Smooth seas do not make skillful sailors."
African Proverb

Day 69

***

Cup (1184 BC)
Homer, *Iliad*, 16:220–250

***

The enraged Myrmidons, warriors from Thessaly, prepared for the assault. Lined up tightly before the ships' sterns, their backs to the sea, a thousand horsehair helmet plumes gleamed, an undulating crimson tide shivering beneath a morning sun. Shield pressed upon shield as Patroclus and Automedon, the two combat veterans, stood before the troops.

With sacred reverie, the warriors steadied themselves and stared with awe as Achilles, their king, raised his wine cup for the libation. This *cup* of rare artistry had lain in the mysterious depths of the wooden chest silver-footed Thetis had given Achilles as he sailed for war years earlier. She had filled it with shirts, woolen cloaks for winter, and cleverly woven rugs. But in one corner of the container, Thetis had placed an ornamental cup of exquisite beauty. Only Achilles could drink from it, and it was this cup he raised before the soldiers.

Having cleansed it with sulfur and rinsed away all impurities with water, he lifted the wine-filled goblet toward Zeus. "King Zeus, lord of Dodona, who lives amid the Sille, those sacred priests who sleep upon the ground with unwashed feet, I pray for your blessings upon these troops." As the wine drizzled upon the sand, a whispering murmur passed through the trembling troops.

***

Cups, like magnets, are drawn to higher causes. They summon the deepest prayers from our hidden places and elevate our tasks for the highest good. God, Himself, holds a cup as he scans the earth. Let the blessed rejoice and the wicked tremble:

***

"For a cup is in the hand of the LORD, and the wine foams; It is well mixed, and He pours out of this..." (Ps. 75:8).

***

Find your cup and consecrate something today.

***

"Pour libations, cover your head with ivy, join the dance!"
Euripides

Day 70

***

Daggers (428 BC)
Euripides, *Hippolytus*, 765–890

***

The queen dangled piteously from the palace bedroom's rafters. A guilty, twisted noose claimed her as she died, tangled up in secrets that dared not speak. They must not speak, for with voice, they would have shredded Phaedra's excellent reputation.

Lustful desires for Hippolytus, her stepson, would surely have cracked the foundations of her husband's reign. Hippolytus, the best of Athens' young men, whose virgin heat longed only for the purest endeavors, knew nothing of this plague. But still, it raged in the queen's heart until she could bear it no longer.

The queen's nurse first discovered the still quivering body swaying over the bed. "Help!" she screamed, the strident notes ringing through afternoon corridors. "Our queen is dead! Someone bring a knife. Help me cut her down." A cluster of terrified feet rushed to the bedroom. Amid screams of disbelief, they laid the pale body upon purple coverlets and wept.

Theseus, her king, and husband, home from a business trip, entered to the direful sounds. "What has happened?" he asked. The servants, choking on explanations, told the sorry tale. Racing to her body, he found a tablet fastened to her lifeless hand.

Desperate to tame the tragedy, he broke the seal and read the lying accusation, *dagger*-tipped: "Hippolytus raped me!"

***

The false accusation, unproven but living, is a common *dagger* in a hostile world. Often there seems no defense capable of quenching the lie. So it was with Joseph, a man after Hippolytus' heart. This Egyptian queen, too, flung a lying tablet at an innocent man:

***

"he came in to me to lie with me, and I screamed" (Gen. 39:14).

***

Lay the dagger on heaven's altar. God knows the truth.

***

"Courage is to feel the daily daggers of relentless steel and keep on going."
Douglas Malloch

Day 71

***

Dancing (AD 41)
Suetonius, *Lives of the Caesars*, 4:54

***

Another sleepless night for Caligula dragged on and on. Long walks through dark corridors eased the stress. Often, he would order the sun to rise, desperate for streaks of gold across the Palatine horizon.

It was one of these nights when after intensely conversing with sea ghosts, he bolted to his closet. Flicking through a bevy of sparkling women's garments, he settled on an ankle-length tunic in bold vermillion topped with a dainty shawl of bumblebee yellow. With butterfly strides, he flew through the palace halls, reaching the stage where he often *danced* before bleary-eyed staff roused from sleep.

Quickly writing invitations for three consular senators to hasten to the palace, he ordered his couriers to summon them to the performance. The clock struck midnight as the terrified senators entered the auditorium to the sounds of crashing castanets and flutes tuning and blaring out unrehearsed melodies. The ever-watchful Caligula noticed their arrival and, with an exuberant song and dance, bellowed out odes to love, swaying seductively as if courting the moon. And then, as quickly as it all began, he slipped into the mists of the backstage without a word.

***

Glance eastward toward Palestine and listen for the castanets. Herodias makes them sing as she sways erotically before Herod and his guests assembled in the luxurious Machaerus fortress east of the Dead Sea. She, too, *danced* in the late hours. The ovation won her the head of John the Baptist on a plate.

***

"and when the daughter of Herodias herself came in and danced, she pleased Herod and his dinner guests" (Mk. 6:22).

***

Sleepless at midnight? Rise and dance before the Lord.

***

"While pensive poets painful vigils keep, sleepless themselves, to give their readers sleep."
Alexander Pope

Day 72

***

Deadlines (431 BC)
Euripides, *Medea*, 270–355

***

Medea, the Black Sea princess from faraway Colchis, cursed the day she fell in love. Jason had won her when he first leaped from his Argonaut ship, striding purposefully ashore on Colchis' white beaches. In search of the Golden Fleece, he scooped up a princess and carried Medea back to Thessaly.

But the fates are fickle, and when alluring temptations from Corinth drew Jason toward its palace, Jason fell in love again. This Corinthian princess promised him wealth, prestige, and blue-blooded love. Jason took the bait and dumped his wife, Medea, and their small children for this new Peloponnesian fantasy.

Medea cursed him and her broken dreams. How far she had fallen from Black Sea privileges to now, on bended knee before Corinth's King Creon. "I'm begging you," she pleaded, grasping the king's legs. "Don't banish my small boys and me. We have nowhere to go."

Creon, unmoved, kicked her away. "I will not be swayed. Go now, or I will throw you out myself!"

Medea raised her swollen eyes and pleaded one last time. "Just give me one day, and I will be gone forever."

The king, hesitating, grudgingly agreed. "One day. It's a *deadline* I will not alter. Then be gone forever!"

***

Deadlines hover over our horizons every day. Some are silly, but others haunt us, shading our days in black. These ephemeral lines in the sand can torment us, box us in, create unbearable stresses. Solomon spoke of deadlines that can't be altered apart from God's grace

***

"There is an appointed time for everything ... a time to die ... a time to heal" (Eccl. 3:1–3).

***

A deadline glares at you. Act swiftly with faith.

***

"If we didn't have deadlines, we'd stagnate."
Walt Disney

Day 73

***

Death (25 BC)
Virgil, *Aeneid*, 6:320

***

Death looms on the misty horizon for us all. Woody Allen famously quipped, "I'm not afraid of death; I just don't want to be there when it happens."

The ancients had the same dread of the afterlife. Virgil described an alarming gathering at the River Cocytus known as the wailing river in the ancient underworld. Here an innumerable multitude of beleaguered souls gathered, waving wildly for Charon the ferryman to take them across. This filthy boat captain with the unkempt white beard and eyes like fiery jets summoned only a select few.

Virgil, in a solemn voice, bade us scan this foreboding landscape packed with the trembling dead. "See how they anxiously loiter there as thick as the leaves that fall at Autumn's first frost. How pitiful they are with their thin arms outstretched, hoping, waiting for the ferryman to take them across the river where *death* could claim its final victory. Virgil sighed and then continued. "Those unable to board the boat are the miserable folks that were never buried properly on earth. Now, alas, they have to wander like miserable waifs for a hundred years before they get another chance at the ferryboat."

***

Death's goal line could be just the motivator you need to grasp your dreams.

Jesus told His friends not to be troubled about *death,* for God has many homes waiting for them.

***

"For in my Father's house are many dwelling places; if it were not so, I would have told you; for I go to prepare a place for you" (Jn. 14:2).

***

Forget the ferryman! This is your day to live with joy and purpose.

***

"Death is not the greatest loss in life. The greatest loss is what dies inside us while we live."
Norman Cousins

Day 74

***

Deception (AD 14)
Tacitus, *The Annals of Imperial Rome*, 1:22

***

The mutiny was raging in Pannonia. Caesar Augustus' grave was still wet with tears, an ideal time for rebellious troops to relieve frustrations. Insubordination swept the army camps, swelling discontentment. Sensing an opportunity, Percennius, a mere private who once was a professional applause leader in Rome's theaters, took the stage. Prancing before the troops, he whipped up a feverish mutiny.

As the rebellion grew, some rabid soldiers hoisted another private named Vibulenus upon their shoulders as a crowd hastily assembled. Raising his hands as if he were Julius Caesar, he began to rail against the camp commander, Blaesus. "Where is my brother, general? Where did you bury him? You dirty dog, where did you bury my brother? He only wanted to talk to you calmly about our common demands."

By now, the livid countenance of the army flared as the wild-eyed private continued, his lips drooling with a phantasmagorical tale. "Even enemies honor a man's corpse. But not you!" He beat his chest and struck his face in mourning. Then he fell to the ground crawling to this and that soldier begging for help.

The only problem was that Vibulenus was making it all up. All of it! Nothing but *deception's* drivel.

***

147

Vibulenus and Judas were contemporaries with similar faults. Judas, like the disconsolate soldier, also *deceived* his friends.

***

"Why was this perfume not sold for three hundred denarii and given to the poor people? Now he said this not because he was concerned about the poor but because he was a thief, and as he had the money box, he used to pilfer what was put into it" (Jn. 12:5–6).

***

Be authentic. Keep a clean money box.

***

"The greatest deception men suffer is from their own opinions." *Leonardo da Vinci*

Day 75

Decisions (1183 BC)
Virgil, *Aeneid*, 3:540–570

***

Standing on the ship's bow, Anchises kept an ever-watchful eye on the foaming waves, ready to implement quick *decisions* needed to save the ship. Aeneas and his ship's vagabonds, ever vigilant as well, sailed toward Italy. New world hopes danced in their minds mingling with dreams of a future beyond Troy's burning walls.

Suddenly, Anchises, peering through sea mists, sensed danger. Thunderous waves, throbbing on shallow rocks, mingled with furious shoals boiling with sand. The old man, his voice edged with disaster, screamed. "It must be Charybdis!" This dreaded monster on Sicily's shore thrice daily gulped down ocean water and spat it out again, her lips belching dead zones in the sea, spinning turbulence, whirlpools lusty for careless sailors.

On the opposite side of the straits loomed Scylla, her wild hair flapping in the fierce wind. Wild-eyed dogs about her waist snapped, and the serpent heads lunged at the passing craft.

"All hands on deck!" shouted Anchises as sailors scrambled to port, the vessel creaking. Caught between monsters, the ship tumbled into the trough and plummeted to the Pit below, scratching sea bottom, and then barreled skyward, spitting spindrift into vacuous snake eyes.

***

Our lives are often littered with spent *decisions* made on the run. We lunge left and then over-correct by forcing the ship to port. Decisions must not be ignored. Choose carefully. Joshua, aged and alarmed like Anchises on the ship's bow, summoned his people to the summit of Shechem to make a decision.

***

"Now, therefore, fear the LORD and serve Him in sincerity and truth;... If it is disagreeable in your sight to serve the LORD, choose for yourselves today whom you will serve..." (Josh. 24:14–16).

***

Your decisions today will echo forever.

***

"Choices are the hinges of destiny."
Pythagoras

Day 76

***

Defeated (AD 62)
Tacitus, *Annals of Imperial Rome*, 15:15

***

The defeated Roman soldiers shuffled, heads down, out of Tigranocerta. The Parthians lined the Roman fortress's streets, mocking the army as they crept away in silence. The enemy tore the clothes off their once fierce foes as they passed by and seized their weapons, piling them in the street. Humiliation swept the legion out of their city.

Paetus, the impulsive Roman commander responsible for this *defeat*, marched his disillusioned forces past heaps of rotting corpses, men he had once led with pride. Beside the dead were all their weapons looted by the Parthians, forming hillocks of disgrace. Once the survivors escaped the city, Paetus forced forty-mile marches, abandoning the wounded as he fled. The panic-stricken flight resembled a chaotic retreat in battle.

Paetus' army met the replacement forces led by the Roman commander Corbulo at the Euphrates River several days later. As the soldiers passed, Corbulo's men, eager for military glory, stared in shock at the disheveled forces. They began to weep so bitterly in pity they could barely utter a greeting. There was no valor, conquerors' bravado, or decorations displays. Only stricken eyes and sunken features remained. Tacitus tells us with grand brevity that "the prevailing emotion was pity."

***

Defeat is inevitable in life. Who wins all the time? Some flee death's shadow with whimpers, while others find treasure within its scowl. Paul, caged in a Roman city facing certain death, did not dwell on defeat; instead, he celebrated.

***

"I have fought the good fight, I have finished the course, I have kept the faith; in the future there is laid up for me the crown of righteousness..." (2 Tim. 4:7–8a).

***

Turn your defeat into a crown.

***

"Never confuse a single defeat with a final defeat."
F. Scott Fitzgerald

Day 77

***

Delirium (AD 38)
Suetonius, *Lives of the Caesars*, 4:22

***

Caligula lay in his bed, turbulently tossing, gasping. His lover, the distant moon, seemed to toy with him, preening with her daring dalliances. The emperor pleaded for her to come closer, enter his bedroom, and lie with him in a lover's embrace. It was the same each night, a routine that led him to the edge of *delirium*, the moon's delicious rays pirouetting on his balcony but coming no closer.

Upon awakening in the morning unsatisfied, he would seek his day devotee, Jupiter, who resided in Rome's premier temple on the Capitoline Hill. There, Caligula would approach the king of the gods with a rare familiarity unknown to humanity.

Whispering so none could hear but the god, he would spill the secrets of his tortured soul. Jupiter, busy with loftier tasks, shunned these intrusions, refusing to answer. Caligula, however, would press his ear to the god's mouth, demanding responses, listening for the briefest sighs, concessions that might ease his inner torment. But, when no breath could be heard, he would shout in angry language and hurl threats at the throne.

Then, one day, he caught a whispered invitation to live with the deity in his heavenly splendor. Caligula, so excited, began preparations to build a home beside Jupiter's temple.

***

Caligula's affairs with the moon and the god of thunder present a portrait of daily *delirium* that stuns the modern reader. And yet, he was not the first to desire the moon's embraces. Jeremiah wrote with utter disgust as Judah worshipped her as well:

***

"the sun, the moon and to all the host of heaven, which they have loved and which they have served..." (Jer. 8:2).

***

Surrender your delirium to the Savior.

***

"The moon is a friend for the lonesome to talk to."
Carl Sandburg

Day 78

***

Delusion (60 BC)
Lucretius, *On the Nature of Things*, 1:150

***

Lucretius sat musing at his desk overlooking the harbor of Pompey. The gaiety of dancing maenads tastefully graced his bedroom wall while deeper thoughts plagued him. Glancing at Vesuvius in the distance, he wondered about life's mysteries and then scowled at the *delusionary* chains that bound humanity.

Picking up his pen, he began to write again, scrawling his sponsor's name, "Memmius," on the parchment. "My dear friend," he wrote, "why do we all fear death and succumb so easily to life's brutish superstitions? Surely Epicurus has set us all free from such silliness and crushed this monster beneath our feet."

Once again, the young philosopher paused, pondering the evils of fear and the dread of unknown forces about us. Remembering the story of Agamemnon's brutality at the altar of Aulis, he recalled its chilling details, shuddering at the altar's bleeding victim:

"The headband bound Iphigenia's virgin tresses that hung so innocently over her cheeks. Suddenly she caught sight of her father, Agamemnon, standing teary-eyed in front of the altar. The attendants beside him and other family members began weeping when they saw the knife in his hand. Terrified and speechless, she fell to her knees, a sinless victim to superstition."

***

Paul made it clear to Timothy that he should avoid such tawdry diversions. Knowing well the *deluded* Roman world about him, he urges us all to find nourishment in faith and sound doctrine. It's a disciplined life that yields heaven's reward.

***

"Have nothing to do with godless myths and old wives' tales; rather, train yourself to be godly" (1 Tim. 4:6–7).

***

Quit knocking on wood. Knock on heaven's door instead.

***

"Superstition is the death of a thinking mind."
Dr. T.P. Chia

Day 79

Departures (438 BC)
Euripides, *Alcestis*, 232–257

***

Through the palace doors, the little troop of mourners trudged behind the sorrowing litter. Alcestis, her life nearly vanquished, fought time, desperate to live. Beside her, Admetus wept openly, counting his innumerable woes as the sun rose merrily over Pherae's distant sea.

"Don't leave me now," cried Admetus imploringly. "Raise yourself!" But his demands, caught in death's web, died their slow death, unable to stir her fading pulse.

"I see him now," she cried! "Charon stands impatiently in his little sea boat with one hand ready on the oar." Her eyes, suddenly lit with a late, defiant flame, widened, afraid. "Husband, he makes demands upon me!"

Charon screamed over the turbulent waves. "What keeps you? Hurry. It is *departure's* time, and you hold me back." The other travelers, bow-huddled in masses beneath thin blankets, stared emptily at some distant shore.

Admetus moaned, unseeing but not doubting. Holding tightly to her hand, he followed beside the bobbing litter approaching the cemetery monument. Spring sparrows flitted among the orchard's branches, oblivious. Suddenly, she whimpered. "Somebody has me; somebody takes me away." His dark eyes shelter a frown. She paused for air. "Oh! He has wings. Death has me. I must go now."

***

Departures, like summer's last breath, eventually leave us shivering in fall's early winds. Families separate, children leave the nest, and marriage bonds dissolve prematurely. We, like Alcestis, hear voices calling. So did the disciples:

***

"I go to prepare a place for you... Thomas said to Him 'Lord, we do not know where You are going, how do we know the way?'" (Jn. 14:2/5).

***

Embrace a friend today before departure's clock calls.

***

"There are no goodbyes for us. Wherever you are, you will always be in my heart."
Mahatma Gandhi

Day 80

Descents (1177 BC)
Virgil *Aeneid*, 6:200–300

***

Aeneas' *descent* began at dawn. Growling mutterings underground rumbled as he approached the cave to hell. In dawn's half-light, he heard a distant baying of hounds and knew Hecate, the goddess of the crossroads, was coming. "Draw your sword now!" shouted the Sibyl, his guide to the underworld. Then, with her wild eyes spinning, she leaped into the darkness with Aeneas close behind.

Following a wending trail, barely illuminated, they stumbled forward toward a gate where demonic Furies lay in disarray, their viperine hair tucked beneath blood-soaked headbands. A monstrous dark elm tree hovered over the entranceway where freakish ghosts hissed and darted. Aeneas drew his sword but knew it was useless, the vaporous bodies morphing here and there.

Drawing ever closer to Acheron's riverbanks, the rotten scent of a boiling whirlpool spitting up slimy sand startled him. Amid the chaos, he caught the ferryman's taut shadow skittering on the shore's edge. Aeneas gasped at Charon's fiery eyes as they locked menacingly upon him. Covered in a filthy cloak, knotted at the shoulders that draggled among the boat's wooden ribs, the ferryman's features raged as he shouted ferociously at the Sibyl who dared to bring the living to these shores.

***

Descents are inevitable on life's erratic coaster ride. Mountain tops, those wondrous elixirs of life, are evanescent, fading all too soon, often leaving us stranded at hell's gate. But it is when chains hold us fast that we can feel the Lord's intimate presence.

***

"When He got out of the boat, immediately a man from the tombs with an unclean spirit met Him, and he had his dwelling among the tombs..." (Mk. 5:2).

***

Turn descent's dark eyes toward God Who waits for you on the shore.

***

"I must lose myself in action, lest I wither in despair."
Alfred Lord Tennyson

Day 81

***

Desertion (370 BC)
Xenophon, *Anabasis*, 4:1–90

***

The two generals whispered of *desertion*. A flickering candle blown by bay winds warned of trouble as Xenias and Pasion argued for and against their treacherous act late into the night. As Cyrus rested his army here at Myriandus Bay beneath the glare of the Cilician Gates, the traitorous generals weighed the risks.

It was only recently that two thousand of their fiercest warriors had walked out of camp fed up with war. They wanted to go home to Greece. Cyrus had refused to punish them, insisting that every man should choose their fate. This angered the generals, who had ordered a midnight ship to weigh anchor secretly nearby.

"Let's just go," muttered Xenias. "If Cyrus won't punish our soldiers for deserting us, we'll desert him." He stepped to the tent's door and studied the bobbing warship's masts.

"You know he'll come for us," said Pasion.

"We have to risk it," countered Xenias. "Cyrus ruined our reputations. I say let's go now while the young moon beckons."

Both men stood, hesitated, and then shaking trembling hands, called for their wives and ordered all their valuables loaded onto the ship.

***

John warned his church to be alert for those climbing aboard a ship, running from God's call. Those who scorn the communal meal, the Christian kiss, the hand of fellowship, or the joy of worship are none other than *deserters*, apostates from the spiritual calling of God in Christ Jesus.

***

"They went out from us, but they were not really of us; for if they had been of us, they would have remained with us" (1 Jn. 2:19).

***

Be cautious. Desertion has its price.

***

"She mixes religion with desertion to make it sound noble."
Graham Greene

Day 82

***

Despair (27 BC)
Tibullus, *Elegies*, 1:5

***

"Delia, O Delia. You've got me spinning, wobbling like a top on a marble floor. Why can't you love me like you used to?"

Poor Tibullus. Delia won't play by the rules. One day she serves him soft caresses, and the next, she spurns him for another. He demands justice but whimpers softly that she can spin him again and again. He doesn't mind.

Then, one glorious day, Delia coughed. And then coughed again. Delia, her radiant eyes dimmed by some silent foe, was sick. "It's my chance!" he mused. "I'll tend to her day and night."

She conceded with a faint sigh.

He began with sulfur rubs as the town's enchantress sang magical melodies while dancing beside an open window, moonlight fed. Three times he forced the powder upon her limbs, cursing the invisible foe. She glanced at him with adoring eyes, seeing him closely again, absorbing him.

Tibullus, next, offered crumbs from his cake, specially prepared and sprinkled thrice with medicinal drops, sure to chase away the night phantoms. She nibbled, and the cough took flight like a receding tide. Still not finished, he donned the healer's robe and, through the silent night, prayed to Diana nine times.

All for nothing. Once recovered, she returned to another lover, and the dark *despair* returned.

"All my prayers and tears have birthed my worst fears— another lover," he mused, sobbing.

***

Paul found himself spinning top-like too. In bondage to innumerable sins, *despair* blotted out the joy of God.

***

"Wretched man that I am! Who will set me free from the body of this death?" (Rom.7:24).

***

Despair yields to the heavenly Healer.

***

"Think of all the beauty still left around you and be happy."
Anne Frank

Day 83

***

Destinations (AD 120)
Suetonius, *Lives of the Caesars*, 4:19

***

Caligula, ever the histrionic showman, sat regally upon his spirited charger, scanning the bridge to nowhere. Stretching from Baiae, near Rome, the playground of the rich and famous of his day, to the mole at Pueoli, three miles away, the bridge served only one purpose—spectacular madness.

Conceived, perhaps, on one of the emperor's sleepless night ramblings, the construction shocked the ancient world. Commandeering all available merchant ships nearby, he strung them out across the sea in two lines anchoring them side by side. Heaping wagonloads of dirt upon planks, he made a superhighway that floated on the bay.

When sunrise rose over his imaginary kingdom, he led his skittish horse to the starting line. Wearing Alexander the Great's actual golden breastplate he had stolen from the king's tomb, he played a role fit for Hollywood. A civic crown gleamed upon his head, hovering over a cloak of golden cloth. With a quick kick, he charged forward as if the Persian Gates beckoned, one of Alexander's greatest victories.

The following day he stepped into a gleaming chariot in full costume with a team of two famous steeds before him. And so it was, back and forth with no *destination* in mind.

***

Destinations usually require certainty. However, Abraham walked a sliver of land to a place unknown. His bridge to nowhere was built on planks of faith—nothing more.

***

"By faith Abraham, when he was called, obeyed by going out to a place which he was to receive for an inheritance; and he went out, not knowing where he was going" (Heb. 11:8).

***

Where will your bridge take you today?

***

"All journeys have secret destinations of which the traveler is unaware."
Martin Buber

Day 84

Destiny (1184 BC)
Virgil, *Aeneid*, 3:440–461

The leaves, wind-blown, lay in disorder within the Sybil's cave. Ancient letters scribbled hastily upon the leaves long ago, notes that once spelled out travelers' *destinies* no longer conveyed truth. The mystic lady of the leaves, prone to fits and starts, mood swings that swirled like the north winds, had laid them all out in perfect order. They once spelled out esoteric insights into the future and had been carefully stacked in perfect order. The dark cave tunnels held them safely, ready, and waiting for those who sought answers.

But, oh, the wind! The wind had its own mind. And when the cave's door swung open now and then, the leaves would rustle and flutter, dancing whimsically on their hidden ballroom floor. Later, when the weather's fever abated, and the breeze departed, the rune-inscribed leaves littered the floor, spelling words that did not exist, messages twisted and empty.

The old Sybil merely shrugged as she shuffled through these untold destinies. The inquirers waiting impatiently at the cave's door left angrily at her blank stare. No futures foretold on this day. Nothing but leaves of grass, gagged and silent.

You're standing today at a crossroads, diverging paths obscuring your *destiny*. You need answers, but the leaves are scattered, and you can't see the way. The best you can do here is lean heavily upon faith as Abraham did long ago. God will guide you with silent nods and reassurances.

***

"By faith Abraham, when he was called, obeyed by going out to a place which he was to receive for an inheritance; and he went out, not knowing where he was going" (Heb. 11:8).

***

God *made* the wind-blown leaves. He knows your destiny.

***

"It is not in the stars to hold our destiny but in ourselves."
William Shakespeare

Day 85

Destitute (AD 120)
Juvenal, *Satires*, 3:203–210

***

Codrus smelled the fire and trembled.

His pathetic attic room on a Roman back street was a human shrine to utter poverty. The bed, sized for a midget, mocked his lean frame each time he huddled beneath its dingy sheets. Beside it, a leaning cupboard held six little jugs and a tankard of half spoiled wine. On top, a defeated and cracked statue of Chiron, noblest of the centaurs, lay in pieces. An old locker, crammed into a dusty corner, cradled some of Codrus' golden Greek books filled with words of wisdom half-eaten by roving rats.

Smokey tendrils floated greedily through the room, searching, licking the torn pages, ruffling the sheets, sniffing the wine. Codrus, shackled by fear, lay engulfed in *destitution*, unable to see a future. Soon, his room would bow to the flames, and then the streets, his unwanted inheritance, would greet him, laughing.

Finally, hearing the urgent whispers of Chiron on the shelf, he rose and scrambled to the door. Down the back stairs, hobbled by hopelessness, he stumbled to an exit and slithered into a mass of wailing, smoldering victims.

***

We live in a world of *destitute* shadows, frail, impoverished people across the globe who struggle every day for life's basics.

Such was the woman whom Jesus admired. She came into the temple amid the flurry of silken robes and tossed her final two coins into the treasury.

***

"Calling His disciples to Him, He said to them, 'Truly I say to you, this poor widow put in more than all the contributors to the treasury'" (Mk. 12:43).

***

Destitute? Savor the eyes of an admiring Savior.

***

"A world without delight and without affection is a world destitute of value."
Bertrand Russell

Day 86

Deterrents (157 BC)
Plutarch, *Cato*, 27

***

The check engine light was blinking in my old truck. I slapped some black tape over the nuisance and forgot all about it. Sweet! Warning signs are everywhere, it seems. Sometimes, though, we need to pay attention.

Plutarch gave a poignant illustration of this when he wrote about the elder statesman Cato who had just returned from a trip to Carthage. Rushing to the senate, he issued a unique *deterrent* as he shouted to the senate about the dangers of Carthage.

Then, he paused and did something that got their attention. He shook the folds of his toga and spilled fresh Libyan figs on the senate floor. The politicians smiled, admiring their size and beauty. Cato continued in a calmer voice. "These figs," he said, "are only three days sail from Rome. Carthage is bristling with young soldiers, so you better strike now while there is still time."

Every time he addressed the senate, no matter what the subject matter, he always ended by shouting, "Carthage must be destroyed!"

***

Warnings, like flu vaccines, are never pleasant, but they often keep death's tinkling bells at bay. Lincoln's speech, delivered on June 16, 1858, was a *deterrent* the nation needed to hear. The divided country must settle the issue of slavery. It was a messy but necessary theme.

Jesus, too, had a warning about impending tribulation.

***

"Now learn the parable from the fig tree; when its branch has already become tender and puts forth its leaves, you know that summer is near. Even so, you too, when you see these things happening, recognize that He is near, right at the door" (Mk. 13: 28–29).

***

Has God scattered any figs at your feet recently?

***

"One thorn of experience is worth a whole wilderness of warning."
James Russell Lowell

Day 87

***

Diadem (AD 63)
Tacitus, *Annals of Imperial Rome*, 13:28

***

The Parthian royal prince, Tiridates, with his regal purple robe fluttering softly in the Armenian breeze, was the first to dismount. He stood proudly before twenty Persian cavalry escorts, all in war regalia. Across from him sat Corbulo astride his war steed, the Roman general backed by twenty Roman cavalries.

The prince dismounted first and approached the conquering Romans, aware of the precedent unfolding. The men met on foot with a firm handclasp, exchanging compliments. Then Tiridates made a solemn pledge to travel to Rome. There he would personally lay his royal *diadem* at the feet of Nero. The submission was startling; the surrender, total.

Several days later, before the armies parted, they met again with spectacular closing ceremonies. Both forces paraded splendidly before the other. The prancing Parthian horses strutted before the sacred deities of the land. The Romans, likewise, displayed their glittering Eagles and standards.

Finally, the culmination of the morning arrived. Sitting on the dais was an official Roman chair bearing Nero's effigy. After the customary religious sacrifices concluded, the prince, with regal attire, strode augustly toward the statue and bowed, laying his golden diadem at its feet.

***

In utter humiliation, Tiridates laid his golden diadem at Nero's feet—the defeated before the debauched. But Isaiah whispers words with different hues: "You **are** the *diadem* in God's hands." With this melody in my ears, I offer praises before the true King.

***

"You will also be a crown of beauty in the hand of the LORD, and a royal diadem in the hand of your God" (Isa. 62:3).

***

Let Nero keep the trinket. You *are* the diadem.

***

"Nature, like us is sometimes caught without her diadem."
Emily Dickinson

Day 88

Disappointments (AD 53)

Tacitus, *Annals of Imperial Rome*, 12:57

***

Spectators streamed from as far away as Rome to Fucine Lake to watch the spectacular naval battle. After eleven grueling years of chopping a tunnel through Mt. Salviano, the show was about to begin. The nightmare of 30,000 enslaved people living and dying in the endless shafts had morphed into Claudius' grand theater.

Anxious tourists covered the coast, slopes, and hilltops surrounding this lake. Each guest clamored for the best vantage point to watch the display of Roman power before the emperor drained the lake.

Claudius took his seat high above the fracas, wearing a splendid military cloak. Beside him sat the empress, Agrippina, in a mantle of sparkling gold. Beneath them on the lake, warships with 19,000 combatants prepared to fight to the death. On rafts stationed here and there among the warships were catapults and stone-throwing machines ready to thrill guests sitting on nature's valley ledges. Droves of banqueters dipped their fingers into delicate sauces and supped with cheer while they waited.

However, when the military display ended, and the sluices opened, something dreadfully wrong swept the raging waters over the surrounding valley, crashing over celebrants who rushed in horror for higher ground. The malfunction swept away everything within the vicinity, leaving the *disappointed* spectators scrambling for safety.

***

Disappointments often come in torrents leaving us breathless and disoriented. Paul knew them well. But Demas, well, that was so personal. With Paul's death nearing, Demas succumbed to this world's elixir and abandoned his mentor in Paul's hour of greatest need.

***

"for Demas, having loved this present world, has deserted me..." (2 Tim. 4:10).

***

Let disappointments take you higher.

***

"We must accept finite disappointment, but never lose infinite hope."
Martin Luther King Jr.

Day 89

***

Discord (1184 BC)
Homer, *Iliad*, 11:1–10

***

Dawn rose over the bloody Trojan fields as the combatants slept fitfully. Nearby, night sweats and heavy sighs drifted over the beach where the Greek ships lay in harbor, their prows lodged in sand, waiting. The war vessels of Ajax and Achilles, the mightiest warriors, bookended the fleet nestled tightly along the shore's curving line. Center place in the harbor lay Odysseus' black-hulled boat, strategically placed so messages could be sent either way up and down the beach.

Here, *Discord*, that fierce Olympian goddess, hurried to her summons. Zeus leaned over his mighty throne on Mt. Olympus and stared at this divine disrupter, the spreader of lies and gossip. Pleased with her acquiescence, he whispered his orders:

"Go at once, Discord, to Odysseus' ship, and there, upon his stout prow, stir the soldiers. Fill their hearts, gorged on death, with renewed courage. Challenge them to fly across the sand to crimson fields of glory. Charge them to kill Trojans from dawn to dusk. Go!"

Flying swiftly to the golden shores, she mounted the center ship's prow and screamed toward Ajax's vessel and then toward Achilles'. Her voice, laden with deceit and turmoil, shattered night's fragile dreams and sent the soldiers once again racing toward death.

***

Discord, ever filled with mischief, still wanders today. She spins conspiracies on tabletops and kitchen counters. She strides, ever confident, among main streets and Capitol hallways. Beware her dark designs. King Solomon heard her whispers and warned all who would listen:

***

"For lack of wood the fire goes out, and where there is no whisperer, contention quiets down" (Prov. 26:20).

***

Put your weapons down and shame Discord on the ship's prow.

***

"Gossip is the Devil's radio."
George Harrison

Day 90

***

Disguises (218 BC)
Appian, *Roman History*, 7:6

***

Hannibal led the shivering African war elephants through the treacherous Alps seeking glory. Cracking mountain passes with iron sledgehammers, he made a road and urged his starving troops onward. After six months of struggle, he slithered silently down the Alpine passes onto the Celtic plains.

Bewildered by such a feat, the native Celts watched as he sent the Roman cavalry fleeing for the hills. The Boii imagined Hannibal to be some invincible god. Ever the shrewd tactician, Hannibal observed the Celtic tribes' awe and decided to exploit this weakness.

Playing on their barbaric imaginations, he became a magician who turned into various stage characters. One day he would put on a gray wig and tattered clothes. He leaned heavily upon an old walking stick and hobbled and shuffled among them like an elderly beggar. However, the next day, he would transform himself into a youthful warrior brimming with energy and athletic movements. And yet again, on the following morning, he would craft the *disguise* of a composed middle-aged man.

***

I once lived in New Orleans, where my friends dressed in costumes and slipped masks over their faces every year. This was all fun, but all too often, we take permanent shelter behind facades.

David once wore a *disguise*. Running for his life from King Saul, some local villagers spotted him. David thought fast and slipped on insanities' mask:

***

"So he disguised his sanity before them, and acted insanely in their hands, and scribbled on the doors of the gate, and let his saliva run down into his beard" (1 Sam. 21:13).

***

Quit pretending. The world doesn't need more charlatans.

***

"Be yourself; everyone else is taken."
Oscar Wilde

Day 91

***

Dissatisfied (AD 40)
Phaedrus, *Fables*, 2

***

The country pond sparkled with morning dew. A slight breeze ruffled the nearby willow, and the rising sun crept along a curved cart path to the sea. Swallows darted here and there, snapping insects in flight and playing joyfully over the pasture. The frogs, however, sat indolently on the pond's muddy banks waiting for Jupiter's reply, whose face remained cloaked in silent mystery.

The pond's joys seemed stale to the frogs, who found themselves bored and *dissatisfied*. The harsh but joyful challenges of earlier days when discipline reigned were long gone. The last frog summit at the pond's north end had been unanimous. They had mailed Jupiter a letter demanding an old-fashioned king.

Finally, Jupiter tossed them a rotten stick sending it splashing into the water where it lodged in the thick mud. Awed by the new potentate's presence, they rejoiced until one day, a curious frog poked it and found it lifeless. The news spread, and soon everyone was leap-frogging over it, ridiculing the water-logged king.

The frogs demanded better. "We want a real king," they insisted.

So, Jupiter sent a water snake that began gobbling them up one by one. Horror swept the few remaining citizens who nostalgically remembered how blessed their boring lives had been.

***

Are you sitting with frogs, muttering? Have the riches of your present life grown stale? *Dissatisfaction* spreads like fog, and before long you no longer see the horizon. This happened once in Palestine:

***

"you said to me, 'No, but a king shall reign over us,' although the LORD your God *was* your king" (1 Sam. 12:12).

***

Burn the letter to Jupiter. Abandon the frogs.

***

"The world is nothing but a great desire to live and a great dissatisfaction with living."
Heraclitus of Ephesus

Day 92

***

Dissimulation (431 BC)
Euripides, *Medea*, 1135–1230

***

Jason strolled gallantly into the princess's bridal chamber. When she saw Jason's children still lingering nearby within the city, dreadful reminders of his first wife, Medea, the princess grimaced. Turning away in disgust, she muttered something disgusting.

He touched her shoulder gently. "My darling, you must love those whom I love. Here, my sons, bring you gifts to woo your friendship." She looked down upon a dress shimmering in delicate golden strands, a goddess's garment. The other child held up a bejeweled Black Sea diadem from Colchis, Medea's homeland. Stunned at the exquisite gifts, she quickly acquiesced, smiling at their thoughtfulness, obsessed by the golden gestures.

Jason and the boys bowed and left, smiling. The princess, shivering with expectation, summoned her maids, who dressed her before a shining boudoir mirror. Her golden curls spilled over the diadem's burnished scenes as she pranced gaily over the palace floors, admiring her extended legs one by one.

But something seemed amiss; *dissimulation* in the shadows. Nearly falling, the princess stumbled to a chair where white foam dribbled from her lips. Her dilated pupils rolled as her face turned pasty white. The maids screamed. The gown constricted, biting into her flesh. Attempting to run, flames from the diadem devoured her face until she fell in a smoldering heap to the ground.

***

Shakespeare reminded us that "all that glitters is not gold." Imposters have dangling keys that open our locked doors, slipping us *dissimulating* gifts that, though alluring, hide dangerous stings. We must beware as Jesus warned his followers.

***

"Beware of the false prophets who come to you in sheep's clothing but inwardly are ravenous wolves" (Matt. 7:15).

***

Study the hearts of those who offer you shimmering dresses.

***

"Sincerity is the face of the soul, as dissimulation is the mask."
Joseph Sanial-Dubay

Day 93

***

Doom (1184 BC)
Homer, *Iliad*, 14:1–60

***

Nestor slipped from his tent upon Troy's beach into a maelstrom of war whoops. Trojan forces had breached the defensive wall and charged with relentless ferocity toward the Greek ships. Oblivious to it all as he had nursed his wounds in seclusion, he now felt the inevitable specter of death.

Instantly aware of disaster's predicament, he raced down the shoreline, hoping to find Agamemnon and Odysseus, the wounded kings holed up in hospital tents nursing their wounds. Spotting them in the distance leaning on their spears, faces aghast, he approached, breathing heavily.

King Agamemnon, filled with dismay at the din of war cries, greeted Nestor. "What brings you here? Are you wounded like us?" He paused and, with a contorted face, asked the dreadful question: "Are we *doomed*? Is Hector's dreaded prediction coming true? He boasted that he would never return to Ilium before he torched our ships and killed us all."

Nestor, his eyes sunken and sorrowful, nodded gravely. "Yes, it is, my Lord. The Trojans have broken through our impregnable wall. Their battle cries ascend to heaven itself. Let's think quickly before fate swallows us whole. Maybe there is something we can still do."

***

Doom, depression's ghost, haunts millions of us daily. We move in heavy increments, dragging our limbs through dark days. But even the darkest doom has an exit. Abraham found that path with God's grace:

***

"But he hesitated. So the men seized his hand and the hand of his wife and the hands of his two daughters, for the compassion of the LORD was upon him; and they brought him out, and put him outside the city" (Gen. 19:16).

***

Take God's hand today and breathe freedom.

***

"Beginning with doom in the bulb, the spring unravels."
Dylan Thomas

Day 94

Dread (467 BC)
Aeschylus, *Seven Against Thebes*, 320–355

The seven-gated fortress of Thebes moaned. Screaming soldiers threatened to flood through its formidable doors, setting fires that would burn the city's soul. Smoke from enemy campfires belched a dirty victory song, billowing black intentions heavenward. A moving wall of fierce combatants surrounded the perimeter, arms locked, preventing escape as their spears punched the sooty air.

Grain, birthed and bagged with love from previous harvests, shivered on Theban shelves. Storekeepers gripped ready swords to prevent pillaging, guarding with their lives the dried figs, and moist dates picked several sunrises earlier. House shelves laden with cucumbers, radishes, and onions would never surrender to the screaming warriors outside the gates.

Maidens clung to shadowy corners, *dreading* the inevitable. Should the gates fail, panting men would drag women by the hair like spirited, unbroken horses, ladies young and old perfumed and coiffed with Theban riches, now nothing but weeping chattel. Frenzied victory-whoops would cram the narrow streets as warriors displayed new wives roped and yanked against their will. Pitiful calls among the newly enslaved girls would echo back, helpless sirens on smoky thoroughfares, dreading the night's impending backroom celebrations with some lucky stranger.

Nothing locks the heart and dampens aspirations like *dread*. Sunrises that once caressed are now daggers in a dark workday. Wedding bells tinkle like rusty ankle weights dragged through dark routines. Will joy ever return? Will your heart ever sing again? Such were the thoughts of Babylon's exiles as Isaiah valiantly offered hope:

***

"For I am the LORD your God, who upholds your right hand, who says to you, 'Do not fear, I will help you'" (Isa. 41:13).

***

Every dark room has an exit. Find yours today.

***

"I have a new philosophy: I'm only going to dread one day at a time."
Charles M. Schulz

Day 95

Dreams (AD 10)
Ovid, *Metamorphoses*, 10:245–290

Pygmalion lay alone, night after night, smothered by loneliness. Daybreak brought no relief, his mood dampened by continual isolation and the dread of another restless evening beneath a dreary moon. Then one day, he began chiseling an ivory companion in his studio. Bit by bit, he smoothed her rugged features, searching for beauty late into the evenings until an exquisite, angelic statue stood before him.

The woman's loving gaze stole his heart. Pygmalion's infatuation grew daily as he shared his darkest secrets with the tender-eyed visitor. His kisses seemed to spark a reaction. At times, he felt as if his fingers had left an imprint on her limbs.

Overwhelmed with new joy, Pygmalion brought her shells gathered on a nearby beach along with smooth pebbles, flowers with a thousand colors, and little pet birds. He combed the nearby dress shops for the latest silk fashions and dressed his love daily with rainbowed robes. He bedecked her bosom with ribbons and draped a necklace of gold upon her neck.

When Venus' holiday came round, he prayed, arms outstretched: "If possible, give me a wife like my ivory girl." When morning came, his *dreams* came true as the statue, her limbs warm and fluid, kissed him intensely.

Dreams still happen, even in our modern world, stiff and unmoved by miracles.

When all seemed lost, Ruth dreamed. One night, lying at the foot of Boaz's bed on the threshing floor, her aspirations of a wondrous love-filled future blossomed.

***

"It happened in the middle of the night that the man was startled and bent forward; and behold, a woman was lying at his feet" (Ruth 3:8).

***

Rise this morning and dream!

***

"You have to dream before your dreams can come true."
Abdul Kalam

Day 96

***

Duplicity (687 BC)
Herodotus, *The Persian Wars*, 1:8–10

***

Betrayal is surely one of the darkest shades of vice, mingling like a chameleon among its friends and associates, hiding its potential for destruction. Herodotus gives us a shocking glimpse of *duplicity*.

He tells the story of Candaules, king of Sardis, who admired the beauty of his wife, Nyssia, so intensely he was not content to keep this to himself. One day he decided to flaunt her elegance to Gyges, his favorite palace attendant. "I will show her to you one night as she undresses," said the king. "She's a real knockout."

"Oh, no, sire. It would not be proper for me to drool over her."

"Nonsense," said the king, laughing. "She will never know. I will hide you in the closet, and when she undresses before bed, she will never notice you."

Since Gyges could not wriggle out of the king's demand, he consented and hid in the closet as instructed. When bedtime came, Nyssia came in and prepared for bed by slowly undressing. After Gyges witnessed the private act, he slipped out the door. But she noticed him and was ashamed.

Disgusted by her husband's betrayal, she married the voyeur and murdered the king! So, Candaules lost everything while Nyssia gained the world, proving betrayal's destructiveness.

***

Duplicity stings with eternal complications. This sweet elixir has a bitter sting, as Judas discovered when he betrayed the Lord, spinning his life into a death spiral.

***

"While He was still speaking, behold, Judas, one of the twelve, came up accompanied by a large crowd. Now he who was betraying Him gave them a sign, saying, 'Whomever I kiss, He is the one; seize Him'" (Matt. 26:47–48).

***

Live without betrayal today.

***

"Each betrayal begins with trust."
Martin Luther

Day 97

***

Dust (AD 110)
Juvenal, *Satires*, 10:147

***

Juvenal set the banker's scale on a table and called us to gather round him. As the room quietened, he picked up a small burlap bag and untied the string. He poured its contents, *dust*, and dirt, upon the scale with a dramatic flair and looked intently at us all.

"Here lies Hannibal, the greatest general. Africa's boundaries couldn't hold him. He saw beyond these petty limitations. Conquering Spain, he leaped over the Pyrenees, splitting Alpine glaciers until he held all of Italy in his palm."

"Do you remember the gloating days after Cannae? Nothing is won," he declaimed, "until I plant the Carthaginian flag in the Roman forum."

Juvenal wiggled the scales, finding the balance. "What a general! Look. With one eye patched, he rode an African elephant on toward Rome like a stage actor before screaming fans." Juvenal tapped the little dirt mound sending tiny tremors along the scale's bar.

"But what did it get him? In the end, exiled in remote Bithynia, he plucked a golden ring from his finger. Filled with poison, Hannibal sipped its deadly nectar and died alone, choking on memories of grandeur. And who is he now?" Juvenal studied his audience with narrowing eyes. "Nothing but an epic poem in schoolboys' mouths."

***

The Lord God summons us now to gather around His table. Wagging His head in dismay at the first couple's fall from Grace, he pronounces a *dusty* verdict that resonates with a familiar strain.

***

"By the sweat of your face you will eat bread, till you return to the ground, because from it you were taken; For you are dust, and to dust you shall return" (Gen. 3:19).

***

The saint's dust is a door to heaven.

***

"Our lives are but specks of dust falling through the fingers of time."
Socrates

Day 98

***

Eavesdropping (AD 28)
Tacitus, *The Annals of Imperial Rome*, 4:69

***

Sabinus was a lonely man.

He had once served in the Roman army with honors. Now his life had settled into a solitary ritual of dull mornings and evenings—all the same. With a desperate need for friendship, Sabinus fell into a trap set by Tiberius' spies during the reign of terror.

Latiaris, a palace official, knew that Sabinus liked to complain about the emperor and Rome in general. To snare this easy prey, Latiaris befriended the lonely knight, stopping by at his humble home in the evening to chat.

Sabinus loved these meetings. He often released his hidden miseries while sipping brandy beside a cozy fireplace. An emotional man, tears would accent his complaints and sorrows while Latiaris made secret notes.

Finally, he set the trap. Three notable Roman senators recruited by Latiaris were stuffed in the poor man's attic. With their ears pressed to the chinks in the ceiling, they *eavesdropped* as the vulnerable knight poured out his complaints and terrors to Latiaris and other confidentialities. Having heard it all, the senators raced back to the senatorial chambers, where they squawked about the traitor's admissions.

***

If only Peter could have shared the couch that night in Sabinus' living room. He would have warned the gregarious knight to guard against *eavesdroppers*. He could have nodded at the ceiling or winked a few times to awaken the loquacious Sabinus. Peter's words, though, can be an encouragement to us who seek to live lives of faith.

***

"Be of sober spirit, be on the alert. Your adversary, the devil, prowls around like a roaring lion, seeking someone to devour" (1 Pet. 5:8).

***

Keep an eye on the rafters today.

***

"When sorrows come, they come not single spies, but in battalions."
William Shakespeare

Day 99

***

Education (423 BC)
Aristophanes, *Clouds*, 960–980

***

The older man dragged his wayward son, Pheidippides, to the famous academy where Socrates taught. Lost to life's basest urges, the once-promising student now lounged at the town's racetrack, gambling on horses, losing his dad's money, dreaming of easy fame and quick riches.

Down the street they trudged, the boy whining, his father determined. Entering the schoolhouse, he shoved the rowdy kid toward the revered philosopher in disgust. "He used to be a quick learner, Socrates. As a little boy, he built mud-houses, fashioned toy warships, and made little racing cars out of leather. But now he's useless. Can you do anything with him?"

Socrates studied the lad and recalled the olden days when kids behaved at school. "I remember," he told the frustrated father, "when all the village kids marched off to school in utter silence, their faces sternly set. No chatter at all; nobody dared. Even on the coldest days, we marched like soldiers off to battle, chanting military songs as the old men taught. Lunches were simple sandwiches, nothing fancy."

He paused, the recollections misting his eyes. "Yes, those were the good ole days. Everybody sat on the ground modestly, getting an *education*. When it was time to leave, the kids brushed the soil lightly to erase their imprint."

***

Where would we be today without those early years of old desks, scratchy blackboards, and paddlings at the principal's office? Tough days at times, but we learned the mechanics of life. Paul valued his privileged *education*.

***

"I am a Jew, born in Tarsus of Cilicia but brought up in this city, educated under Gamaliel, strictly according to the law of our fathers..." (Acts 22:3).

***

Quick step! School is starting. What will God teach you today?

***

"Education is the movement from darkness to light."
Allan Bloom

Day 100

Elderly (AD 110)
Juvenal, *Satires*, 10:200–250

***

"Everybody wants to live forever," said Juvenal mockingly. "I mean, if I ever heard someone praying to Jupiter, they always pleaded, 'Please, God, give me a long life.'"

Juvenal just shook his head in disgust as he put pen and ink to the side for a moment. "Why?" he asked. "Why does everybody want to be old? Longevity is nothing but trouble."

Understanding Juvenal like I do, I knew a boatload of sarcasm was about to unload. His angry eyes flashed. I just settled back in the chair and let him go.

"Have you ever just gazed into an old man's face? It's disgusting! All those leathery wrinkles. Ugh. Reminds me of a mother baboon's mug."

Juvenal's cruelty animated him, poking some hidden fire within as he continued his tantrum.

"Look at how they dodder along, their arms dangling and swaying. Ridiculous. Runny noses, bald heads, I could go on and on. Poor things can't even chew their food anymore. They gum their bread, masticating like pasture cows."

He paused, remembering a recent venture to the theater.

"I was sitting in the fourth row from the stage just last week, and I could tell that this *elderly* lady couldn't hear a thing. When it was time to go, her partner had to bawl into her ear."

***

It's too bad Juvenal never met Moses. When he was 120, he climbed to the peak of Mt. Nebo, full of vigor and strength. With clear vision, he looked across the valley to the Promised Land.

The culture of ancient Israel honored the *elderly*.

***

"You shall rise up before the gray-headed and honor the face of the elderly..." (Lev. 19:32).

***

Hug a senior today and see God smile.

***

"Those who love deeply never grow old."
Benjamin Franklin

Day 101

Eloquence (374 BC)
Plutarch, *Demosthenes*, 5

***

The teachers in the little academy in Athens were buzzing about the pending court case. The area's greatest orator, Callistratus, was coming to town. There was talk of closing school for the day.

Demosthenes, a young pupil at the academy, listened to the teachers' buzz and begged his tutor to take him. "I'll be quiet, he pleaded. No one will know I'm even there." His misty eyes tore at the teacher's heartstrings.

"I'm telling you, children aren't allowed!" barked the tutor.

But the kid wouldn't stop begging. Yielding finally, the tutor managed to secure coveted tickets. When the celebrated day arrived and the courthouse doors opened, Demosthenes' tutor hid the boy on the edge of the courtroom. "Stay put and don't even breathe!" he muttered.

For the next few hours, Callistratus mesmerized everyone at the proceedings, pacing in front of the jurors and flinging *eloquent* legal phrases upon the audience. His gestures punctuated lethal arguments while his charm and literary skills fell like stars from heaven upon an adoring audience.

When the final gavel fell, Callistratus sashayed out through the pressing mob of admirers, victorious. Demosthenes watched with fascination as citizens pressed to congratulate the champion, following in his departing wake, utterly hypnotized by the hero's prowess.

***

If you stand today on ancient Marble Street in Ephesus and stroll quietly toward the grand theater carved into the slope of Mt. Pion, you will hear the echo of another *eloquent* orator. His fluid style punctuated the public theater as onlookers gazed with admiration.

***

"Now a Jew named Apollos, an Alexandrian by birth, an eloquent man, came to Ephesus; and he was mighty in the Scriptures" (Acts 18:24).

***

Raise *your* voice today and change the world.

***

"Eloquence is a painting of the thoughts."
Blaise Pascal

Day 102

Embraces (1180 BC)
Virgil, *Aeneid*, 6:684–717

***

Aeneas, desperately searching for his deceased father in the underworld, stood at a crossroads. The blissful path to the right led on toward Elysium, the happy place where light and pleasure graced the mingling souls. The opposite road led to Tartarus' battlements, enclosed by a circling wall girdled by Hell's fiery river. The bottomless pit consumed blaspheming souls, evildoers who lived in greed's grasp.

Turning right, he strode toward Elysium, where he noticed a jovial gathering, men and women feasting and singing in unison among a fragrant grove of bay trees. Aeneas paused before them. "Has anyone seen my beloved father, Anchises? I have crossed the underworld to find him."

"You will find him there in the valley below these upland heights," they said, pointing to a path beyond the cliffs.

Hurrying toward the valley floor, Aeneas spotted his father and ran across the grassy meadow toward him joyfully. Anchises greeted his son with joy. "Pause, my son. Let me gaze at your face. I never lost hope you would come!"

Aeneas tried three times to *embrace* his father, flinging hungry arms about his neck only to find the wispy wings of a fleeting dream.

***

Embraces are the elixirs of life, sweet confections that lighten life's onerous burdens. Often taken for granted, embraces, like delicate smiles, wait patiently for their time.

***

"So he got up and came to his father. But while he was still a long way off, his father saw him and felt compassion for him, and ran and embraced him and kissed him" (Lk. 15:20).

***

Embrace your truest friend today while you can.

***

"When someone hugs you, let them be the first to let go."
H. Jackson Brown Jr.

Day 103

Empathy (AD 150)
Apuleius, *The Golden Ass*, 1:7

***

Aristomenes stared gloomily at the empty shelves. His competitor, Lupus, had beat him to the bargains, and now he would have to travel to other small Greek villages to find his honey and cheese. As a wholesaler, he had learned to be quick when breaking news of honey sales surfaced. But Lupus beat him to it, so now all he could do was head for the baths and soak away his miseries.

Arriving midday at the spa, he noticed a beggar by the roadside. His face, partially hidden beneath a tattered garment, looked familiar. With sudden *empathy*, he wondered, "could this be Socrates, long taken for dead?" The emaciated man looked like a streetwalker, barely clinging to life.

"Is that you, Socrates?" he asked.

Hearing his name, the man pulled the filthy cloak over his head, ashamed. "Everyone gave up on you!" shrieked Aristomenes. "Your poor wife mourned forever, and your children now have court-appointed guardians."

Although Socrates resisted, Aristomenes made him get up, putting one of his garments over him. They hobbled off to the baths, where he scraped Socrates' nasty skin and bought him some oils and ointments. When he was all cleaned up, his benefactor took the poor fellow to a local inn, put him to bed, and gave him some food and wine, hoping to lift his spirits.

***

The Bible's good Samaritan and Aristomenes never met, but they both demonstrated the value of *empathy*.

***

"But a Samaritan, who was on a journey, came upon him; and when he saw him, he felt compassion, and came to him and bandaged up his wounds..." (Lk. 10:32–33).

***

Look around today. Release your empathy.

***

"Empathy is walking a mile in somebody else's moccasins. Sympathy is being sorry their feet hurt."
Rebecca O'Donnell

Day 104

Enemies (AD 80)
Suetonius, *Lives of the Caesars*, 8.2

***

The two guilty patricians, leading citizens in Rome, feared their imminent death. The emperor, Titus, had not ordered their deaths though the court convictions demanded it. Instead, the noblemen stared at palace dinner invitations on Tuesday and Colosseum tickets for the following day's gladiatorial contest.

Fearing sinister retributions, the men dressed for the arranged dinner and arrived on high alert. To their astonishment, Titus, ever gracious, seated them in prominent places about the table. Though every guest knew the suppressed treachery, they spoke kindly to the convicted patricians, establishing renewed friendships.

The following day, as throngs flooded into the amphitheater to watch the gladiatorial exhibition, these same two conspirators sat beside Titus as prominent guests. Suddenly, the emperor stood quieting the crowds. He ordered his attendants to bring the gladiator's swords to his throne. Unsheathed, the blades, sharpened for maximum effect, glared menacingly before the silent observers.

Titus stood and handed the weapons to the two disloyal *enemies*. "Go ahead," he said to them. "Test the blades. Feel the edge. Tell me what you think."

***

Titus' willingness to forgive and treat his *enemies* with kindness echoes a similar affair in ancient Palestine. Elisha had blinded the host of Arameans, whose sole mission was to slay him at his country home. Now, with the Arameans corralled, vulnerable, and awaiting inevitable slaughter, Elisha warned the king of Israel against harming them. Instead, he held a feast on their behalf.

***

"Set bread and water before them, that they may eat and drink and go to their master. So he prepared a great feast for them..." (2 Kings 6:22–23).

***

Who will you hand your sword to today?

***

"Love your enemies, for they tell you your faults."
Benjamin Franklin

Day 105

Ennobling (401 BC)
Xenophon, *Anabasis*, 6:5

***

The army stood, stumped, at the deep ravine, unable to pursue the Bithynian army. "It can't be passed," said general Sophaenetus, staring at the crevasse before them. "It's too deep and risky. Let's turn back."

While the soldiers grumbled, Xenophon rode up in a frenzy, asking why the army had stopped moving. "It's the ravine, sir," barked Sophaenetus, the oldest general.

"Nonsense!" said Xenophon, who, after a brief pep talk to the hesitant force, led the men step by step down into the treacherous deep. When they gathered victorious on the other side, Xenophon ordered his men into battle formation and said this one notable thing: "Listen, men. The enemy is just beyond that ridge. So as we march on, call the names of those marching beside you. Inspire them. And remember to do something *ennobling* today, something memorable, so that no matter what happens in combat, people will whisper your name in awe for generations to come."

Then, marching with purpose, they pursued the Bithynians. Suddenly, the trumpet sounded, striking up the paean; they raised the battle cry, couched their spears, and sent the enemy running for the hills.

***

Ravines often bring out the worst in us, forcing us to turn away from a destination or goal in frustration. But they can be a turning point, a rare chance to say or do something *ennobling*.

Paul said to Titus,

***

"In all things show yourself to be an example of good deeds, with purity in doctrine, dignified, sound in speech which is beyond reproach, so that the opponent will be put to shame..." (Titus 2:7–8).

***

Strike up the paean! Do something ennobling today.

***

"Make each day your masterpiece."
John Wooden

Day 106

Ensnared (20 BC)
Propertius, *Elegies*, 1:1

***

It was all in her harlot eyes. Cynthia's glances had sparkled and forced an awkward surrender, leaving Propertius captive to a dangerous woman.

There was a brief time when love had flowed like a wilderness dream between them. Cynthia's glances, coy and supreme, had once received his overtures. The game was well played by both lovers. But, alas, no more. Her soft lips, now kissed by another, left him trembling beneath a moonless night. Her dark eyes crippled his emotions. He was a prisoner to memories now cold and fractured, though fondly remembered.

Twelve moons passed with no relief. Propertius wandered aimlessly, continually begging the gods for relief from a broken heart. Over and over, on restless night rambles, he pleaded for divine assistance.

"Venus, prove you care. Sift love's fickle sand, and summon Cynthia to my hand."

But moons came and went, mocking his loneliness as if love were but a game. He searched far and wide for some mysterious potion, some antidote to his despair, but found none. If only he could return to his first love, faithful and tested. But Cynthia's eyes had *ensnared* him.

***

How easy it is to stray. Propertius' wandering eyes had caught the glances of a harlot and quickly *ensnared*, never recovered. Better by far, it is to turn our eyes toward God, who always loves us.

"And let your eyes delight in my ways."

***

"For a harlot is a deep pit and an adulterous woman is a narrow well. Surely she lurks as a robber..." (Prov. 23:26–28).

***

Kiss your wedding ring and live with joy.

***

"A successful marriage requires falling in love many times, always with the same person."
Mignon McLauglin

Day 107

***

Enticements (65 BC)
Lucretius, *On the Nature of Things*, 4

***

Lucretius sounds like a love-stricken cowboy singing the blues.

I can almost see him at midnight, leaning on a French Quarter stage, beer-sobbing, wondering why his girl deserted him—again. Jerome, the translator of the Bible, said Lucretius died of a spoiled love potion. Who knows? Lucretius certainly had some dark opinions of romance. If we wander closer to the stage where he sits mumbling, we can listen to how it all went wrong for him:

"I used to have lots of money, but then she came along. Now she's got it all. Look at how the green emeralds play on her brow. Every darting glance dances in jingling gold. Those shoes cost me a week's pay, and look at that crumpled robe at her feet, creased with a thousand embraces that aren't mine!"

"Watch her strut across the floor with those *enticing* robes trailing like a wedding train. That perfume she wears smothers me. I saw her put all this on last week before she left. She must have spent an hour smearing makeup on her greasy face with that other girl assisting. She's got a spell on me that I can't shake."

He waves his hand erratically. "Bartender! Another round of Hurricanes, s'il vous plaît."

***

Enticements come in all shapes, sizes, and genders. Sometimes they can take over a disciplined life once dedicated to God. Paul knew such a person. He shook his head in wonder when he thought about him. Was Demas in that bar room with Lucretius?

***

"for Demas, having loved this present world, has deserted me and gone to Thessalonica" (2 Tim. 4:10).

***

Skip the bar. Head to the chapel.

***

"The scars of others should teach us caution."
St. Jerome

Day 108

***

Entreaties (AD 117)
Tacitus, *Annals of Imperial Rome*, 16:10

***

Nero's temper blazed undiluted.

Lucius Vetus, former governor of Asia, lived in happy retirement with his daughter Pollitta, and her Rubellius, until Nero murdered Rubellius out of envy. Pollitta grieved hysterically, clasping his bleeding neck as the assassins laughed. She kept his bloodied clothes and lived daily, unkempt and starving, disdaining food.

But unsated, Nero sent assassins again to kill her father, Lucius Vetus. His only hope was to send his grieving daughter to Nero's palace, hoping her *entreaties* might curb his wrath. Pollitta hastened to Neapolis where Nero vacationed. She begged to see the emperor. Refused admittance, Pollitta waited for him at the door. When he finally passed by, she pleaded incessantly for understanding and mercy. Nero scoffed. Pollitta screamed furiously—all to no avail. Cold and unmoved, Nero slammed the door upon the exhausted penitent.

Knowing the end was imminent, Vetus, Pollitta, and her mother-in-law cut their veins and were carried by devoted attendants to the baths, where they sat in crimson water gazing into one another's eyes, longing to be the first to cease breathing.

***

Watching Pollitta whimpering, abandoned at the emperor's slammed door, leaves me pale and distraught. I desperately want to slip my hand through the veil of time and touch her feverish brow. If only I could have told her of One whose door is never closed, whose throne of grace welcomes all *entreaties*.

***

"For we do not have a high priest who cannot sympathize with our weaknesses....There, let us draw near with confidence to the throne of grace, so that we may receive mercy and find grace to help in time of need" (Heb. 4:15-16).

***

Your first teardrop summons all of heaven's grace.

***

"Sweet mercy is nobility's true badge."
William Shakespeare

Day 109

***

Escape (423 BC)
Aristophanes, *Wasps*, 200–400

***

The Athenian night was still, the evening winds calm.

Philocleon, the withered old judge, crept through his house checking locks. Every door was bolted tight, and slaves watched the windows.

"But the chimney! Why not?" mumbled the judge who longed to elope with his fellow magistrates who were warbling secretly for him outside.

Hurrying, he stood on a rickety stool in the chimney's ashes and managed to shimmy up its sooty path. Undetected, he scrambled out upon the rooftop and stared in disbelief at the trammeling net.

A sweet whippoorwill whistled from a distant tree. Taking courage, the prisoner inched his way to the roofline and slid down to the net's edge.

"What's wrong?" screeched his buddies in breathy, hushed tones below on the road.

"My son's got me locked up. He doesn't want me to go a-courting anymore. Says my bench days are history. Says I should retire and take it easy like all old folks do."

"Take this rope," motioned one accomplice below. "Slide down the rope, and let's get going. The first case is waiting."

The roof tiles click-clacked beneath nervous feet as he chewed the netting.

His son, Bdelycleon, awoke and sounded the alarm. "He's *escaping* down the roof. Get him!"

***

Are you stuck in a chimney longing for freedom? You can't see much but a few twinkling stars through the cracked cap, but you're desperate. St. Paul was there. He knew how to *escape*.

***

"They were also watching the gates day and night so that they might put him to death; but his disciples took him by night and let him down through an opening in the wall lowering him in a large basket" (Acts 9:25–26).

***

Heaven has a lifeline for you. Escape today!

***

"To escape fear, you have to go through it, not around."
Richard Norton

Day 110

***

Excuses (401 BC)
Xenophon, *Anabasis*, 3:4

***

The race was on. Xenophon's army was hustling to beat the Persian soldiers to the top of a strategic ridge. The winners would have a substantial military advantage. Xenophon, the general on horseback, urged his men upward. But Soteridas, a weary foot soldier, would have none of it, hurling a barrage of *excuses* at the general.

"It's easy for you to be a cheerleader sitting on top of that horse. Look at me carrying this heavy shield. You wouldn't be so energetic if you were in my shoes."

When Xenophon heard the challenge, he leaped down, shoved the soldier out of his way, and grabbed the man's shield while at the same time carrying his weapons. Then, from the ground, he rallied the troops and pushed forward until the soldier was shamed and took back his gear.

***

God was looking for a leader to lead His people to freedom. He called Moses and repeatedly passed the baton to him. But Moses fumbled it with endless excuses:

***

"Then Moses said to the LORD, 'Please, Lord, I have never been eloquent, neither recently nor in time past, nor since You have

219

spoken to Your servant; for I am slow of speech and slow of tongue'" (Ex. 4:10).

***

Moses and Soteridas must have read the same "excuse" book. How many *excuses* did you make yesterday for not getting something done? Don't let the Promised land, your bright future, fade beneath a sweltering mirage because you failed to take action.

***

Quit your fake stutter, pick up your shield, and just do it!

***

"Ninety-nine percent of the failures come from people who have the habit of making excuses."
George Washington Carver

Day 111

Execution (221 BC)
Livy, *History of Rome*, 21:2

***

The slave ran helter-skelter through the tumultuous mob. His hands still dripping with murderous blood, he searched frantically for an escape route. There were no regrets. General Hasdrubal deserved *execution*. After all, he was the one who had killed the slave's master.

It was only minutes earlier that the angry servant had tucked a dagger beneath his robe and trailed Hasdrubal as he strolled casually through the city streets. Drawing closer, he heard his prey's light laughter. Hasdrubal's sing-song dalliances with the women along the roadside fueled the stalker's hatred. As admiring spectators clamored to touch the general's garments, the servant pounced. With a glance into Hasdrubal's eyes, the dagger hit its mark. Stumbling, the general fell dead in a crimson pool.

Bolting frantically now for a quick exit, the murderer caught the wrath of shocked citizens. They surrounded the fugitive flinging him to the ground. Retribution fueled the lynching. The blows, however, seemed like kisses to the slave who saw only the love in his dead master's eyes. The more the servant suffered, the more he smiled, his face contorted with happiness.

***

The misguided servant above died without regret defending his slain master's honor. A young Saul saw a similar joy in

221

Stephen's eyes as he lay bleeding to death. The rabid assembly *executed* him with stones and kicks. But all the while, it was the martyr's peaceful eyes that caught Saul's focus.

***

"Then falling on his knees, he cried out with a loud voice, 'Lord, do not hold this sin against them!' Having said this, he died" (Acts 7:60).

***

Look past your pain today. The Savior is watching.

***

"The freedom of the soul-bird Death cannot take away."
Sri Chinmoy

Day 112

Exhaustion (401 BC)
Xenophon, *Anabasis*, 3:4

***

The snow was falling softly in the mountains of Armenia, choking the ground, burying everything beneath six feet of suffocating flurries. Xenophon's men struggled onward, hoping to reach the pass at the summit's peak before the pursuing enemy soldiers caught up. A large body of frozen soldiers stopped at a dell where a gurgling creek had melted a patch of snow. There they collapsed, refusing to go on.

When Xenophon, lingering with the rearguard, finally caught up, he saw them sitting motionless, staring into the white abyss "Get up, men!" he shouted. "The enemy is near and closing in. Come on, get up. We have to go now!"

But the men wouldn't budge. Xenophon, angry, drew his sword. But the *exhausted* soldiers merely stared, their eyes blissfully hollow, taunting their general with icicle words. "Go ahead and kill us now. We can't go any further."

***

Let us all stand with the Savior, blood-smeared from tears of grief at Gethsemane, as he looks down at the sleeping disciples, too *exhausted* to go on. The enemy was near, but sleep had seduced them, drugging his friends with blissful scenes beyond the garden's pain.

How disappointed the Savior was as he loomed over them, knowing His hours were limited. He urged them on, but they couldn't see the Cross and retreated into sleep's tangles.

***

"Again He came and found them sleeping, for their eyes were heavy" (Matt. 26:43).

***

Exhausted? Rediscover your purpose and live.

***

"He felt like an old sponge steeped in paraffin and left in the sun to dry."
Douglas Adams

Day 113

Exiles (AD 24)
Tacitus, *The Annals of Imperial Rome*, 4:13

***

The stage dancers, sweating profusely, took their final delirious bow before the cheering audience. This traveling troupe had not performed in Rome for some time. Night after night, they filled the theaters as the lewd vaudevillian show played to catcalls from the rowdy audience.

As the spectators filed out laughing at the scandalous scenes just witnessed on stage, the actors assembled for a hastily called meeting. Authorities from Rome's courts stood in drawn faces holding eviction papers. The troupe's leader read the legal notice and scowled. "What is this? You're forcing us out of the country? That's absurd. You heard the applause. The crowds love us."

The officers had come from the senate with Tiberius' seal. "Your dancing is scandalous, and the emperor will have no more of it. You are ruining our youth and the city's morals, so pack your bags and get out!"

The performers, shocked at the turn of events, slipped sullenly through the darkened theater into the streets. From heroes on stage to *exiles*, the transformation had been swift and traumatic. "Where will we go?" they uttered in fear as sullen moonbeams led them to a destination unknown.

***

In many ways, all believers are *exiles*. This world is just a stage, and we're evicted dancers wandering in the dark. The writer to the Hebrews tells us that our spiritual ancestors lived in this mindset:

***

"All these died in faith, without receiving the promises, but having seen them and having welcomed them from a distance, and having confessed that they were strangers and exiles on this earth" (Heb. 11:13).

***

There are no exiles in Heaven.

***

"I know how men in exile feed on dreams."
Aeschylus

Day 114

***

Exits (429 BC)
Sophocles, *Oedipus at Colonus*, 1575–1660

***

Oedipus stumbled slowly, unaided by his daughters, toward the mouth of hell. Beneath him, the dark rumbles of underworld gods followed his progress. When he arrived by the slab of Thoricus, he sat down beside an old pear tree's hollowed trunk and began to peel off his squalid clothes. The pit's brass steps, coiling ever downward, reflected the sun's morning rays, waiting.

"Daughters, please fetch water from the spring," mumbled the old man, wistfully distant, his heart set on the *exit*. The girls, weeping softly, carried water to their father, bathing and dressing him. Grumbling thunder beneath their feet rumbled again, impatiently. The sobbing girls fell at their father's feet, trembling.

"Girls, my time has come. You know I have loved you, but now I must go on." These brief sentiments softly expressed brought them all to tears until sorrow finally subsided, leaving them spent and breathless. Then a voice from the deep curdled their senses. "Oedipus, Oedipus, why are you waiting so long. It is time now!"

Standing on wobbling legs, he kissed his daughters and urged them to leave. "You must not see my departure. It is forbidden." Walking away, the girls turned and saw nothing but a bright light fading over Cape Sounion.

***

The *exit* doors are always swinging. Night terrors still make their demands leaving an endless wake of mourning loved ones weeping. Whether we depart on Elijah's chariot of fire, swept up in a whirlwind, or slip away, suffocating on Covid's stranglehold, exits hurt. But John lifts a sparkling promise before us:

***

"And He will wipe away every tear from their eyes; and there will no longer be any death…" (Rev. 21:4).

***

Let's pause and contemplate the thousands of Covid exits and weep.

***

"Every exit is an entry somewhere else."
Tom Sheppard

Day 115

***

Extinction (65 BC)
Lucretius, *On the Nature of Things*, 3:1170

***

Lucretius was a keen observer of his neighbors. He noticed that so many everyday people were unhappy. Everybody seemed to be lost, always searching for something more. This endless desperation only led to sorrowful dead ends.

"I've noticed," said Lucretius, "that the fellow who felt cornered by difficulties at home decided to dash for freedom. He hopped into his chariot, rode for lush lands over the distant ridge, and found more emptiness.

"The woman who lived in town wished nightly to live in the country where the air was sweet and birds sang. But when she got there, the bugs bothered her, and she longed to be back in the city."

Lucretius shrugged. "Everybody is hustling, trying to cheat death. Chariots are flying here and there to no avail," he muttered. "If only people realized the basic principle of life that I have found, they would relax. If they could see that life would eventually slip into nothingness. Death ends everything. You don't have to live in fear of endless torture after you die. There isn't anything after you die but *extinction*. Know this, and you will be content to enjoy life while you have it."

***

Lucretius must have missed Paul's letter. I guess he wasn't on the mailing list. Paul wrote it with death's veil dangling perilously before him, but he longed to pass through *extinction's* gate.

***

"For to me, to live is Christ and to die is gain.... But I am hard-pressed from both directions, having the desire to depart and be with Christ, for that is very much better" (Phil. 1:21–23).

***

If you get a chance today, send Lucretius the memo.

***

"The song is ended, but the melody lingers on."
Irving Berlin

Day 116

***

Farewell (AD 37)
Tacitus, *The Annals of Imperial Rome*, 6:50

***

Aged Tiberius, in obvious decline, felt the cumbersome weight of his 77 years. A lifetime of crimes against humanity now haunted him as he faded away on Cape Misenum up the coast from Capri. The sycophants about him, sensing the imminent end, summoned Charicles for a medical consultation. The Greek medic chatted amiably over dinner with the emperor, covertly searching for clues.

Finally, under the ruse of an intimate farewell, he grasped the emperor's hand and coyly felt for a pulse. This dissembling gesture was merely a search for medical gossip. However, the astute patient noticed it and ordered the evening's dinner extended. Some think Tiberius might have been annoyed by the doctor's tactic and pretended to conceal this over an extended supper.

Upon leaving, Charicles hurriedly summoned Macro, Tiberius' military guardian, and whispered the bad news. "He's almost gone so you better say *farewell* soon. I would say he won't last but days."

***

When I ponder Charicles' easy dismissal of the world's most powerful man, a disingenuous parting that led a few days later to Tiberius' horrible smothering to death in his bed, I think of another *farewell*.

231

Paul was racing down the Asian coastline to get to Jerusalem. He paused anxiously at Miletus and summoned his Ephesian friends. On the beach beside the ship, they embraced, smothering one another with genuine kisses.

***

"And they began to weep aloud and embraced Paul, and repeatedly kissed him, grieving especially over the word which he had spoken, that they would not see his face again. And they were accompanying him to the ship" (Acts 20:37).

***

Only a genuine farewell has meaning.

***

"Don't cry because it's over, smile because it happened."
Dr. Seuss

Day 117

Fascination (60 BC)
Lucretius, *De Rerum Natura*, 2

***

Life has *fascinations* that we no longer notice. When I lived in Japan, my dad loaded my sister and me into our tiny VW and drove out into the countryside. A crowd had gathered, and I was confused. Then suddenly, the sky lit up with bursts of color and streams of fire. I have often thought of the marvels of that day.

Lucretius, that ancient philosopher, lay outside one evening and gazed at the firmament. "So many people never even notice the miracle of nature anymore," he thought. "If only they could remember how it must have been when they first saw a sunrise."

"The sky," he mused, "is amazing with all its mysteries that seem beyond understanding. What would happen if some folks looked up for the first time and saw the moon smiling through the darkness? Can anyone even remember the first time they watched a swirling cumulous cloud drift calmly toward a distant horizon? It would have to seem like a fanciful dream."

***

This very thing happened to the disciples of Jesus one day when he took them to the top of Mt. Tabor. One by one, the select disciples followed the Savior in single file up the mountain, expecting nothing but familiar landscapes seen since birth. They had dragged Him down dusty roads for months and had grown

233

accustomed to His humanity. But this! This was *fascination* that sent their imaginations soaring.

***

"And He was transfigured before them; and His face shone like the sun, and His garments became as white as light" (Matt. 17:2).

***

Start your day this morning with new eyes. Wonderment awaits!

***

"Wonder is the first of all the passions."
Rene Descartes

Day 118

Faults (35 BC)
Horace, *Satires*, 1:3

***

Horace, an insightful poet of the era just before Christ, gave some salient advice to those of us too quick to find fault with others:

"Why are we all so quick to find *fault* with others? We have eagles' eyes that are quick to find the scantiest faults. If this is you, remember that others will return the favor and babble about your faults.

"I knew a guy once who was like a country bumpkin. He must have cut his own hair, and his clothes didn't fit right. Oh, and his worn-out shoes barely stayed on his feet when he walked. But in truth, he was a fine fellow—just a little out of touch.

"Let's learn to be more tolerant. Do you remember Balbinus, who was in love with Hagna? The poor lady had a wart on her nose, but Balbinus saw a beautiful face.

"Here's what I think. Let's treat everyone like a father who loves his kid no matter what. You know how parents can be. If their son is always squinting, he doesn't criticize. He just smiles and lovingly calls him 'Blinky.' If there is a dwarf in the family, loving parents should call him 'little dear.' We should learn to turn each other's faults into blessings. For example, if a fellow is a tightwad, let's call him 'thrifty.'"

***

Paul's Corinthian members would have profited from Horace's little book of tolerance. But they didn't read it. Instead, they mumbled about Paul's *faults*, sputtering criticisms like,

***

"his presence is unimpressive and his speech contemptible" (2 Cor. 10:10).

***

Let's meet tonight at Horace's house. We're going to bury criticism.

***

"Some people find fault like there's a reward for it."
Zig Ziglar

Day 119

Fearless (1184 BC)
Homer, *Iliad*, 7:130–160

***

Hector strode majestically between the two angry armies bristling with shields, helmets, and swords. Gripping his battle spear, he separated the Greek and Trojan warriors, who sat down to hear Hector's address. Leering from a nearby oak tree in the likeness of vultures, Athene and Apollo smirked as this play began to unfold.

"I challenge you Greeks to send forth a hero," shouted Hector, "a fighter who dares to stand before me. If I win, let him strip my armor and take it to your ships. But if I win, I will do the same, taking my opponent's weapons to Troy's mighty walls."

A nervous twitching among the Greeks rippled through their ranks. No one stood; nothing but wide eyes and hot cowardice. Finally, the old warrior, Nestor, known for his *fearless* renown beneath the citadel of Pheia, stood in disgust. "I wish I were young again! I remember when Ereuthalion made this same challenge. No one dared to rise against him. I was the youngest, but I fought this beast, the strongest man I ever killed. When I finished, he lay sprawled upon the bloody ground."

***

Giants often dot our landscapes, fearful obstacles severing us from success and daily victories. We find ourselves sitting like the Greeks, trembling. David witnessed a similar sight among the Israelite soldiers when Goliath mocked them in the valley of Elah. But David was *fearless*:

***

"David said to Saul, 'Let no man's heart fail on account of him; your servant will go and fight with the Philistine'" (1 Sam. 17:32).

***

The fearless heart always beats the odds.

***

"He who is not every day conquering some fear has not learned the secret of life."
Ralph Waldo Emerson

Day 120

***

Feuds (AD 128)
Juvenal, *Satires*, 15:35–90

***

Two sleepy Egyptian villages, Ombi and Tentyra, barely tolerated the fragile *feud* between themselves. Each mocked the other's gods and customs, the feud simmering beneath the desert sun, baking festering wounds. Passionate fury against one another lived in the hearts of each township.

One day a week-long festival began with innocent frivolity in one of the villages. The people celebrated night and day, smearing themselves with sweet-scented unguents and wearing flowers for hats. They danced with drunken joy late into the Deltan nights, stammering and staggering, lost in a delightful delirium.

Their feuding neighbors detested this unsavory reveling and decided to crash the party. A sober hatred rose as men gathered on the party's fringe and began taunting, stirring the vitriol between them, challenging the disgusting orgy. This, in turn, brought boisterous retorts that led to fisticuffs and hand-to-hand violence.

Soon, everyone rumbled about with bloody noses and broken jaws as tensions escalated quickly into deadlier violence. One man hurled a stone while another responded with rocks. The mob ebbed and flowed until one resident tripped and fell. The invading combatants dragged him to the fringe and cut him into small bits, eating him raw, licking blood drops from the sticky sand.

***

If only the folks above could have shared the festivities. How delightful would that have been? James' insightful comments on *feuding* offer us hope.

***

"What is the source of quarrels and conflicts among you? Is not the source your pleasures that wage war in your members?... You fight and quarrel. You do not have because you do not ask" (Jas. 4:1–2).

***

Settle a feud peacefully today, and light a lamp of hope.

***

"Life is too bitter already, without territories and wars and noble feuds."
T.H White

Day 121

***

Fidelity (AD 150)
Apuleius, *The Golden Ass*, 9

***

In one of the earliest Latin novels ever written, Apuleius told a frolicking story about broken promises. A man named Barbarus had to leave town on business. He had a beautiful wife, and he didn't want any hanky-panky going on while he was gone. So he told his house slave, Myrmex, to guard her with his life or else!

He threatened the slave with prison, heavy chains, tortures untold, and a shameful death if a single man strolling by so much as grazed her arm with his fingertip. The master summed all this up with an ocean of dirty words and threats and then left town.

The servant was shaken to the core. Summoning *fidelity*, he played it straight, guarding her like a hawk. But then, one day, a guy offered him a bucket of gold if he could have one amorous night with the lady. Greed took over, and Myrmex consented.

But then the husband surprised everyone by sneaking home early and banging on the door. Nobody answered so he knew something was up. He slammed the portal with a heavy stone, demanding entry, but there was no response. "Open this door now, or you know what I'll do," screamed the irate husband.

***

Jesus, too, told of an unfaithful servant lacking in *fidelity* who was surprised by a late-night return of the master:

***

"Therefore be on the alert, for you do not know which day your Lord is coming ... the master of that slave will come when he does not expect him and at an hour which he does not know..." (Matt. 24:42–50).

***

Keep your promises. Be faithful in the least of things.

***

"Many persons have a wrong idea of what constitutes true happiness. It is not attained through self-gratification but through fidelity to a worthy purpose."
Helen Keller

Day 122

Fighting (1184 BC)

Homer, *Iliad*, 5:590–610

***

The battle raged on as battles tend to do. Hector, screaming threats against the Greeks, led the charge against the invaders from distant lands. With death-defying hostility, he urged his battalions to follow him to glory.

Diomedes, his Greek opponent, shook with passion as he saw Hector's troops kicking violent dust storms in his face. With fearless zeal, Diomedes plunged toward the enemy. But suspecting foul play, he soon ordered his forces to stop. Seeing the shadows of Ares and Enyo mingling ferociously among the enemy forces, he knew the danger of fighting against heaven's forces.

Calling his men together, Diomedes warned them against further pursuit. "Men," he said heroically, "the gods fight with our enemy. I see Ares' monstrous spear stirring the dust ahead. Let us move slowly backward, for we cannot *fight* God on these Trojan plains. We are like a traveler who suddenly stops before a raging river and must turn back. So retreat, men, and let us not be eager to battle with spiritual forces."

***

Now we can hear this same warning in the New Testament when Gamaliel, a teacher of the Law and one respected by all the people in Jerusalem, knew the odds of *fighting* against God. Gamaliel advised the high priest and the Sanhedrin to leave

Peter and the apostles alone. After all, if their movement were of man, it would die a natural death.

***

"but if it is of God, you will not be able to overthrow them; or else you may even be found fighting against God" (Acts 5:39).

***

Sheathe your sword. Better to love God than fight against Him.

***

"Fight if you must on the path of righteousness and God will be with you."
Mahatma Gandhi

Day 123

Finish (1178 BC)
Vírgil, *Aeneid*, 4:600–660

The majestic pyre of pinewood and ibex towered above the palace's ivory floors. Assembled deep within the inner sanctum, it trembled at its hushed purpose. None must know. It would smother the last sobs from a heart broken by love's betrayal. Dido, the queen, ordered Aeneas' bejeweled sword, which still dangled on pegs in her bedroom, to decorate the pyre's floor. Its burning would blot out the last pleasurable memories of their affair.

Hovering forlornly beneath the ascending pyre, she gave a final command to her nurse to fetch Anna. "Tell my sister to wear the holy headband that Jove demands at such times and to come quickly!" Carefully had she veiled the pyre's purpose, its horrible fate presented as a rue to rid herself of Aeneas' memory.

But now, alone before Hade's yawn, she sprang to action. With bloodshot eyes and quivering cheeks blotched from worrisome fear, she climbed to the pyre's peak. Drawing Aeneas' sword, her love gift to him, she lay on the branchy bed next to an effigy draped in his clothes. "I have lived and run life's course to the *finish* line," she sputtered to the gods. Then, as sunlight caught the departing sails of Aeneas' fleet, she fell upon his sword, blood spurting over her hands as she lay defeated and dying.

A *finish* line looms before us all, its thin fingers calling, making demands. It need not be a tragedy. Let us approach our final curtain with joy as Paul did:

***

"the time of my departure has come. I have fought the good fight, I have *finished* the course, I have kept the faith" (2 Tim. 4:7–8).

***

Sing atop the pyre. God awaits with your crown.

***

"Unable are the loved to die, for love is immortality."
Emily Dickenson

Day 124

***

Forgotten (AD 150)
Pausanias, *Description of Greece*, 1:1

***

Pausanias, our tour guide to the mysteries of ancient Greece, stood upon the Sounion promontory at the edge of the world, so it seems. This tip of land rose high above the Aegean Sea, about 43 miles south of Athens. Upon it rested the slender ivory pillars of Poseidon's temple, where Lord Byron once etched his name into one of the columns and wrote memorable words about the sweeping waves and murmurs buried within his heart.

Pausanias, lingering in the shadow of the glorious temple atop the promontory, pointed to the harbor ahead and then bade us glance at the ancient town of Laurium. He mentioned in a passing breath that this was where the Athenians once exploited silver mines:

Sighing like the cliff-breezes, he urged the tourists to gather the distant groans, "Can you hear them," he asked? "It was from those mines that untold scores of unfortunate slaves toiled night and day, scraping out the precious silver to make Athenian coins. As many as 20,000 pitiful souls, many of them children, worked in deplorable conditions and died *forgotten* in those ghastly silver-sprayed shafts of the deep."

***

For Pausanias, the mines were a mere novelty, and he didn't linger more than a few moments before leading the restless troop on to grander themes. But I wonder? Are you *forgotten*? Do you call Laurium home? Isaiah reminds us of a golden truth:

***

"Can a woman forget her nursing child, that she should have no compassion on the son of her womb? Even these may forget, yet I will not forget you" (Isa. 49:15).

***

God has not forgotten you.

***

"We sometimes think we want to disappear, but all we really want is to be found."
Anonymous

Day 125

Fortunes (30 BC)
Horace, *Satires*, 2:3

***

How many *fortunes* do you have tucked under your bed?

Horace, a favorite writer of Caesar Augustus, mocks all who fanatically hoard treasure. He reminded his friends of the billionaire Staberius who wouldn't spend a penny. When he died, Staberius, in his will, ordered his heirs to open the locked vault and count every gold coin he had. Then came this last demand: I want the total engraved on my tombstone so that the world will remember me.

Horace just sneered at this foolishness. He went on to reason with us:

"Imagine a guy with a shed packed with corn or grain. He guards it each day, pacing back and forth with a club in his hand but goes to bed hungry each night, eating only bitter leaves. Or how about the old fellow with a cellar full of the most expensive wine who only drinks sharp vinegar at dinner. And don't forget about the old fool who has a closet full of silken coverlets stuffed in his mothy closet while he sleeps on a straw bed.

"Try this," said Horace, frustrated. "Pour some expensive oil on your salad tonight. And while you're at it, dabble some high-priced perfume on your scruffy head."

***

Jesus didn't know Horace, but they both understood about *fortunes* and those fragile threads that bind us to this world. Jesus said:

***

"Do not store up for yourselves treasures upon earth, where moth and rust destroy, and where thieves break in and steal. But store up for yourselves treasures in heaven,... for where your treasure is, there your heart will be also" (Matt. 6:19–21).

***

Go ahead. Crack a piggy bank today. Life is short, remember?

***

"I make myself rich by making my wants few."
Henry Thoreau

Day 126

Foundations (AD 27)
Tacitus, *The Annals of Imperial Rome*, 4:63

***

Atilius, formerly a Roman slave, clapped his hands in glee. The amphitheater he built stood three stories high with wooden beams locked and gleaming in solidarity. The public, starved for the brutality of blood-soaked colosseums banned by Tiberius until recently, lined the streets for blocks, waiting impatiently for the gates to open.

Atilius knew little of architecture or the building arts. He cut corners when he could. Rather than call in experts, he had proceeded with incompetent optimism. He had neither rested its *foundation* on solid ground nor fastened the wooden superstructure securely.

On opening day, the swollen stands creaked and groaned as rowdy fans screamed for action. When the first combatants entered the stadium, they grimaced at the tiered rows as the crowd erupted. The first sword blows missed their marks as delirious spectators berated them voraciously, screaming for blood.

When the first gladiator fell, a head gash spurted blood. The crowd stomped in glee, and the stadium collapsed! Fifty-thousand men and women of all ages tumbled to their death in Rome's worst public disaster. When the smoke finally cleared, those still living rushed to kiss the corpses of their loved ones, mangled and broken like gladiators in pools of sandy blood.

***

At about this same time on history's timeline, a young prophet rose to address a crowd in Galilee. "Good *foundations* in life are essential," he told them. "Only foolish people build their houses on sand."

***

"The rain fell, and the floods came, and the winds blew and slammed against that house; and it fell—and great was its fall" (Matt. 7:27).

***

Foundations are everything. Lay your planks carefully today.

***

"And so rock bottom became the solid foundation on which I rebuilt my life."
J.K. Rowling

Day 127

***

Freedom (AD 35)
Phaedrus, *Fables*, 2:5

***

Tiberius scanned the Sicilian sea, breathing sweet respite from his imperialist duties at Rome. His villa on the Misenum summit seemed to touch the clouds. Here, without pretension, he could stroll the lush gardens and seek the solace he desperately pursued.

As he strolled one morning down a hidden path on the promontory's edge, he touched the verdant shrubs and savored the subtle fragrance of purple bougainvillea blossoms tumbling down toward the harbor. Suddenly, a slave slipped from the foliage, dressed in flowing Egyptian linen embellished with dangling fringes. Without a word, he began to drench the dusty path before the emperor with his wooden watering pitcher. Desperate to prove his worth and secretly hoping to win his *freedom*, he clambered ahead of the smiling prince.

Slipping back into the fringes of the shrubs, the slave reappeared, sprinkling dust further down the trail. As Tiberius approached, the servant once again began watering steps ahead of the great man. The emperor stopped and called him forward. "It will take more than these silly efforts to win your freedom slap," he said with a smirk. "That comes at a much higher price."

***

In late antiquity, enslavers could merely slap their servant's cheek a few times before a magistrate and bestow *freedom*. This represented the final humiliating violence that an enslaved person would have to bear. But today, the process avoids the slap. We merely seek God's mercy:

***

"Out of my distress I called on the Lord; the Lord answered me and set me free" (Ps. 118:5).

***

Put down your wooden pitcher and call for heaven's freedom.

***

"From every mountainside, let freedom ring."
Martin Luther King Jr.

Day 128

***

Frescoes (AD 60)
Petronius, *Satyricon*, 5:29

***

Guests arrived at Trimalchio's Roman mansion eager for the enchanted evening to begin. Petronius shuffled toward the front gate with the others, and running headlong into a ferocious leashed dog, he fell and nearly broke his leg. When he realized it was only a vibrant *fresco* painted on the wall, the others about him laughed until breathless. Beneath the screaming dog were these words scrawled in huge letters: Beware of the Dog!

Once he got up and shook himself off, he noticed that the frescoes loped gracefully down the wall replaying Trimalchio's entire life. First, there was a scene when he was a young man with long, curly hair like the slaves wore. He walked with a staff and entered Rome for the first time.

Next, as a young man dreaming of success and fame, the frescoes depicted him as an apprentice accountant and then a paymaster, each step scrupulously labeled.

Finally, several frescoes further down the wall, he saw a picture of Mercury lifting him to a platform of lofty eminence. Beside the stage, the three Fates were busily spinning out Trimalchio's life in threads of gold.

***

This comical scene reminds us all that we, too, are making *frescoes* of our lives each day. David's life wanderings caught the eye of God, who paused at several sorrowful scenes, catching

David's tears in His bottle. The Psalmist reminds us all that God does keep a book of tear-stained frescoes that line the infinite pathways of heaven.

***

"You have taken account of my wanderings; Put my tears in Your bottle. Are they not in Your book?" (Ps. 56:8).

***

What's on your wall? Paint some memorable scenes today!

***

"Your deeds are your monuments."
R.J. Palacio

Day 129

***

Friendship (1177 BC)
Virgil, *Aeneid*, 9:400–450

***

Lost in a thicket behind enemy lines, Euryalus panicked. Lunging this way and that, he could not find a clear path, nor could he call for his friend Nisus somewhere ahead beyond the moon's lamp. Hearing enemy horses panting heavily over the rise, he fought the brambles futilely. Suddenly, a warrior spotted him, and then a mob pounced, surrounding him, clucking.

Nisus, hearing the ruckus, turned back and watched in horror as they dragged his closest friend away. Euryalus, swordless and overpowered, fought vainly as the braggadocios foe toyed with their moonlight captive.

Nisus, crouching behind a tree, raised his spear and, after a brief prayer, hurled it through the darkness. Swishing through the shadowy night, it struck Sulmo in the back. The shaft snapped, but the pointed head pierced Sulmo's heart.

A raging Volscens, the troop captain, turned about blindly, seeking the source. Finding none, he lunged at Euryalus, his sword drawn. It was then that Nisus rose from the forest veil and screamed. "Here I am. I did it! Turn your weapon on me. Spare my *friend*!" But Volscens had already thrust his sword deep into Euryalus' chest.

Nisus, now surrounded, fought wildly through the crush of combatants, lunging for Volscens. Hurling himself toward certain death, his sword found its mark, slashing the captain before Nisus fell over his friend's body, whispering Nisus' name.

***

Friendship, molded in heaven's furnace, leads us through golden gates where hearts pledge unbreakable fealty. Nisus passed through these gates, as did Jesus, our Savior. At a moonlight meal one Jerusalem night, he said this:

***

"Greater love has no one than this, that one lay down his life for his friends" (Jn. 15:13).

***

Who would you die for?

***

"Two friends are always together in spirit."
L.M. Montgomery

Day 130

***

Frustration (219 BC).
Livy, *History of Rome*, 21:10

***

Hanno, the elder statesman of Carthage, stood to address a silent senate. The heat of a budding war across the sea singed the room. With fists clenched, the senators longed for revenge against Rome and prayed for war, as farmers called for rain. But Hanno stood alone and aloof in his opposition. Raising his trembling hand, he called for silence. "You all know how I despised Hannibal's father. All he did was fight endless battles for decades. What do we have to show for it? Nothing but rising desperation. I hated that man, and I was glad when he died."

The senators stared, blank-faced at the bitterness in Hanno's thunderous voice. Only his years of credible service quenched their open revolt. Hanno continued. "And I have to say that I hate Hannibal, his son, as well. He's just like his father—war crazy. While I stand here, he is jabbing with catapults at the walls of Saguntum, a Roman city. I wish he were dead too."

A few senators stood angrily, but others pulled them down. "Let him finish," they urged. Hanno felt the tension in the room, but he could not suppress his *frustration*. "The Roman ambassadors who just left our city have given us an ultimatum. They demand we surrender Saguntum and ship Hannibal in chains to Rome at once. I agree! And when they drag him to the emperor, I hope they slay him before the masses."

***

Frustration can be deadly if left untreated. I hear Hanno's vitriol just outside of a little home in Capernaum. Jesus is dining with local sinners while the Pharisees peek in through the window.

***

"Why is He eating and drinking with tax collectors and sinners?" (Mk. 2:16).

***

Turn your frustration into praise today.

***

"Expectation is the mother of frustration."
Antonio Banderas

Day 131

***

Games (401 BC)

Xenophon, *Anabasis*, 4:8

***

Laughter, cheering, and exuberant shouting ricocheted off the mountainside, tumbling to the Black Sea. While the Greek soldiers waited for Cheirisophus to gather many ships from afar for their journey home, the idle men decided it was time for games and fun. They laid their weapons aside and put on their competitive faces.

Draconius became the manager of the *games*. He selected a hardscrabble section of the mountain with a steep slope for fun. Immediately, the wrestlers complained about the hard ground. "Just don't get thrown to the ground," said Draconius with a grin.

The events began with a short race for the boys, mostly war captives. Then came the cross country with over sixty runners eager to prove their speed, followed by wrestling, boxing, and a unique sport that combined boxing and wrestling without rules, the pankration.

While these events drew cheers and great crowds, further up the mountain, the horse races began. Skilled equestrians plunged recklessly down the steep mountainside to the shore and back up again to the altar. Many horses tumbled head over heels on the sprint down, with spectators cheering on the riders.

***

Despite the new Covid-19 world, it's common to see people of all ages flocking to the beaches for fun and *games*. It seems everyone needs an outlet, as did Xenophon's Greek soldiers. St. Paul loved the games as well and used the spectacle to teach a spiritual thought:

***

"Do you not know that those who run in a race all run, but only one receives the prize? Run in such a way that you may win" (1 Cor. 9:24).

***

Play a game today and lift your spirits.

***

"Just play. Have fun. Enjoy the game."
Michael Jordan

Day 132

***

Garden (AD 53)
Tacitus, *The Annals of Imperial Rome*, 12:57

***

Agrippina often strolled in the evening past Titus Taurus' exotic gardens and sighed. The flow of delicate bushes between the mulberry and cypress trees that summoned heaven's smile taunted her. She would often return dejected as she looked with disdain at her scraggly plants.

Titus Taurus worked in the local mint, spitting out coins and amassing a vast fortune. After a long day at the job, Agrippina often spotted him caressing the roses and hyacinths and cooing at his purple saffron angels. Each day this silent dialogue between the empress and the minter's *gardens* roiled her evil heart.

Titus was an honorable man who had served as governor of Africa. He had returned to Rome after years of dedicated ambassadorial effort and found life's joy in gardening. It caught him by surprise that the court had summoned him on charges of extortion and magic. Agrippina invented these accusations without evidence. Hauled into court, he vigorously denied the allegations. Nightly, however, he suffered an undeserved humiliation that crushed his spirit.

Unwilling to wait for the senate's verdict, he took his own life beneath a cypress tree, his blood mingling with the cassia and thyme of his beloved garden—that now belonged to Agrippina.

***

Another *garden* of olive trees sleeps beneath a saddened moon on a hill overlooking Jerusalem. Beneath their dreamy branches, scented with the Mediterranean Sea and sun, Jesus wept, his blood mingling with the garden's soil.

So sad. One woman coveted a garden, while Jesus, in a garden, bled love drops for the world.

***

"and His sweat became like drops of blood, falling down upon the ground" (Lk. 22:44).

***

Pause at a garden today and remember Jesus.

***

"I covet wings more than crowns, for my dreams are of flight, not of thrones."
Pepper Blair

Day 133

***

Girded (200 BC)
Plautus, *Captives*, 770–790

***

It was such a sad tale. Hegio, a wealthy Greek man from Aetolia, grieved daily for his lost son. One of his slaves had stolen the four-year-old boy years ago and fled to Elia, another country. Time passed, and the father wondered if he would ever see his son again. But then, on one serendipitous day, Hegio's slave saw the lost son getting off a ship at the local harbor.

"Oh boy, this is big," thought the slave. "I've got news that will change my life forever! When I tell Hegio that I've seen his boy getting off a ship at the harbor, why, he'll treat me like a king. Let me tuck this robe in tight so I won't trip because I'm going to be running as fast as I can."

So there he goes, all *girded* up, his loose cloak wrapped around him tightly. The slaves in the ancient world wore the "pallium," a loose-flowing garment that had to be tucked in for running. A "tucked up" servant meant he was on some critical mission.

Hegio was at home when he glanced outside and saw this slave bolting through the crowd gyrating his arms and screaming. "What in the world is going on with this slave?" wondered Hegio from the window. "He's running this way girded up like he's on some crazy mission."

***

Paul, hobbled by shackles in a Roman prison, nevertheless felt an ongoing urgency to tell the world of the mystery of the gospel. He pleads with us to *gird* our robes and run God's errands with purpose and speed.

***

"Stand therefore, having girded your loins with truth, and having put on the breastplate of righteousness" (Eph. 6:14).

***

Find your mission today and run!

***

"Without a sense of urgency, desire loses its value."
Jim Rohn

Day 134

***

Glances (1177 BC)
Virgil, *Aeneid*, 5:1–10

***

High on the ship's poop, Aeneas slept deeply. His failed romance with Dido, the Carthaginian queen, was now condemned by heaven's frown. The ship's stern moaned beneath restless waves while in the distance, the queen's tragedy bloomed. The pyre she had built, nestled in the palace's inner chambers, was lit, its smoke drifting ominously toward the sky as she lay bleeding with unfathomable regrets.

Slumbering Aeneas, oblivious to the queen's distant suicide, suddenly heard the breath of Mercury, heaven's messenger. He hovered above the poop, mingling with dreams, urging Aeneas to rise and run. "Get up and go, now!" he urged. "You never know what a grieving woman will do. Go, now!"

Aeneas flung the bedding off and screamed to his comrades. "Ready the ship! We sail at once. Hurry everyone. Now is the time." Finding his sword, Aeneas clambered to the stern's ropes and severed the line. The oars struck the sea with savagery, finding the westward wind, sailing toward Rome with rigorous strokes.

As morning's saffron lights swept the horizon, Aeneas *glanced* backward one last time, noting the glow of fires atop the city's walls, wondering what it meant, but sensing a woman's tortuous grief.

***

Nostalgia can have dark fingers, pulling us backward toward previous failures. When morning urges escape, we should fling off the bedding and run toward any open doors God sets before us. Lot's wife, ever-shackled by Gomorrah's dark shadows, lingered and *glanced* backward to her demise:

***

"But his wife, from behind him, looked back, and she became a pillar of salt" (Gen. 19:24–26).

***

Cut the lines today and sail boldly into your future.

***

"What is past, one cannot change, so each backward glance is a bit of the present slipping away."
James Conroyd Martin

Day 135

Goodbye (AD 69)
Suetonius, *Lives of the Caesars*, 7.2

***

Sensing his end, Otho, the emperor of Rome for a mere 85 days, summoned his friends. Vitellius' angry legions were on the march, closing in, leaving just enough time for hasty farewells. Otho first embraced his older brother, Lucius, remembering the happy days of youthful bliss at Ferentium, where they often attended the local theater. Then he kissed his nephew *goodbye* as many other friends pressed him for a few final words.

After all his close associates had departed, as grief and silence settled in his bedroom, he sat and wrote two final letters: one to his beloved sister and Messalina, whom he had meant to marry, begging her always to remember him. Next, he burned his private letters to block any future gossip and set aside any loose cash for his faithful household staff.

In the evening's solitude, he drank a glass of cold water and left his bedroom door open if any late visitors might wish to speak with him. Then, after testing the points of two sharp daggers, he put one under his pillow and drifted off into peaceful dreams.

When morning broke on the hills of Brixellum, Otho rose, plunged the dagger into his heart, and collapsed in a crimson pool of regrets.

***

Goodbyes are complicated, often severing long-standing ties of affection. Paul knew this well as he boarded a ship in Miletus. Rising from a final prayer session with his closest friends, they all trudged toward the boat, continually kissing the departing apostle.

***

"And they began to weep aloud and embraced Paul, and repeatedly kissed him…" (Acts 20:37).

***

Sad farewells sometimes lead to happy reunions.

***

"Don't cry because it's over, smile because it happened."
Dr. Seuss

Day 136

Gossip (431 BC)
Euripides, *Medea*, 50–95

***

The slave skipped homeward beneath Corinthian skies as dusk fell over the harbor. With a little child holding the tutor's hands, they laughed at games played on city streets earlier. Approaching the children's home, the tutor paused, noting the family nurse's familiar profile musing downheartedly upon the front porch. "What's wrong?" he asked. "Why aren't you inside consoling the mistress?"

With wringing hands, she replayed Medea's horrid betrayal by her husband. "She can't stop fretting over Jason running off with the princess of Corinth. I just had to get out of the house."

"She should be done crying by now. It's getting late," he said.

"Are you kidding? She's just getting started."

The tutor shook his head. "She doesn't know half of what's coming."

"What do you mean?" asked the nurse.

"Oh, it's nothing. Sorry, I said that." He gathered the children and started inside.

She stopped him. "What do you mean? Tell me. I won't say a thing, but I need to know what's going on."

He looked about and then, with hands shading his voice, continued. "I've heard some *gossip* through the vine that King Creon intends to banish her and the kids from Corinth. It's what people in the palace are whispering."

***

Gossip's wings flutter constantly about us, luring us to gather at the porch. Paul thought it worth his pen to scribble a few salient warnings about it all.

***

"At the same time they also learn to be idle, as they go around from house to house; and not merely idle, but also gossips and busybodies, talking about things not proper to mention" (1 Tim. 5:13).

***

Avoid the porch gossip today.

***

"Great minds discuss ideas. Small minds discuss people."
Eleanor Roosevelt

Day 137

***

Grasshoppers (431 BC)
Thucydides, *The Peloponnesian War*, 1:6

***

Both elderly Athenian men walked with a grace that wealth and prestige bestow. Meandering through Athens' old marketplace, these aristocrats, giddy with anticipation, disregarded the locals' envious stares.

Pausing here and there to stroke silken scarves and marvel at intricately carved ivory knife handles, they quickly resumed their mission to the goldsmith stall. Their long braided hair, glistening gray against the morning sunlight and gracefully tied in knots, awaited the prize, the golden *grasshopper* clasps used to secure the hair knots.

Only the highest-bred men wore them as a badge of distinction along with linen vests, a token of luxury and status. But it was the golden grasshoppers that set them apart, buzzing softly in their windblown braids, telling the world of the Greek's noble breeding.

***

Peter, the crusty old fisherman from Palestine, had little love for such trinkets mentioned in Thucydides' history. However, this man of the sea with blistered hands knew the attraction of such baubles for those newly minted saints living in the distant Asian Pontus. These saints, not long removed from barbarianism, loved status-shouting *grasshoppers*. Peter offered guidance:

***

"Your adornment must not be merely external—braiding the hair, and wearing gold jewelry, or putting on dresses; but let it be the hidden person of the heart, with the imperishable quality of a gentle and quiet spirit, which is precious in the sight of God" (1 Pet. 3:3–4).

***

Wear the golden grasshoppers if you must but favor the gentle spirit within.

***

"In the long run, the sharpest weapon of all is a kind and gentle spirit."
Anne Frank

Day 138

Greatness (55 BC)
Catullus, *Poems*, 22

***

Suffenus loved to play the poet. Nothing made him happier than writing verse. The problem was that he couldn't write. Sure, he was gently bred, a man who loved the pastries of life, but he was no poet; he merely pretended *greatness*.

Catullus smiled at the imposter and muttered softly, "Yeah, he wrote a lot of poetry, but man was it awful!"

Suffenus was so impressed with his ten thousand poems that he put them down on the best paper and tied them with expensive bows. Catullus explained Suffenus' creative process with a smirk:

"Suffenus didn't work on scraps. Oh, no. He started with royal sheets of gleaming paper that he smoothed out with an elegant pumice stone. But that's not all. He embroidered each page with gleaming bosses and then bound it with scarlet ribbons. It was truly a work of art—until you read it and groaned."

Catullus tried to take a few lessons from the imaginative huckster: "We're all Suffenus with our allusions of grandeur. But when you think about it, we're just carrying piles of poetic junk on our backs."

***

The disciples of Jesus seemed to walk with the same limp. Once on a trip to Capernaum, Jesus overheard his disciples whispering about *greatness*. When they arrived in town, he stopped and asked them what they had been discussing so intently on the road.

***

"But they kept silent, for on the way they had discussed with one another which of them was the greatest" (Mk. 9:34).

***

Are you strutting like Suffenus? Try a little humility.

***

"Nothing is more simple than greatness; indeed, to be simple is to be great."
Emerson

Day 139

***

Greetings (1184 BC)
Homer, *Iliad*, 15:1–90

***

Zeus woke slowly, the evening's bliss still caressing his turbulent mind. Sitting on the edge of his locus bed, dew-spangled and soft with crocus and hyacinth sprouts, he reached for Hera, his wife, who still slumbered in her Mount Ida wonderland. Stretching peacefully, Zeus smiled at the night's sweet memories. Rising, he peered over the mountain's edge and glanced casually at the sea coast where the endless war raged on between Hector's Trojans and Achilles' Greeks.

Then, like a spark ignites a fire, he understood. Hera had lulled him to sleep so the Greeks could rally and thrust their sharp spears at the fleeing Trojan soldiers. His rage inflamed, he woke his wife and called her hand. "I see what you have done, but it won't work. Get dressed and send messengers to the armies. I will reset this battle to favor Troy. He glared at her. I ought to hang you up by your ankles like I once did."

Hera knew his rage and quickly obeyed, ordering Iris and Apollo to deliver her husband's threats. She, in turn, dressed quickly and flew to Mt. Olympus, where the gods were gathered. Thrilled to see this long-missed friend, they gathered about her holding out their heavenly cups as a *greeting*. She glanced at them but selected lovely Thetis' chalice, a gift from a concerned goddess.

"Why are you here, Hera? You seem troubled," noted Thetis, suspecting Zeus' temper.

***

A pleasant *greeting* among friends is often all we have to save a blusterous day. As the cups clink, we gather ourselves and restore life's calm. Paul had a different tradition for *greetings*:

***

"Greet one another with a holy kiss" (2 Cor. 13:12).

***

Extend your cup today. Someone needs it.

***

"The usefulness of the cup is its emptiness."
Bruce Lee

Day 140

***

Grief (1184 BC)
Homer, *Iliad*, 18:1–100

***

Achilles sat by the tall ships in melancholy brooding. A light breeze ruffled his new silk shirt, which brought him little pleasure. The endless Trojan war seemed a nightmare he could not escape, its phantasmagorias relentless. The distant dust troubled him as it swirled ever closer to the coast where he guarded the ships. "Are the Greeks fleeing again, racing from Hector's brutal sword?" he wondered. Why can't they stand and fight?

He knew as he scrawled runes in the sand that his closest friend, Patroclus, was in that dust cloud somewhere wearing the armor Achilles had loaned him. Moaning at the dark possibilities, he grew more agitated when he saw Antilochus, the fleet-footed messenger, hurrying toward him. "Surely this is an omen," he thought, rising to face the ominous uncertainties.

Antilochus approached with bad news. "I hate to be the one to tell, Achilles, but Patroclus is dead. The armies are fighting for control of his naked body, and Hector now wears your armor."

A dark cloud, *grief* infused, settled upon the listener. Then without words, Achilles stooped down, filled his hands with dirt, and drizzled it over his head, smearing his disfigured face, blotting the fluttering white shirt. He flung himself upon the beach, tearing his hair, screaming against fate.

***

Perhaps this is you at this moment, lying beside Achilles, engulfed in *grief*. Moments like these seem bottomless, hopeless. Jesus, Himself, was not spared the disfigurement of profound loss. Lazarus, His closest friend, lay four days dead in a tomb:

***

"Jesus wept. So the Jews were saying 'See how He loved him!'" (Jn. 11:35–36).

***

Behind grief's bolted door, there is Light.

***

"In the garden of memory, in the palace of dreams ... that is where you and I shall meet."
Alice Through the Looking Glass

Day 141

***

Grudges (26 BC)
Cassius Dio, *Roman History*, 56:43

***

Corocotta mocked as he read the wanted poster from Caesar Augustus. The emperor's *grudge* over this pirate's endless attacks upon Roman legions drove the bounty higher, now a million sesterces for anyone who could drag this criminal before Caesar Augustus.

Corocotta laughed when he saw it. Fearless in his defense of Spain's northern coastline, he took a warrior's delight in causing havoc upon the Roman settlers strangling the native customs of his beloved land. Sitting before a campfire one night with his gang, he brashly declared, "I will go to Rome myself and claim this reward." The others laughed as they prepared to launch another raid by morning light.

"I'm serious," said Corocotta. "I will go to Rome and stand before Augustus and claim the reward."

At first light, Corocotta set sail for Rome. Upon arrival, he knocked upon the emperor's door on the Palatine Hill. Augustus, astonished at the robber's boldness, invited him in and listened to tales of life beneath the Spanish sun where the Bay of Biscay laps sweetly on golden shores.

Augustus saw the love of Spain in the pirate's eyes and summoned the treasurer, bestowing the full bounty to Corocotta, releasing him unharmed.

***

The willingness of Augustus to put aside his *grudge* is a challenge for all believers. It seems everybody has some grudge in a pocket somewhere. Augustus appears to resemble the spirit of James' advice to us all.

***

"But everyone must be quick to hear, slow to speak and slow to anger; for the anger of man does not achieve the righteousness of God" (Jas. 1:19–20).

***

Don't let a grudge ruin your budding friendship.

***

"We cannot embrace God's forgiveness if we are so busy clinging to past wounds and nursing old grudges."
T.D. Jakes

Day 142

Guilt (AD 110)
Juvenal, *Satires*, 13:190–210

***

The Spartan inquirer, his eyes squinting *guilt*, approached the Pythian shrine with trepidation. He fell to his knees before the priestess, who sat regally upon a golden tripod. A scarlet shawl draped her head, casting shadows of intolerance over her forehead. An imperious nod implored the visitor to speak.

The Spartan, his voice quivering, sought guidance for a shady business arrangement. "My friend asked me to guard his money while he's gone on a long journey. I told him I would, but secretly I intend to steal it all. What do you think?"

The Delphic priestess shivered at this grand deceit and issued her proclamation as vapors rose from a crack in the earth beneath her feet. "Punishment awaits you!" she said in whispery tones, her eyes dilated and distant.

Stumbling forth from the cave, the Spartan hurried home, the verdict hissing in his soul. He returned the money, desperate to avert hell's chaos from striking. But it was too late. As Juvenal tells us in this satire for a defrauded friend, "the mere wish to sin brings on retribution. Even if you never commit a crime, or mention it to others, the guilt of the thought lives."

***

Achan went one step further than the Spartan above. He breached God's ban on Jericho's booty and hid a golden bar

283

and an exquisitely embroidered mantle beneath his tent floor. Punishment for the *guilty* was swift.

***

"Joshua said, 'Why have you troubled us? The LORD will trouble you this day.' And all Israel stoned them with stones; and they burned them with fire after they had stoned them with stones" (Josh. 7:25).

***

Your guilty eyes sing a dark melody. Don't do it!

***

"You wear guilt like shackles on your feet, like a halo in reverse." *Depeche Mode*

Day 143

Harbors (1184 BC)
Virgil, *Aeneid*, 1:55–179

***

The seven ships filled with Troy's survivors limped, broken and battered, into a *harbor* somewhere on Libya's coast. The brine-crusted masses huddled in frigid bows stared at the mystical mirage, disbelieving their eyes. Twin peaks atop lofty cliffs towered toward heaven, cradling a curtain of overhanging woods. The seaward harbor, set like some smooth theater before the woodland spectators, welcomed the exhausted refugees.

At the foot of the cliffs above the shore, there lay, nestled at the forest's edge, a cave spiked with stalactites, dripping fresh water upon naturally hewn stones, smoothed by the hidden nymphs.

Bobbing gently on this sheltered sea, the seven tired ships lay, untethered by taut cables and anchors' biting teeth. Led by Aeneas, the weary Trojans aching for dry land, unfolded from bow and stern and tumbled upon the sandy beach, their limbs crusted with salt. Achates struck a flint, spitting sparks upon dry branches. Sweet solace mingled with drenched hope rose into the African sky as the sojourners paid homage to Ceres. Then, with fire blazing, they began to grind the soggy grain, wondering what tomorrow would bring.

***

Part your fears today and see in the distance the *harbor* that awaits you. God knows your limits, and soon the mists will

285

clear as He points to some peaceful shore prepared for you. Look ahead! The dark clouds are parting, and quiet melodies summon you. The harbor awaits. Come and rest.

***

"He caused the storm to be still, so that the waves of the sea were hushed. Then they were glad because they were quiet, so He guided them to their desired haven" (Ps. 107: 29–30).

***

When all seems lost, there is always a harbor.

***

"The house with an old grandparent harbors a jewel."
Chinese Proverb

Day 144

***

Hatred (219 BC)
Livy, *History of Rome*, 21:1

***

Though just a boy of nine years, Hannibal watched the army loading the warships on the northern coast of Africa. At early sunrise, the troops would set sail to Spain. General Hamilcar, the boy's father, bellowed orders to soldiers as he had done for years during the recent revolt in Africa.

Hannibal dreamed of heroism and fame on Spanish terrain. He admired his father's swagger and wanted desperately to follow him across the Mediterranean. Pumped with visions of grandeur, Hannibal requested permission to go aboard.

Hamilcar paused from his labors and studied the boy's intensity. With an imperial wave, he summoned Hannibal to the altar, where sacrifices scented the night air. Prayers for safety always preceded a new venture, and these would ensure safe passage across the ever boisterous waters.

Hannibal obeyed, awed by this sacred ritual that demanded piety and an intense awareness of the gods. Taking his son's hand, Hamilcar laid it upon the smoldering blood-smeared carcass, its heavenly incense pleading with heaven's deities. "Swear, my son, by all that is sacred, that you will stir an ever-increasing hatred for Romans. This altar will bind you to this oath. When your *hatred* for Romans reaches its zenith, you will be ready."

***

If only Hannibal, fueled by *hatred*, could have heard love's melody in Jesus' retort to a trap-scented question by a mischievous Pharisee.

***

"Teacher, which is the great commandment in the Law? And He said to him, 'YOU SHALL THE LORD YOUR GOD WITH ALL YOUR HEART, AND WITH ALL YOUR SOUL, AND WITH ALL YOUR MIND'" (Matt. 22:37).

***

Place your hand upon the Cross and Love.

***

"Hatred does not cease by hatred, but only by love; this is the eternal rule."
Buddha

Day 145

Healing (1184 BC)
Homer, *Iliad*, 4:190–220

***

The blood dripped down Menelaus' thighs, pooling at his feet, reminding him of war's wrath. The arrow's tip, lodged in the intricate mail of Menelaus' cuirass, had missed its death mark, leaving, however, a nasty gash. King Agamemnon called for his *healer*, Machaon, to come immediately. As search parties scoured the battlefield searching for him, attendants laid the warrior on the ground as a crowd of Achaean soldiers pressed in tightly, gazing with concern.

With a sudden flurry, Machaon, a healer of renown, arrived. Agamemnon met him; fear etched into the king's face as he led the physician through the crowd. Pushing through the circle of chieftains, Machaon kneeled beside the blood-smeared warrior and calculated the damage. Then, with the utmost care, he tugged at the arrow, pulling it through the mail and leather, bending back the death barbs until he stared with disgust at the deadly shaft.

Flinging it aside, he undid the burnished belt, removing Menelaus' armor until, finally, he stared at the bleeding gash. Anguished signs resonated throughout the gathering as Machaon rummaged through his bag of ointments and medicines. Wiping away the blood, he then sprinkled various soothing drugs upon the wound as his father, Aesculapius, the great physician, had taught him.

***

We all stumble, arrow-bit, from time to time. Our wounded spells often sideline us forcing us to ponder more deeply life's meaning and purpose. Surely such was the case when Peter's mother-in-law fell to a burning fever. Summoning the *healer*, Jesus passed through the circle and touched her brow.

***

"And standing over her, He rebuked the fever, and it left her; and she immediately got up and waited on them" (Lk. 4:39).

***

Wounded? The Great Physician is kneeling over you.

***

"Make peace with your broken pieces."
r.h. Sin

Day 146

Heartless (AD 24)
Tacitus, *The Annals of Imperium Rome, 4:28*

***

They stood side by side, father and son, in a Roman court of law. The father, Vibius Serenus, dragged out of exile from a remote island for petty crimes, stood before an intolerant judge. His tattered clothing draped over rusty manacles binding his hands. He smelled of urine and filth, his beard unshaven, his hair tangled and graying, reminders of the lost years.

Beside him stood his *heartless* son, also named Vibius Serenus, named, in fact, by this ruined man in tatters. The younger Vibius, his hair carefully coifed and perfumed, wore an elegant robe from Rome's best shops. He refused to glance at his father, preserving an imperious front before the court officials, while winking at his privileged admirers who strolled in to watch the circus act unfold.

The son took the stand first. "He's guilty, your honor, of plotting against Tiberius." The crowd giggled as they studied the old man's reactions. "He hired a mess of subversive agents and sent them to aid the Gauls with stolen money. I couldn't remain silent, your honors."

Finally, the father stood before the judge but faced the son. He shook the rusty manacles in Vibius' face and called on the gods for vengeance. "You're lying, and I pray that the gods punish you in the pits of Hades!"

***

Heartless acts are everywhere. Remember Solomon? Two harlots, living in the same house, had given birth to baby boys. One had died in the night; both claimed the living baby.

***

"Then the king said, 'Get me a sword!'" (1 Kings 3:24).

***

Resist your heartless impulses today. Practice graciousness.

***

"He lives down in a ribcage in the dry leaves of a heart."
Thomas Harris

Day 147

***

Heaven (27 BC)
Tibullus, *Elegies*, 1:3

***

Tibullus, that poet of soft elegies, lost on some distant war-shore apart from his beloved Delia, imagines. He stares, homesick and lonesome, at his tombstone and reads the chiseled epitaph:

A wandering poet who lost his way
Paused here in anguish humbly to pray
For Delia.

Then he follows love's mystical trail to *heaven*, discovering ceaseless joy and revelry. His parched soul hears soothing music floating on the winds, and sees painted warblers hopping gaily in this celestial orchard. His love-torn heart smells the untaught hedges, scented with cassia and rich perfumes. As he turns, dreamlike, here and there, the vista is painted in purple fields and flooded with brilliant light. Everyone is free from pain and hurt. Heaven's residents, crowned with myrtle, wander wherever Love leads them.

But heaven cannot hold love so profound as his. Delia calls! With divine help, he slips from the blessed Elysian Fields and descends unannounced, a wandering vagrant, fallen from heaven into the arms of his beloved.

***

Our love-consumed poet's brief visit to *heaven* reminds us of a permanent abode for God's privileged saints. Those who stroll its gardens will never again feel the burden of hunger or thirst.

Midday suns will no longer torment them, nor will heat-laden days oppress. Instead, our heavenly Shepherd will guide each beloved resident to springs of living water where banished sorrow no longer lives.

***

"for the Lamb in the center of the throne will be their shepherd, and will guide them to springs of the water of life; and God will wipe every tear from their eyes" (Rev. 7:17).

***

Heaven, but a fantasy to our poet, is ready for you.

***

"Earth hath no sorrow that heaven cannot heal."
St. Thomas More

Day 148

***

Hecklers (1184 BC)
Virgil, *Aeneid*, 3:210–255

***

Free from the flames of burning Troy, Aeneas and his small fleet of vagabond ships sailed the Aegean searching for a homeland. After four days of frothy turbulence, they spotted the coast of the Strophades, a welcome sight for waterlogged sailors. Gliding into the white sands, they beached their vessels stern first on the shore and set up an altar and tables for a feast. Rambling goats browsed nearby, and from this herd, a sumptuous dinner delighted the souls of every weary traveler.

But as the feast unfolded in this halcyon moment, a terrible sound of hoarse wings vibrated the tables as Harpies swept down from the mountains. These winged beasts with angelic faces but filthy, bestial bodies swooped over the gracious tables, defiling the food with their excrement and stench.

Racing for cover beneath cliff tops, the people waited until all was calm and then, beneath the cliff's arms, set up their makeshift tables and continued the festival. However, again the Harpies marshaled their forces and flew, screeching and belching over the tables. The lead monster, Calaeno, *heckled* the band of travelers predicting hard times and famine when they found their dreamland across the seas.

***

Beware when skies are blue, and your heart drifts merrily along with song. Envious *hecklers* thrive on disruption. Without cause or invitation, they will swoop down, disrupting your celebration. Knowing no bounds, they will even challenge your pain:

***

"They spat on Him, and took the reed and began to beat Him on the head. After they had mocked Him, they took the scarlet robe off Him…" (Matt. 27:30–31).

***

Stay grounded and faithful today when the Harpies swarm.

***

"Never argue with stupid people. They will drag you down to their level and then beat you with experience."
Mark Twain

Day 149

Heralds (431 BC)
Thucydides, *The Peloponnesian War*, 1:29

***

The Corinthian delegation was angry. One of their colonies along the coast, Epidamnus, was under siege by local barbarians. Nearby cities refused to help, leaving the citizens in a panic. They had issued an immediate appeal to its motherland, Corinth, which summoned their herald. "Go and tell those who seek to destroy Epidamnus that Corinth is on the way with 75 ships and a large force. We'll destroy them unless they all back down and get out of town."

The *herald* took it all in, absorbing the raw emotion so he could pass it on accurately to the distant foes. With his herald's staff in hand, he sailed off under the protection provided for all such mediators. When he arrived at the city, he disembarked, noting the hectic war preparations underway along the coast. Watched with glaring eyes, he proceeded with his staff held high to the general's tent. "The Corinthians sent me to announce impending war," cried the herald in his powerful voice.

The Corcyraean general scoffed and handed the ambassador his reply in a scroll. "If they want war, tell the Corinthian fools that we will oblige." Scurrying back to his ship, the herald hurried home with the news. Within days, war cries filled the sea coast.

***

These ancient *heralds,* renowned for their stentorian voices and staffs, skittered from city to city, passing official messages back and forth between grieving parties. Paul says that is our task as well:

***

"Therefore, we are ambassadors for Christ, as though God were making an appeal through us; we beg you on behalf of Christ, be reconciled to God" (2 Cor. 5:20).

***

Don't forget your staff this morning.

***

"We have it in our power to begin the world over again."
Thomas Paine

Day 150

Heroes (1184 BC)
Homer, *Iliad*, 2:535

***

Agamemnon called his armies to battle. He sent criers out, whose voices pierced the sea winds, summoning those who would win glory against Troy. Athene, too, moved among them, carrying her priceless shield from which a hundred tassels of pure gold, each worth a hundred oxen, waved gloriously upon the Scamander Plains.

The Greek warriors, their hearts burning for battle, rallied before their great king, marching with their armor flashing heavenward. They were like flocks of geese that scream above the Cayster River, flying gloriously until noisily settling among the wakening fen. As the troops sprang from their ships, they seemed like leaves blooming in summer, bespangled flowers finding new purpose beneath the sun.

These *heroes*, names that will live on in history's pantheon, came from throughout the Greek world. The Abantes called Euboea home. Fierce warriors, they rallied, their long hair flouncing as they grasped their long ashen spears. They brought fifty ships, each bursting with valiant soldiers. Ajax brought twelve ships, and the men of Argos led by Diomed, who had a loud battle cry, came with eighty ships. King Agamemnon, glorious in his gleaming armor, boasted a hundred ships from Mycenae. Heroes all.

***

This boisterous rallying of *heroes* from a distant past almost seems to touch another list of ancient heroes. They, too, step forward, sharing the spiritual limelight, urging us to follow them to heaven's gate. There is Enoch who pleased God, and Noah, hammer in hand. Abraham came, too, searching for his city.

***

"Now faith is the assurance of things hoped for, the conviction of things not seen, for by it the men of old gained approval" (Heb. 11:1–2).

***

It's roll call. Step forward heroically.

***

"Heroes are people who rise to the occasion and slip quietly away."
Tom Brokaw

Day 151

***

Hesitation (54 BC)
Caesar, *Gallic Wars*, 5:56

***

Sometimes, hesitating can be fatal. Julius Caesar noted a remarkable example of this in his Gallic Wars. A Gallic chieftain named Indutiomarus thought he had Caesar on the run. Throughout the winter, he sent deputies across the Rhine, inviting the various Gallic clans to join him in a revolt against Caesar. He promised large sums of money and claimed that much of Caesar's army was scattered or slain. Though some refused to join him, many deputations hastened from all directions.

Quickly, Indutiomarus called for an armed convention which is how the Gauls started their wars. Every grown man must come at once with their weapons and without excuse. The one who *hesitated* and came last to the assembly was tortured to death slowly in front of everyone.

***

Hesitation in the Gallic world could cost a man his life.

In the Old Testament, no one dared to enter the Holy of Holies except the high priest (Lev. 16:2). I can only imagine many a priest lingering nervously at the edge of the sacred veil before entering. Tradition tells us that people tied a scarlet rope to the priest's ankle before entering the holy area. If he died, they could pull him out. But now, we who know the Lord can slip quietly into this mysterious place without hesitating.

***

"Therefore, brethren, since we have confidence to enter the holy place by the blood of Jesus, by anew and living way which He inaugurated for us through the veil, that is, His flesh, and since we have a great priest over the house of God, let us draw near with a sincere heart in full assurance of faith..." (Heb. 10:19–22).

***

Come early to the holy place. Don't be last!

***

"He who hesitates is last."
Mae West

Day 152

Hiding (AD 69)

Suetonius, *Lives of the Caesars*, 7:16–17

***

Vitellius, the gluttonous emperor, closed the curtains on his palanquin, a Roman litter, and ordered his servants to run. Vespasian's threatening troops were on the fringes of Rome. Panic-stricken, Vitellius bolted for his father's house on the Aventine Hill, where he hoped to slither away to safety in the night. Having no time to pack for this quick exodus, he gathered only the essentials: his pastry cook.

No sooner had he arrived than he began to hear sweet overtures of peace. These faint rumors tempted him back to the palace. Returning cautiously, he slipped through the grand entrance and feasted on a deserted home, abandoned and eerily silent. Realizing the trap, he scrambled to pack his girdle with gold coins and then raced to the doorkeeper's quarters. He tethered a dog outside, jammed a mattress against the door, and crouched, whimpering inside a closet.

When Vespasian's soldiers searched the Palatine Hill, they found a sniveling man *hiding* behind locked doors and yanked the supposed slave out, not recognizing him.

"Where is the emperor?" they demanded. Vitellius, his voice quavering, pointed to the mansion nearby. The diversion failed, and the soldiers tied the tyrant's hands behind his back. Fastening a neck-noose, they dragged him in tattered clothes to the Forum.

***

David, too, had been running. The ghostly images of a lonely night's pleasure with Bathsheba leered now before his cold bed, demanding justice. Humiliated and exhausted from *hiding*, he finally turned toward God and heard unexpected melodies of grace.

***

"You are my hiding place; You preserve me from trouble; You surround me with songs of deliverance" (Ps. 32:7).

***

God's palanquin awaits you. Step in and breathe again.

***

"His will is our hiding place."
Corrie ten Boom

Day 153

Homeless (1184 BC)
Virgil, *Aeneid*, 3:1–10

***

The night fires raged across Troy as embers of a once regal city now drifted skyward. Aeneas stumbled through the smoky back streets calling for Creusa, lost in the hysterical scramble from the furnace. Finally, she appeared, ghostlike, a phantom now, who bade her husband goodbye, forever. Thrice, Aeneas tried to embrace her, but each time his arms slipped through wispy air as Creusa faded gently away.

Dawn crept solemnly over Mt. Ida. Aeneas accepting defeat gathered with a few survivors and headed for the mountains, *homeless*. Cutting down trees, these weeping pilgrims, in the shadow of their burning city, built a small fleet. Then, in the first days of summer, Aeneas and his aged father, Anchises, along with the fragile remnants of a lost life, shoved off into the Aegean. Tears were the common language of those aboard as they lifted glazed eyes one last time toward the plain where mighty Troy once stood, a beacon now broken and desolate.

Gathered about a small altar aboard ship, they kneeled before the charred home-gods salvaged from the burning hearth and prayed for fair winds and an eternal home.

***

Calamities, fickle and hard-hearted, befall us all. One night, we sleep peacefully beneath starry skies only to awaken *homeless* beneath Troy's smoky horrors. Such was the case with King

David, whose palace in the Judean hills reigned supreme until Absalom came calling.

***

"While all the country was weeping with a loud voice, all the people passed over. The king also passed over the Brook Kidron, and the people passed over toward the way of the wilderness" (2 Sam. 15:23).

***

Treasure your home, but keep the pilgrim boots close.

***

"Seven out of 10 Americans are one paycheck from being homeless."
Pras Michel

Day 154

Homesick (57 BC)
Catullus, *Poems*, 31

***

In the classics, there is a poignant story of a *homesick* young poet whose job sent him to a faraway land for a year. Catullus owed one year of military duty to the Roman governor Gaius Memmius, and so, in 57 BC, he left with high hopes for Bithynia. But the cold, bleak shores of this province nearly killed him. All he could think about was Sirmio, his fairytale estate in Italy with its lake views. Knowing his beloved brother had just died only intensified this longing for home with its sweet memories.

At last, the final detested day in Bithynia ended. He packed his bags, raced to the wharf, and sailed off to Sirmio's beloved embrace:

"Just the thought of you, beloved Sirmio, changes everything. All of my worries are gone now that I am finally home. I feel safe at last here among all my familiar sights. Those disgusting Bithynian plains are merely memories now. Ah, just relaxing on my old feather bed is like heaven without worries. And to think that the twisting roads to Bithynia have all led me here back to Sirmio—sweet home. So hail, dear Sirmio. Go ahead, hold your sides and laugh with gusto for your master, Catullus, who is home again."

***

Abraham could have commiserated with young Catullus. The patriarch felt out of place, living like a *homesick* alien in a foreign land. But he kept the vision of his eternal home before him always:

***

"for he was looking for the city which has foundations, whose architect and builder is God" (Heb. 11:10).

***

Smile a little. Home is waiting for you.

***

"All exiles carry a map within them that points the way homeward."
Jacqueline Carey

Day 155

***

Honor (1184 BC)
Homer, *Iliad*, 6:150–200

***

Queen Antea fumed, pacing back and forth across the palace portico. Looking off over the lush hills of Argos where she lived in quiet luxury, she played, repeatedly, her dark disdain of Bellerophon, a recent refugee from Corinth. Prince Bellerophon had fled Corinth after slaying his brother in some petty dispute. His father, king of Corinth, sent the lad far away hoping time would diminish the mistake.

Antea, the queen, had noticed the lad when he had first disembarked at the nearby harbor and made inquiries. His golden hair caught her eye as he strolled through the seaside village. That evening she paced restlessly in her palace boudoir drenched in moonlight, wondering how she might seduce him.

One day she summoned him to her bedroom. Draped in a sheer silken gown, she fluttered before him like a crowned jewel. But Bellerophon resisted the temptation and fled through a palace backdoor, his *honor* intact.

Humiliated, Queen Antea, in utter exasperation, lied to her husband, stitching a tale of deceit. "He tried to seduce me," she claimed tearfully to the gullible king. "You have to do something about this, darling. Kill him, I say. Just kill him!"

***

Honor shines brightest in moonlight. It is there beneath a darkened horizon when no one sees, that our true nature shines.

Joseph fought the same allurements while living in Potiphar's house.

***

"Now it happened one day that he went into the house to do his work, and none of the men of the household was there inside. She caught by his garment, saying, 'Lie with me!' And he left his garment in her hand and fled, and went outside" (Gen. 39: 11–12).

***

Sometimes, true character is measured in flight.

***

"Day by day, what you choose, what you think, and what you do is who you become."
Heraclitus

Day 156

***

Hostility (AD 51)
Tacitus, *The Annals of Imperial Rome*, 12:42

***

Ominous signs abounded in the city of Rome. The people were restless, spooked, uneasy. Ill-omened birds had settled on the Capitol. Earthquakes continued to rattle the houses sending frenzied inhabitants spilling onto the roads, trampling one another as they fled the unknown. Adding to these miseries, food was scarce. Some said that only a 15-day supply of corn remained in the entire city.

Amid these uncertain times, Claudius, the emperor, ventured into the Forum on official business. Within minutes, a belligerent mob gathered surrounding him, hurling insults, shaking their fists. Claudius, alarmed, searched for an exit. There was none. Back-stepping in troubled increments, each promising avenue was immediately blocked. Claudius was cornered.

Hostility, that implacable enemy of evildoers, leered at him from the packed throngs. Angry eyes threatened vengeance as Claudius stumbled about in a rising delirium. Just when things had hit some sinister nadir, troops entered the Forum, pushing toward the emperor. Marching in step, swords at the ready, the soldiers came to conquer as if they stood on one of Gaul's distant hillocks facing a tribal revolt.

***

Another mob gathered in Nazareth about 20 years earlier. Jesus' synagogue sermon had not gone well, and a *hostile* horde

311

of villagers surrounded the teacher. Dragging Him from the building, they forced him to the edge of a cliff. With Mt. Tabor watching unapprovingly in the distance, they prepared to fling him over the cliff.

***

"And they got up and drove Him out of the city, and led Him to the brow of the hill ... to throw Him down the cliff" (Lk. 4:29).

***

Cornered by a hostile world? Jesus knows the exit.

***

"Anger is fleeting, whereas hostility is enduring."
Deborah Sandella

Day 157

Humblebrag (AD 14)

Tacitus, *The Annals of Imperial Rome*, 1:11

With the death of Augustus fresh on the minds of the senate, Tiberius rose and addressed the senators. He shuffled humbly on the Curia floor with its stylized rosettes all worked in green and red porphyry. Bragging on Augustus' exploits and the greatness of the empire, every phrase highlighted his unpretentiousness.

"Nobody will ever match the glory of Augustus," he stressed, his eyes lowered. "Least of all me."

The noble audience stared silently, sniffing the political air perceptively as Tiberius continued. "I was asked once by the emperor to share his duties, and I learned how impossible it was. I could never do it. Never!" Then pausing for effect, he added, "I am convinced, senators, that it would be better to divide the vast responsibilities among a plethora of talented leaders."

No one listening took him seriously. It was all seen for what it was—*humblebrag*.

This technique of inner concealment and distortion was a skill Tiberius had mastered along the way, and now he humblebragged himself before his detractors who dared not counter or resist this political actor on Rome's most prestigious stage.

John the Baptist lived in the shadow of Tiberius. Many people thought John was the Messiah. After all, he commanded great crowds and had a dynamic personality. But John didn't *humblebrag*. His dreams were all cradled in the heart of Jesus. No fakery or false pretensions existed on John's stage.

***

"So this joy of mine has been made full. He must increase, but I must decrease" (Jn. 3:29–30).

***

Ditch the humblebrag. Live with sincerity beneath the shadow of God.

***

"False humility is thinly veiled ego disguised as self-confidence." *Dov Davidoff*

Day 158

Humiliation (AD 55)
Tacitus, *The Annals of Imperial Rome*, 13:15

***

As the Saturnalia, that Roman Mardi Gras, unfolded in all its joyful naughtiness, Nero worried. His mother's recent outbursts against him left him annoyed and uneasy. Still, the party beckoned. This was the December day when all of Rome celebrated without fear. Slaves were served by their masters, and gambling took center stage with raucous laughter, excessive drinking, and goodwill.

The young men at the party quieted the crowd and prepared to roll the dice. When the cubes quieted on the tabletop, they pointed to Nero. As king of the night, anything he said would be obeyed. Nero smiled, and then an insidious idea formed. He would call his throne-rival Britannicus forward, celebrating his fourteenth birthday and entering manhood. Pointing to Britannicus, he commanded in jest: "Come, my friend, and sing a song." Nero hoped for an utter *humiliation*.

Britannicus shuddered. Unused to parties or drunkenness, the young man shuffled into the limelight. With the room silent, but for a few giggles, he began to sing shyly a poem that bared his emotions, a song of pain and longing for his deceased father and his rightful reign. The crowd grew restless and then began to sympathize with him.

Nero's scheme collapsed, and he hated Britannicus all the more.

***

Handling *humiliation* is a peculiar dance with the devil. The insidious melody can either cripple or elevate; only the dancer can decide.

David heard this tune on his flight from Jerusalem. When the miscreant Shimei hurled abuses at him and kicked dust into his face, David hummed quietly with humility:

***

"Let him alone and let him curse, for the LORD has told him" (2 Sam. 16:11).

***

Humility makes a great dance partner.

***

"Humiliation is the beginning of sanctification."
John Donne

Day 159

Humility (401 BC)
Xenophon, *Anabasis*, 1:5

***

Cyrus the Younger, delirious with ambition, struck off across the Arabian desert to defeat his brother for the Persian throne. Passing fragrant bushes that smelled like spices and living off of fleet-footed gazelles or clumsy bustards which could only fly a short distance, Cyrus pushed forward with little rest.

Once, he found himself mired in mud at a narrow ravine. Impatiently he screamed for the barbarian troops to pull the wagons from the mire. With slight effectiveness and losing time, Cyrus turned his vitriol toward some Persian nobles watching it all beneath shady parasols. "Can't any of you do something about this delay?"

Instantly, these men of culture and polish sprang into action. They tossed off their purple cloaks, expensive tunics, and embroidered trousers and, with picturesque *humility*, raced down the steep hill. With no thought for their golden neck chains or emerald bracelets, they leaped into the mud, silk trousers billowing in the hot air, and within minutes dragged the wagons onto dry ground.

***

There is an elegant power in this exhibition of *humility*. A difficult task became easier when egos disappeared. Surely the machinery of this modern world would spin and hum more

317

efficiently if we would but nod to the Persians and follow their lead.

Paul would have been the first to shed his robe and help. He wrote:

***

"For through the grace given to me I say to every man among you not to think more highly of himself than he ought to think; but to think so as to have sound judgment, as God has allotted to each a measure of faith" (Rom. 12:3).

***

The wagons are stuck again. Off with the Armani jackets.

***

"A great man is always willing to be little."
Ralph Waldo Emerson

Day 160

***

Hunger (AD 10)
Ovid, *Metamorphoses*, 8:817–865

***

The monarch, Erysichthon, scorned the gods, refusing to bring incense to their altars. Ever hateful, he decided to attack an ancient tree in a sacred grove devoted to Ceres, god of agriculture. Centuries old, it hovered above bountiful forests surrounded by cheerful, dancing dryads. It took a dozen little creatures, with arms linked to circle the wondrous giant. Still, Erysichthon picked up an ax and slaughtered the icon sending it crashing to the ground.

The mourning dryad sisters, heartbroken, prayed for revenge. A fleet-footed messenger raced to the Scythian mountains searching for *Hunger* and found her alone in the stony fields digging the scanty grass. Pale and hollow-eyed, she rose, her skin wrapped tightly about her stick-figure spine. Her knees seemed like swollen balloons, and her ankles like lumpy tubers. Upon hearing the plight of the dryads, she wept. Abandoning her food quest, she raced to Erysichthon's palace and, finding him sleeping peacefully, breathed hunger into his nostrils.

When the king awoke, ravenous cravings clawed at his soul. He demanded food, but nothing satisfied him. His appetite, an unquenchable fire, consumed every thought. Having sold his kingdom for the final scraps of food, he turned to his flesh, gnawing on arms and legs, salivating over an ever-shrinking self.

***

Jesus once quieted a hungry crowd and motioned them to sit on a mountain slope. Overlooking the Sea of Galilee, as a dying sun slipped gently toward its nightly rest, He felt their *hunger*. Raising His hands, he reassured them all.

***

"Blessed are those who hunger and thirst for righteousness, for they shall be satisfied" (Matt. 5:6).

***

Forget Erysichthon! Jesus has eternal bread.

***

"There are people in the world so hungry, that God cannot appear to them except in the form of bread."
Mahatma Gandhi

Day 161

Husbands (188 BC)
Plutarch, *Cato*, 20

***

Marcus Cato, a Roman statesman, orator, and writer of the highest reputation, knew how to appreciate his wife. He loved Licinia above all things and worked hard to be the best *husband* he could. He chose Licinia not for her riches because she didn't have any; instead, he was attracted by her noble lineage, treating her like a queen.

"I would never harm my wife. She is the most sacred thing in the world to me. Being a good husband is more praiseworthy than being a famous politician or a great senator. I admire Socrates because he was always gentle and considerate with his wife, who was, by the way, quite challenging to live with along with his children, who were not the brightest. Still, he loved them and treated them with care and tenderness.

"Loving and helping my wife is one of my highest priorities. I think nothing of leaving Rome and my duties to sprint home to my farm in the Sabine hills near Rome to help her bathe and swaddle our baby. Loving Licinia is my life's highest priority. Without her, I would be nothing."

***

I think Paul would have admired Cato's priorities. Both men focused on life's duties and placed the highest esteem on family loyalty. Paul knew the value of happy family life and urged *husbands* to love their wives. His words to the Ephesian disciples say it best:

***

"Husbands, love your wives, just as Christ also loved the church and gave Himself up for her" (Eph. 5:25).

***

Heed the whispers of Cato and Paul: "Love your wife!"

***

"No matter how much I say I love you, I always love you more than that."
Anonymous

Day 162

***

Hymns (467 BC)
Aeschylus *Seven Against Thebes*, 830–875

***

The Theban city, lying in smoldering ruins, whimpered in liberation. The seven gates had held, but at what price? Death mingled with lamentations as the living gathered around the dead whose eyes, locked on invisible horizons, smiled no more.

As countless dripping corpses were dragged to holy biers for cremation, everyone suddenly stopped their ghoulish labors. The royal brothers, Eteocles and Polynices, blood-smeared and breathless, were carried to the palace floor and laid side by side. With heads hung low, the Theban citizens began a cadence of grief, a somber beating of hands upon heads that sifted in a muffled cadence through the palace doors and beyond.

Dueling with one another at the seventh gate, these kingly brothers, their feverish hatred sweating beneath a hot sun, were now silenced forever. Their hatred fed the death hymn that now spread its dark melody up and down silent city streets.

Hastening to the palace, sisters Antigone and Ismene kneeled beside their beloved. Moaning Fury's *hymn*, each sister sang Hades' hateful paean. Wearing torn garments waist-bound with death's sashes, their voices were a discordant cacophony of hopelessness. With muffled tears, they bade their brothers farewell as the black-sailed ship moved forlornly across the Acheron, never to return.

***

I find myself standing at these palace doors, distant but within range of the wails. The sadness is overwhelming. I can't help but think of another genre of *hymns* that celebrate life, not death. If only the brothers had loved the Lord, the tune would have differed:

***

"speaking to one another in psalms and hymns and spiritual songs, singing and making melody with your heart to the Lord" (Eph. 5:19).

***

Hades' paean or Heaven's song: which hymn will you sing today?

***

"My poems are hymns of praise to the glory of life."
Edith Sitwell

Day 163

***

Illumination (525 BC)
Herodotus, *The Persian Wars*, 2:62

***

The quaint Egyptian village of Sais, nestled in the Western Nile Delta, was the seat of power for the 26th Dynasty of Egypt. Once a year, the citizens gathered for the Feast of Lamps, worshipping Osiris, the god of death and life. On the night of the sacrifice, people carried small saucers full of salt and oil and placed floating wicks in them that burned all night. The soft lights mingled with the Nile air summoning the god's favors.

Those who couldn't make the journey to Sais still lit their lamps all across Egypt, carefully watching the dancing wicks, making sure they burned throughout the night.

On this sacred night, once a year, the country flickered with hope's *illumination* beneath starry skies as small wicks carried the prayers of millions heavenward. Looking down from above, green-faced Osiris smiled benevolently upon his followers, counting the flickering lights as signs of genuine devotion.

***

Follow the laughing candles to the inner courts of Jerusalem's temple. It is the Festival of Tabernacles, known for the ceremony of light. Here, four massive candelabras in the Court of the Women, each 73 feet tall, spun their grand *illumination* upon the eloquent temple. At the Savior's feet lay a fallen woman cast there by seething Pharisees. Jesus, however, merely scribbled

325

on the court floor. When the accusers left in shame, he stood beneath the candelabras and said,

***

"I am the Light of the world; he who follows Me will not walk in the darkness but will have the Light of Life" (Jn. 8:12).

***

Osiris' lights have long been quenched, but the light of the Savior shines on for all eternity.

***

Choose your light carefully.

***

"Illumination by the Spirit is the endless end of every virtue."
Symeon the New Theologian

Day 164

Imitation (401 BC)
Xenophon, *Anabasis*, 3:2

***

Clearchus was the best general in the Greek army. Unfortunately, the Persian king tricked him and other top generals into attending a night peace conference and slaughtered them all. Xenophon, one of the younger soldiers, called the troops together in the middle of the night and set out a master survival plan, brilliant in its simplicity and inspiring in its core truth.

"Men," he said as the soldiers gathered in tightly. "The Persians assumed that if they massacred our leading generals, as they did like cowards, we would all lose heart and surrender. I say we are not defeated, and here is what we must do:

"First, we should burn all the wagons so we can travel lightly. Secondly, we should torch our tents since they are cumbersome to carry. Finally, let's abandon all our unneeded possessions."

Then, he paused and looked into their frightened faces. "They murdered our top general, Clearchus. So, now, let us all be Clearchus! When the enemy mocks us tomorrow, let them see ten thousand *imitations* of Clearchus. We will be him, and we will be victorious."

***

Thomas a Kempis, a Christian theologian of the fifteenth century, wrote one of the most popular devotional books of all time. He said of Christ that we should "imitate the life and habits of the Savior." Who are you copying in your life? Peter, like Xenophon, urges us all to *imitate* someone great.

***

"For you have been called for this purpose, since Christ also suffered for you, leaving you an example for you to follow in His steps" (1 Pet. 2:21).

***

Imitate Christ. Change the world.

***

"Kings in this world should imitate God, their mercy should be above their works."
William Penn

Day 165

***

Immobilization (AD 33)

Tacitus, *The Annals of Imperial Rome*, 6:18

***

An ugly paralysis reigned in Rome during Tiberius' final cruel years. Terror haunted anyone who had supported or spoken to Sejanus, Tiberius' most trusted assistant. Age, sex, eminence, or obscurity mattered little to the police who hunted the thoroughfares and back alleys of the city for supposed traitors against the emperor.

Frenzied with bloodshed, Tiberius' shadow hovered over many rotting corpses filling Rome's gutters, those unfortunates who had once whispered dark, silent conspiracies against Tiberius. Now they lay strewn about in heaps, stinking under a noonday sun.

Relatives or friends were forbidden to mourn their loved ones or even stand in silent grief near them. Occasionally, the imperial guards would drag bloated bodies to the Tiber, where they floated away or grounded themselves on some obscure shoreline. Common sympathy was now *immobilized*, shackled with fear. The rising tide of brutality slit compassion's throat, leaving only ghosts walking Rome's streets.

***

We see another pitiable form of paralysis when we gaze at the dying body of Jesus. His forearms are nailed to the shoulder crossbeam and his ankles to the vertical post. He can only move in tiny, exhausting increments, movements to gather

329

gasps of air. And yet, in this torturous *immobilization*, he exudes sympathy and love to the dying prisoner beside Him.

***

"And he was saying, 'Jesus, remember me when you come in your kingdom!' and He said to him, 'Truly I say to you, today you shall be with Me in Paradise'" (Lk. 23:42–43).

***

Today, defeat spiritual paralysis as you mingle with the world.

***

"Our fingerprints don't fade from the lives we touch."
Judy Blume

Day 166

Immortality (1177 BC)
Virgil, *Aeneid*, 9:65–120

***

Turnus, ruthless king of the Rutuli, paced restlessly beneath the Roman battlements. His soldiers gripped their spears and waited for a command to charge, but no order came. The walls were sealed, and the fortifications impregnable. But then wily Turnus had an idea. Glancing at the ships banked on the Tiber's shore, he called for every soldier to find a firebrand. "We'll burn their fleet!" he shouted. Soon a frenzy of resinous torches gave forth a murky glare as hordes of ravaging warriors raced to the ships.

Aeneas' forces watched in sorrowful disbelief from their watchtowers as the ground crawled with innumerable fireflies, soldiers jabbing their flambeau's skyward as they sped toward the ships.

But in the midst of this frenzy, a strange light rolled over the distant horizon. Closer and closer, it swirled a cloud of brilliant hue. Then the loud crashing of Cybele's cymbals stopped the mutiny in its tracks. The Rutuli stared heavenward, their mouths agape. "No one will harm these ships!" said a dreaded heavenly voice.

Immediately, the barques snapped their moorings. Then they slipped into the depths of the Tiber, bearing the shape of God-blessed maidens. The once mortal ships now laughed in new, vibrant *immortality*, changed forever.

***

Our mortality mocks us daily as it slowly drags us toward inevitable ends. Our joints ache, our minds tilt, and our vision dims. Yet, like aging Trojan ships on Tiber's banks, we know some *immortal* destiny awaits us. Paul gives us this insight:

***

" in a moment in the twinkling of an eye, at the last trumpet; for the trumpet will sound and the dead will be raised imperishable, and we will be changed" (1 Cor. 15:52).

***

Take hope. The twinkling is near.

***

"Life is only precious because it ends, kid."
Rick Riordan

Day 167

Impatience (467 BC)
Aeschylus, *Seven Against Thebes*, 375–400

***

Tydeus, the Aetolian hero, stood ankle-deep in the Ismenus River, staring at the Proetid Gate. Charged with flattening this first of seven gates guarding the terrified residents of the Theban town, he trembled waiting for the trumpet. He just needed the signal from Amphiaraus, the priest, but the signs were not good. Sacrificing animals repeatedly on the river shore, the gods turned away, leaving Tydeus fuming.

Up and down the bank, he strode in full battle attire, screaming insults at the priest. Like a hissing snake at noon, he demanded clearance. But still, the priest delayed. The noonday sun lingered overhead, listening to Tydeus damning the seer's cowardice. But the priest held firm. The signs warned of failure.

Tydeus shook his helmet violently in protest, its three crests casting impudent shadows across the gurgling stream. Raucous bells tethered on the belly of his bronze shield bonged and clanged their battle demands. Still, the priest held firm.

Tydeus' shield, boasting a blazing firmament with a full moon intricately etched upon its surface, heightened his cocky *impatience*. Like a horse panting to bolt for freedom, the warrior stood at the river's edge, screaming at the gate.

***

Significant accomplishments often creep along a slow path. They have hidden agendas with their own tempo. Mastering *impatience* is critical to success, something Martha never did.

***

"But Martha was distracted with all her preparations; and she came up to Him and said, 'Lord, do You not care that my sister has left me to do all the serving alone? Then tell her to help me'" (Lk. 10:40).

***

Stop screaming at the gate. Impatience has its cost.

***

"Patience is the art of concealing your impatience."
Guy Kawasaki

Day 168

Impossible (423 BC)
Aristophanes, *Peace*, 1–200

Trygaeus paced impatiently near the garden as two slaves toiled in the latrine. "This is the worst job I've had yet," said one slave as he formed another dung paddy.

"Stop complaining and do your job," muttered his accomplice in the pit. "The master is in a hurry. I've got to fatten this beetle up fast." As he spoke, he crumbled another dung patty, sprinkling it at the beetle's feet.

Trygaeus leaned over the slave's shoulder to inspect his progress. "Okay. That's good. Step aside now and observe the *impossible*." Having so uttered, the master leaped upon the little beast and secured his legs beneath its wings. Kicking both spurs gently, the beetle stirred and fluttered its pinions, hovering in the air a few feet before settling back to earth.

The slaves screamed in disbelief. "What are you doing?" They turned and ran for the house, summoning help. Trygaeus' little daughters came running. "Father, where are you going? Are you leaving us alone to starve?"

"I won't be gone long, my sweets. I have to fly to heaven and meet with God. Somebody has to stop these incessant Greek wars. Maybe God will end them and order Peace out of her jail cell."

With a blown kiss, he kicked the beetle and fluttered, singing, toward heaven's throne.

***

Trygaeus scoffed at the *impossible* and flew to heaven's gate. Why does "impossible" form impassable roadblocks for us? God expects every believer to move mountains. He reminded Mary once of this truth:

***

"and she who was called barren is now in her sixth month. For nothing will be impossible with God" (Lk. 1:37).

***

Still hesitating? Take wings and challenge the impossible.

***

"Nothing is impossible, the word itself says 'I'm possible'!"
Audrey Hepburn

Day 169

***

Imposters (AD 120)
Juvenal, *Satires*, 1

***

I put a mask on once and strolled down Bourbon Street during Mardi Gras. It was exhilarating! Nobody knew me. As a rule, though, it's best not to be masked in life. *Imposter* is not a career choice with promise.

Juvenal watched clients paying homage to their patron in first-century Rome. The tradition was to gather at the big boss's house every morning and flatter him. But sometimes, underserving people came in disguise, hoping for a free handout. Here's how Juvenal described it:

"I stood off in the shadows this morning and watched the disgusting ritual. First, the old patron set one small basket of goodies at the doorway. Then the circus began as hungry clients crammed forward with their best rags on, ready for inspection. But there's a new precaution now. The boss knows unapproved cheaters are trying to feed at the trough. So now the owner is inspecting for imposters. He stares hard at every face. One by one, he calls the folks forward, and as they rummage through the baskets' treasures, he squints at their eyes, looking for masks.

***

Even in the early church, the desperate widows stood in line, hoping for a handout. But there were rules: you had to be at least sixty with a clean record. Any *imposters* were sent packing (1 Tim. 5:9–16).

Jesus also inspected faces. He could tell when a lamb was a wolf. It's all in the eyes. Ravenous, corrupt eyes don't lie. Jesus put it this way:

***

"Beware of the false prophets, who come to you in sheep's clothing, but inwardly are ravenous wolves" (Matt. 7:15).

***

Toss that Mardi Gras mask. It's time to come clean.

***

"Every Christian is either a missionary or an imposter."
Charles Spurgeon

Day 170

Incest (AD 59)
Tacitus, *Annals of Imperial Rome*, 13:57

***

The midday sun cast a suffocating shadow over Nero's palace. Labor stumbled beneath the oppressive heat, and efficiency was a fairy tale. Nero escaped into the coolest corner of the royal rooms and there, upon a coiffured chaise lounge, drank liberally from various chilled wine flasks. The liquor heated passions that offered pleasant dalliances, respites from the sun's scorched grip.

Agrippina, always plotting, found this an ideal time to secure influence over her wayward son. According to Cluvius Rufus and Fabius Rusticus, historians of the day, she would wait seductively outside his room until the wine flushed his soul with blurry freedom.

Selecting her most delicate rose-scented negligee purchased from silk road merchants, she draped it eloquently over her body, the garment unbound and flowing as freely as the Nile. Then with the grace of a night shadow, she slithered into his bedroom with coy glances and fluttering eyes. Her kisses were gentle at first, suggesting forbidden love that aroused Nero's inner flame. Then caresses followed that defied description leading to dark *incestual* intimacies that Nero loved.

***

Glance eastward from Nero's palace veranda, and you will hear the echoes of a similar sin in some Corinthian backroom 600 miles away. The sin grows darker when we learn that the *incest* featured two members of the Corinthian congregation. Paul was incensed when he heard about it.

***

"It is actually reported that there is immorality among you and immorality of such a kind as does not exist even among the Gentiles, that someone has his father's wife" (1 Cor. 5:1).

***

Forbidden love tastes of poison.

***

"You have witchcraft in your lips."
Shakespeare, Henry V

Day 171

Indifference (AD 48)

Tacitus, *The Annals of Imperial Rome*, 11:36

***

Messalina, Rome's naughty empress, cast her sensuous web over Silius, Rome's most handsome young nobleman. She blushed at the pleasurable prospects. Though married to Claudius, the emperor, she winked at that insignificant detail and moved into Silius' home with her prize furnishings.

Soon, a new and more daring dream danced in her soul. Why not marry Silius and tell the world? This idea, outrageous and colored with lunacy, became her obsession. Soon, wedding invitations summoned dignitaries from Rome's elite families to a formal banquet where the couple exchanged wedding promises. Lifting her veil, Silius embraced and kissed the forbidden fruit. Later that evening, bidding the patrons adieu, the couple eloped to the mansion's bedroom.

Claudius panicked. "Am I still emperor?" he kept asking. "Is Silius really married to my wife?" Once the emperor's mental fog cleared, he stormed to the couple's home. Personal heirlooms littered the room. With anger rising, Claudius returned home while his attendants rushed to find the adulteress. Lacking the courage to kill herself, an officer thrust his sword into the delirious empress.

As Claudius dined that evening, a servant handed him a note declaring Messalina's death. Pausing momentarily before a silent and trembling room, he scanned the death notice, searching for meaning. Then, with *indifference*, he clapped his hands, calling for more wine.

***

It's the *indifference* that stuns me.

I see the same blank look in Pilate's eyes. An attendant handed him a note urging him to acquit Jesus. Tossing the missive aside before a bleeding Savior, he washed his hands with cold apathy and condemned Jesus to death.

***

"he washed his hands in front of the crowd..." (Matt. 27:24).

***

Cast aside your manacles of indifference.

***

"The opposite of love is not hate, it's indifference."
Elie Weisel

Day 172

Indignation (59 BC)
Suetonius, *Lives of the Caesars*, 1:20

***

Caesar's temper flared as the crowd pressed the steps of the Temple of Castor and Pollux in the Roman Forum. He presented a bill to award land to Pompey's veteran soldiers for battles fought and won. Bibulus, the presiding magistrate, grumbled, ordering the throng to disperse. "I'll have nothing to do with it," he groused. Rising with *indignation*, he denounced the pending legislation. "The gods tell me to repudiate this political impudence."

Caesar, the highest-ranking religious authority, quickly approached the magistrate. As Bibulus protested, grizzled soldiers who favored the bill grew restless. Caesar, sensing victory, urged the agitated protesters to rise against Bibulus. Suddenly in a chaotic rush to the temple steps, the veterans dragged the impudent priest by his purple-bordered toga off the throne.

Hurling him to the ground, they broke the temple's sacred rods, symbols of religious authority and dumped feces upon Bibulus in a final humiliating act. Shamed beyond words, the magistrate urged someone to kill him as some in his entourage helped him up, leading the shamed consul to a quiet room in a nearby temple.

Caesar, rising with a newfound authority, smirked, having cleansed the temple of its ills.

***

Politics and personal ambition motivated Caesar to cleanse the temple. When I reflect on his shocking actions, I think of Jesus, who rose with holy *indignation* in the Jewish temple. He acted to further the agenda of His heavenly Father.

***

"And Jesus entered the temple and drove out all those who were buying and selling in the temple, and overturned the tables of the money changers and the seats of those who were selling doves" (Matt. 21:12).

***

Reserve your indignation for the highest causes.

***

"There is no more sovereign eloquence than the truth in indignation."
Victor Hugo

Day 173

***

Indulgences (401 BC)
Xenophon, *Anabasis*, 4:8

***

The Greek army stood in silence before the altar, praying for success. Their weapons at the ready, the men awaited their fate as they prepared to rush the summit of the last mountain before reaching the Black Sea. When the last prayer echoed off the mountain cliffs, the men raised their mighty war paean, singing victory's song as they always did before a battle. And then, at the signal, they rushed the Colchians armed with wicker shields and lances.

The Colchian's bravado soon evaporated, however, surrendering the mountaintop. The Greek soldiers celebrated by visiting the numerous small villages nearby and setting up temporary quarters.

Looking about for something to do, the Greeks noticed hundreds of bees here and there and soon tracked down the honey. The taste was heavenly, and the soldiers couldn't resist. After gorging themselves on this mountain delicacy, they all settled down for a nap.

Within minutes of eating the honey, the men began to feel dizzy and drunk. They stumbled about falling in heaps here and there, unable to move. The commanders, alarmed, watched their army surrender in defeat to a mass of bees and the honey's *indulgences*. The bees were the only army that ever defeated the Greek army.

***

I find it amazing that these undefeated Greek warriors, called the Ten Thousand, surrendered to honey bees. It was simply a matter of over-*indulgence*. We all do it to some extent, whether it's ice cream, chocolate, wine, or leisure.

Paul told the Ephesian saints that they, too, once over-indulged.

***

"Among them we too all formerly lived in the lusts of our flesh, indulging the desires of the flesh and of the mind..." (Eph. 2:3).

***

Beware your honey pot!

***

"There are limits to self-indulgence, none to restraint."
Mahatma Gandhi

Day 174

Inhibitions (401 BC)
Xenophon, *Anabasis*, 5:5

***

When the soldiers reached the Mossynoecian's country on the Black Sea shores, they stopped in disbelief and stared. The people were lily-white and plump from eating boiled nuts. They tattooed their backs in a rainbow of colors and had intricate floral patterns etched onto their breasts.

They were the most unique people the Greeks had stumbled upon on their long journey home. These folks had no *inhibitions*. They begged the Greek men to have sex with them in public since this was their custom. The Greeks were stunned since, in Greek culture, this was a very private matter.

Even when they were alone, these people would talk and laugh as if a crowd of friends was with them. They would dance wherever they might be as if they were putting on a show — with no one there. Because of these observations, the Greeks considered them the most uncivilized of the tribes discovered on their trip.

***

When was the last time you tossed your *inhibitions* out the window? Inhibitions have their place, but free expression brings a unique joy. David experienced this as he led the ark of God into the city of David.

***

"And David was dancing before the LORD with all his might, and David was wearing a linen ephod... Then it happened as the ark of the LORD came into the city of David that Michal the daughter of Saul looked out of the window and saw King David leaping and dancing before the LORD; and she despised him in her heart" (2 Sam. 6:14/16).

***

Tear off your mask today and dance!

***

"I like to give my inhibitions a bath now and then."
Oliver Reed

Day 175

Innocence (1177 BC)
Virgil, *Aeneid*, 7:480–500

***

It was Tyrrheus, warden of the royal herds, who first noticed the faun. Suckling in the brush beside a gurgling stream, Tyrrheus called his daughter, Silvia, to see this tender scene. "Oh, Father, please can I have it? I promise to take care of it and..."

He cut her off. "The faun is wild, my darling. We must leave it with its mother." But Silvia persisted, pleading with passionate tears. Finally, with a sigh, the warden relented, and his daughter entered motherhood's joyous realm.

Daily, Silvia groomed the faun, bathing it in the valley stream beneath Mt. Aurunci's loving gaze. As time passed, the pet sported high-branched antlers and walked regally beside his soulmate. She often wreathed its antlers with soft-leaved garlands whispering poetic couplets as they strolled happily along the pilgrim's road toward the castle.

Respecting its natural instincts, she released it each evening to wander the woods, where it delighted in nature's abundance. But the pet always wended its way home when night fell, following moonlit paths to Silvia's familiar, well-known door. But on this fateful night, *innocence* died when a hunter's whirring arrow streaked across the pilgrim's path, piercing a dream.

***

Innocence is fragile. Like dried fall leaves, it crumbles easily and scatters, wind-blown into God's hands. Such a day came in another garden long ago. Bitten by the serpent's arrow, it withered on history's saddest day.

***

"He said, 'I heard the sound of You in the garden, and I was afraid because I was naked; so I hid myself?' And He said, 'Who told you that you were naked?'" (Gen. 3:10–11).

***

Guard the faun and your innocence.

***

"Come with me where dreams are born and time is never planned."
Peter Pan

Day 176

***

Inspiration (1177 BC)
Virgil, *Aeneid*, 6:1–100

***

Aeneas' roving adventurers slid their vessels upon Italy's shores. When their sterns bit sand, the men tumbled out, excited to feel the land that would be theirs through prophecy. As others scattered among the forest's edge, gathering flint and wood, Aeneas made straight for Sibyl's cave, hollowed out on a vast flank of Cumae's hill.

Passing through Daedalus' temple with its hero-decorated entrance, he gasped at the sight beyond — a hundred shut doors carved into the cave's jaws. It was from these hundred mouths that Sibyl's cryptic replies would occasionally bellow with divine *inspiration*.

Suddenly, his heart skipped as he saw the prophetess standing beneath the cave's dome. "The time has come to ask your destiny, for God is with me," she said, thundering from a distance. Having spoken, her complexion morphed into mystical hues, and her hair whipped wildly. With heaving breasts, she prepared for an utterance as Apollo stirred her soul. The Sibyl, however, not yet utterly submissive, fought Apollo, striving with the god until finally, she relented, broken and quivering.

Then as she lay limp and submissive, a hundred doors flung open, releasing Sibyl's mystical revelations. Wrapping truths in enigma, she foretold future glory for Aeneas and his fellow outcasts. When finally the storm calmed, and Apollo had departed, she fell silent, twitching upon the cave floor.

***

When did heaven's shrill voice last breathe upon you? "Find guidance in God's *inspired* words," said Paul to the youngster, Timothy. "They are His breath infused in Holy Scripture. They will lead you through life's dark and threatening corridors."

***

"All Scripture is God-breathed and profitable for teaching..." (2 Tim. 3:16).

***

The doors are open now! Listen and live.

***

"No one was ever great without some portion of divine inspiration."
Cicero

Day 177

***

Instigator (AD 40)
Phaedrus, *Fables*, 1

***

The wolf, desperately thirsty, stood lapping water at a quaint brook. Life beneath a broiling sun had come to a sluggish halt, the thick air hard to breathe. Glancing downstream, he perked up when he saw a wooly lamb drinking, its nose buried in the stream.

"Hey, you! Why are you muddying the water?" He shook his head threateningly and narrowed his eyes.

The lamb, trembling, made a quick reply, hoping to deescalate the mood. "Please, Mr. Wolf, I'm far downstream, so I could not be guilty of such a grievous crime." She smiled when she said it, hoping to soothe the wolf's temper.

The wolf saw his error at once but made no concessions, his stomach growling. After a few more sips of water, he hurled another charge. "I think I recognize you. Yes, I'm sure you cursed me in the glade not far from here six months ago."

Quivering at the blunt attack, she laughed nervously and fluttered her eyes. "That would not be possible, sir, since I wasn't born six months ago."

Weary of this civilized tone, he shouted, "well, if it wasn't you, it must have been your father." Then he pounced upon the lamb and ended the discussion forever, proving that *instigators* will always bring false charges.

***

Are you downstream, running from a wolf? Instigators abound, and often they hang out at brooks or office clusters or classrooms. They will face justice soon. Meanwhile, cling to faith as Jesus did:

***

"Now the chief priests and the whole Council kept trying to obtain testimony against Jesus to put Him to death, and they were not finding any" (Mk. 14:55).

***

Take the Shepherd's hand. Let Him handle the wolves.

***

"There's an instigator in every family."
Imgur

Day 178

Integrity (AD 110)
Juvenal, *Satires*, 13:60–70

***

It was just an old leather wallet filled with rusty coins, but it meant the world to the owner. It had sentimental value as well, along with a few odd artifacts from his past. With some trepidation, he handed it to a trusted associate for safekeeping. "Guard it with your life," he told him. "I'll get it back from you when I return." And with those words, the wallet exchanged hands.

Some days passed, and the friend returned to claim his valuables. The keeper of this treasure smiled assuredly and slipped a hand into his cloak's hidden folds, his fingers dancing in the cloth. "Here it is," he beamed.

When told of this affair, Juvenal, our writer, seemed stunned that such *integrity* still existed in Rome's mangled ethics. "Amazing!" he exclaimed to the wallet's owner. "An honest man lives among us. Let's garland and slaughter a lamb!"

As Juvenal shuffled home later, he talked to himself. "Man, this is like seeing a three-legged boy or finding fish swimming in your garden! It's like a pregnant mule, or stones falling in a rainstorm, or a milk river spilling into the sea...."

***

Is *integrity* so elusive? Take a moment and glance at a fig tree near the Bethsaida shore. Jesus, for some time, had been watching

Nathaniel sitting there beneath its branches. His eyes lingered because He admired Nathaniel, a man who lived without deceit.

***

"Jesus saw Nathaniel coming to Him, and said of him, 'Behold, an Israelite indeed, in whom there is no deceit!'" (Jn. 1:47).

***

Do you *still* have the wallet?

***

"In looking for people to hire, look for three qualities: Integrity, intelligence and energy. And if they don't have the first, the other two will kill you."
Warren Buffett

Day 179

Intermediary (AD 51)

Tacitus, *The Annals of Imperial Rome*, 12:42

***

Agrippina fumed. She threw the letter in the air, exasperated. "How dare they accuse Lucius of such a thing. There is not a treasonous bone in his body! The old man is a gem, three times a consul, and I will not stand for it!" she said, muttering.

Pacing restlessly on the veranda overlooking Rome, she gathered her things and marched, an incensed *intermediary*, to Claudius' office, her husband, Rome's emperor. Brushing past the office attendants, she shook the summons in his face. "Surely, darling, you don't take this seriously, do you? This is Lucius Vitellius, one of my closest friends! He's no traitor."

Claudius ordered the room cleared. Glancing at the document, he sighed. Junius Lupus, a junior senator, had made the accusation and could not easily be ignored. "I know how you feel about him, honey, but these accusations come from the senate and must be considered." He rose to comfort her, but she backed away.

"I won't stand for it. I won't!" she warned. A tear slipped down her flushed cheek. He winced. She had him. An hour later, after pleading like a star prosecutor, she flipped the court upside down, bringing virulent charges against the young senator who had dared to confront Agrippina.

***

Such grit. What an *intermediary*! If only we could have such a friend on our side.

But wait, for I hear a distant voice interrupting my reverie with assurances that Christ is our advocate standing

***

"in heaven itself, now to appear in the presence of God for us" (Heb. 9:24).

***

Forget Agrippina. Your advocate is the Savior.

***

"Our lives begin to end the day we become silent about the things that matter."
Martin Luther King

Day 180

***

Intractable (1184 BC)
Homer, *Iliad*, 9:180–430

***

Ajax and Odysseus, ambassadors from the king, strolled briskly along the roaring Trojan seashore. The fatherly Phoenix, who had raised and tutored Achilles, tottered along beside them. When they arrived at Achilles' tent, they paused outside, listening as Achilles strummed whimsical melodies on his silver-barred lyre, booty from a recent faraway battle.

Entering the tent, the mighty warrior sprang up and warmly greeted his friends, ushering them to favored seats covered with purple rugs. Placing a large bowl of pungent wine before the guests, Achilles ordered a feast with lamb's loins spit-roasted on a burning fire.

With the formalities settled, old Phoenix stood and reminded his host of spending years teaching him the rudiments of war and life. He then passed on Agamemnon's urgent pleas for the *intractable* Achilles to rejoin the battle. "The king is sorry for taking your woman. He offers riches beyond imagination if you return to the army and fight."

Achilles listened, his face steeled against the overture. Phoenix, tottering on old legs, continued. "He pledges you seven tripods in mint condition, ten talents of gold, twelve prize-winning horses, and seven beautiful women from the island of Lesbos."

When the old man sat down, Achilles grimaced. "He treated me like a tramp before my men. I will never fight for him again!"

***

We've all worn Achille's mask, refusing to listen or yield. But it only leads to isolation and woe. This reminds me of the followers of Baal, who screamed futilely at their *intractable* god, who refused to listen. But one sweet prayer from Elijah saw God's swift response.

***

"Answer me, O LORD, answer me..." (1 Kings 18:37). And He did.

***

Today, refuse Achille's mask and fling away your stubbornness.

***

"Stubbornness and stupidity are twins."
Sophocles

Day 181

Invisible (680 BC)
Plato, *Republic*, 2:359–360

***

Gyges ran for cover, huddling his sheep near the Lydian forest's edge. Lightning struck the ground, and thunder tumbled across the pastureland. Staring hopelessly across the stricken vista, he felt the ground rumble and shift. Then, following another powerful bolt to the earth, he fell back in horror as the land split, forming a crevasse near his flock. Hours passed in terror until, eventually, the winds calmed, and the sun emerged.

Gathering his sheep, he moved cautiously toward the fresh cavern yawning beneath blue skies. Curiosity displaced fear, and he crawled to the edge, peering into the chasm. Slipping down a slight incline, he slithered to the base of the cleft earth and discovered, among other marvels, a hollow brazen horse with doors. Pushing one open, he gasped at an enormous human corpse with a golden ring. Stripping it off, he scrambled back to the surface, admiring the glint of the exquisite jewel on his finger.

Later that week, when he traveled to the king's palace to report on the sheep, he noticed that he could become *invisible* by turning the ring slightly. Stunned at this sudden power, he used invisibility to seduce the queen and slay the king.

***

Would you welcome the ring? How would it change your life? Plato, who told this story, would have been amazed at how

Jesus used His *invisibility* for a noble cause, encouraging the frightened disciples.

***

"So when it was evening on that day, the first day of the week and when the doors were shut where the disciples were, for fear of the Jews, Jesus came and stood in their midst and said to them 'Peace be with you'" (Jn. 20:19).

***

Take the ring today and find a noble cause.

***

"She had the oddest sense of being herself invisible; unseen; unknown..."
Virginia Woolf

Day 182

Invocation (423 BC)
Aristophanes, *Wasps*, 800–890

***

The little ramshackle courtroom outside Athens opened for business at the old man's country cottage. Nothing fancy here, just the basics: a pot for the judge's bladder, a few snacks for hunger, and a bird to crow if the judge dozed off during the case.

The retired judge seemed amused. "What's the first case, gentlemen?"

Bdelycleon, the judge's son, stepped forward. "A blatant case of gluttony and robbery, your honor."

"Explain, sir. What do you mean?"

"Well, your honor, this dog, Labes, dashed into the kitchen, grabbed a Sicilian cheese sandwich, and gobbled it all down without permission."

"Very well. You're the prosecutor, then, I suppose," mumbled the judge settling into his chair.

"No, your honor. The mad dog who claimed the sandwich will prosecute."

Philocleon, the judge, gestured impatiently. "Very well, bring him on. You're wasting time! I don't stand for dawdling in my court. Make the summons."

"Excuse me, your honor," said his son. "I forgot the voting urns."

"Just use some saucepans in the kitchen," said the judge gruffly. "And don't forget the coals, incense, and myrtle. We've got to start with a proper *invocation*."

363

"Silence in the court!" shouted the bailiff. "Prayer time."

"Phoebus Apollo, bless the work of this court today," intoned Bdelycleon, his head bowed. "Keep the judge calm, and may he favor the accused. Amen."

***

Invocations are more than courtroom props or humorous words from a naughty playwright. Faithful prayers drop like tearful diamonds before the throne of God:

***

"But the tax collector, standing some distance away, was even unwilling to lift up his eyes to heaven, but was beating his breast, saying, 'God, be merciful to me, the sinner!'" (Lk. 18:13).

***

Steal away. Discover the power of a private invocation.

***

"Prayer is aligning ourselves with the purposes of God."
E. Stanley Jones

Day 183

***

Isolated (550 BC)
Herodotus, *The Persian Wars*, 1:174

***

Panic stirred the Cnidian villagers living on a narrow strip of coastal land jutting into the Aegean. The Persian army was coming!

Time was short, so the villagers opted for a brilliant plan. They would dig across the Turkish isthmus and make themselves an island. They rolled up their sleeves and stared at the half a mile of land they had to excavate. Then with a war-whoop, they began digging the trench. As they cut into the stubble and split rocks, they dreamed of the splendid *isolation* that would soon be theirs. They would make a paradise of the emerging island that slipped into the surrounding sea.

However, it wasn't long before the workers began to feel the ravages of daily toil. Many were blinded by flying rock chips from axes biting the boulders. They halted work and sent off for advice from the Oracle of Delphi. The Oracle's stinging rebuke cut them to the quick.

"Stop mangling the isthmus," wrote the priestess. "If Zeus had willed this land an island, he would have done it himself."

Immediately submissive to these prophetic words, they threw down their shovels and surrendered to the Persians.

***

The church began on an island called the upper room. It was the place disciples and early believers gathered after the ascension.

It was safe, quiet, *isolated*. But it didn't remain an island long. Soon, in multiple languages, they began to proclaim the love of God to the world, a task still relevant today.

***

"When they had entered the city, they went up to the upper room where they were staying" (Acts 1:13).

***

Quit digging your trench. Open up and love your neighbor.

***

"Isolation is a self-defeating dream."
Carlos Salinas de Gortari

Day 184

***

Jealousy (AD 40)
Phaedrus, *Fables*, 3

***

Four jackdaws sat preening their black feathers high in a pine tree. A lazy afternoon sun dappled a stream beneath them as they chattered and danced. One of them was at the end of a branch alone. "Why don't you scoot over a little closer to us?" asked one of the birds. "You're way out on a limb there."

Ignoring the summons for comradery, the isolated jackdaw stared *jealously* at several peacocks passing along the stream's edge. He adored their playful antics as several spun around, spreading rainbows that ruffled deliciously in the breeze.

The jackdaws, feeling snubbed, tried again to reason. "Our wings glisten in the sun. Don't you think so?"

But he never heard them as he fluttered down to steal a few peacock feathers left behind by the traveling troupe. Greedily balancing them upon his back, he tucked them tightly beneath his outstretched pinions. Abandoning his friends, he hopped hurriedly along the brook's edge until he caught up with the winged aristocrats, pushing his way into the peacocks' inner circle.

The reaction was swift. Stripping the felon of his stolen feathers, they pecked him mercilessly until the jackdaw took flight, barely escaping with his life. Scurrying back to the pine tree, he flew with a forlorn face to his old branch. But the jackdaw tribe turned their backs.

***

Jealousy usually leads us to the limb's edge, where we live in false fantasies. We drool over scattered feathers refusing to see our beauty. Paul saw too much of this in the Corinthian flock.

***

"Love is patient, love is kind and is not jealous; love does not brag and is not arrogant..." (1 Cor. 13:4).

***

Look within. Celebrate your unique qualities.

***

"It is not greed that drives the world, but envy."
Warren Buffett

Day 185

***

Jerusalem (168 BC)
Josephus, *Antiquities of the Jews*, 13:3

***

The city of Jerusalem lay smoldering. The Greek general Antiochus spared nothing, wreaking havoc upon the once regal home of the Jewish nation. Undeterred by its storied past, he sacked the sacred temple, forcing the priest to sacrifice swine upon the altars, which continued unabated for three and a half years.

Onias, the high priest, wept openly. It was more than he could bear. He summoned a midnight meeting of his followers and shared a breathtaking vision of a new beginning. "We shall flee to Egypt and there build a new *Jerusalem!*"

Those in the room gasped at the prospects sensing the impossibility of such a task. But Onias delineated his dream. "We will solicit the help of the Pharaoh and place within our new city a replica of the temple. Here, gentlemen, we shall worship again as we did in the olden times."

Grasping tightly to the fragile vision of a sparkling Jerusalem in the Egyptian desert, the men fled silently beneath a stale moon to make their dreams a reality, settling in Heliopolis, the land of the Pharaoh.

***

Under Domitian's reign, Josephus wrote this stirring tale late in the first century. But lift your eyes eastward toward a little island named Patmos. In Domitian's reign, another man

369

sat quietly dreaming of new beginnings, sharing his vision of Jerusalem. The *Jerusalem* in Egypt is now a wasteland, a skeleton of broken stones; John's Jerusalem sparkles for eternity like a bride.

***

"And I saw the holy city, new Jerusalem coming down out of heaven from God, made ready as a bride adorned for her husband" (Rev. 21:3).

***

Choose your beginnings carefully.

***

"Learn from yesterday, live for today, hope for tomorrow."
Albert Einstein

Day 186

Journeys (401 BC)
Xenophon, *Anabasis*, 3:2

***

Wise pilgrims often travel lightly through life, carrying only the simplest of possessions. They recommend unpacking before every journey. "Leave behind your grudges," these pilgrims advise, "since they only darken the road you travel. Toss your past mistakes aside as well. After all, they will bog you down. And those elusive dreams you never captured should be left under your sagging mattress at home."

Xenophon, the famous Greek general, had this same strategy. As his renegade army of 10,000 soldiers fled the Persians, he counseled the soldiers to travel with only the basics. This way, they could react quickly to the *journey's* challenges.

"I think we should burn all our wagons," he told the men, "so we can take any escape route that seems best. We should also burn our tents because we have to carry them and they slow us down. I urge you to jettison almost everything except your weapons and a cup for drinking, and a few eating utensils. After all, this stuff will go to the enemy if they conquer us, but if we defeat the enemy, all their possessions are ours."

***

What's in your baggage train that's slowing the *journey*? Keep your knapsack small. Go ahead and jettison life's trivialities. If it doesn't sparkle with God's love, then leave it behind.

223

Peter saw the rich young ruler balk at discarding all his possessions and gloated about leaving behind all his valuables. Secretly, though, he wondered what this would mean.

***

"Then Peter said to Him, 'Behold, we have left everything and followed You; what then will there be for us?'" (Matt. 19:27).

***

Discard something today. Travel lightly.

***

"A nomad I will remain for life, in love with distant and uncharted places."
Isabelle Eberhardt

Day 187

***

Judging (423 BC)
Aristophanes, *Wasps*, 1–130

***

The two slaves sat outside the Athenian house guarding the front door so the patriarch, Philocleon, wouldn't escape. Weary of the task, they grumbled back and forth.

"Well, what exactly has old Philocleon done?" asked Sosias.

"He's got a weird addiction," replied Xanthias. "Don't even try to guess."

Sosias scribbled in the dirt with a stick. "What is it? Tell me."

"It's crazy. You wouldn't believe me if I told you." Xanthias, bored, stared off at a distant stream where he had left his fishing pole. "Man, I could be down there, catching dinner."

"Is he some kind of gambler, a dice-lover?" persisted Sosias. "Did he lose the family's fortune?"

"Oh no, nothing like that," said Xanthias, refusing to yield the shielded secret.

Sosias, frustrated, tried again. "I'll bet he's a drunkard, staying up all night at the local hot spots making a fool of himself. That's it, isn't it?" He smiled as if he had opened the family vault, stirring up suppressed histories.

"Nope. That's not it either." Xanthias saw the frustration. "All right. I'll tell you." He moved close and whispered. "He's addicted to *judging* others." He paused for effect, then continued. "The family sent him off for help, but nothing worked. So they've got him locked up."

***

As the curtain went up on this play, one of the slaves spoke to the audience. "Ladies and gentlemen, this is not a vaudeville act. Litigation is rampant in Athens, and all of us are too quick to *judge* others."

Jesus, too, once quieted a crowd and brought up the same topic:

***

"Do not judge so that you will not be judged" (Matt. 7:1).

***

A little less judging; A little more loving.

***

"You cannot judge people because they sin differently than you."
Erykah Badu

Day 188

Keys (1184 BC)
Homer, *Iliad*, 14:155–190

***

Hera, queen of heaven, dangled the golden *key* in her hand, plotting. A fierce battle raged at the Greek ships she loved, and all seemed lost. The Trojans, led by mighty Hector, were threatening the fleet. "I must do something," she gasped. "Zeus will soon gloat over his Trojan victory, and the Argive fleet will be nothing but burning planks in the dread sea."

She caressed the key, her painted fingernails tracing its exquisite contours crafted by her son, Hephaestus. The key's bow, embroidered with golden tendrils, wove concentric circles pleasant to touch. The heavy shank with its god-driven cuts was uniquely made so no other god could open the door to her room.

As she toyed with the heavenly key, a plan with sinister intentions taunted her. "Yes," she thought, "I will seduce Zeus, and after our love-making, he will sleep. And then the tide of war will turn."

With a determined gait, she walked quickly through heaven's palaces until she came to her dressing room. Inserting the key, the acacia wood door swung open. Quickly closing it, she sat at the mirror and cleansed her body with ambrosia. Then she anointed her delicate skin with olive oil, scented uniquely by palace parfumiers, scheming.

***

Even a heavenly *key* can be misused. When our Lord handed one to Peter, His expectations were high. "Open great things and free your dreams," He said. That same key now lies in your hand. Take it and open a closed door today.

***

"I will give you the keys of the kingdom..." (Matt. 16:19).

***

That key dangling from heaven is yours. Use it today for good.

***

"A very little key will open a very heavy door."
Charles Dickens

Day 189

Kiss (AD 62)
Tacitus, *Annals of Imperial Rome*, 14:54

***

Seneca, Nero's famed tutor, knew of the attacks. He and Burrus had tutored the deviant emperor for 14 years, pointing the despot's restless soul toward truth and justice—all to no avail. Nero's hands dripped with blood as his inner circle buckled beneath his unpredictable rages. Burrus lay dying with a throat tumor at his home. Nero sent assassins to paint his gullet with a poisonous feather.

Seneca, ever astute, made the first move. He called for a private meeting with Nero, catching his sinister advisors off guard. Speaking softly to the pacing emperor, he reminded him in glowing words of their many intimate years. "I will gladly return to you the vast riches you have bestowed upon me, my mansion and gold. All I need now is a humble home where I can read and work in my garden."

When he finished, Nero's eyes misted. Expressing gratitude for the years of service, he clasped the philosopher's hands and *kissed* him. Tacitus, our guide to this sensitive moment, didn't buy it. "Nature and experience had fitted Nero to conceal hatred behind treacherous embraces." Time would soon reveal the treachery of this last kiss.

***

It takes a dark soul to poison a *kiss*. When highjacked by evil motives, this most sensitive gesture of a loving heart is treachery's darkest moment. We see the sacred kiss mangled in Nero's hands, but we hear its wail in the garden that gazes across the Kidron Valley.

***

"Now he who was betraying Him gave them a sign, saying, 'Whomever I kiss, He is the one; seize Him.'" (Matt. 26:48).

***

Guard your kisses with a pure heart.

***

"Faithful are the wounds of a friend; but the kisses of an enemy are deceitful."
Solomon

Day 190

***

Labor (200 BC)
Plutarch, *Marcus Cato*, 3

***

Did you wake up this morning with the blues? It happens. Nothing can cure a depressed spirit better than hard, honest *labor*. When D.H. Lawrence got the blues, he stopped thinking about the future with all its uncertainties and instead started making marmalade and scrubbing floors. It always cheered him up.

Marcus Cato found purpose and joy in laborious work on his Sabine farm in the Rieti valley near Rome. He would head to town early every morning, where in the market place he would help various folks with legal matters. Then, later in the day, he returned to his farm, where he worked side by side with the servants in his field. In the winter, he wore a sleeveless smock, enduring the cold, and during the sweltering days of summer, he stripped down to a few thin garments. When the sun slipped beyond the horizon, he would head to his house and eat with the workers sharing his bread and wine.

***

Paul must have had a little of Cato in his blood. He believed in purposeful *labor*, traveling the world with the gospel, and working as a tentmaker. He had this advice for the Ephesians that still rings true today:

***

Let him who steals steal no longer; but rather let him labor, performing with his own hands what is good, in order that he may have something to share with him who had need (Eph. 4:28).

***

Shred some oranges today, and join hands with Paul and Cato heading out to the fields.

***

"He who works with his hands and his head and his heart is an artist."
Saint Francis of Assisi

Day 191

***

Labyrinths (1177 BC)
Virgil, *Aeneid, 5:550–600*

***

On remote Sicilian shores, the Trojan boys gathered outside nature's arena, straddling spirited horses. When the signal came, they marched in, three troops of twelve, led by the squad's major, riding high in the saddle. Admirers stood clapping, stunned at the miniature armies' sophisticated beauty in perfect dress guiding their bridled steeds into the stadium.

With their heads garlanded by well-trimmed ceremonial leaves, each lad carried several steel-tipped, cornel-wood lances, famed for their Macedonian hardness. Prancing in precision, the troops advanced through the arena, their polished quivers, shoulder slung, bouncing with a menacing flair. Flexible golden torques worn around their necks reflected the morning sun drawing coos of admiration from the crowded spectators and family elites.

A sudden whip crack echoed off the mountain slopes as Epytides ordered the battalions to launch well-rehearsed maneuvers and counter-maneuvers. The troops kept their order and wove subtle patterns charging and then retreating. It was like they were creating a *labyrinth*, a maze of confusing designs that kept everyone guessing. Like gamboling dolphins in the sea, the young combatants spun an exotic tale of sham warfare that elicited pride in the spell-bound assembly.

***

Life's paths are often seen as *labyrinth*-like, weaving promises down ever-changing lanes. We stumble about daily in moonlit forests, never sure of diverging intersections. Paul, a man of skilled intuition, often stared into smoky mirrors, struggling to decipher God's signals.

***

"For now we see in a mirror dimly, but then face to face; now I know in part, but then I will know fully just as I also have been fully known" (1 Cor. 13:12).

***

The blood-spattered tracks of the cross will lead you home.

***

"The measure of intelligence is the ability to change."
Albert Einstein

Day 192

Lasciviousness (428 BC)
Euripides, *Hippolytus*, 435–515

***

Phaedra paced back and forth across her palace bedroom. The nurse, her trusted assistant, watched anxiously, listening to endless mutterings about chastity.

"I did my best not to love him," said Phaedra. "I know it's wrong. Depression has buried me alive, and I can't go on. What am I going to do?" She asked the question to the walls, but the nurse listened with wringing hands.

"It's not like I didn't try," cried the queen, her eyes smeared with guilt. "I swore to myself I would be silent about it. But silence only whets the appetite further."

The nurse wanted to whisper comforting words, but the tense drama spinning before her suffocated them. "My lady, please let me…"

Phaedra cut her off, still deliriously jabbering. "I thought that perhaps my will could prevail against these *lascivious* urges to have my son, but I had no choice. This slide into hell cannot be checked by good sense or rationalizations." The queen sat heavily on the bed and sighed. Then staring into the nurse's eyes, she whispered bitterly, "Death! That is my only plan now. I will slay the demon within and put this evil from me."

The nurse took the queen's hands. "My lady, there is another way. There are magic love charms, spells of enchantment that will rescue you."

***

Our modern world drowns in sensuality. Like Phaedra, a queen consumed by *lasciviousness*, we, too, see its shadows winking at us. Even St. Paul watched it wriggle through the Corinthian congregation, cooing among the pews.

***

"It is actually reported that there is immorality among you ... someone has his father's wife" (1 Cor. 5:1).

***

Touch God's heart and commit to purity today.

***

"When you doubt, abstain."
Ambrose Bierce

Day 193

***

Leisure (546 BC)

Herodotus, *The Persian Wars*, 1:155

***

"I'm sick and tired of these Lydians," griped Cyrus, the king. "All they do is cause me trouble. I think I will crush them and make them all enslaved people. That should do it."

"Don't do that," said Croesus, his friend and confidant. "Why not just turn these rebels who love to fight and cause trouble into men of *leisure*. Just lay a few simple rules down to them and watch the magic happen."

"What do you mean?" asked the king.

"Here's what you should do to tame those wild bucks. Just turn them into sissies. Tell them they have to turn in their weapons, for starters. Then give them all silk underwear and tunics and measure them for soft, comfortable boots. Next, sign them up for lessons on harp playing and other musical stuff. Oh, and teach them how to sing, dance, and have a good ole time going to parties. And, while you're at it, show them how to sell trinkets on pushcarts, not a real job. Turn them into old-fashioned hucksters."

The king was amazed. "You think this will actually work?"

Croesus smiled cagily. "Yep. Before long, these men will be like ladies of the night, and you won't ever have to worry about any more revolts."

***

Such a clever trick to get the ruffians all tamed down and useless for warfare. St. Paul said just the opposite. Instead of *leisure*, he ordered us in the Lord's army to soldier up and prepare for battle.

***

"Put on the full armor of God, so that you will be able to stand firm against the schemes of the devil" (Eph. 6:10–11).

***

Enjoy leisure with your weapons on!

***

"The end of labor is to gain leisure."
Aristotle

Day 194

***

Letters (AD 10)
Ovid, *Metamorphoses*, 9:515–546

***

Byblis lay upon her couch, trembling with a forbidden passion. This obsession for her brother, an unstoppable force within, left Byblis breathless, agitated, perversely determined. "There must be a way," she thought, pacing dark corridors. Then an idea tripped cautiously across her mind: "I could write him a letter. Yes, a *letter*!"

Gathering supplies, she lay upon her couch, pen in the right hand, tablet in the left. The stylus hovered inches above the waxen surface as she realized the implications. "He's going to actually see it, and then he will know this crazy passion I have for him. Oh, my!"

Nearly breathless with excitement, she began composing. A few words here, a few phrases there with quick erasures, the waxen surface blushing, awaiting the replacement. Frenzied scribbling followed with a frown and then a nod of approval. Occasionally, she put the letter down and paced dreamily on the portico, staring at the distant mountains. Then, with a flurry, she would rush back to the couch and scribble again, love words melting the wax.

Her face, a missive all its own, reflected the journey, first beaming boldness, followed instantly with shame and then confusion. She once realized that she had written sister and quickly replaced it with a lover of yours. So it went, an assault followed by a retreat, until the letter, shivering, awaited delivery.

***

There is such power in a little stream of words waltzing through wax. This *letter* ultimately destroyed Byblis' life, much like Jezebel's wicked words were forever shackled to ignominy's skirt.

***

"So she wrote letters in Ahab's name and sealed them with his seal..." (1 Kings 21:8).

***

Your tablet is blank. Write a love letter today.

***

"Behold me going to write you as handsome a letter as I can. Wish me good luck."
Jane Austen

Day 195

***

Lies (1184 BC)
Homer, *Iliad*, 2:1–15

***

The Greek army, weary of staring at Troy's impenetrable, interlocked walls thirty feet above the plain, slept soundly. Dreams of hearth and home comforted each soldier as they camped on the moonlit plains beyond the sea.

But Zeus could not sleep. Ever restless, he pondered how to keep his promise to Thetis, sea-goddess, and mother of Achilles. She had received his approving nod to destroy the Greek army because their king, Agamemnon, had forcibly taken Achilles' woman, Briseis, leaving the warrior sullen and despondent.

Zeus sighed heavily, the weight of the world upon his shoulders. My wife will nag me to death over my involvement in this war. Finally, he had an idea. "I will send a Lying Dream to the Greek king and tell him he must gather his troops and charge the walls of Troy." Satisfied, he quickly summoned *Lying* Dream. "Go at once and whisper in Agamemnon's ear that Troy will fall today. He must charge the walls today!"

And so Lying Dream hastened on his mission, hovering over the sleeping head of the king, whispering of quick and easy victory that would not come.

***

The same *Lying* Dream scampered across the plains of time and settled beside Peter inside the high priest's court. As the disciple warmed himself by a fire, listening to the frosty abuse

389

hurled at his Savior, Lying Dream tickled his ear as a rooster crowed nearby.

***

"So they said to him, 'You are not also one of His disciples, are you?' He denied it, and said, 'I am not'" (Jn. 18:25).

***

Send Lying Dream on his way. Wake up to truth.

***

"A lie can travel half way around the world while the truth is putting on its shoes."
Charles Spurgeon

Day 196

Life (AD 50)
Seneca, *Phaedra*, Act 3:825–850

The World Health Organization estimates that each year approximately one million people die from suicide. As you start your day this glorious morning, please choose to live!

There is a fascinating story in the ancient world of a man who did this very thing—but in strange circumstances. Seneca, a philosopher of St. Paul's time, tells the story of the Athenian king, Theseus, who had died and gone to the underworld, though he continued to follow the troubles of his family. He wondered whether he should remain in Hades or live again and help his family in crisis.

"I just don't know which I should choose," he muttered. "Should I stay here in the fiery depths or take a chance to live again? I belong in hell, but something draws me upward. My family needs me."

As it turns out, he managed, with help from Hercules, to escape the tortures of Hades and returned to his earthly home. In other words, he chose *life*!

Paul also had such a choice to make. He lived under house arrest in Rome but often wondered what it would be like to leave his troubles behind and join his beloved Savior in Heaven. Paul chose *life*! And so both of our characters made choices: Theseus sought to escape hell, while Paul fought his heavenly impulses and elected to remain on earth.

***

"For to me, to live is Christ, and to die is gain.... But if I am to live on in the flesh, this will mean fruitful labor for me; and I do not know which to choose" (Phil. 1:21–22).

***

This is your day to live anew!

***

"How lucky I am to have something that makes saying goodbye so hard."
Winnie the Pooh

Day 197

Light (AD 69)
Suetonius, *Lives of the Caesars*, 7:8

***

Vitellius was flat broke. His creditors haunted his every move in Rome, demanding payments for outstanding debts. But just as the sun occasionally shines through stormy clouds, good news fell into his gluttonous lap one day. The emperor, Galba, had appointed him to be governor of Lower Germany!

He stuffed his wife and children into a rented attic on Rome's dirty streets, hastily kissing them goodbye. His own tiny house, he leased for the remainder of the year. Realizing he had no money to finance his journey abroad, he remembered his mother Sextilia's pearl earring. Brushing her aside as he stormed into her bedroom, he snatched the pearl from her jewelry box and hocked it at the neighborhood pawn shop.

When he reached the camp in Germany, the soldiers were ecstatic to see him. One night, a gang of soldiers broke into his bedroom, saluted him as emperor, and paraded him, pajamas and all, through the neighboring village streets. Unknown, however, to the jubilant throngs, a fire broke out in the dining hall at headquarters. This unlucky portent worried some. But Vitellius shouted to the troops, "It's wonderful news, my friends. *Light* is given us!"

***

Not all *lights* shine favorably. It was only eight months into Vitellius' short reign as emperor that palace soldiers mangled

393

him with the torture of the little cuts. Then, they dragged his bloody body to the Tiber River with a hook and threw it in.

***

I much prefer Matthew's starlight that shone upon a budding king in Bethlehem. "When they saw the star, they rejoiced exceedingly with great joy" (Matt. 2:10).

***

Which light is leading you today?

***

"If light is in your heart, you will find your way home."
Rumi

Day 198

Lighthouse (AD 10)
Ovid, *Metamorphoses*, 11:390–410

***

A humble, wood-built chapel stood meekly beside an ancient grove near a marsh spiked with willows. "It's a sacred place," said a sailor to a local herdsman who was tending his cows near the sea. "This is the home of the god Nereus and his daughters," he said. Suddenly, a ferocious stirring nearby broke the reverie. A wild wolf, smeared with marsh mud, hurtled past the temple toward the beach where a flock of docile cattle frolicked in the shore's wavelets.

The wolf, its eyes blazing with rage, tore into the herd, its jaws chomping, flecked with bloody foam. It began mangling the cows, to the shepherd's dismay. Before long, the crimson shore wept before the small temple as the slaughter continued. When Aeacus, the island's king, heard the pleas for help, he climbed to the lighthouse nearby to beg heaven's intervention.

The *lighthouse*, a beacon on the mountaintop to storm-tossed vessels, welcomed the king. From its highest observation point, Aeacus looked down in dismay at the bloody beaches as the wolf continued its rampage unchecked. Holding his hands skyward, the king prayed to the Nereid, the sea goddess. Glancing ashore at the carnage, the goddess answered the call, and just as the wolf buried his fangs into a young heifer's neck, she turned the wolf into marble.

***

What would this world be without *lighthouses*? Daily let us climb the mountain and find the light that saves and renews our purpose.

The Psalmist understands.

***

"O send out Your light and Your truth; let them lead me; Let them bring me to Your holy hill and to Your dwelling Places" (Ps. 43:3).

***

Be the lighthouse for others.

***

"Lighthouses are more helpful than churches."
Benjamin Franklin

Day 199

***

Limitations (AD 120)
Juvenal, *Satires*, 3:40–60

***

Juvenal sat down heavily at his desk, weary of Rome's hustle and bustle. "There are so many things I can't do and won't do," he thought. "I'll never make it here." Sighing, he began to scribble down his *limitations*:

"I'm not a good liar, and that's the pulse of this Roman hell hole." He scoffed at a book half-read lying on a nearby chair. "That book sucks. It's got no soul, no brilliant phrases, or lofty themes. I'm certainly not going to pretend it's a classic and tell people to buy it. I'm not a good liar."

Pessimism primed the pump, and soon all his cant's streamed forth: "I can't read the stars, so I'll never make my fortune as a merchant in pursuit of exotic destinations." Then, remembering an encounter at a nearby temple, he reflected. "I see the religious folks at their altars reading the guts of animals. Shoot, I couldn't even read a frog's innards."

He leaned back, thinking of the criminals he knew who flourished in Rome. "I can't do that stuff. I can't be a lookout for thieves, and I don't dare blackmail anybody. I wouldn't know what to do with a bribe." He remembered a friend who set up affairs for bored housewives. "I wouldn't even know how to start doing that."

***

Limitations can paralyze the best of us. Any one of us could make a list of cant's like Juvenal. Before long, however, paralysis will take over as it did for Moses, who made his own list:

***

"But Moses said to God, 'Who am I, that I should go to Pharaoh... Please, Lord, I have never been eloquent...'" (Ex. 3:11/4:10).

***

Burn your *cant's* list today.

***

"Argue for your limitations, and sure enough they're yours."
Richard Bach

Day 200

***

Loathing (429 BC)
Sophocles, *Oedipus Tyrannus*, 1232–1270

***

Oedipus smashed through the double doors of the palace bedroom, sending bolts and hinges flying. Besieged by guilt for mistakes etched with eternal implications, he stood mesmerized by the swinging of the corpse. She dangled, tangled in moonlight beams that filtered through the double windows. Jocasta's beautiful body, twisted in innocent misdeeds, swayed gently. Oedipus dropped to his knees, quivering. His maddening shrieks echoed through the valley beyond the window.

Struggling up from his knees, he lunged for the noose, freeing his wife from failure's entanglements, and laid her gently on the bed. Tracing the links that had led to this death, a dreadful chain forged from mistakes along life's journey, he moaned. Sweet familial memories of laughing children and afternoon strolls by the lake hovered in the dead space between him and her, accenting the dirge.

Enraged, he ripped the golden brooches from her gown, gifts from a happier time, and rammed the pins into his eyes. "Wicked, wicked eyes!" he gasped. "Never again will you gaze upon our shame or this horrid scene." Repeatedly he stabbed his eyes, feeling the blood drops drip down vanquished cheeks. Then, calling for his daughter Antigone to lead him from the palace, he stumbled forth from a once treasured kingdom into a vagabond's life, wandering the hills and woods in *loathing*.

***

Failures, like golden brooches, can destroy a worthy life, darkening forever any visions of remaining happiness. And yet, who lives without loss? We are all prone to the disease and the *loathing* that follows. Judas knows.

***

"And he threw the pieces of silver into the temple sanctuary and departed; and he went away and hanged himself" (Matt. 27:5).

***

Lay all your self-loathing upon the Shepherd's shoulder.

***

"I'm self-loathing, introverted, and neurotic."
Megan Fox

Day 201

Loneliness (438 BC)
Euripides, *Alcestis*, 910–960

***

Admetus, king of Pherae, stood staring tearfully at the palace's closed doors. His two small children tugged at his robes, motherless. The funeral wails now seemed but empty echoes, his wife's name fading softly into the valley forests. Alone now before the home that once rang with joy and festivities, he clung to these fleeting fantasies, joyous mirages that now sang a *lonely* tune.

He stood forlornly, remembering the sweet bride that once, long ago, took his arm at this very place where now he stood. Revelers had escorted them to these doors carrying Pelian pine torches that danced in midnight shadows. It was here before the palace entrance that he had held her tightly, humming wedding melodies so brightly flung at them by friends and well-wishers. Her fluttering hair and dancing eyes had made promises now broken.

Still, the entrance beckoned, but its voice was strangely hollow, and he dared not step across the threshold. "Who will I speak to when I get inside?" he asked himself. "What will I do when I glance upon Alcestis' empty bed or when I see the chair where she used to sit knitting children's socks? How will I comfort these weeping children who beg for their mother?"

***

Loneliness's melancholy moan haunts us all at one time or another. Happy thresholds can turn bitter in an eye's wink, and many of us will sway to its somber melody alone. Even Jeremiah, a stalwart voice from the past, felt the sting of loneliness.

***

"I did not sit in the circle of merrymakers, nor did I exult. Because of Your hand upon me, I sat alone..." (Jer. 15:17).

***

Walk with loneliness but know a bright day is coming soon.

***

"All great and precious things are lonely."
John Steinbeck

Day 202

***

Loss (688 BC)
Herodotus, *The Persian Wars*, 1:150

***

The men of Smyrna moved like midnight revelers down the Street of Gold, winding like a woman's necklace around Mt. Pagus to the harbor. Dionysus, the god of wine and religious ecstasy, was summoning them to gather outside the city walls for a festival of drunken fantasies. The moonlight glittered upon the road leading through the town's gates to the harbor's edge.

Once they were gone, temporary guests, exiles from a nearby city, moved in quickly. They locked the city gates and claimed Smyrna as theirs, an audacious move forever recorded in history.

The following day, the groggy revelers stumbled home and found the gates locked shut. They shouted at the walls to no avail as the abandoned women and children within sobbed helplessly. The city fell without bloodshed! After negotiations, a few men were allowed to retrieve their wailing wives and other possessions. Before them was a destination unknown to lives haunted forever by the fading memories of a dream upon a hill now *lost* forever.

***

Loss comes in all hues. David felt this in the extreme when God cursed his newborn son. Before the baby died, David grieved and refused consolation, lying on the ground all night, refusing food and drink (2 Sam. 12:16–17).

403

Should you find yourself outside the walls of your fortress, locked out of a dream, remember the words of Jesus still valid for us today:

***

"Therefore you too have grief now; but I will see you again, and your heart will rejoice, and no one will take your joy away from you" (Jn. 16:20).

***

Loss often leads to a new land of bliss.

***

"Those we love don't go away, they walk beside us every day."
Anonymous

Day 203

***

Loyalty (429 BC)
Sophocles, *Antigone*, 400–450

***

The sentries, clutching swords and spears, settled upon the ridge overlooking the corpse. Polyneices, decaying under the hot sun, lay exposed to both beasts and vultures, the Theban king's decree. "He dared to attack Thebes, his own city," muttered King Creon. "Now let the traitor bake beneath the sun for his treachery."

Antigone wept silently from a distance for her unfortunate brother. Aware of his faults, love prevailed. A defiant rage at the king's cruelty roiled her blood, and at midday, she rose, *loyalty* making its demands. With tears, she swept down towards the rotting corpse, its stench scenting the valley floor.

A sentry shouted from the hillock as Antigone's swift steps betrayed the king's edict. "Someone is here!" screamed the watchman. "Someone approaches the body." The soldiers leaped to observe, but as they rose, a whirlwind swept across the plain, whipping up choking dust that veiled the rescue.

When the wind calmed, Antigone stood shrieking over her beloved brother's mutilated body. Like a bird's poignant cries over a pillaged nest, she raged against the desecration. Scooping handfuls of earth, she sprinkled the body with nature's veil and poured libations from a brazen urn over his disfigured face.

Swooping down, the soldiers shackled her without resistance. When confronted with the crime, she admitted the deed, denying nothing.

***

The very word, *loyalty*, rings with a golden charisma. It draws the angels' praises and pricks the best of our souls. Sad is the day when we fail its call. No one knows this more than Peter.

***

"Peter said to Him, 'Even if I have to die with You, I will not deny you.' All the disciples said the same thing too" (Matt. 26:35).

***

A rooster crows. Will your loyalty stand?

***

"Faithless is he that says farewell when the road darkens."
J.R.R. Tolkien

Day 204

***

Magic (27 BC)
Tibullus, *Elegies*, 1:2

***

The lover's gate was bolted; Tibullus locked out. Delia played her cruel game again, leaving him in desperate longing. That shut door was killing him. "I'll pray," he said forlornly. "That will bring help." He closed his eyes and, with solemn utterance, summoned the aid of heaven.

With pleasure sweet, he imagined sympathetic deities scurrying to his rescue. He watched as they jiggled her gate's lock noiselessly and swung love's possibilities open. They tiptoed across her forbidden floor until they caught Delia's smile. She looked past them with fluttering, conceding eyes, and raised her hand alluringly to Tibullus.

Living in this sweet dream, he cursed the night ramblers, spirits up to no good, who dared to linger near the couch. Cursing them all, he warned them of the sin of babbling tongues. What they see had better remain unseen!

He wagged his finger at the inquisitive ghosts, still probing his dream, and warned them of his divine protector who wove *magic* spells. This spirit guide gave him a secret chant to melt Delia's heart. "Thrice I was to spit, and then thrice I was to repeat the secret chant."

***

Lovesick souls will try anything to gain some advantage. A little *magic* seemed to help poor Tibullus. Magic also tempted some

new believers under Paul's sway. The aprons he released upon
the Ephesian streets wrought miracles by God's power alone.
"There is no magic here," he warned them.

***

"And many of those who practiced magic brought their books
together and began burning them in the sight of everyone"
(Acts 19:19).

***

Shun the sorcerer's bag. Miracles aren't magic.

***

"She's as old as the hills, evil as a snake, all malevolence and
magic and death."
Neil Gaiman

Day 205

Manipulation (AD 66)
Josephus, *The Life of Josephus*, 1:6

***

Jewish fanatics danced into the night beneath the Fortress of Antonia, celebrating their astonishing defeat of the Roman garrison. Against all odds, the ragtag Jews with their hand-me-down weapons had humiliated the elite Roman fighters who surrendered the Jerusalem citadel.

The victors, ecstatic over their success, spilled out into the countryside and soon attacked the town of Scythopolis, a pagan metropolis loyal to Rome. The residents, shocked at the screaming Jewish fanatics outside their city walls, devised a wicked but successful strategy. They shoved the peaceful Jewish town's residents to the front lines. With diabolical *manipulation*, they forced them to fight the Jewish rebels, an act forbidden by Jewish law. Families now slaughtered each other. Brothers killed fathers, and fathers slew sons until the blood trickled to the Jordan humbled in crimson despair.

When nightfall settled over the darkening horizon, 13,000 men, women, and children lay silent beneath a weeping moon. All Josephus could do was groan, the horror of the devastation breathtaking.

***

This seems like a scene out of the American Civil War, a national calamity that wrenched families apart. Whether it was Bulls Run or the calamity at Antietam, dark forces still find ways to shatter peace and silence love's appeal. Even our sacred gatherings are prone to *manipulation* as Paul reminds us:

***

"and that no man transgress and defraud his brother in the matter because the Lord is the avenger in all these things,..." (1 Thess. 4:6).

***

Josephus and Paul saw the shame in it. Are you still manipulating others?

***

"If they do it often, it isn't a mistake; it's just their behavior."
Dr. Steve Maraboli

Day 206

Mansions (AD 8)
Ovid, *Metamorphoses*, 1:163

***

It's more than just a residence. Slip under the skin of 432 Park Avenue's Penthouse Model Residence 92B and experience the closest thing to a heavenly home. When the evening sun's expiring breath blows across the bedroom, you can sit on the cushioned window seat and watch New York below spread its lights like a million festive fireflies.

Ovid described something similar once in the days of Augustus. He urged us to dally as we walk heaven's main boulevard, the same road to Zeus' house:

"Just follow the Milky Way, that ivory path in the sky. Pause along the way and stare at the deities' breathtaking *mansions*, their courtyards quietly summoning the restless gods as they fling their gates open one by one. Stroll on a little further, and you will see the royal palace itself, where Zeus, the god of thunder, lives in his heavenly home."

***

Ovid, who died in 18 AD, just missed John's lecture on the mansions of heaven. The great apostle doesn't use the poetry or the wizardry of magical words to describe the homes on heaven's thoroughfare. But what he does tell us is profound. The *mansions* that lead to God's throne are inside the palace of God. You can sit in your window seat and see more than Central

411

Park or the Hudson. Here, nestled beneath the warm glow of God's light, you can see God Himself!

***

"Do not let your heart be troubled; believe in God, believe also in Me. In My Father's house are many dwelling places; if it were not so, I would have told you; for I go to prepare a place for you" (Jn.14:1–2).

***

Your mansion is waiting for you.

***

"My home is in heaven. I'm just traveling through this world."
Billy Graham

Day 207

Memories (AD 79)
Suetonius, *Lives of the Caesars*, 8.2

Tertulla's *memories* still resonated long after dying in her country estate near Reati. As Vespasian's grandmother, she won his soul, opening her home and heart to his childhood ramblings. Memories of the joyous vintage season in nearby Cosa played in the emperor's mind throughout his adult life. During this festive time, the area's population would swarm the hamlet's streets, their wagons pulled by cumbersome country oxen crowned with leafy garlands snatched from dangling grapevines.

Vespasian never forgot Tertulla or her genteel country manners. As emperor, he would often travel back to the old home place and sift the pleasant ghosts of childhood days spent beneath Mt. Terminillo's snowy brow. His treks down to the Velino River coaxed the carefree smiles of playful friends.

He insisted on the villa remaining unchanged throughout his lifetime. Everything held its form and place, just as he remembered it. And during Roman festivals, when he could not make the beloved journey home, he would often take from his palace cupboard her little silver cup, Tertulla's chalice, and sip the sweet nectar of a grandmother's love.

Nothing lifts somber spirits more than pleasant *memories* of a beloved past. Paul urged his followers to ponder beauty, drawing from its soul hope and life that sustain us through difficult times.

***

"Finally brethren, whatever is true, whatever is honorable, whatever is right, whatever is pure, whatever is lovely, whatever is of good repute, if there is any excellence and if anything worthy of praise, dwell on these things" (Phil. 4:8).

***

Find your silver cup today and stir the memories.

***

"I love that a scent can make memories come alive."
Anonymous

Day 208

***

Mercy (1178 BC)
Virgil, *Aeneid*, 3:560–620

***

The Trojan wanderers slept fitfully on Sicily's smoky shores. Their battered ship, nestled in the sand beneath Aetna's fuming mouth, still quivered at yesterday's death dives in the murky whirlpools offshore. Hiding, now, beneath night's shade at the forest's edge, they cowered beneath Aetna's belching fireballs spewing sporadically over the straits.

As first light spun its morning web across the sky, Aeneas awoke to a mirage, an unknown man shivering at the forest's edge. Emaciated and dressed in rags stitched together by thorns, the human creature stretched out his hands imploringly to the shore's vagabonds. Aeneas gazed up and down the shoreline but saw no one else. The beggar was alone, appallingly dirty with an overgrown beard and sunken eyes.

At first, the man studied the Trojans, fearing retribution, but then, fearful no more, ran frantically toward them, sobbing, screaming for mercy. "Rescue me! I admit I once was a Greek soldier fighting against Troy, but now I've been abandoned in the cyclops' cave. My life is a nightmare. It searches for me every day. Please. Rescue me!"

He clasped our knees, writhing beneath us until Anchises, Aeneas' father, stepped forward and offered him his hand, a gesture of *mercy* and reassurance.

***

Mercy. What a wondrous portrait painted by God's fingertips upon our hearts daily. Without heaven's artwork, we would all be this marooned man, living in daily fear trembling beneath some cyclops' shadow. Such was the fate of a blind man Jesus once encountered on a Jericho road:

***

"And Jesus stopped and said, 'Call him here.' So they called the blind man, saying to him, 'Take courage, stand up! He is calling for you'" (Mk. 10:49).

***

Today, show mercy. Rescue the perishing.

***

"I have always found that mercy bears richer fruits than strict justice."
Abraham Lincoln

Day 209

***

Mirage (430 BC)
Euripides, *The Heracleidae*, 1–50

***

Iolaus wept with joy. The old man's hopes for safety soared, lifting him and Heracles' orphaned waifs, into the ether where freedom lives. Life on the run had been brutal for Iolaus chasing dreams of refuge from the unceasing pursuit by Eurystheus the Argon king, who held a relentless vendetta against Heracles' memory. Finally clambering to safety in Zeus' Marathon temple, the frightened boys and girls, Heracles' only living lineage, huddled trembling but secure at the altar's base.

Iolaus could scarcely constrain his tears. Safe harbor, that tantalizing *mirage*, ever-elusive, embraced his motley vagabonds. "Remember this day forever, children," Iolaus said, gathering the kids around him at the altar. "Justice still lives in this world. You are safe now, forever."

Yet before these golden words crystalized in the children's hearts, the dreaded voice of their pursuers echoed at the temple's door. The king's herald, Copreus, had tracked them down, storming the inner sanctum beneath the towering pillars of Zeus' inner sanctum, hurling Iolaus to the floor.

Then yanking the screaming children from the altar, Copreus castigated the old fool. "There is no safety here in this temple or anywhere," he screamed. "The Argon's shadow is long and will drag you and your renegade flock back to justice wherever you flee."

***

417

We stride daily forth through deserts shimmering with *mirages*. They rise and fall with misadventure, failures, and dashed hopes. Such was the lonely woman who dropped her bucket into the well at high noon. Five times love had evaporated on the sands of heartache. Dare she try one last time for peace?

***

"The woman said to Him, 'Sir, give me this water...'" (Jn. 4:15).

***

Cling to the Lord's promises. They are mirage-proof.

***

"Mirages enchant us up to the very moment we die of thirst."
Marty Rubin

Day 210

Misfortune (1178 BC)
Virgil, *Aeneid*, 5:300–350

***

The spectators fluttered from the Sicilian shore toward a grand amphitheater of surrounding forests rising on natural bluffs. Beneath their shadows lay a fertile valley where throngs of festive Trojans, Greeks, and Sicilian natives gathered for the running event. Aeneas displayed the first prize, a caparisoned stallion taken in battle. Second place promised an Amazonian quiver filled with Thracian arrows slung upon a golden belt.

Bent low and quivering at the starting line, the athletes, dreaming of glory, waited for the starting signal. A grand hush swept the grassy seats across the stadium, all eyes locked on the line. Then, the call shot forth, and the runners bolted like greyhounds from the blocks, thundering around the first turn.

Nisus set a substantial lead from the start, followed at a great distance by Salius and Euryalus. When the runners rounded the final corner, Nisus, already claiming first prize with his eyes set greedily upon the finish line, slipped.

A gasp filled the stadium. Headlong he fell, spinning wildly into a gory, bloody mess left from a morning's sacrifice. Slime, mingled with battered intestines, dripped from Nisus' face, who, try as he might, could not stand as Euryalus darted past unexpected *misfortune* claiming the top prize and the crowd's adulation.

***

Misfortune stalks us all, rearing its head at inopportune moments. Like a squall offshore, it slams us to the ground and strolls casually away, leaving us breathless, pondering uncertainties.

Paul knew this foe well. His privileged background evaporated as he followed the Light.

***

"I have suffered the loss of all things, and count them but rubbish so that I may gain Christ" (Phil. 3:8).

***

Misfortune brought you down; now rise and finish the race.

***

"My expectations were reduced to zero when I was 21. Everything since then has been a bonus."
Stephen Hawking

Day 211

***

Mistakes (547 BC)
Herodotus, *The Persian Wars*, 1:86

***

Cyrus, the Persian conqueror, pointed his finger mockingly at King Croesus as his Pergamum empire blazed before him. Bound in chains upon a massive pyre, the humbled Croesus surveyed his burning kingdom of clifftop temples and exquisite buildings. The 10,000-seat stone amphitheater, with its granite seats plummeting down the mountainside, now mocked him, the lead actor in a tragic play. As billowing smoke drifted languidly over the valley floor, the glories of Pergamum seemed trivial now.

Cyrus ordered 14 slave boys to be tied upon the pyre next to the former king. Through it all, the defeated ruler never uttered a word. Cyrus marveled at this stoic behavior and clapped his hand for the torches. "Set it ablaze!" he commanded and then sat back to watch the play unfold.

Croesus began to mumble strange words foreign to Cyrus. "What does he say?" asked the king of his translators.

"He repeats the word 'Solon,' your majesty."

Intrigued, Cyrus demanded its meaning. "He tells a strange story, your majesty, of Solon, a visiting wise man, who mocked his kingdom and told him it would tumble one day."

When Cyrus heard this, he became frightened, realizing that this humiliation could happen to him. "Take him down," he ordered immediately. "Stop the fire!"

But the *mistake* was too great to correct. The fire raged beyond control.

***

Mistakes are often hard to stop.

David, another king centuries earlier, stood atop his palace portico late one night and stumbled. Spotting a beautiful woman bathing beneath a glorious moon, he summoned her setting adrift an irreversible failure.

***

"So David sent and inquired about the woman..." (2 Sam. 11:3).

***

Be careful today. Some fires are hard to quench.

***

"People just make stupid mistakes and suddenly, they can't dig themselves out."
Karen Slaughter

Day 212

***

Mothers (1177 BC)
Virgil, *Aeneid*, 9:275–300

***

The Trojan army slumbered in the heavy mists of the fourth watch. The burdens of warfare ceased their bellicose whines as warriors dreamt of home fires and cozy beds. Only the chieftains, leaning upon their long spears with shields at the ready, lingered by soft fires, whispering uneasily. Beyond the battlements, a fierce Rutulian army slept restlessly, preparing for a final dawn advance against the camp.

As the leadership probed the unknown, two valiant soldiers approached and, risking etiquette, interrupted their seniors. "Gentlemen, pardon the intrusion, but Euryalus and I, Nisus, have a proposal."

The elders nodded consent. Nisus spoke first. "We have studied the enemy's position and see a weakness near the seaward gate where two ways fork. The fire rings are broken there; some are out completely, while others smoke heavily. Let us steal away now and get news to our commander, Aeneas."

The elders listened in awe and deep respect for this valor. With tears, Aeneas' son, Ascanius, stepped forward weeping and pledged wealth untold to them for this daring mission.

Then Euryalus spoke. "I have one simple request before we leave. My *mother* knows nothing of this. I could not bear to tell her, for her tears would have unmanned me. I merely ask that you all console her in my absence. With this assurance, I will go forth with bravery."

***

On a thunderous mountain curtained by sacred smoke, a few sanctified words fell like solitary comets from God's voice. One of these holy nuggets commanded all humanity to honor their *mothers*. This heavenly priority, later etched in stone, still stands:

***

"Honor your father and your mother..." (Ex. 20:12).

***

Say your mother's name today and give thanks.

***

"A mother's arms are more comforting than anyone else's."
Princess Diana

Day 213

Music (AD 8)
Ovid, *Metamorphoses*, 11:1–80

***

Orpheus, plucking a mellifluous melody upon his lyre, drew sighs of joy from the waving trees as he skipped along a mountain road. Forest beasts ceased their toils and hummed while river pebbles danced merrily beneath the wavelets.

But far off on Thracian mountain tops, wild Ciconian women with their tresses flaying the air screamed in madness. Spotting him faraway, they declared war and flung spears across distant valleys. Missing the mark, others slung stones that flew against their will, falling harmlessly at his feet, begging forgiveness.

But anger, never satiated, summoned others, and soon there was an orgy of hatred aimed at Orpheus. Shrilling flutes, braying trumpets, and drums that bellowed out dark syncopations, overcame the poet's sweet *music*. Falling beneath their relentless blows, he raised desperate hands in supplication. His voice, silent now, moved no one to tears.

He died, and the birds wept for him as the trees shook their leaves, a tribute in sorrow for the valiant minstrel. The Hebrus River, mourning, carried the corpse gently to Lesbos' white sands, where they lay Orpheus to rest, his head still dripping with sea spray.

***

Ovid led us somberly to the graveside of *music*. Gone were the melodies of life, the orchestral crescendos at our rare accomplishments, the singing at weddings and nuptials. Imagine a silent globe where nothing is heard but street congestion and guns popping angrily.

But wait! I hear whispering on heaven's corridors. God is sending a messenger our way with an urgent command:

***

"speak to one another with psalms, hymns, and songs from the Spirit. Sing and make music from your heart to the Lord" (Eph. 5:19).

***

Sing some glorious song today.

***

"Music, once admitted to the soul, becomes a sort of spirit, and never dies."
Edward Bulwer Lytton

Day 214

***

Mysteries (AD 150)
Apuleius, *The Golden Ass*, 11:248

***

Lucius' long nightmare neared its end. A lovely witch had turned him into a donkey and forced him into a seemingly endless nightmare. He wandered the globe from place to place, suffering humiliation due a dumb animal.

But one day, the goddess Isis whispered to him in a dream, promising to restore him to normalcy. The next day he joined a holy procession strolling to the sea. A priest carrying in his arms a rattling sistrum and a crown of roses stopped the throng and urged Lucius to nibble the sacred flowers. Suddenly the miraculous transformation stripped away the donkey's form leaving Lucius naked and startled.

Back at the temple later that day, Lucius took the old priest's hand and entered a spacious temple. The cleric slipped behind a veil and produced a *mysterious* old book written in strange, unreadable characters. Some were hieroglyphs of painted animals and twisted and wreathed letters with a fancy script of swirls and spirals woven together like tendrils on a vine. Lucius finding it impossible to read, called for the high priest who interpreted it all for the befuddled disciple as part of his mystical preparation.

***

The natural man picks up the New Testament, and what does he see but squiggly lines and colorful shapes. It makes no sense to him. Without guidance from the Spirit, it is just a book of *mysteries*, dots, and dashes tucked away in some mystic shrine.

***

"But a natural man does not accept the things of the Spirit of God, for they are foolish to him; and he cannot understand them, because they are spiritually appraised" (1 Cor. 2:14).

***

God's mysteries are lingering for you in the Scriptures.

***

"All silence is the recognition of a mystery."
Vladimir Nabokov

Day 215

***

News (AD 9)

Cassius Dio, *Roman History*, 56:23

***

Augustus groaned. The *news* of the Teutoburg Forest disaster nearly killed him. While gazing into a waning sunset on the Palatine Hill in Rome, he tore his imperial garments and collapsed on the palace floor. For years he moaned, "Varus, give me back my legions!"

Varus, the general in charge of Rome's illustrious 17th, 18th, and 19th legions, had fallen victim to a brilliant ruse. The German prince, Arminius, who seethed with silent anger at the Romans for conquering many German villages, sought revenge. Meeting with Varus, he and his fellow tribesmen feigned friendship, urging Varus and the legions to follow him deep into the forests to aid his suffering people. Varus agreed, not listening to his staff who urged caution, even rebuking those who had such little faith in the tribes.

Once deep in the valley crags, the Romans could barely move. Making matters worse, a violent thunderstorm fell, making the slopes muddy and treacherous. Suddenly, in the gloom of night, from beneath the Black Forest canopy, screaming warriors charged the Roman legions and slaughtered them in the forest muck. When all hope was lost, Varus pulled his sword and committed suicide, leaving Rome's worst military nightmare in his wake.

***

Six centuries earlier, in the king's palace of Jerusalem, Shaphan the scribe rushed to meet King Josiah with *news*. "Sire, we have found a book!" he said breathlessly. Opening the scroll, the words of a long-forgotten God tumbled from the dusty pages, and the king trembled, knowing the consequences.

*****

"When the king heard the words of the book of the law, he tore his clothes" (2 Kings 22:11).

*****

When bad news comes, weep humbly before a loving God.

*****

"Bad news has good legs."
Richard Llewellyn

Day 216

***

Nostalgia (AD 40)
Phaedrus, *Fables*, 3:1

***

The clutter of spent wine glasses covered the table. The comissatio, that infamous drinking party the Romans loved, had staggered to its inevitable close by early morning as drunken revelers departed into the morning mists. An old slave woman, broom in hand, began sweeping the floor; her tattered robe trailed behind her fluttering silently among the party ghosts.

Scanning the majestic hall with its intricate wall mosaics, she paused to daydream. "What if I had been a guest at the night's revelry?" she mused. Her sweet childhood, nestled in shadows beneath Theban mountains, had ended abruptly when an army passed through. This life of domestic futility was all she knew now but for those flittering memories of happiness.

She paused in her reverie before an empty wine jar shipwrecked among a cluster of dinner debris. Lifting it, she paused and sniffed the aromas from the Falerian dregs at the jar's bottom. "Ah," she purred *nostalgically*, her voice mingling with the sun's shafts dappling the table, "you, sweet wine, once had a life of grandeur like me."

***

Nostalgia, those golden dreams we all relive from time to time, comfort and amuse us as we age. Glances backward soothe frayed nerves and steer us into calm waters. But at times, the past can shackle us to a time long gone. Paul, raised with privilege in a fine home, preferred the forward gaze:

***

"Brethren,... but one thing I do; forgetting what lies behind and reaching forward to what lies ahead, I press on toward the goal for the prize of the upward call of God in Christ Jesus" (Phil. 3:13–14).

***

Don't linger long in the past. Press on to a new summit.

***

"Nostalgia is a seductive liar."
George Ball

Day 217

***

Nuisance (35 BC)
Horace, *Satires*, 1:9

***

Horace, the renowned poet, was strolling down the Sacred Way toward the Roman Forum, sifting his cares, pondering trifles, when a strange fellow intercepted his gait. Out of the blue, the shifty fellow struck up a conversation with the poet. Grabbing Horace's hands, he asked, "How's it going, old chap. How's the world treating you?"

His reverie broken, Horace replied with a curious "fine," followed quickly by "goodbye." But the stranger didn't leave. Instead, he waddled on beside the poet, talking drivel and rattling incessantly about nothing.

The pest noticed the poet's vain attempt to get away. Ever the inquisitor, he asked, "Just where the heck are you going that is so important, anyway?"

With an impatient sigh, Horace responded. "I'm going across the Tiber to visit a sick friend near Caesar's Gardens."

"Oh, how lovely," said the *nuisance*. "I'll just follow along."

"Don't you have some parents to visit or close friends?"

"Nope. Not a one. All dead."

When they passed Vesta's shrine, a quarter of the day was already lost. But then, fate winked. The stranger had a court summons. Horace smiled. Surely this will end it all, he thought.

But the man deferred. "I will just do court later. I'd rather be with you."

***

Look yonder near the Mount of Olives. Do you see the dust clinging to a bent and weeping king passing the orchard? As David fled his son Absalom, Shimei, an annoying *nuisance,* taunted him.

***

"and Shimei went along on the hillside parallel with him and as he went he cursed and cast stones and threw dust at him" (2 Sam. 16:13).

***

Patience. The dust always settles.

***

"You must learn to forgive a man when he's in love. He's always a nuisance."
Rudyard Kipling

Day 218

***

Oaths (52 BC)
Julius Caesar, *Gallic War*, 7:2

***

The Carnutes, a fierce tribe of ancient Gaul, gathered secretly at midnight in a remote forest. A bonfire illumined their savage faces as eerie sparks floated into the upper canopy. They spoke in whispers, fearing Caesar's ghost. They replayed over and over the brutal public flogging of Acco, their chieftain, at the hands of Caesar. "We must fight back," they all muttered in the darkness. "If not, we might be next."

They all agreed and called for the war standards, the flags that led them into battle. Each bowed his head before the sacred symbols understanding the implications of this venerable ritual of *oaths*. "We swear to be loyal and true to one another as we take vengeance upon the brutality of Caesar."

The oath bound them by blood. Each warrior stared solemnly into the waning fire, and then they shuffled silently out of the dark forest to gather their armies.

***

The embers of this bonfire seem almost to drift forward in time to the courtyard of Caiaphas, the high priest. There beside a flickering fire, Peter too shouted an oath. "I do not know the man" (Matt. 26:74). A rooster suddenly crowed, and Jesus "turned and looked at Peter" (Lk. 22:61).

***

Consider these two nighttime *oaths*. Savage warriors in Gaul's dark forest swore loyalty to one another as they sought revenge on Caesar; Peter's oath was one of abject disloyalty. Both held severe consequences for those who uttered them.

***

Guard your oaths. Jesus is listening.

***

"Eggs and oaths are easily broken."
Danish Proverb

Day 219

***

Oblivious (539 BC)
Herodotus, *The Persian Wars*, 1:191

***

The dimensions of Babylon defied the imagination.

Herodotus tells us the walls ran 15 miles long in a perfect square with a width and height of 85 by 335 feet. Hovering over the city were 250 defensive towers making the city impregnable.

Cyrus and his generals studied it from afar, wondering how to take it. Suddenly, the king snapped his fingers. "I've got it!" he shouted to his staff beneath a Babylon moon. "We will slip in with the Euphrates that runs through the city." And so, at midnight, his ablest soldiers slithered into the murky stream and rode the flow beneath the gates. Bit by bit, the army assembled on the inner fringe of the walls.

Far off in the distance, beyond sight, the inner neighborhoods danced at an all-night festival, *oblivious* to the danger. The sounds of distant decadence tickled the ears of the drenched soldiers. Cyrus' command to attack filtered silently down the ranks. The party-goers never saw them coming—until it was too late.

***

The widow was also *oblivious* in the temple. Bent and lost beneath the prominent givers, she shuffled along, immersed in her silent marital memories, holding two thin coins tightly. Jostling amidst the fluttering robes of Jerusalem's nobility gilded in gold, she waited humbly as they tossed in clutches of gold, listening for the symphony to slide round and round the trumpet chests.

Her pennies slid without song into the depths. Unnoticed by all but an admiring Jesus, she turned and left unnoticed.

***

"And He saw a poor widow putting in two small copper coins" (Lk. 21:2).

***

Step outside yourself today and see.

***

"I would rather die now than to live a life of oblivious ease in so sick a world."
Nate Saint

Day 220

Omnipotent (1184 BC)
Homer, *Iliad*, 8:1–20

***

When Morning rose in the eastern sky, her saffron robe billowing over the horizon, Zeus snapped his regal fingers. The gods, scattered here and yon on personal business, stopped and noted the summons. Dropping their affairs, they scurried toward lofty Mt. Olympus, settling upon their thrones, wondering.

When all was still, Zeus, in foul mood, addressed his subordinates. "Gods and goddesses, listen carefully. I won't say this twice." Pausing, he glared at them, daring a reaction. "And if any of you try to thwart my will, I will beat you black and blue and shove you into the darkest levels of Tartarus behind its iron gates."

Trembling, the gods ruffled their embroidered robes, twitching in fear. He continued. "I'm tired of you choosing sides in this Trojan war. This stops now! I'm in charge of this bloody campaign. You know I am the mightiest of all heaven's deities. So, back away."

A profound silence gripped the assembly. Zeus, fuming, tossed a golden chain from heaven's portals, letting it dangle to earth's valley below. "Go ahead, all of you. Grab, hold and pull as hard as you can. You will never drag me from my throne. I am *omnipotent*."

***

I can see Jeremiah scoffing at an earthly Zeus, Nebuchadnezzar, the Babylonian king who besieged Jerusalem. Glancing heavenward from his prison door, Jeremiah praised God almighty who, in His *omnipotence*, also dangled a golden chain earthward, promising loving kindness to thousands and a restoration of Jerusalem.

***

"Ah, Lord God! Behold, You have made the heavens and the earth by Your great power and by Your outstretched arm! Nothing is too difficult for You, who shows loving kindness to thousands..." (Jer. 32:17–18).

***

Today, grab God's golden chain, and feel His love for you.

***

"Prayer is weakness leaning upon omnipotence."
W.S. Boyd

Day 221

***

Orator (AD 69)
Suetonius, *Lives of the Caesars*, 4:53

***

Caligula, one of history's most infamous characters, considered himself a world-class *orator*. He loved to strut back and forth before his captive audience, gesticulating madly, his movements frenzied and erratic.

Suetonius conceded that this hated emperor had a measure of eloquence, especially noted when he pretended to prosecute a defendant in court. His voice would carry to the backbenches with ease. He would often begin with a melodramatic proverb. Staring at his mock audience, he would say with a clarion voice, "Today, I draw the sword which I have forged in my midnight study."

Ever the exhibitionist, Caligula often composed court speeches for both the prosecution and the defense of influential men currently on trial by the Senate. He would then set up a sham court and invite the city's nobles. Thus, while the actual case unfolded in the Senate, his court nearby became a theater for the emperor, who would strut before the audience presenting elaborate arguments. When his eloquence reached its zenith, he would pronounce the verdict, knowing the actual trial proceeded in the authentic courthouse down the street.

***

I see another audience gathering in a distant Greek city. Corinthians, curious about a visiting *orator*, gathered to hear his presentation. When Paul rose to address the working-class Corinthians, he fumbled for his words. Disappointing glances from the audience told the tale. This was no orator. This was no Caligula swinging a midnight sword.

***

"And when I came to you, brethren, I did not come with superiority of speech ... my message and my preaching were not in persuasive words of wisdom..." (1 Cor. 2:1–4).

***

Let your life be your oratory.

***

"Oratory is the art of making a loud noise sound like a deep thought."
Bennett Cerf

Day 222

Origins (65 BC)
Lucretius, *On the Nature of Things*, 2:1055–1060

Lucretius' head was spinning. He couldn't stop seeing atoms whizzing and spinning all over creation. It's all he talked about. He's got an idea that we all came from lifeless atoms. He clapped his hands with glee when he pondered these invisible specks that are the *origins* of life.

Some say his wife, Lucilla, served Lucretius a toxic love potion one evening at dinnertime, and he never really recovered. Perhaps, but his theories of origins do seem to swim in the fumes of an imbalanced mind.

"Life," he used to say, "arose out of the lifeless!"

"Well, how exactly did that happen?" I asked him.

With eyes swollen with lovesickness, he replied. "It's like this. It all happened very slowly over a long, long time. The lifeless matter had to go through many stages before it bloomed. Only rare, unique circumstances could shake the atoms awake, drawing them from lifelessness to life.

"Stare long enough at mundane earth clods, and you will see tiny wriggling worms surface, seeking light and sustenance. It's amazing! One minute the worm is a swirling mass of lifeless atoms, and the next, he plows the dirt like a farmer. So, you see, we have all arisen out of inanimate things."

Lucretius means well, but I think those potions might have fermented his mind. Stroll with me through an ancient mist-covered garden and listen to another voice speak of *origins*.

***

"Then the LORD God formed man of dust from the ground, and breathed into his nostrils the breath of life; and man became a living being" (Gen. 2:7).

***

Today, dig up a worm and wonder.

***

"Pursued by our origins ... we all are."
Emil M. Cioran

Day 223

***

Overboard (1178 BC)
Virgil, *Aeneid*, 5:90–170

***

The shores of Sicily glistened beneath a morning sun. The ninth day of mourning over, Aeneas' sailors trembled with glee at the Trojan Games' commencement. Following a regatta on the first day, other events would soon follow. There would be running, archery, javelin throwing, and rawhide-gloved boxing. A glut of prizes spread out on the beach set dreams flaming.

The regatta began first with four ships quivering at the starting line. Far off in the distance, the surf beat upon a solitary rock projecting above the sea top. Competitors would circle that point and then storm the shore for the grand finish.

Tensions gripped each team as they awaited the trumpet's signal. Finally, the clarion call spat forth, and the ships lifted from the sea. Delirious oars smacked the water, spitting foam, as shore spectators howled for their favorite vessel. Nearing the halfway point, near the boulder slab bedecked with an ilex tree, the Whale and the Centaur battled for the lead.

"Turn to port!" screamed the captain to Menoetes, the coxswain. "Make the oar blades scrape the rock." But Menoetes hesitated and instead pulled starboard. Like a flash, the Scylla slithered into the gap and took the crag. The captain, enraged, flung Menoetes *overboard*, abandoning him to the deep.

***

It's a competitive world today. This game we play daily can often jade our spirit. "Victory at any cost!" can soon become our mantra shouted at daybreak and whispered in night's dreams. Jonah's shipmates, ever competitive, tossed Jonah *overboard*.

***

"So they picked up Jonah, threw him into the sea, and the sea stopped its raging" (Jon. 1:15).

***

Are you bobbing in a restless sea? Take God's hand.

***

"In the world of ruthlessness, I found him humane."
Deepa Srinivas

Day 224

***

Panic (1178 BC)
Virgil, *Aeneid*, 5:600–660

***

Iris, sliding elegantly down her heavenly rainbow, landed greedily on the Sicilian shores, looking for trouble. Aeneas and his noble Trojan vagabonds had landed here with their fleet of swift ships, wet and weary. Seven long years had passed since the burning of Troy, their beloved homeland. Now, after skimming endlessly upon the dark seas, they hugged the land. Once disembarked, the restless immigrants strolled restlessly over the emerald shore, longing for play.

Aeneas announced the games would begin on the morrow after sacrifices and worship to the gods. The following day, as the athletic contests sparked joyful challenges, many Trojan ladies remained behind at the ships where they brooded. It was here that Iris came, mumbling discordant lines about roaming endless seas. "Why not settle here? Burn the ships and make this your home," she whispered. Snatching a firebrand from the coals, Iris hurled it at the nearest boat.

Her words roused fresh visions of a new Troy. Rushing to gather twigs, greenery, and torches, the women torched the ships. The fire galloped over the thwarts, the oars, and the poops of painted pinewood until the flames licked the sky, signaling disaster.

The men raced pell-mell over the dunes to the shoreline in full *panic*. Rending their garments, they prayed to the gods for mercy while the women trembled in the bushes.

***

Unwanted fires seem to breed along our daily journeys. Quench one, and three more erupt. But *panic* fans faithlessness. Ask Joshua as he stared at unknown obstacles across the Jordan.

***

"Be strong and courageous! Do not panic or be dismayed, for the LORD your God is with you wherever you go" (Josh. 1:9).

***

Don't panic. The swift ships will sail again.

***

"He who is not every day conquering some fear has not learned the secret of life."
Ralph Waldo Emerson

Day 225

***

Paradise (1177 BC)
Virgil, *Aeneid*, 8:300–350

***

As eventide crept over the Latium hills, Evander, Rome's king, strolled home from Hercules' festival with Aeneas, leaving the waning fires behind. The sacred rites drifted into time's memories as the king talked freely about the *paradise* this Roman citadel once knew.

"There was a time long past," said the king, "when Saturn bolted from Olympus, exiled by powerful Jove. Lost and seeking refuge, these hills and valleys rich with promise drew him into its graces. He smiled as he observed men and women living off nature's vegetation. No one knew how to plow or toil beneath a glaring sun. Instead, they hunted for dinner's fare and suckled fruit from the meadow trees."

After walking in silence, Evander continued reminiscing with Aeneas, eager to learn. "Saturn united these intractable wayfarers, gave them laws, and passed on a deeper understanding of life's joys. He called this place Latium and ushered in a golden age. Absent were the rumblings of war and hostile drums. Everyone lived in harmony."

When the men reached Evander's humble palace, he urged Aeneas to enter, as Hercules once did. As evening settled, he gave his guest a couch of leaves to lie upon with a Libyan bear skin coverlet for comfort.

***

King Evander shared his peaceful reverie as war brewed about him. The image of *paradise* still stirred him, and he shared it with his guest. Even in today's turbulent times, you can find paradise walking daily with God.

***

"God saw all that He had made, and behold, it was very good. And there was evening and there was morning, the sixth day" (Gen. 1:31).

***

Look beyond your personal wars. See the garden.

***

"Paradise is always where love dwells."
Jean Paul Richter

Day 226

***

Paralysis (AD 60)
Tacitus, *Annals of Imperial Rome*, 14:30

***

The flat-bottomed Roman war boats smacked rough waves as they lunged methodically for Mona Island, north of Wales. Suetonius, the freshly minted governor of Britain, seeking fame and desperate to bolster his military reputation, saw the island as a bold first step. Alongside the naval flotilla came the cavalry swimming in deep water beside their horses.

A dense armed mass of frenzied islanders lined the foggy shore, waiting. Black-robed women with disheveled hair drifting in the breeze like Furies made threatening gestures toward the Romans. Each held a torch that swung like battle-tested swords, spitting light, daring the soldiers to make a final lunge through the surf. Close by stood the long-robed Druid men with their hands raised toward heaven, their tangled imprecations calling for blood.

A battalion of Roman soldiers paused at the water's edge, staring with a superstitious chill, *paralyzed*. They could neither flee into the strait nor press forward. They stood locked in a soggy formation, aghast at the witches' hive they had pricked. It was only with the greatest difficulty that they broke the spell and surged forward.

***

There are black days of *paralysis* that rise in mockery, keeping us off balance. "Is this happening to me?" you ask, bewildered as you stand lock-kneed in life's turbulent surf. John had such a moment. Struck with an apparition of heavenly brilliance, he too fell to the ground in utter paralysis, overcome and unable to breathe.

***

"His face was like the sun shining in its strength. When I saw Him, I fell at His feet like a dead man" (Rev. 1:16–17).

***

Break your paralysis today. Plunge through the surf and dominate.

***

"Nothing will ever be attempted if all possible objections must first be overcome."
Samuel Johnson

Day 227

Parenting (AD 110)
Juvenal, *Satires*, 14: 1–74

***

Juvenal offers four wicked portraits of *parenting*, haunting images that provide our modern eyes with valuable glimpses into ancient homes. Juvenal believed every child deserved the greatest respect during the impressionable early years.

First, he bids us peer through a shameless cottage window on an unnamed Roman street. A father bends low, his hand shaking a small, cylindrical dice box. A midnight candle dances on a table as several local miscreants place their bets. After a frantic prayer, the dice clatter on the tiled floor as a young son watches, bewitched, behind a curtain.

Next, we visit a kitchen where a gluttonous old man feverishly peels delicate truffles and seasoned mushrooms. Like a maestro, he turns to stir gravy destined for the delicate beccaficos and orders his young son to put away his books and hurry with the plates.

Then, in a home down the street, several siblings watch in horror as a poor slave cowers on the floor. A few stolen towels, cheaply woven and worthless, demand justice. The father, whistling, pulls a hissing brand from a kettle and shoves the glowing metal upon the slave's flesh. The children run from the screams, laughing.

In our final portrait, we hear a mother's bedtime whispers to her daughters. She gloats over countless sexual escapades before kissing them goodnight.

***

"Shun such damnable deeds or our children will repeat these crimes," said Juvenal, disgusted. This blunt truth reminds us of Solomon's *parental* advice:

***

"Hear my son, your father's instruction and do not forsake your mother's teaching; indeed, they are a graceful wreath to your head and ornaments about your neck" (Prov. 1:8–9).

***

Make positive memories tonight.

***

"Don't worry that children never listen to you; worry that they are always watching you."
Robert Fulghum

Day 228

Partings (1184 BC)
Homer, *Iliad*, 6:490–520

***

Hector, on a brief respite from battle, raced to find his wife. The home hallways and backrooms were silent but for the maids' gentle weeping. Delirious with fear, haunted by her scent lingering in the shadows, he begged the slaves for guidance. "Have you seen Andromache? Did she flee to her sisters or perhaps the temple? I must find her!"

His housekeeper answered gravely. "Sir, she left for the city walls where she could search for you in the dust of combat."

Hector hastened down side streets toward the Scaean gates. Andromache, the Theban princess, spotted him and came running toward her husband. Behind, bobbing in the nurse's arms, Hector spotted his darling baby boy, the one named Scamandrius, but called Little King by the locals.

The two embraced without words beneath the great walls, their love smothered by tears and war's realities. Hector smiled as the frightened boy stared at his father's mighty horsehair plume that nodded fiercely from his helmet.

Andromache's desperate pleas, muffled upon his chest, begged him to stay. "You're all I have," she cried. "Achilles killed my father and brothers. I have nothing but you."

Hector, weeping, took off his helmet, kissed the baby, and with sorrowful *parting*, trudged off to battle, leaving behind a trail of tears.

***

The ties that bind are often severed. Ships leave to somber farewells; failed relationships sever bonds fused with sacred memories. *Partings* are always difficult. Ask David and Jonathan:

***

"When the lad was gone, David rose from the south side and fell on his face to the ground, and bowed three times. And they kissed each other and wept together, but David wept the more" (1 Sam. 20:41).

***

God, ever with you, sees your sorrowful parting.

***

"Parting is such sweet sorrow."
William Shakespeare

Day 229

***

Passion (401 BC)
Xenophon, *Anabasis*, 2:6

***

Clearchus, that high-spirited general, was on the run. The Spartan ephors had ordered him to return home and pursue peace. Clearchus, however, passionate about war and adventure, ignored his summons and jumped a ship from Corinth to the Hellespont, looking for a battle. Ignoring the death sentence on his head posted by the Spartan authorities, he quickly found himself cozying up with Cyrus, the Persian prince who was gathering an army.

Cyrus looked the renegade over and saw war's *passion* in his eyes. "Just the man I need," he thought. When Clearchus agreed enthusiastically to join Cyrus' march against the Persian king, Cyrus handed him bags of Persian gold—10,000 darics worth millions today.

Xenophon tells us that Clearchus could have retired and lived in luxury on this loot. Instead, he chose war. He could have indulged every fancy in endless pleasure, but he preferred the toils of endless battles, swaggering about in distant lands.

"He loved war more than anyone I have ever known," said Xenophon. "Oh, and by the way, the Persian king, Artaxerxes II, beheaded Clearchus at fifty."

***

I remember St. Francis, who abandoned his life of luxury and pleasure as a youth, preferring to wander as a peace-loving

457

beggar, *passionately* searching for truth as did St. Paul. It is compelling to contrast the lives of these ancient men: Clearchus loved war, while Paul and St. Francis loved God.

***

"Indeed, I count everything as loss because of the surpassing worth of knowing Christ Jesus my Lord. For his sake I have suffered the loss of all things and count them as rubbish" (Phil 3:8–10).

***

Find your passion. Find your life.

***

"The most powerful weapon on earth is the human soul on fire."
Ferdinand Foch

Day 230

***

Peace (425 BC)
Aristophanes, *Acharnians*, 1040–1070

***

It was sleight of hand, unseen by roving eyes. Dicaeopolis, desperate for peace among endless Greek wars with Sparta, gestured for Amphitheus, his friend. Handing him a secret note cloaked in mystery, he whispered, "Here's a bag of money. Take this letter to Sparta and ask them to craft a private *peace* just for my family and me."

As weeks passed, Dicaeopolis began to prosper as merchants flocked to and from his humble country abode. All the delicacies from forbidden markets flowed into his little farm. He planted a row of delicate vines and some fig plants next to them. A border of tempting olive trees marked his garden.

One evening as he savored peace's pleasantries, a stranger banged on his door.

"Who is it?"

"I'm the groomsman from a wedding banquet across town."

"What do you want?" asked Dicaeopolis impatiently.

"Could you please send my master one ounce of Peace?"

"I won't do it, not for a million dollars!" screamed Dicaeopolis, slamming the door.

Another knock came, this time from a bridesmaid. She whispered in Dicaeopolis' ear, making him laugh. "Okay. Anything to help a lady. Bring your myrrh box and hold it carefully. I will pour you a small portion of peace. Make sure you rub it every night upon your husband, who is considering war's glories."

***

Peace is a commodity meant for sharing. Lock it away, and it will search for the light where it thrives. Share peace with those around you. Pour it into empty myrrh boxes and count your blessings. Jesus did:

***

"Peace I leave with you; My peace I give to you; not as the world gives do I give to you" (Jn. 14:27).

***

Someone's knocking at your door. Bring your peace.

***

"Peace begins with a smile."
Albert Einstein

Day 231

***

Perfume (AD 60)
Petronius, *The Satyricon*, 5:70

***

The banquet skipped forward merrily, with guests indulging in an endless feast worthy of the gods. Trimalchio, the former slave and host turned multi-millionaire, loitered pleasantly in the grand landscape. "How far I have come," he thought. "How far!"

Without warning, he clapped his hands, startling everyone, who ceased their gluttony temporarily and gazed at the miracle man. The dining hall seemed hung in exotic suspension. Trimalchio, without a word, clapped again. A bevy of young slaves waltzed in, their long locks drifting on a window breeze gracefully salted by the distant sea. Each servant selected one guest and genuflected before them, displaying an obeisance reserved for royalty.

The visitors stared down with unreserved glee. The servants selected summer garlands imbued with variegated fragrances from distant Elysian Fields. Little by little, they festooned the noble patrons' legs with rose petals from heaven. Then each slave pulled a small silver bowl from a floating table filled with an exquisitely aromatic *perfume*. Their fingers dripping with scented liquid, they caressed the feet of the astonished guests. When finished, they poured any remaining perfume into oil lamps and even dribbled some into wine bowls that littered the table.

***

Look there! I see a small home nestled on Bethany's hillside near the Mt. of Olives. Within its cozy folds, a small intimate dinner is underway. The mood is quietly festive, the food simple but fresh, *perfume* flowing freely.

***

"Mary then took a pound of very costly perfume of pure nard, and anointed the feet of Jesus and wiped His feet with her hair, and the house was filled with the fragrance of the perfume" (Jn. 12:3).

***

Pause today and perfume the feet of the Savior.

***

"Love is bending down to wash another's feet."
Andrew Peterson

Day 232

***

Perspectives (423 BC)
Aristophanes, *Clouds*, 180–240

***

The old man, Strepsiades, banged and kicked at the schoolhouse door. It was his last hope. If his worthless racetrack-gambling son didn't learn an honest trade, he would have to go back to school, bad memory and all. Buried in debts, he had to find a way. Creditors had his number.

Bent and forlorn, he banged on the door, praying for a miracle. "Maybe Socrates can teach me to be a smooth talker. Then I'll go to court and win all my cases against these bill collectors."

Pushing his way past the doorkeeper, Strepsiades saw the school floor littered with students in grotesque poses. "What is this?" he asked.

"They're studying," said a pupil. "Those with their faces buried in the dirt are sniffing out hell's mysteries while others explore the stars."

Amazed, the old man saw legs dangling in a basket from the ceiling. "Who are you, and what are you doing up there?"

Socrates peered down from the basket, irritated. "I'm walking on air and contemplating the sun."

"Why not just come down here and do it?" asked a bewildered Strepsiades.

"It's all about *perspective*," replied Socrates. "My head spins up here, and I make amazing discoveries."

***

Nine to five lifestyles make deep ruts. Blinders shut out the most promising views of life, leaving us stuttering the same worn phrases. Maybe a lofty basket, some new *perspective*, might help. Jesus tried this approach when he opted to don the form of a slave:

***

"but emptied Himself taking the form of a bond-servant, and being made in the likeness of men." (Phil. 2:7).

***

Walmart's got a sale on baskets. Sale ends today.

***

"Often it isn't the mountains ahead that wear you out, it's the little pebble in your shoe."
Muhammad Ali

Day 233

Persuasion (1184 BC)
Homer, *Iliad*, 4:70–130

***

Athene, disguised as a spearman, walked urgently through the Trojan ranks, searching for Pandarus, the great archer. Intent on mucking up the fragile truce between Troy and Greece, she spotted him milling about with the Trojan heroes. Pulling him aside, she whispered with *persuasive* sighs. "I can make you a Trojan hero greater than all if you do one simple task."

He listened, intrigued, his bow fingers twitching. "Go ahead," he replied, "I'm listening."

With a sly smile, Athene continued. "Take your mighty bow and sling an arrow at Menelaus. If you kill him, the Trojans will pour honors upon you, and Paris will make you rich."

Pandarus, his fool's heart easily persuaded, agreed. He took his bow, a gift from Apollo, and laid it on the ground. Made from ibex horns sixteen palms long, its gold-tipped ends sparkled, eager for action. Soldiers gathered, placing their shields protectively about him. Taking a virgin arrow from the quiver, he notched it and pulled the bow back to its breaking point. With a twang, he sent it singing toward Menelaus, who, wounded and bleeding, survived.

***

We all have fickle hearts, prone to persuasion. Yield easily, and rippling regrets will likely haunt you with its poisoned arrows.

I am reminded of another whispering incident when the serpent *persuaded* Eve to eat forbidden fruit.

***

"When the woman saw that the tree was good for food, and that it was a delight to the eyes, and that the tree was desirable to make one wise, she took from its fruit and ate; and she gave also to her husband with her, and he ate" (Gen. 3:6).

***

Put your bow down; Resist persuasion's tickle.

***

"The most important persuasion tool you have in your entire arsenal is integrity."
Zig Ziglar

Day 234

***

Petition (58 BC)
Caesar, *The Gallic War*, 1:20

***

Diviciacus, the Druid, stood forlornly in Caesar's war tent. Caesar, agitated, paced back and forth before this trusted confidant whose brother, Dumnorix, was secretly plotting against the Romans. "You know what he's doing, don't you? He's stirring up the tribes, building a dark hidden conspiracy against me, Caesar!"

Diviciacus kept his eyes lowered, his face shamed. Caesar continued. "I just left an assembly of Gaul's top leaders. They smell a rat here, and they want your traitorous brother punished. I told them I would take care of it!"

Diviciacus slowly raised his head, partially concealed by the long warlocks draping his shoulders. Tears began to flow, and before words could come, he stepped forward and embraced Caesar. Speaking softly into the general's ear, he began pleading for Dumnorix's life. "I know he is guilty. No one feels this betrayal more than I do. I was the one who helped him rise through the ranks. He turned against me as his power grew, but I couldn't bear to see him killed. He's my brother, and I love him still."

Overcome by this warrior's *petitions*, Caesar took his hand and begged him to be silent. "No more tears, my friend. I will deal gently with him for your sake."

***

Caring for others lifts us all to humanity's highest spheres. I hear the general's empathy for Diviciacus in Stephen's *petitions* as he fell beneath a barrage of stones:

***

"They went on stoning Stephen as he called on the Lord and said, 'Lord, receive my spirit!' Then falling on his knees, he cried out with a loud voice, 'Lord, do not hold this sin against them!'" (Acts 7:59–60).

***

Take someone's bereaved hand today and plead.

***

"Is prayer your steering wheel or your spare tire?"
Corrie ten Boom

Day 235

Phantoms (1177 BC)
Virgil, *Aeneid*, 10:630–670

***

Toying with death's rigid requirements, Juno received frail permission from her husband, Jupiter, who told her, frowning: "You may rescue Turnus from the battlefield for a little while. Just a little while, mind you," he said sternly. Savoring her victory, she quickly went to work.

Fashioning an apparition from thin dreams, she dressed it in Aeneas' war costume. She gave it an exquisite imitation shield and plumed helmet, exact copies of Aeneas' battle panoply. She made it walk with the general's gait and shaped the wraith's voice to mimic Troy's hero. Then she spun the *phantom* out onto the battlefield beneath the ramparts by the Tiber.

When Turnus, that brutish Trojan enemy, came stalking for prey seeking Aeneas' blood, the apparition screamed abuses, luring him into its web. Turnus hurled his spear at the ghost. Dancing past the whirling projectile, the wraith turned and ran for the shore, where a ship's bow bobbed innocently.

"Why do you flee from me?" shouted Turnus, his temper flaring. "I have a gift for you. Six feet of our Latin land!" He laughed as the cowardly specter leaped aboard the ship. Turnus scrambled aboard, his thirsty sword raised for blood. Then, with silent precision, Juno cut the cables and pulled the vessel off into the mists of the open sea.

***

Phantoms crisscross our paths daily, spinning tall tales and endless lies, baiting us to follow. Many of us go astray and drift endlessly on an apparition's journey to nowhere. The disciples, stuck in nadir's trough, spotted a phantom and weighed their choices:

***

"When the disciples saw Him walking on the sea, they were terrified, and said, 'It is a ghost!'" (Matt. 14:26).

***

Deception abounds. Choose your phantoms carefully.

***

"It is far harder to kill a phantom than a reality."
Virginia Woolf

Day 236

***

Philosophies (58 BC)
Caesar, *Gallic Wars*, 6:14–15

***

Every day we hear the phrase "fake news," and we have learned
to doubt everything in our modern society. When we look back
to the Druids, who lived in ancient Britain, we glimpse strange
philosophies that guided thousands.

Caesar wrote about this in his Gallic Wars. He said that the
Druids were the respected priests of the people. They gathered
once a year in central Gaul in a consecrated conclave and heard
disputes from the people. These Druids did not believe in war
and were exempt from war taxes. Parents sent their children
to learn in these academies where they had to memorize their
religious beliefs since the Druids did not inscribe them in books.
Initiates into this secretive society often needed twenty years to
master the core doctrines.

One of their cardinal tenets was reincarnation. Caesar
explained it this way:

"This is one of their central teachings since they believe that
souls pass after death from one body to another." As a result,
Druids didn't fear death and exhibited great valor in battle. They
also taught theories about the motion of stars, earth's origins,
nature's mysteries, and the majesty of the immortal gods.

***

Paul saw similar pagan *philosophies* creeping into the new
congregation at Colossi. Some congregants got caught up in

rules and a false asceticism similar to what the cynics and stoics taught. But Paul believed in joyous freedom that came from the Spirit of God:

***

"See to it that no one takes you captive through philosophy and empty deception, according to the tradition of men ... such as, 'do not handle, do not taste, do not touch!'" (Col. 2:8, 21).

***

Just live simply and joyfully in the Spirit.

***

"The worst of all deceptions is self-deception."
Plato

Day 237

***

Pity (1177 BC)
Virgil, *Aeneid*, 10:800–840

***

Young Lausus stepped boldly from the battlefield's shadows. Facing Aeneas, the veteran Trojan warrior, Lausus blocked, sword for sword, Aeneas' death dance as he sought to kill the boy's despotic father, King Mezentius. Lausus, though inexperienced, nonetheless drew cheers from his surprised comrades, who watched in awe as the crippled Mezentius dragged himself, bleeding, to safety. Lausus, loving the moment, taunted Aeneas as a thousand arrows hailed down upon the Trojan general.

Aeneas crouched beneath his shield as a thunderstorm of enemy missiles clouded the sky. Waiting for the blizzard of war to lessen, Aeneas toyed with the brazen youngster. "Boy, you're too young for this battle. Why do you tempt fate? Go home to Momma." But Lausus gained courage and cursed his foe.

Aeneas, fueled by contempt, twirled his sword as the Fate-spinners spun the boy's last threads of life through their fingers. Then, lunging at the toy soldier, Aeneas rammed his sword up to the hilt into the boy's chest. The lad's thin shield, inadequate for such affairs, yielded, and blood covered the golden-threaded tunic woven by his mother.

But after the young warrior collapsed into death's arms, Aeneas felt a sudden *pity* for Lausus. Aeneas sighed deeply, respecting Lausus' courage. Rather than stripping the armor, he lifted the boy in his arms and handed him to his comrades for burial.

***

Pity, genuinely offered, is the lubricant of our souls. Without it, we calcify and move with a wooden gait through life's self-centered rituals. Jesus taught us this virtue over and over. He watched one day as a mother wept behind her only son's coffin.

***

"When the Lord saw her, He felt compassion for her, and said to her, 'Do not weep'" (Lk. 7:13).

***

Find the notes for pity's song today.

***

"Try to be a rainbow in someone else's cloud."
Maya Angelou

Day 238

Pleading (1184 BC)
Homer, *Iliad*, 16:1–100

***

It was midnight in the Achaeans' hearts as the gloom of imminent defeat drifted along Troy's dusky seashore. Ajax, the mighty Greek warrior, did his best to lift morale as he leaped from stern to stern among the packed fleet, stirring the melancholy soldiers to fight on with courage. But even his best efforts dissipated beneath the relentless Trojan sallies.

When Patroclus felt the desperation among the besieged ships, he hurried to Achilles' tent. With tearful eyes, he *pleaded* for help. Lost for words, he merely stood before the mighty warrior and wept, his tears falling like a crystal stream over a wilderness precipice.

Achilles feeling deep grief for his life-long friend, roused himself from the couch where he lay in stubborn pride. "Why are you crying like a silly girl tugging on her mother's skirts? Tell me your heart and any late-breaking news from the battlefield."

"I weep," said Patroclus, "for the unfolding tragedy among our ships. Our best soldiers lie wounded or dead." He hesitated, turning away, but then continued. "You are so pitiless. Don't you care anymore? You could at least give me your armor to wear; the enemy might think I am mighty Achilles in the battle."

***

Pleading, life's emotional adrenalin, lives in our tears for others. Pleadings stir the humanity within us and focuses our hearts on others. Listen in Gethsemane's night air, and you can still hear its echo:

***

"And He went a little beyond them, and fell on His face and prayed, saying, 'My Father, if it is possible, let this cup pass from Me'" (Matt. 26:39).

***

Plead your cause today before a loving heavenly Father.

***

"Every great movement of God can be traced to a kneeling figure."
D.L. Moody.

Day 239

***

Pleasures (AD 110)
Juvenal, *Satires*, 11:180–208

***

One by one, the invited men took their places around Juvenal's rustic dinner table. Nothing fancy here. Just simple *pleasures*.

Before the meal began, he rose and spoke. "I want all of you to forget that hectic world out there. It's time for a day of rest. Let me lay down a few rules for our evening of bucolic pleasure.

"**Number one:** Let's not talk about money at all. You know very well what it does to your soul. So, no bragging about bank accounts this evening or fulminating over pending foreclosures.

"**Number two:** I want you to forget your marriage problems. So what if your wife is slipping out of the house at midnight. We won't worry about all that around this table.

"**Number three:** No grumbling about the servants. I know they are constantly breaking and losing things. But this evening, we want to think of life's happy moments.

"**Number 4:** All your thankless associates at work and in the neighborhood who don't appreciate you—well, let's forget them too."

Juvenal offered a toast for life's joys. The glasses clinked, and everyone sipped their chilled wine. Then the festivities began on a light note. "I hear the Greens won at the chariot races in Rome," said Juvenal, his eyes sparkling. Everyone smiled.

***

I think Mary would have fit in with the boys here. As Jesus talked in her little cottage in Bethany, Mary sat immersed in Jesus' glow savoring the *pleasures* of His presence. Martha, however, missed the point.

***

"Martha, Martha, you are worried and bothered about so many things; but only one thing is necessary..." (Lk. 10:41–42).

***

Today, savor life's daily pleasures.

***

"That man is rich whose pleasures are the cheapest."
Henry David Thoreau

Day 240

Plunging (AD 100)
Juvenal, *Satire*, 12

***

The little sailboat burned like a match, bobbing on the sea with its sails on fire. The Tyrrhenian lighthouse was nowhere in view. All was lost. The sky throbbed with anguish, belching out lightning bolts, heaving waves ten feet tall. Catullus said his last windy prayers and then got to work. "Throw my stuff overboard, every bit of it!" he shouted to the small crew of terrified sailors.

Soon, the purple garments fit for a king were flung overboard along with the silver plate and priceless wine bowls. They all *plunged* like weights. As fast as they could gather valuables, they tossed them seaward: baskets from Gaul, dishes by the thousands, and engraved goblets that sovereigns had once held in their jeweled hands.

Still, the boat wallowed in danger. "We've got to lighten it more," screamed Catullus. "Cut down the mast!"

With nothing left to jettison, Catullus huddled in the bow with only three-inch planking beneath him and a sputtering death. But then, a miracle. The sea grew calm, and a light wind shoved the splintered craft into the harbor.

***

Paul felt the same terror at sea as his ship, including 276 passengers and crew, faced the frothy Adriatic Sea for 14 days, with death imminent at each moment. He stood in the boat's bow with sea spray blasting his face and still prayed with confidence.

Perhaps today, you feel as if you're *plunging*. Hope seems beyond the horizon, and you can't see the lighthouse through the fog.

***

"The next day as we were being violently storm-tossed, they began to jettison the cargo..." (Acts 27:18).

***

You're sinking but the lighthouse *is* near.

***

"Life isn't about waiting for the storm to pass. It's about learning to dance in the rain."
Anonymous

Day 241

Poison (AD 41)
Suetonius, *Lives of the Caesars*, 4:46

***

Caligula, bleary-eyed and restless, sat alone at his palace desk, writing.

The sleepless city beneath the Palatine Hill likewise yawned and creaked on through the midnight hour, celebrating life's miseries at local taverns. The emperor, summoning evil from the moon, selected a royal pen and made new entries into his death ledgers. Determined to slaughter the most distinguished senators and equites, he meticulously scrawled their names upon the parchment. Images of these detested faces hovered before him in the candle's glow. "All of them will die," he muttered as his pen hurried on its inky death trail. "None will live," he whispered to no one. "They will all die!"

Finished, finally, with his murderous intents, he tucked these two notebooks, *Dagger and Sword*, back into their hidden space beside a huge chest filled with *poisons*, an array of viperous concoctions potent enough to kill thousands.

It was Claudius who found this witchy chest and the notebooks. After Caligula's murder, his secret intentions shocked the new emperor with their breathtaking cruelty. Claudius ordered the poisonous crate to be thrown into the sea. Witnesses tell of beached and bloated fish by the score littering the beaches the following morning.

***

James can only sigh at the *poisonous* possibilities buried within all of us. Caligula's chest of toxins is a restless evil stirring earth's residents, and only by God's grace can the lid be closed. Burn your *Dagger and Swords* notes and cling to heaven's joy.

***

"But no one can tame the tongue; it is a restless evil and full of deadly poison" (Jas. 3:8).

***

Burn the chest! Ban all poisons from your life.

***

"We drink the poison our minds pour for us and wonder why we feel so sick."
Atticus

Day 242

Portrait (459 BC)
Pausanius, *Description of Greece*, 1:2

Pausanias, our ancient travel guide, only said it in passing.

Gazing at the Parthenon, that stately temple revered by the world, he paused and sighed. "There's an old portrait of poor Themistocles hanging somewhere in those dark corridors. Such a pathetic end for so great a general," he said to the tourists gathered near him. "He saved Athens from the Persians, but in the end, he got arrogant, and his people ran him out of the city."

One listener spoke up. "Who put the *portrait* there?"

"His loving children," he said. Then, with a twirl of his fingers in the hallowed air, he was on to other ancient vistas in the city.

But that image of parental reverence echoes in my mind. I can see the disgraced general's kids walking with solemn grace up the steep ascent, past gawking eyes, placing the portrait on a prominent wall that no eye could avoid. Once revered by all the citizens of Athens, Themistocles had fled to Magnesia, where he died by sipping a cup of poison. But in this single, loving act, his children erased the shame.

In a strange twist, it was the enemies of Jesus who painted a living *portrait* of the Savior. John, our guide, points to the hill called Golgotha, where the Roman soldiers crucified the Son of God. That portrait caught the world's attention, who see at Golgotha the singular act of unequaled love.

***

"There they crucified Him, and with Him two other men, one on either side, and Jesus in between" (Jn. 19:18).

***

Let's weep and then rejoice over the portrait.

***

"Are we to paint what's on the face, what's inside the face, or what's behind it?"
Pablo Picasso

Day 243

***

Possessed (1177 BC)
Virgil, *Aeneid*, 7:350–450

***

Allecto, the snake-infested Fury from the underworld, changed forms. Tucking vipers under an olive-wreathed chaplet, she assumed the shape of an old crone, a priestess of peace, her white hair drizzling in disarray over her wrinkled brow. Allecto, known for explosive anger, pasted a thin, deceptive smile upon her mouth and slithered unannounced to the bedside of Turnus, king of Ardea, a seaside town south of Rome.

The gods had canceled his pending wedding with the local king's daughter favoring Aeneas, the Trojan prince. Allecto, infuriated over this slight, sought to rouse the king and foment war upon the Trojan drifters. Slipping to his bedside, she spoke sweet words of revenge, urging him to rise and retaliate.

Waking from his sleep, Turnus resisted the witch, belittling her. "You've made all this up, lady. Go back to your temple! Leave warfare to men."

Allecto exploded with rage at these impudent words. Standing tall with eyes boiling and snake horns wriggling on her head, she hurled a blazing torch at him, which buried itself deep within his heart, *possessing* him. Shaking with a sudden palsy, the king bolted to his feet, his nightclothes sweat-drenched. Racing through palace corridors, he scoured the corners for his shield and sword, ordering his commander to gather the army.

***

Possession has many faces, each one with endless possibilities. Turnus, possessed with fresh rage, now lived for war. But Peter, that New Testament sage, watched it spread unfettered in a small upper room in Jerusalem.

***

"And suddenly there came from heaven a noise like a violent rushing wind and it filled the whole house where they were sitting" (Acts 2:2).

***

Ride possession's winds to new hopeful heights today.

***

"The purpose of art is washing the dust of daily life off our souls."
Pablo Picasso

Day 244

Potential (1184 BC)
Homer, *Iliad*, 18:368–427

***

Thetis, goddess of the silver feet, strode gracefully toward the Olympic palace where Hephaestus lived. Lame from early life, Hephaestus, whose life was a tragedy ever-unfolding, was toiling at the bellows making twenty tripods that would grace the outer walls of his heavenly abode. He had just finished setting the golden wheels under them, so they could go and come on their own, mechanical wonders, inexplicable to mortals, when she spotted him.

She watched from a distance as he finished hammering the rivets of the tripod's ears. Sighing, Thetis remembered the years she had spent with him in a cave by the ocean's edge. Rejected and hurled from heaven's halls by his mother, intolerant of the blacksmith's lame foot, he had fallen to this hidden cave. There to the sweet sounds of ocean spray, Thetis had nurtured him and whispered daily of his great *potential*. He repaid her by making beautiful spiral armlets, cups, and chains to grace her neck.

Slipping away quietly, not wanting to disturb his work, Thetis wound her way to the palace door where she called for Charis of the graceful head-dress, Hephaestus' wife. Thrilled at this unexpected visit, Charis led the goddess to a richly decorated seat inlaid with silver. Propping her silver-footed shoes upon a footstool, the ladies chatted about the past.

***

Follow Hephaestus' dragging footprints into the cave, where he lies downhearted. It is here you will feel the pulse of your *potential*, for surely the possibilities for your life are endless. So it was for the teenager Uzziah:

***

"And all the people of Judah took Uzziah who was sixteen years old, and made him king..." (2 Chron. 26:1).

***

Look through your disability, and see endless potential.

***

"The flower that blooms in adversity is the most rare and beautiful of all."
Mu

Day 245

***

Pressure (375 BC)
Plato, *Republic*, 1:350–351

***

Thrasymachus paced brashly back and forth before Socrates as if he were toying with a ladybug. "Criminals always win," he said impudently. "The honest guy is nothing but a loser. In a business partnership, the cheater walks away with the profits. He's smarter than the honorable man. And what about taxes? The noble sucker pays the most, not the sleazy fellow hiding his money." Back and forth, strutting like a mob boss, Thrasymachus made his points one by one to a hesitant Socrates.

Having made his brutal ethics known to spectators lingering in the room, Thrasymachus hurriedly prepared to leave. But Socrates urged him to stay a little longer. "I don't think you're right about all of this. Would you mind if I just asked a few questions?"

"Well, uh, sure, but I'm in a hurry." A thin line of sweat creased his brow.

"Okay. I won't keep you long," said Socrates. He then chipped away at the arguments, pulling concessions like rotten teeth bit by bit. Pacing calmly before the now trembling defendant, the case for truth and justice began to blossom, its verdant tendrils climbing vine-like through the mob boss's psyche.

Thrasymachus, buckling under the *pressure*, wiped his brow. Sweat poured from his face in torrents, and then an unusual thing happened: the defendant began blushing as if his face had pitched a white flag on a losing battlefield.

***

Pressure points on life's path are inescapable. Remember the principal calling your name over the intercom? Moses felt the pressure, too, as the Pharaoh's 600 chariots chased him down. But Moses knew this singular truth:

***

"The LORD will fight for you while you keep silent" (Ex. 14:14).

***

Evade the pressure in inspired silence.

***

"Courage is grace under pressure."
Ernest Hemmingway

Day 246

Pretense (AD 400)
Avianus, *Fables*, 5.

***

A disillusioned donkey shuffled miserably through the hot Saharan sand avoiding his farm work. Leaning lazily against a scraggly cork tree, he imagined a different life. Feeling the cool breezes of the faraway Atlas Mountains, he muttered wistfully, "I could be so much more than a mule."

It was then that he spotted a Gaetulian lion's skin abandoned at the farm's edge. With exhilaration, he wrapped himself in the lion's robe and roared. Prancing about beneath the cork limbs, splendid courage spread through his soul like vineyard tendrils enveloping a supporting fence. "Look at me," he exclaimed. "Now I am somebody!"

The *pretense* firmly established, he strode off to a nearby pasture where quiet sheep lolled about in thick grasses. Bellowing with African ferocity, he sent the sheep and other cattle scurrying for their lives. The confusion and horrific bleating alerted the farmer, who came running. Seeing his delinquent mule racing about stirring up trouble, he yanked off the silly disguise, tied him with cords, and thrashed the fool violently. "You don't trick me," he said, scolding. "You'll always be just a donkey."

***

Discontent is often a self-imposed exile. We hide behind insecurities and half-truths, having never discovered our actual value. If only the donkey could have seen how much the farm depended upon his strength and loyalty.

Adam and Eve once wore disguises. Clothed in *pretense*, they were afraid to face God honestly.

***

"Then the eyes of both of them were opened, and they knew that they were naked; and they sewed fig leaves together and made themselves loin coverings" (Gen. 3:7).

***

Ditch the lion suit. Find your true value today.

***

"No one can long hide behind a mask; the pretense soon lapses into the true character."
Seneca

Day 247

Privilege (AD 51)
Tacitus, *The Annals of Imperial Rome*, 12:41

***

Agrippina's ornate carriage clattered upon the Sacra Via that led past the Forum in Rome's Capitol. Owning such a carriage was an honor rarely bestowed on any citizen. However, Agrippina, the empress of Rome, was a rising star in the glittering city, and the constellations were in her favor.

Wife to Claudius, she used her influence to amass unprecedented power. It was just one year earlier that her husband had named an entire town, Agrippinensis, after her. Now, as she entered the most powerful city in the world, she did so in style, as her mother by the same name once did similarly.

When she made her appearance, people stopped everything to stare. Drawn by a pair of mules, the cart, richly adorned with carved panels on the doors and caryatides at the four corners, astounded the commoners and nobility. Customarily reserved for priests and sacred emblems, this carpentum glowed with the presence of a determined woman who would stop at nothing to amass power and wealth. Reverential awe swept the narrow streets as the *privileged* cart rumbled by on its bumpy, wooden wheels.

***

Jesus did not request a carriage. He, too, prepared to enter a great city, but He did not demand such *privileges*. He would shelter within the closed doors of humble villagers who also

escorted Him down Bethany's grand slopes toward the Via
Dolorosa. He waved to crowds atop a simple colt which ambled
over humble peasants' garments tossed upon the road.

***

"They brought it to Jesus, and they threw their coats on the colt
and put Jesus on it" (Lk. 19:35).

***

Step out of your carriage today. Walk humbly with Jesus.

***

"What separates privilege from entitlement is gratitude."
Brené Brown

Day 248

***

Procession (AD 59)
Tacitus, *Annals of Imperial Rome*, 14:10

***

Nero lingered in the Campanian cities after Agrippina's murder. The seacoast seemed to weep turquoise tears beneath a wailing moon as Nero futilely tried to escape the murderous deed done at his command. Each night he paced restlessly, hearing his mother's wails from the grave echoing among the cliffs hovering over the Bay of Naples.

"Should I return to Rome? Will the senate still give me free rein?" Nero's panic choked him nightly as the ghostly face of Agrippina haunted his every move.

His closest advisors reassured him. "Go and enter the city boldly! Your subjects remember Agrippina's cruel temperament. Nobody is grieving for her now." Slowly, these diseased words danced in his guilt-stricken mind until, with his seared conscious fading, he rose and left for home.

As he approached the city, he saw, to his astonishment, senators and their families lining the thoroughfare in their finest clothes. Crowds pressed along his route as if he were a general receiving a Triumph. Relieved that his crimes seemed forgotten, he *processed* majestically to the Capitol and paid his vows. Then he plunged into the wildest improprieties without Agrippina's voice to quell his darkest vices.

***

As Nero's *procession* yields to a night of riotous banqueting, I see another crowd gathering along the twisting path toward Jerusalem's hallowed walls. Trumpets blared as a lone figure wearing only a linen ephod danced wildly before the Ark of the Covenant. Winding his way into the city, all of heaven rejoiced.

***

"So David and all the house of Israel were bringing up the ark of the LORD with shouting and the sound of the trumpet" (2 Sam. 6:15).

***

Choose Jerusalem's procession and make heaven smile.

***

"A procession is a participant's journey, while a parade is a performance with an audience."
Rebecca Solnit

Day 249

***

Promises (54 BC)
Caesar, *Gallic War*, 5:48

***

Julius Caesar distributed his weary legions and commanders throughout Gaul for the winter. Everything seemed calm for a few weeks until the restless Gauls, feverish for revolt, attacked the Roman fort of Atuatuca. The Romans fought with courage, but many brave men died. Huddled and starving in the winter camp, several dispatches pleaded for Caesar to come quickly.

One of the attacking kings, Ambiorix, sought a meeting with two Roman generals in charge. "Leave your fort, and my men will give you safe passage to anywhere you would go." But this deception proved fatal. The Gauls ambushed the fleeing legionnaires in a valley several miles from the camp.

The beleaguered survivors fought their way back to the fort's safety and waited. When Caesar heard of these events, he sent a messenger with an urgent letter bound to a javelin. He told the courier, "If you manage to sneak through enemy lines, hurl this javelin over the wall *promising* my swift return."

Against all odds, the courier found the camp and hurled the spear over the rampart. It stuck accidentally high up on a tower and was unseen for two days. On the third day, a soldier saw it and, running, delivered it to the general, who read Caesar's promise to delirious cheers. Soon, in the distance, they saw the burning fires of villages proving Caesar was coming.

***

Promises can save lives. As you start your day, remember the promise Jesus made to His disciples at the ascension:

***

"and lo, I am with you always, even to the end of the age" (Matt. 28:20.

***

Today, toss someone a note over the wall.

***

"A promise must never be broken."
Alexander Hamilton

Day 250

***

Protection (1178 BC)
Virgil, *Aeneid*, 1:405–440

***

Aeneas and his friend, shipwrecked wanderers in a strange African land, lay atop a hillock staring with disbelief at the massive Carthaginian city below. Rising from the desert, like mystical irises, soared lofty towers, impressive buildings, and bronzed gates. On the paved streets of this wilderness fortress, Tyrian artisans were frantically cobbling a citadel unequaled on earth. As exquisite buildings bloomed, other laborers hewed out a harbor basin where a fleet of ships would soon reside.

Aeneas lay in wonderment upon his distant hill perch in disbelief. Far off beside an eastern battlement, a stone theater's graceful columns loomed over a nascent stage where elite actors would strut and sing one day. It seemed to Aeneas like the beehives of Troy. In his youthful days, he had often observed the earnest industry of the little winged creatures stuffing cells with nectar, laboring endlessly, building a honeyed palace fit for their queen.

Aeneas urged his friend Achates to follow him. Slipping down the hillside, cloaked in a cloud of invisibility provided by Venus, his mother, they stepped upon the thoroughfare of the rising metropolis, undetected, though surrounded by the crowds, *protected* behind their veil of darkness.

***

So often, we feel vulnerable and exposed to a caustic world around us. Who is watching? Who can be trusted? Such were the thoughts of Zion's exiles until Isaiah reminded them that they, too, were *protected* from threatening eyes.

***

"I have put My words in your mouth and have covered you with the shadow of My hand, to establish the heavens, to found the earth, and to say to Zion, 'You are My people'" (Isa. 51:16).

***

Walk today with confidence in the shadow of God's hand.

***

"A woman's best protection is a little money of her own."
Clare Boothe Luce

Day 251

***

Punishment (35 BC)
Horace, *Satires*, 1:3

***

Horace, who lived in the days of Caesar Augustus, urged us all to be more understanding. "After all," he said, "we've all got faults. Let's say a slave is waiting on folks at the dinner table, and when he takes away the dishes, he gorges himself in the kitchen on the leftover fish and warm sauce. You wouldn't crucify him, would you? For just eating a little of the leftovers? No, that's crazy."

Horace paused and then continued. "And what if this same fellow accidentally knocked over a cup and ruined the table cloth or clumsily broke a valuable bowl? Should I think him stupid or worthless?

"Let's say a boy steals some cabbages from a neighbor's garden. That's not nearly as bad as a fellow breaking into the temple at night and snatching the sacred vessels of the gods. So let's not whip the poor cabbage stealer, ripping his back to shreds for such a trivial fault. That's too much! Let's use commonsense and mercy when we assign *punishment*."

***

I see a little of Horace's pleading for merciful *punishment* in the great apostle Paul's demeanor. The Corinthian congregation had censured one of its members, and now the whole church was gloomy and the morale low. Paul wept about it, urging everyone to lighten up a bit (2 Cor. 2:4).

501

***

"Sufficient for such a one is this punishment which was inflicted by the majority, so that on the contrary you should rather forgive and comfort him, otherwise such a one might be overwhelmed by excessive sorrow" (1 Cor. 2:6–7).

***

Still mad at your neighbor for stealing cabbages? Give Paul a call.

***

"Returning violence for violence multiplies violence, adding deeper darkness to a night already devoid of stars."
Martin Luther King

Day 252

***

Quiet (27 BC)
Tibullus, *Elegies*, 1:1

***

Happy to be home from plundering raids with Messala's army, Tibullus wandered in tranquility over his Pedum farm under the close eyes of Mt. Prenestine. He detested war's fortunes. He clearly remembered braving the boisterous seas frothy with cold wind and waves in pursuit of battles and loot. But no more. Now and forevermore, he would be content with the sunny valley's caresses.

Each morning he rose from his *quiet* cottage and slipped out among the scented vines, heavy with promise. With expectant joy, he waited patiently for the harvest when his vats would swell with a purple haze. At eventide, returning homeward, he would lay upon his couch with Delia and let balmy sleep take them both down.

How cozy it was to lie with his sweetheart when the storm winds howled. Tibullus would clasp Delia to his breast and, holding her tightly, sink into slumber to the rhythm of beating rain. Drifting into night's embrace, he would dream of grazing sheep on the rolling pastures below his cottage, pear trees on the distant slopes, and then at peace, snuggle into Delia's arms.

***

Slip away to the city's edge today and breathe *quiet* air void of contracts and deals.

Perhaps Paul, who knew the ancient poets well, thought of Tibullus and his quaint farm when he sat to compose a letter to the Thessalonians.

***

"Make it your ambition to lead a quiet life and attend to your own business and work with your hands, just as we commanded you" (1 Thess. 4:11).

***

Find your farm today. Leave the crowds behind.

***

"It is neither wealth nor splendor, but tranquility and occupation which give you happiness."
Thomas Jefferson

Day 253

Racing (AD 10)
Ovid, *Metamorphoses*, 10:560–700.

***

Atalanta, the most beautiful woman in ancient Greece, threw down a challenge to all the men who adored her. "Beat me in a *race*, and I will marry you; lose, and you will die!" Men lined up to race her but always failed.

One day a handsome young bachelor, Hippomenes, challenged her. Atalanta was smitten by his good looks. She accepted the challenge and, crouching low at the starting line, waited for the trumpet. Once the clarion note sounded, they were off. They both could run on waves without their sandals getting wet and on grain fields without bending the stalks.

After some time, however, Hippomenes began to breathe heavily, gasping for air. His only hope lay in three golden apples he possessed. Tossing one into the air, it glittered across the road catching Atalanta's eye. Curious, she tracked it down, bemused with wonder at the fruit.

Hippomenes took the lead, but not for long. Desperately, he threw another golden apple into a field. Again, she chased but returned quickly. Sighing and greatly discouraged, he flung his last apple far off. This time, her reckless pursuit cost Atalanta the race. Hippomenes lunged for the finish line and won his prize.

***

Atalanta took the *race* for granted. She had always won. Easily distracted, she wandered once too often from the challenge and forfeited a certain victory.

Paul abhorred second-place trophies.

***

"Do you not know that those who run in a race all run but only one receives the prize? Run in such a way that you may win" (1 Cor. 9:24).

***

Are you chasing golden apples?

***

"The winner ain't the one with the fastest car. It's the one who refuses to lose."
Dale Earnhardt

Day 254

***

Reaper (23 BC)
Horace, *Odes*, 1:4

***

Horace, with a writer's sleight of hand, revealed the glory of spring glistening like a newly found pear in his Ode titled Spring's Lesson. But he hid a brutal truth in the Ode's last verses.

"Ah, spring is finally here, and the meadows no longer hide beneath snow's chilly blankets. The West Wings are blowing softly, and bleary-eyed oxen drag dry winter ships down to the welcoming sea. The lovely Nymphs are dancing beneath a glowing moon, and smiling faces wear spring garlands stitched with the meadow's finest jewelry."

And then, just when he has us singing spring's eternal praises, he drags us over to Death's hot door:

"But wait a minute," frowned the poet. "Here comes the *Reaper* strolling impartially along the road knocking at humble cottages and ivory palaces. Riches won't shelter you. Your short life span won't let you look far down the road. Before you know it, your party days will be over."

***

It was the custom among the Romans when they gathered for a spring party to choose someone to throw the dice and kick off a celebration for the new year. But when Death knocks, the dice days are over.

I wonder if James ever read any of Horace's poems. James spoke with a similar sentiment about the *Reaper's* knock:

***

"Come now, you who say, 'Today or tomorrow we will go to such and such a city, and spend a year there and engage in business and make a profit.' Yet you do not know what your life will be like tomorrow. You are just a vapor that appears for a little while and then vanishes away" (Jas. 4:13–14).

***

The cherry blossoms call, but death knocks louder.

***

"Our dead are never dead to us, until we have forgotten them."
George Eliot

Day 255

Recognition (498 BC)
Plutarch, *Coriolanus*, 3

***

Do you crave *recognition*? It often seems to evade those most qualified. Employees often complain that no one in the organization cares about their accomplishments. They feel unwanted, as if their efforts don't count. I felt this way when I taught middle school for a few years. I instructed with creativity, but never once was my name submitted for an award.

Coriolanus, too, longed for recognition. As a rising soldier who dreamed of fame, he wondered why no one noticed his talents.

But everything changed in a battle outside Rome. Latium armies surrounded the city, fearing Rome's rising power. As the ensuing battle raged beneath the fortress's walls, a solitary tragedy unfolded. A Roman soldier lay bleeding after a ferocious assault by the Latium warriors. Coriolanus, fighting nearby, reacted instantaneously. Leaping over the bodies of other slain combatants, he attacked the front line, killing the lead soldier with a volley of sword thrusts.

Unaware that the general was observing him, he blocked the assault and saved the wounded man's life. When the battle ended and the victory fires burned brightly, the commander surprised Coriolanus with a garland wreath of oaken branches praising him before all the troops.

***

Your day, too, will come. As a Christian, *recognition* awaits you, glistening with unfading glory. Your life of sacrifice and achievement does not go unseen. God follows your every act of heroism and selflessness. When you think no one cares, the Lord Himself will stand before you:

***

"And when the Chief Shepherd appears, you will receive the unfading crown of glory" (1 Pet. 5:4).

***

Your wreath is ready. Prepare yourself!

***

"Don't worry when you are not recognized, but strive to be worthy of recognition."
Abraham Lincoln

Day 256

***

Reconciled (1184 BC)
Homer, *Iliad*, 7:280–300

***

Night was falling, and still, the two warriors fought on, their clanging swords echoing off the distant Trojan walls. Suddenly two heralds appeared, separating Hector and Ajax from their brutal combat. "Night falls quickly, brothers," spoke Idaeus. "Please cease fighting. Go home now to loved ones weeping at hearths."

Both men, sweat dripping from their fierce bodies, stepped back, breathing heavily. Their swords dangled loosely, pointing groundward as the reality of a truce crawled slowly through their agitated minds.

Finally, after suspicion settled, Hector spoke with admiration for his opponent. "Ajax, without doubt, you are the best fighter of the Greeks. Your skill with that spear is unmatched. Let's honor the truce and go home. Perhaps we will fight again, but now let us celebrate *reconciliation*."

With these trembling words, Hector took off his silver-studded sword with its sheath and leather baldric, handing it to his opponent. Ajax, pleased with the gesture, gave Hector a girdle dyed with purple. A dusky quiet fell over the battlefield as both men parted ways; savage enemies reconciled beneath first stars. Cheers erupted on the Trojan walls as wives rushed to the Scaean gates sighing as they slowly opened.

***

It is breathtaking when genuine friendship appears out of hatred's mists. Even fierce foes long for *reconciliation*. Such was the day when Abner shouted to Joab in the heat of battle at Gibeon.

***

"Then Abner called to Joab and said, 'Shall the sword devour forever?...' So Joab blew the trumpet; and all the people halted and pursued Israel no longer, nor did they continue to fight anymore" (2 Sam. 2:26–28).

***

Night falls. Grant peace to your enemy this evening.

***

"Reconciliation is more beautiful than victory."
Violeta Chamorro

Day 257

***

Reconsider (429 BC)
Sophocles, *Antigone*, 1065–1115

***

The old prophet Tiresias, blind and bent, confronted King Creon. The king, giddy from his guilty venture to the rock vault, leaned forward over his golden throne and ridiculed the old man. "You money-grubbing old preacher, what do you want? Say it quick, and then get out."

Refusing to cringe, Tiresias spoke softly, each word a dagger. "I sat in my ancient augur's chair beneath swamp trees, reading the birds as they darted among the branches. Suddenly, a brutal pandemonium assaulted my ears as screaming fowl fought unseen demons above the dark waters. A violent pattering of wings and bared talons ripped nature's calm veil. Shocked, I quickly kindled a sacrifice, but I could keep no flame. The gallbladders burst and grease oozed down the thigh bones. The reading was terrifying!"

Pausing for composure before a startled king, he breathed deeply and continued. "This is what it means, sire. You are guilty! You just locked poor Antigone in a rock vault with a cup of water and a biscuit for merely caring for her brother. Before the sun sets, you will pay a heavy price." Then abruptly gathering his robe, Tiresias left.

King Creon shifted uncomfortably, sifting the raging words. Then, *reconsidering* his affairs, he commanded his servants to free the girl.

***

Learning to *reconsider* is an artform often neglected. Our decisions, locked in pride, often remain unmovable. "Leave the vault locked!" you say. "My mind is set." Such was the command one brutal night in Egypt's past until the Pharaoh reconsidered:

***

"Pharaoh arose in the night,... for there was no home where there was not someone dead. Then he called for Moses and Aaron at night and said, 'Rise up, get out from among my people, both you and the sons of Israel: and go, worship the LORD, as you have said'" (Ex. 12:30–31).

***

The dark vault screams. Reconsider!

***

"A little consideration, a little thought for others, makes all the difference."
Winnie the Pooh

Day 258

***

Refusal (1177 BC)
Virgil, *Aeneid*, 7:580–620

***

King Latinus stood unmoved. Packing the palace steps, a mob of yelping citizens demanded war on the Trojan intruders. Shepherds from the battlefield dragged their dead to the palace weeping with hysterical tears. Women, known for peaceful traditions, suddenly streamed into town from nearby woods screaming for revenge. "Open the Gates of War!" they shouted.

But the grizzled king *refused*, withstanding the howling mob, pointing his trembling finger at them all. "You are the cause of this trouble. You all set this rage in motion, and you will pay." Having thus uttered his decision, he wheeled about, relinquished the reins of government, and retired to his palace reverie.

Shocked at this breach of ancient tradition, the terrible Gates of Hell, sanctified by the indwelling presence of Mars, remained locked. A hundred bronzed bolts still held the iron bars fast. Only the king, clothed in Quirinal robes bound by the sacred Gabine knots, could shove the rusty doors open. Only then would trumpets blare the onset of war, with soldiers scrambling for swords.

But Latinus refused. Turning from this clamor for war, he buried himself from sight, recalling the blessings of peace.

***

Those who study the art of *refusal* will gain tranquility and revel in the joys of peaceful living. Learning to stand unmovable against life's fickle demands will pay generous returns. Latinus refused to play war's silly games just as God does daily:

***

"He makes wars to cease to the end of the earth; He breaks the bow and cuts the spear in two; He burns the chariots with fire" (Ps. 46:9).

***

Make peace with others. Refuse the personal wars.

***

"One of the truest tests of integrity is its blunt refusal to be compromised."
Chinua Achebe

Day 259

***

Regrets (AD 100)
Plutarch, *Lives: Marcus Cato*, 9:6

***

Marcus Cato leaned against an ancient olive tree as the Sabine mists drifted over his orchard. He admired the tilt of the land, the rounded mountain peaks that rolled ever northward along the Apennine chain far from Rome's busy cackle. Glancing about the farm left to him by his father, he sighed, remembering the early days of childhood here.

Some local farmers passed by in the fog, shouting hellos. Calling them over, Cato, ever filled with saucy witticisms, chattered with his neighbors.

"Do you have any *regrets* for leaving home to fight Rome's battles?" they asked.

Motioning for them to sit beneath the knotty branches, he smiled and considered the inquiry. "Fellas, I can only recall three times I ever regretted anything in my life."

The others smiled at this absurdity.

Cato, nibbling on straw, measured their disbelief and then answered. "My first regret was when I entrusted a secret to my wife." The others laughed as men do in small circles.

"And what else?" one countered. "You said there were three."

"Yes. The second was when I paid a fee to board a ship when I could have easily walked to the place." The others nodded, impressed. They knew Cato's reputation for frugality.

"And the third regret was when I lived one day without a will."

***

Paul's brilliant early career as a Pharisee made him a rising star in Jewish circles. Surely, he *regretted* losing these privileges. But he shakes his head, refusing to linger in the past:

***

"More than that, I count all things to be loss ... and count them but rubbish so that I may gain Christ" (Phil. 3:9).

***

Fine-tune the future. Live without regrets.

***

"A man is not old until his regrets take the place of his dreams." *Yiddish proverb*

Day 260

***

Rejuvenation (430 BC)
Euripides, *Heracleidae*, 845–865

***

The two armies glared at each other beneath the shadow of
Athene's hill. Hyllus, son of Heracles, dismounted from his
chariot and strode confidently into the abyss calling King
Eurystheus to meet him. "Let's settle this right now between
the armies. Come out and fight me!"

The Athenians cheered their lusty leader, but Eurystheus
refused, shamefully avoiding the challenge. Hyllus returned
to his troops as both sides rattled their lances against fierce
shields. When the trumpet blared, pandemonium broke loose
as swords collided beneath a brilliant Athenian sun. Hand-to-
hand combat mingled with death shrieks and last gasps. Men
tumbled to their deaths on both sides until the Argive king's
ranks broke and fled the blood-soaked field.

Hyllus whipped his chariot horses and plunged into the
chaotic retreat, searching for the king. Iolaus, the old guardian of
Heracles' orphaned boys, waved him down. "Let me fight, too."
He stood bowlegged and bent, but Hyllus paused and helped
him into the chariot. As they charged into the ruckus, searching
for the king, Iolaus prayed for strength. "Zeus," pleaded the
aged caregiver, "please give me back my youth for one day."

A dark cloud suddenly rolled over the chariot. When it lifted,
Iolaus bore the biceps of a husky warrior and, with *rejuvenated*
strength, pursued and captured the king.

***

We all drag accumulating years like anchors through time's shifting sands. We remember our frolicsome seasons fondly when springtime never ended and hopes flourished. However, daily *rejuvenation* is but a prayer away, as Hezekiah can attest:

***

"I will add fifteen years to your life, and I will deliver you and this city from the hand of the king of Assyria..." (2 Kings 20:6).

***

Find rejuvenation in spiritual pursuits.

***

"Everything you want is on the other side of fear."
Jack Canfield

Day 261

***

Religion (65 BC)
Lucretius, *On the Nature of Things*, 1:62

***

"What is *religion*?" asked Lucretius pondering the deepest issues of life. "I'll tell you what it is," he says, with burgeoning confidence: "it's a monster gazing down from a hidden world beyond ours, with evil eyes and a dark gaze. I used to shudder at this veiled monster, but not anymore."

I watched as Lucretius strolled to his living room window, scowling at the invisible threat in the sky. He continued "All my life, this fiend has scowled at me and everyone else as we lie cowering in the dirt. Those who dare to glance upward at it see its grizzled contempt for all humanity, its hideous head shaking, threatening.

"But there was a man—one courageous man, a teacher who dared to confront the monster, bursting into its lair, learning its ways. And now he has returned, unscathed, with joyful news: religion can and will be crushed by us who understand."

Lucretius paused and studied my reaction waiting for the obvious question.

"Who are you talking about, Lucretius? Tell me his name."

The philosopher then smiled and whispered, "Epicurus."

***

"What is *religion*?" asked Paul, mimicking Lucretius' question. "I, too, know a teacher who peered into unseen realms," he said. "He once wore a crown of thorns. He alone explained life's mysteries and the true meaning of religion: Jesus."

***

"Christ Jesus, who, although He existed in the form of God, did not regard equality with God a thing to be grasped, but emptied Himself, taking the form of a bond-servant ... becoming obedient to the point of death, even death on a cross" (Phil. 2:6–8).

***

Choose your guide today: Lucretius or Paul.

***

"Religion is what keeps the poor from murdering the rich."
Napoleon Bonaparte

Day 262

***

Remembrances (AD 10)
Suetonius, *Lives of the Caesars*, 4:7

***

Perhaps it was the little boy's smile, or maybe just his effervescence. He loved to laugh, making Livia and Augustus, his doting grandparents, happy to watch him play. His sudden death brought such sorrow to the emperor's household. Everyone mourned.

Livia commissioned a statue that captured her grandson's boisterous manners. She placed it in Rome's largest sacred edifice, the temple of Venus beside the colosseum. There she would come daily and summon mournful *remembrances*.

Augustus adored the statue and ordered one for himself. When it was finished, he placed it in his Palatine bedroom. Each morning when he rose and drew the empire's heavy burdens upon his shoulders, he paused in the boy's shadow and kissed him fondly before exiting.

When the long day's labors concluded, the emperor shuffled home and sat with his wife at dinner, remembering. When evening summoned them to bed, he walked with Livia into their bedroom and lingered longingly kissing the boy's cheeks.

***

Remembrances, stirred like mantle ashes, revive fading moments of love lost in tragedy. We see the contours of a lost face again, staring into eyes that once brought such joy.

So it was when Jesus reclined at a table with his closest friends and bid them all farewell. This memorial meal would be His effigy, a sacred window through which they could remember His love for them.

***

"And when He had taken some bread and given thanks, He broke it and gave it to them, saying, 'This is My body which is given for you; do this in remembrance of Me'" (Lk. 22:19).

***

Savor the Bread today and remember.

***

"Come back. Even as a shadow, even as a dream."
Euripides

Day 263

***

Reminiscing (AD 60)
Petronius, *The Satyricon*, 5:44

***

Let's listen in on a rambling, first-century Roman dinner conversation spiked with alcohol. Ganymedes, satiated by a sumptuous dinner, burped and began *reminiscing*:

"Life's so hard now," he said, plucking a grape from the dinner bowl. "I can't even afford a slice of bread anymore. Part of it is that horrible drought, but most of it is those crooked officials. They're in cahoots with the bakers!"

He paused and took another sip of wine. "I remember old Safinius way back when I was just a boy. He lived down by the old archway. That man was pure peppercorn; scorched the ground wherever he went."

Ganymedes stared off for a minute. "But he was a true friend when you needed one. You could match coins with him in the dark. He used to stand up in the town square and make a speech like a bugle blowing. He would tell it like it was, no matter what. He never got ruffled, and he dressed neat as a pin."

Everybody just stared at Ganymedes as they nibbled on lambs' legs. He continued: "Nobody believes in religion anymore. I remember when the women would dress up in their finest and climb barefoot up to the temple on the hill. When they prayed for rain, it fell in buckets. And they would stand there in the rain like a pack of drowned rats."

***

Paul, facing execution in a Roman jail just down the street from the banquet, also *reminisced*, writing a haunting letter to Timothy.

***

"I constantly remember you in my prayers night and day, longing to see you, even as I recall your tears..." (2 Tim. 1:3–4).

***

Stir up your best memories today.

***

"Moments, rather than possessions, are the true treasures of life."
Frank Sonnenberg

Day 264

***

Renewal (1178 BC)
Virgil, *Aeneid*, 1:440–465

***

There was a grove in the city's center, quaint with comforting shade, that caught Aeneas' eye. Shipwrecked and lost, he had stumbled upon this Carthaginian oasis in the desert, a magnificent, rising metropolis. Here resided Dido, herself a recent refugee, who had found this grove with its spirited horse's skull projecting from the sands, a sign from the gods, predicting wealth and future success.

Aeneas stared, awed at the queen's newest project, a temple dedicated to Juno rising with spiritual force above the citadel. A flight of marbled steps led to bronzed doors, signifying *renewal* of life and dreams. Aeneas wove this sacred grove around his heart and felt his hopes rising again for the first time since Troy's fall.

Wrapping himself in a cloak of invisibility, Aeneas meandered past newly minted temple walls. As his eyes supped on the vibrant riches before him, he noticed a series of Trojan frescoes, the paint still fresh with vibrant hues. Stunned that the recent Trojan tragedy lived in distant lands, he stood and wept at the scenes still fresh within him. He traced gentle tears on Priam's cheeks and saw, too, the fierce Achilles raging beneath Troy's battlements. The frescoes fed his soul and sparked visions of salvation for his people.

***

Darkness often settles over all who travel life's treacherous journey. One day we rise and trace endless possibilities on the horizon, and by sunset, fall blinded and wheezing into hopelessness. *Renewal* of dreams must be a daily priority. Even Jesus welcomed the wilderness angels.

***

"Then the devil left Him; and behold, angels came and began to minister to Him" (Matt. 4:11).

***

Sit with Aeneas today in the grove, and breathe again.

***

"When I let go of what I am, I become what I might be."
Lao Tzu

Day 265

***

Repercussions (550 BC)
Herodotus, *The Persian Wars*, 1:129

***

When I was a kid living in Kyoto, I picked up a smoldering cigarette tossed on the Baptist church parking lot. The twinkling embers fascinated me. Eventually, I could resist no more and took a puff or two. I nearly died from coughing and swore nicotine away forever. I learned that life has its *repercussions*.

Astyages, a Median king, fell into this same quagmire scoffing at life's intangibles as if consequences didn't apply to him. When his best general, Harpagus, didn't follow orders one day, the king raged and determined to teach the old soldier a lesson. He ordered his palace staff to prepare a sumptuous banquet. He signed a personal invitation for the general to attend.

Beneath twinkling palace lights, the evening's festivities began. Attendants burst through the kitchen doors carrying savory dishes and decadent desserts. The general praised the king for the delicious meal but didn't realize that the main course was Harpagus' son, boiled to perfection! When the general learned the truth, he maintained his composure, saying nothing.

Time passed, and King Astyages lost his kingdom. Shuffling in chains before King Cyrus, Harpagus confronted the fallen potentate. "So, king, what does it feel like to be a common slave? You've fallen so far."

***

King Saul, too, felt the *repercussions* of poor life decisions. The Philistines hung his bloody corpse on a Philistine wall at Beth-shan.

***

"It came about on the next day when the Philistines came to strip the slain, that they found Saul and his three sons fallen on Mount Gilboa. They cut off his head,… and fastened his body to the wall of Beth-shan" (1 Sam. 31:8–10).

***

Don't let the wall get you. Make good decisions from now on.

***

"Sooner or later everyone sits down to a banquet of consequences."
Robert Louis Stevenson

Day 266

Reprisals (429 BC)
Sophocles, *Antigone*, 160–260

The sentries, shocked at the impossible breach, encircled the corpse. Lying respectfully covered with a thin veil of dust as if sprinkled by heaven's night angels, Polyneices lay at rest, his forbidden funeral rites fulfilled stealthfully beneath a quiet moon.

The sentries remembered the echoing command of the king: "I forbid anyone to bury this fool. He dared to attack Thebes, his city, and now he will pay. He will lay unburied, dinner for the vultures."

Careful inspection of the sight revealed no sign of intruders. Absent were footprints, shovel cuts, or any imprints of intrusion. Nothing. And yet somehow, the traitorous body lay before them, caressed by the sun's golden touch, blissfully at peace.

Pointing fingers at one another, gesticulating like lunatics before a looming cross, they searched for the emissary. "Who will tell the king? It must be you," squawked one. "You stood watch."

"No, I will not go!" was the swift reply. "You were charged with this mission too."

And so, the only solution was to toss the dice. And when it shouted a guilty name, the soldier trudged toward the palace with deadly news, fearing myriad ghastly *reprisals* to fall upon him at the throne. Scurrying at a snail's pace, the sentry approached the Theban palace steps, trembling.

***

Reprisals lurk in the shadows among us all. Our failures often unleash hidden megaphones that tell tales of secrets long buried. Like the sentry forced to confess, we march in slow motion toward doom unless we follow John's advice:

***

"If we confess our sins, He is faithful and righteous to forgive us our sins and to cleanse us from all unrighteousness" (1 Jn. 1:9).

***

Approach the King in humility. There will be no reprisals.

***

"Reprisals are but a sad resource."
Napoleon Bonaparte

Day 267

Requests (27 BC)
Tibullus, *Elegies*, 2

***

Tibullus and his friend gathered around the morning altar, pleased with the cloudless sky above. Sacred incense, scented with Arabian odors, rose beneath a budding sun, summoning heaven to hear an early petition.

Flowery wreaths decorated the altar. The god's brow flowed with sweet unguents, mingling with sugar cakes and flowing wine. As the flames darted skyward, Tibullus glanced at his friend. "What will you ask God for this morning? Anything is possible, you know. Whatever you request will be granted."

Silence mingled with the sacred aroma. No flood of frivolous demands sputtered from his lips. Tibullus' partner kept his thoughts caged, distant.

Tibullus pressed again. "Don't be afraid to ask. The god is cheerfully waiting. Just ask!"

The humble petitioner still could think of nothing he needed. Tibullus, impressed by the worshipper's disinterest in distant gemmy shores or world fame, intervened. "I know what you want. Yes! Let's pray for a beautiful wife who will love you throughout your life. Even when old age mangles your face, she will hover over you with kindness and devotion. And as you age, your lovely children will frolic in your shadows. That will be our *request* this morning!"

***

There is something admirable about these men standing by a morning altar searching for meaningful *requests*. But wait. Glance toward the Sea of Galilee. Jesus, His arms outstretched, urges his listeners to pray boldly.

***

"Ask, and it will be given to you; seek, and you will find; knock, and it will be opened to you. For everyone who asks receives, and he who seeks finds, and to him who knocks it will be opened" (Matt. 7:7–8).

***

Look! The sun rises. What will you ask?

***

"Every great movement of God can be traced to a kneeling figure."
D.L. Moody

Day 268

Rescued (AD 69)
Suetonius, *Lives of the Caesars*, 7:19–20

***

The signs warned Galba, the newly minted emperor, that something was amiss. On his frantic march to Rome, he paused at a small town. A worker spooked an ox accidentally. The animal broke its harness and charged Galba's chariot, rearing up and drenching the emperor in blood. A few days later, when he was sacrificing in the temple, the sacred garland tumbled off his head, and the temple chickens flew away—ominous signs.

Galba, ever confident, rose early a few days later and put on his linen corselet, chuckling that it would never blunt a bevy of thirsty swords. Rumors of unrest swarmed through the city. Hearing false reports of peaceful overtures, he greeted a band of cavalrymen in the Forum. These assassins spotted him alone beside the Curtian Lake, a small pond. With a frenzied war scream, they charged.

Trumpets blared, ordering Galba's protectors to rally. Instead, all the soldiers turned their backs to the slaughter. No one came to his *rescue*. Sensing the end, Galba bared his neck and dared them to strike.

As the clatter of hooves scrambled away, the emperor lay in a pool of mingled blood and pond water. A lone soldier returning from grain duty paused and set down his grain sack. Decapitating Galba's body, he stuffed the mangled head inside his cloak, which he sold for a small profit.

***

We all need valiant *rescuers*, angelic friends who have our backs.

Paul once found himself hunted in Damascus. Death threats abounded. But he had friends!

***

"his disciples took him by night and let him down through an opening in the wall, lowering him in a large basket" (Acts 9:25).

***

Fear not. God has your basket ready.

***

"Love is the only way to rescue humanity from all ills."
Leo Tolstoy

Day 269

Resilience (AD 52)

Tacitus, *The Annals of Imperial Rome*, 12:49

Zenobia, the exotic queen of Armenia, lay a lifeless, bloody mess upon the Araxes River's dark shores. The day before, she and Rhadamistus, her husband, had fled on horseback from political enemies. Galloping through tangled forests and mountainous terrain, they pressed for the Iberian border. Zenobia, many months pregnant, begged him to stop. "Leave me here alone. I can't endure this flight any longer," she cried.

Her husband, a man of violence, nonetheless loved his wife and took her in his arms with comforting words. But knowing she would only impede his flight to safety he succumbed to ingrained violent impulses. Unable to bear the thought of plundering pursuers abusing Zenobia, he unsheathed his scymitar and brutally stabbed her. Placing her bleeding corpse on the riverbank, he abandoned his wife to the wave-swept banks. With barely a glance backward, he raced away beneath a full moon for Iberia.

Shepherds with grazing flocks nearby spotted the bobbing body and, with curiosity, investigated. The woman lived, her breath faint but steady. Her royal gown, blood-soaked but bearing a regal tone, startled them. Using rustic medicines, they brought her back to health and presented her to the Armenian prince, Tiridates, where she lived out her days *resiliently* in the king's court.

From the red-stained banks of the Araxes River, glance westward toward Lystra. In the same year, Paul's blood-soaked but *resilient* body lay crumpled and lifeless beneath a pile of stones cast by angry Lystran crowds.

***

"they stoned Paul and dragged him out of the city, supposing him to be dead. But while the disciples stood around him, he got up and entered the city" (Acts 14:20).

***

Today, live in the light of *resilience*.

***

"A good half of the art of living is resilience."
Alain de Botton

Day 270

***

Restlessness (428 BC)
Euripides, *Hippolytus*, 175–240

***

Phaedra tossed *restlessly* in her palace bed. Nothing suited her. "Nurse. Nurse! I need fresh air. Take me outside. I can't breathe." She shook her sweaty hair side to side, the fever making demands.

Summoning help, the nurse led the mistress to the couch outside beneath a shady Juniper. Fluffing the purple pillows, she tucked Phaedra beneath a gentle Athenian sea breeze and watched her lady drift into an agitated calm. But within minutes, another eruption made its demands.

"Take me inside at once! I can't take this sunshine. It's too bright here. Oh, please, someone, take me inside." The nurse, panicking, called for help, pulling the lady to a feeble sitting position.

"First, you want to go out, and then you scream to go in." Mumbling to no effect, the nurse grasped Phaedra's waist and, stumbling, took her to her palace bed.

But the longer she lay in the smoldering bedroom, the more her secret roared. Uprooting her very soul, her heart's sin devoured all sensibilities leaving Phaedra exhausted, spinning ever deeper into some undisclosed mystical chaos. Within minutes she issued new orders. "Take this hat off my head at once. It's too heavy. Let my hair fall freely upon my shoulders." Then with barely a breath, she shouted, "Take me to the meadows! Let me lie beneath the poplars."

***

Silent anxieties haunt the modern mind sending us all reeling into each new sunrise, unsettled. Perhaps there is a meddlesome secret brewing within. God offers peace to every *restless* heart as the imprisoned apostle wrote to his friends:

***

"Be anxious for nothing, but in everything by prayer and supplication with thanksgiving let your requests be made known to God" (Phil. 4:6).

***

Breathe in your simple blessings and find peace.

***

"She wasn't bored, just restless between adventures."
Atticus

Day 271

***

Restraint (55 BC)
Caesar, *Gallic War*, 6:21

***

When Caesar conquered the Gauls, he encountered the Germans, whose customs he wrote down in his daily journal. "They were people," he noted, "without priestly guidance since they didn't follow the druids in religious affairs. They only worshipped the Sun and the Moon, visible deities. They lived for toil and hardship hunting wildlife and fighting in military pursuits.

"One way they won esteem from their village was to show great *restraint* in sexual matters. This was notable since the young people wore very little clothing, mostly small deer-cloak hides that barely covered their bodies. They considered it normal for both sexes to bathe promiscuously in the rivers.

"This noble restraint among the young men and women was the secret for winning praise from the villagers and society. Those who purposefully remained chaste for the longest time were admired the most. The theory was that restraint promoted physical strength and increased personal power. Sex with a young woman before the age of twenty was considered a disgraceful matter."

***

Our modern culture revels in liberation, casual sex, and quick retaliation for any slight grievance. Disturbed students think little of whipping out pistols and firing at fellow schoolmates.

We would all benefit from Caesar's observation. It was Jesus who admonished Peter to show *restraint*:

***

"Simon Peter then, having a sword, drew it and struck the high priest's slave, and cut off his right ear;... So Jesus said to Peter, 'Put the sword into the sheath; the cup which the Father has given Me, shall I not drink it?'" (Jn. 18:10–11).

***

Sheathe your sword and count to ten.

***

"When restraint and courtesy are added to strength, the latter becomes irresistible."
Mahatma Gandhi

Day 272

Resurrection (438 BC)
Euripides, *Alcestis*, 1038–1160

***

Heracles insisted. "Take the woman. She is my gift to you. I won her fairly in a wrestling match. Now I give her to you to ease your widower's pain. She will comfort you."

Admetus refused. "No, Heracles. No woman will ever sleep in my embrace again. I made a vow to my wife just before her death to never marry again. I meant it."

Heracles gently pushed the woman toward his friend. "You cannot live alone. Take her. Let her ease your pain."

Admetus sighed deeply. "Please, Heracles. I can't. I wish you had never won her. I made a vow!"

"Just take her hand and lead her into your home," persisted Heracles. "You will feel differently." He lifted the slave's hand toward him.

Admetus glanced at her eyes with their familiar warmth. "You have the form of my Alcestis," he whispered hesitantly. "Your body is like hers." But this admission spun him deeper into a dark abyss. Staring harshly at Heracles, he clung to his vow tightly. "You force me to betray my one love. I can't!"

Heracles insisted, guiding the woman's hand toward his. "Do you have it?"

Sighing, he answered. "Yes. I have her hand." His fingers felt a familiar warmth.

"This is your once-dead wife, Admetus," said Heracles softly. "I sprung upon death at her tomb and crushed it with my hands. Your wife lives again, *resurrected* from Hades' horrid grasp."

***

Euripides spins a romantic fable, but Paul fleshed out *resurrection's* truth. He observed death's sting in the cruelty of Roman life. But the Savior forced death's whimper, bringing victory to us all.

***

"O DEATH, WHERE IS YOUR VICTORY? O DEATH, WHERE IS YOUR STING?" (1 Cor. 15:55).

***

Take the Lord's hand and claim life.

***

"Mostly it is loss which teaches us about the worth of things."
Arthur Schopenhauer

Day 273

***

Retaliation (1184 BC)

Homer, *Iliad*, 1:200–220

***

Achilles scowled at King Agamemnon, who threatened to take his war prize, the beautiful Briseis, won in battle. Achilles, ever restless, sat among a small group of measured men who tried to reason with the king. Chryses, the priest, had spoken with respect as had old Calchas, wisest of the augurs. But Agamemnon was furious with them all and refused to yield, preferring to flex his authority.

"You all swarm into this meeting making your demands, telling me the gods are unhappy with me. You pester me to give up my lover, Astynome, the priest's daughter, but I will not." He paused and then stared at Achilles. "But if I do give her up, by god, I will take your lover, Briseis."

Achilles leaped up at these fighting words and gripped the hilt of his mighty sword. Pulling it from the scabbard, he prepared to sweep the others aside and lunge at the king.

"Wait, Achilles! Wait." Athene's soft voice whispered to him as she tugged at his blond hair, an intervention unseen by those in the tent. Turning, he saw her flashing eyes pleading for reason.

"Why are you here?" he asked as time drifted to a halt.

"I have come to bid you not to *retaliate*. Curse him if you will but please return your sword to the sheath."

***

Achilles listened to the goddess and spared the king. Tempering our anger isn't always easy. But Jesus proposed an even bolder plan against *retaliation*:

***

"But whosoever slaps you on your right cheek, turn to him the other also ... love your enemies, and pray for those who persecute you" (Matt. 5:39,44).

***

Bury your sword. Give love and prayer a chance.

***

"Before you embark on a journey of revenge, dig two graves." *Confucius*

Day 274

***

Reunion (429 BC)
Sophocles, *Oedipus at Colonus*, 300–328

***

Old and crushed by life's failures, Oedipus lingered in a sacred grove beneath a blistering summer sun. His ghoulish face, disfigured with mutilated eye sockets, symbols of hopelessness, longed for respite. Wiping his brow, he turned toward Antigone. "Where are we, child? What is this quiet place?"

"I don't know, Father. It bears traces of the gods."

He sighed and sat heavily upon a rock as a cooling breeze stirred the trees. "Perhaps someone will come down the road."

"Oh, my! I think I see someone far off." Antigone paused, her keen eyes sifting the scene. "Father, a woman rides this way straight toward us!"

Oedipus unfolded slowly and wondered at it all, "Tell me more, Daughter. What do you see?"

"She rides hard, Father, a dust storm spinning in her wake. Oh, heavens, she hurries on an Etnean thoroughbred. She is someone special, Father."

"What else do you see?" He stood breathlessly awaiting fate.

"Father, she wears a broad Thessalian hat to shade the sun. I see her face now. Is it?" She paused, choking on the possibilities, a *reunion* framing the portrait. "Could it really be?"

With flashing eyes, the woman pulled up sharply, dismounted, and ran to Oedipus. "Father, it is me, Ismene, your lost daughter!"

***

Nothing lifts the dispirited soul like *reunions*. They remind us we are not alone in our struggles. They bear memories laden with hope and reassurance. Such was the hallowed day another aged man greeted a long-lost child.

***

"But when he was still a long way off, his father saw him and felt compassion for him, and ran and embraced him and kissed him" (Lk. 15:20).

***

You've strayed from heaven's gate. Today will be your reunion.

***

"Every parting gives a foretaste of death, every reunion a hint of the resurrection."
Arthur Schopenhauer

Day 275

***

Revelations (429 BC)
Sophocles, *Oedipus Tyrannus*, 345–365

***

The old seer, Tiresias, shuffled slowly through the dark mists toward the Theban palace. Led by a boy to the city besieged by plagues, famine, and suffering, he came, unwillingly, by order of King Oedipus.

The morning prayers and lamentations still resonated outside the palace gates. Throngs of disheveled and glum citizens had gathered earlier in a farrago of wails and incense to seek the king's help against the suffocating plague. Wearing olive branches wreathed in white wool, they gathered beneath a plume of sacred incense. Marshaled by a village priest, they crowded the palace steps pleading for the king's help.

Oedipus gazed in sorrow at the quivering masses. "I hear your pleas," he told the crowd. "The gods have made it clear we must find King Laius' murderer. I have summoned the mystic priest Tiresias to come and peer through the veil."

After hours of delay, the gloomy-faced seer trudged to the palace doors to face an impatient king. "Why did you insist?" grumbled the seer. "I have nothing to say."

Oedipus recoiled and then castigated the old man. "You miserable old man. Find the killer. Look through your blind eyes and yank him from the shadows where he lurks."

The tense standoff continued until the seer raised his bent frame and pointed a boney finger at the king, releasing a provocative *revelation*: "You, sir, are the man!"

***

Revelations shine brightest in troubled hearts. Our secrets, carefully tucked in dark boxes, can't evade truth's call. David discovered this all too well when another old prophet came calling. Nathan's boney finger also touched a dissembling king:

***

"Nathan then said to David, 'You are the man!'" (2 Sam. 12:7).

***

Come clean today. Don't wait for revelations.

***

"That lingering question; That unfinished sentence—"
Diwa

Day 276

Revenge (1177 BC)
Virgil, *Aeneid*, 10:450–550

***

Aeneas, blood-spattered, opened the official message delivered to him on the battlefield. Each scribbled word seemed a dagger to his heart as he read of young Pallas' brutal murder by Turnus. The spectators of war had witnessed Turnus gloating over the trembling prince's body as he gasped for air, blood streaming from the lad's mouth. With mockery, the general had yanked the spear from the youngster's chest and then delighted in stripping the ornate sword belt from his royal corpse, still hot with war's sweat.

Aeneas tossed the letter aside, rage written large upon his face. Flashes of memory flooded his mind as he fondly remembered Pallas and his father, King Evander of Arcadia, welcoming Aeneas' wandering crew to Italy. The king had spread a banquet for the strangers, the first in this foreign land. His princely robes glittering before the evening fire, Pallas had embraced the Trojans and officially welcomed them to his father's Italian kingdom.

Each fond scene stoked *revenge's* fire as Aeneas picked up his shining shield and stormed from the tent. Shouting Turnus' name, muffled by war's cacophony, he plowed, slashing, through enemy ranks, seeking the foul hand who had destroyed those halcyon memories. Turnus was his sole objective; revenge, his weapon.

***

Revenge, that battlefield specter of last resort, haunts us all, drifting through our spoiled memories. All-consuming at times, it leeches the life from our souls, spinning us toward a never-ending lust for justice. But Jesus rebuked a disciple who had drawn his sword in the garden.

***

"Then Jesus said to him, 'Put your sword back into its place; for all those who take up the sword shall perish by the sword'" (Matt. 26:52).

***

Silence revenge's roar with Divine understanding.

***

"A man that studieth revenge keeps his own wounds green."
Francis Bacon

Day 277

Rhetoric (AD 60)
Petronius, *Satyricon*, 1:1

***

Petronius, a first-century novelist, and critic of Roman society, didn't think much of public education in the Roman classrooms of his day. He mocked the educational system because it seemed to turn out students who couldn't think with originality or speak clearly.

"We don't educate our children at school; we cram useless stuff into their heads and then send them out into the world half-baked. They are utterly ignorant of real life. They don't understand or experience real life; it's all this mythology junk."

We can see one example of this poor training in the subject of *rhetoric* that all schools taught. Petronius noted that true eloquence soars to life through a natural, simple loveliness. But, instead, "the professors are teaching these kids to speak in sticky honey balls of phrases, every sentence looking as though it had been plopped and rolled in poppy seed and sesame. A kid stuffed on this diet will never acquire real taste more than a cook can stop stinking. We pack our schoolrooms with children wasting their time and playing at learning."

***

Paul understood *rhetoric*. He knew the difference between genuine words that meant something to people and the empty, flattering drivel of poppy seed imposters. As he rattled off his farewells to numerous friends in his letter to the Romans, he warned about those who caused dissensions through flattering speeches.

***

"For such men are slaves, not of our Lord Christ but of their own appetites; and by their smooth and flattering speech they deceive the hearts of the unsuspecting" (Rom. 16:18).

***

Make your words count. Speak love clearly from a genuine heart.

***

"False rhetoric and false boastfulness spell moral ruin and lead unfailingly to political extinction."
Vladimir Lenin

Day 278

***

Riddles (429 BC)
Sophocles, *Oedipus Tyrannus*, 30–38

***

Oedipus, prince of Corinth, fled his beloved city, running from an echoing prophecy. The Delphic oracle had predicted that Oedipus would slay his father. Grieved over these dark visions, he packed a humble knapsack and wandered west, deep into the unknown, to escape the oracle's deadly stare.

Homeless and friendless, he approached the town of Thebes, wondering if he might find shelter from life's storm there. Approaching the outskirts of town, a fierce sphinx made demands upon everyone who dared to enter. Shaped like a winged lion but with a woman's face, she flung *riddles* at each one she seized. If an unfortunate traveler could not guess the puzzle, the sphinx gobbled them down.

Oedipus having nothing to live for anyway, decided to challenge the monster. She held him tightly in her grip and issued this challenge: "What creature goes on four legs in the morning, on two at noon, and three when the sun sets?"

Without hesitation, Oedipus answered, "Man. As a toddler, the child crawls on all fours, but two legs are adequate when an adult. When time wears all down, the tottering cane suffices." The correct answer startled the winged sphinx, who killed herself. The happy Theban town made Oedipus their king.

***

There are times in daily life when *riddles* block the road challenging our welfare. Should I marry now or wait till spring? Why am I so unhappy? Even Samson peddled mysteries:

***

"Out of the eater came something to eat, and out of the strong came something sweet" (Judg. 14:14).

***

Are you locked in riddle's box? God has the key.

***

"All riddles are blues. And all blues are sad. And I'm only mentioning some blues I've had."
Maya Angelou

Day 279

***

Risks (401 BC)
Xenophon, *Anabasis*, 4:7

***

The soldiers were starving, shivering in the cold beneath a mountainous fortress. A fierce tribe of Taochians held this high ground that led through a pass to the plains of Armenia. The Black Sea summoned them in the distance, offering to sail the weary army homeward to Greece.

The fortress was unassailable. Each time the men left the safety of the forest to charge upon the stronghold, the Taochians unleashed wagon loads of stone that tumbled down upon them with a tumultuous clatter.

The stalemate lingered with Greek soldiers huddled and broken behind thick oak trees while the fortress defenders laughed atop crenelated walls, confident in their wagons of boulders.

But then Callimachus had a brilliant idea. What if he bolted from his tree for just a few steps pretending to charge the castle, and then dashed back to the forest? At considerable *risk*, he tried it, lunging wildly from the forest's edge. Instantly the enemy unleashed a barrage of tumbling stones and thus used them all up within a short time, leaving them defenseless.

***

At some point in our lives, we have to take a *risk*. Nobody can live forever latched to the skirts of a great tree. Lunging out from the forest can be perilous, but in the end, it pays off.

Peter did this very thing. In the safety of his small fishing boat, he watched the storm rage, the waves crashing, threatening the disciples' safety. But then he heard the Savior call.

***

"And He said, 'Come!' And Peter got out of the boat, and walked on the water and came toward Jesus" (Matt. 14:29).

***

Take a risk today. Dance in the open.

***

"It always seems impossible until it's done."
Nelson Mandela

Day 280

Rituals (177 BC)
Plutarch, *Marcellus*, 5

Tiberius Gracchus, the consul of Rome, sat flipping through some old books in his library. A sweet evening breeze wafted through his open window, and all was well in the empire. Having sent off several governors to distant provinces, officially approved by the priests, he was contented.

Sighing heavily beneath a glowing reading lamp, his eyes fell upon an ancient religious observance he had not heard of before. "If a priest reads the bird formations overhead and must suddenly return home, it is forbidden to return to this same house to continue the *ritual*."

Gracchus bolted to attention. "The priests I used did not do this!" Fearing this breach of protocol, he immediately informed the senate, who recalled the provincial magistrates.

Rituals were essential in the Roman world. Cornelius Cethegus, a priest of a noble family, lost his public job because he didn't properly present the entrails of a slaughtered animal. Quintus Sulpicius got fired because while he was sacrificing, his sacred peaked cap, the apex, fell off his head. And then there was a mouse who dared to squeak during a religious ceremony that cost Minucius and Flaminius their jobs.

Jesus lived in a country obsessed with *ritual* as well. Once, he sat down to eat with a Pharisee but didn't wash his hands first as required by law. The host was upset at this breach of protocol. Jesus only sighed:

***

"Now you Pharisees clean the outside of the cup and of the platter; but inside of you, you are full of robbery and wickedness" (Lk. 11:39).

***

Don't let mouse squeaks and empty rituals muffle the power of God.

***

"Salvation is not in rituals and sacraments but in clear understanding of the meaning of life."
Leo Tolstoy

Day 281

Rousing (1184 BC)
Homer, *Iliad*, 10:1–115

***

Agamemnon, the Greek king, tossed restlessly beneath a canopy of frowning stars. Rising, he stepped from his tent to the hum of surf stirring the Trojan beach. Scanning the plain nestled beneath Troy's citadel, he surveyed the countless enemy watchfires dotting the vast expanse.

When the surf quieted on its momentary exodus, he could hear distant foes humming confidently, some playing flute melodies that mingled with the sound of pipes. These night tinkling's sounded like dirges to him, forebodings of Greek blood painted on morning's ivory sand.

Groaning at the prospects of such imminent humiliation, he put on his shirt, bound both sandals, and flung a lion's skin over his shoulders, letting it tumble to the sand. Spear in hand, he hurried to rouse Menelaus.

Finding his brother restless also, they plotted anxiously to prevent an imminent slaughter. "Run!" whispered the king. "Hurry up and down the seafront calling men to wake and gather. Meanwhile, I will find old Nestor and tell him to go among the sentinels and urge them to *rouse* the regiments by their ships. We must act quickly before the watchfires beyond those hills enflame us all at morning's tide."

***

How easily we succumb to night's cooing, falling day by day into sweet complacency. We no longer see the watchfires melting distant stars. We are comfortable in our death dance. Jesus was stunned at His drowsy disciples asleep at their Gethsemane posts, and He *roused* them with urgency.

***

"Then He came to the disciples and said to them, 'Are you still sleeping and resting?... Get up, let us be going; behold, the one who betrays Me is at hand!'" (Matt. 26:45–46).

***

Rouse yourself, today. Take a new path.

***

"The contented soul is the stagnant soul."
Aiden Wilson Tozer

Day 282

***

Rumors (AD 10)
Ovid, *Metamorphoses*, 12:40–65

***

The mountain summit, hemmed in by land and sea, resides regally at the world's center. Here, atop the highest peak, there is a palace of countless entrances, all without doors. Here dwells *Rumor*, queen of gossip. Nothing is hidden from her; every bold and discreet word tickles her hollow ears.

Here in Rumor's estate, the halls stand open, and the bronze re-echoes, whispering secrets, doubling them, re-invigorating them. The air here is balanced with neither silence nor uproar, nothing but whirring murmurs like distant sea waves or dying thunder. Glance down any hallway and follow the lisping trail of truth and lies blending into dark confusion.

Each morning Rumor selects her missiles for the day and shoots them forth, stories that grow as they sprint across the globe. When received, oblivious hearers retell the stories weaving webs of half-truths that veil clarity.

Within this peaked palace, many associates come and go. Credulity winks at Error while Vain Joy mocks Fear. Sedition whispers in coded language that none can trace while Rumor searches, prying under rocks and crevasses for news.

***

Rumor, though never visible, knows your address. She sees all and loves to send your secrets spinning down side roads.

Often, we unwittingly aid her covert schemes. Be careful, as St. Timothy so eloquently said:

***

"At the same time they also learn to be idle, as they go around from house to house; and not merely idle, but also gossips and busybodies, talking about things not proper to mention" (1 Tim. 5:13).

***

Quick. Flee! Rumor's coming down the hall.

***

"A lie can travel halfway around the world while the truth is putting on its shoes."
Mark Twain

Day 283

***

Sacrifice (52 BC)
Caesar, *Gallic War*, 7:15

***

The wailing was intense. Villagers stood sobbing as they burned their homes and possessions, watching memories rise in the smoke across the valleys and hamlets. Caesar was on the march. It was the only way to stop him.

Vercingetorix, leader of the Gauls, had summoned all the locals together to develop a strategy to stop the incessant Roman advance. "The only way," he said bluntly, "is to burn everything! Burn the wheat fields so his army can't forage and set your homes ablaze. If you don't, Caesar will drag your wives and children into slavery."

The crowd listened sullenly, the somber news falling like a plague upon their once happy lives. All was lost, but still, they agreed. It was a *sacrifice* they would bear somehow to remain free.

At dawn, the citizens wept before their beloved thatched homes and then tossed torches on the pitched roofs. Mingling with the sunrise, the smoky villages blazed, flickering histories blending with a hopeless haze.

The stifling sorrow of this scene is oppressive. What do we value more in this life than our homes spiced with our most personal objects? And yet these Gauls burned them voluntarily to remain free.

***

Jesus asked for a similar *sacrifice* from a young aristocratic man who wanted to follow Him. Blessed with wealth and privilege, he thought it would be a fabulous adventure to follow the wandering prophet. "You may join Me," said Jesus, "if you sell all your possessions first."

***

"But at these words he was saddened, and he went away grieving, for he was one who owned much property" (Mk. 10:22).

***

Go ahead and light the torch. Sometimes, it's the only way.

***

"Great achievement is usually born of great sacrifice, and is never the result of selfishness."
Napoleon Hill

Day 284

***

Sanctuary (429 BC)

Sophocles, *Oedipus at Colonus*, 1–230

***

His regal accouterments long vanished, Oedipus shuffled toward an unknown grove near Athens. Wisps of white hair ruffled in a spring breeze as he dragged his 65 years heavily toward some hero's statue tucked against a grove boulder. Blind and hobbled, he leaned heavily upon his only friend, Antigone, a true daughter who had abandoned personal ambitions to follow her father.

"Daughter, tell me, where is this place? What is it called? Is anyone here?" His questions pricked the silence but for the spring nightingales.

"I'm not sure, Father. But wait, someone is coming. Here he is. Speak to him, Father."

"Excuse me, sir, but I wondered if..."

"Before you toss out questions, I must inform you that you are trespassing on holy ground."

"This is sacred ground?" asked Oedipus, confused.

"Yes. It is the grove of stern goddesses, Earth and Darkness."

"Maybe they will grant an old man *sanctuary*, a man whose life crumbled years ago, leaving nothing but this beloved daughter."

"Wait here while we get the authorities," they said brusquely.

Returning with an angry posse, the men made their demands. "Who are you? What do you want?"

"Sanctuary, friends. I'm too old to go on. I only seek..."

Before Oedipus could continue, the guilty verdict echoed through the pine trees. "Out with you. Leave our land at once!"

***

When clouds gather, as they always do, *sanctuary* becomes the shore upon which we must land. Ezekiel found such a haven as Jerusalem crumbled beneath him. It was then, beneath Babylon's shady trees, he found sustenance:

***

"yet I was a sanctuary for them a little while in the countries where they had gone" (Eze. 11:16).

***

Troubles? Join Oedipus and Ezekiel by the river.

***

"There is nothing wrong with having a tree as a friend."
Bob Ross

Day 285

Scarlet (52 BC)
Caesar, *Gallic War*, 7:88

***

Caesar rode ferociously down the hill's flank outside Alesia, entering the battle at its critical moment. He had been conducting cohort movements from a perch above the town, but now it was time for a dramatic presence. He adjusted the *scarlet* cloak, regally draped over his shoulder, the mark of the commander-in-chief, and dashed into the fray. Caesar's cape, fluttering for all to see, elicited instant bravado from the troops who took courage as their dashing general led them against the rabid Gauls.

A shout of acclamation rose among the forces that scrambled over the ramparts and out of the entrenchments. Leading the cavalry, Caesar, like a scarlet meteor falling from the heavens, summoned the full might of his Roman legions and routed the fleeing barbarians.

***

But wait. I see another *scarlet* cloak in the mists of time. A lusty Roman battalion surrounds a figure in Jerusalem's Praetorium. Jesus, standing alone, smeared with blood from a brutal scourging, has just been condemned to death. Bored soldiers toyed with Him. Having stripped his clothes off, they placed a royal garment about his bruised body, the crimson threads blending with rivulets of blood that slipped from his brow. In mocking derision, they hailed Him as King of the Jews.

***

"They stripped Him and put a scarlet robe on Him" (Matt. 27:28).

***

A scarlet-cloaked king rode a white stallion into battle; another king, beaten and humiliated, wore a roseate robe in a palace destined to fall.

***

Choose your cloak carefully. Only one leads to eternal life.

***

"The blood of the martyrs is the seed of the church."
Tertullian

Day 286

***

Scheming (AD 14)

Tacitus, *The Annals of Imperial Rome*, 1:1

***

Livia, murderous intentions dripping from her midnight pen, sat down quickly and scribbled the letter. It sped out by special courier to Illyricum, urging her son Tiberius to come home at all haste. Augustus was dying!

In the early years of marriage, Livia, Augustus' stolen wife, had learned how to manage her emperor husband throughout their 51 years of marriage. Tacitus called her a feminine bully and said that Livia had the old emperor firmly under control in the emperor's last years. He tells us that her blatant *scheming* led to Augustus' sudden death in Nola, a town south of Rome.

Many suspected this hastily composed letter hinted at murderous intentions. When Tiberius got back, Livia's guards sealed off the neighborhood. Nobody knew for sure whether old Augustus was dead or alive, but it didn't take long for two pieces of news to hit the streets and the empire: Augustus was dead, and Tiberius, Livia's son, was in charge.

***

The ancient Persians educated their kids from ages five to twenty. According to Herodotus, they only taught them three things: riding, archery, and truth-telling. Livia, always *scheming*, missed that last class.

One evening King Solomon picked up his midnight pen and wrote seven truths God hates. Livia checked all the boxes:

***

"Haughty eyes, a lying tongue, and hands that shed innocent blood, a heart that devises wicked plans, feet that run rapidly to evil, and a false witness who utters lies, and one who spreads strife among brothers" (Prov. 6:17–19).

***

No more midnight letters, please.

***

"While I'm dreaming, wake up screaming, cuz I can hear them suckas scheming."
Tupac Shakur

Day 287

School (AD 60)
Petronius, *The Satyricon*, 5:46

***

Professor Agamemnon sat bored and silent at the banquet table. He seemed to endure the sordid conversations of the drunken sots about him. Finally, Encolpius cornered him. "Guess you're above us all, aren't you? Sitting there in snobbish silence while we working-class slugs slobber on about our petty lives."

The professor ignored him, remaining aloof and distant, sipping on Falerian wine.

Encolpius took this as a challenge and decided to ramble on about his kids, who would soon be in the professor's classroom.

"As you remember, prof, I've got two boys almost ready for your class. The little one is smart as a tack. Studies all the time. He's even wading into his Latin and Greek a bit, but that older boy is a dud for sure. He works hard, but he just doesn't have it. I've been telling him repeatedly how important a good education is. I even bought some big red law books. A little law can be valuable, I told him."

The professor shrugged, wishing he was anywhere but at this table.

The guest beside him continued. "If that boy doesn't make it in *school*, I'm going to get him a trade, like barbering or auctioneering. But I tell him every day to get all the learning he can. It's money in the bank, I tell him. A diploma never killed a man yet."

***

The king of Babylon looked the refugees over carefully. He selected several of the most promising young men and pledged them a superlative education in his best *school*. Daniel was one of them.

***

"The king appointed ... that they should be educated three years...." (Dan. 1:5).

***

Study hard today, and make God smile.

***

"Education's purpose is to replace an empty mind with an open one."
Malcolm Forbes

Day 288

***

Scorn (AD 55)
Tacitus, *The Annals of Imperial Rome*, 13:12–13

***

Nero strolled through the closet memories of past empresses, touching their gowns and resplendent garments shimmering in saffron yellows and Tyrian purples. Brooches from exotic lands and studded gems of immense value graced the folds and sleeves of translucent gowns, stirring exotic senses within him.

He paused at one robe with exceptional jewels and decided spontaneously to give it as a gift to his mother, Agrippina. Tensions between them made life in the palace nearly unbearable. Perhaps such a gesture might help. He ordered this coveted gown boxed and sent it to her and then waited for a sweet reunion.

Agrippina received the servant holding a gift box. Aroused, she inquired its origin. "Your son sends this gift with his love," he replied.

Stunned but wary, Agrippina unwrapped it slowly and laid the garment upon her bed, its jewels shimmering in the morning sunlight. A small handwritten note tumbled from the folds of the dress written with Nero's hand: "I hope this treasure worn by Caesar Augustus' wife, Livia, will bring you happiness."

Agrippina frowned. "My son thinks he can buy me off with this hand-me-down. I give him the world, and he sends me a stupid dress!" Stuffing it back into the box, she sent it back with her *scorn*.

***

These scathing remarks stung Nero and elicited a brutal reaction. Nobody likes rejection. There are times, however, when it is justified. Once Jesus stood frail and exhausted atop a high mountain in the Judean hills. The devil's gift of worldly kingdoms shimmered in the desert heat but was met with divine *scorn*.

***

"Then Jesus said to him 'Go, Satan!'" (Matt. 4:10).

***

Shake scorn like salt: sparingly.

***

"Hell hath no fury like a woman scorned."
William Congreve

Day 289

***

Scuttlebutt (AD 19)
Suetonius, *Lives of the Caesars*, 4:5–6

***

When Rome heard that Germanicus was dead, the city convulsed with communal agony. So loved was this young general that when news of his death swept through the city streets, people rushed out in public mourning. Their grief had no bounds. Some hurled stones at temples while others demolished sacred altars, and a few threw household gods residing peacefully on home mantels into the streets.

The tragedy was not locked behind Roman walls only. It spread worldwide, an uncontained wildfire with distant kings shaving their beards and even their wives' heads. Civil wars everywhere ceased as combatants paused to reflect.

But then, suddenly in the evening, false whispering *scuttlebutt* began to circulate in Rome's gloomy byways. "Germanicus was not dead. He had recovered from his illness. He was alive!"

As evening fell, citizens flooded the streets with torches. They raced with their sacrifices to the very temples where they had hurled contemptuous stones and woke the gods with celebration. If temples were slow to open, they broke down the doors.

Tiberius, asleep in his palace, heard the ruckus and rose with alarm. From his veranda, he saw Romans congratulating one another and singing in the streets.

***

Thomas heard a rumor about Jesus, but he didn't believe it. The excited *scuttlebutt* in the shadows didn't crack his skepticism. It couldn't be true; crucifixions tolerate no survivors. But then, on the eighth day of its birth in a shuttered Jerusalem home, Thomas met Jesus face to face.

***

"Thomas answered and said to Him, 'My Lord and my God!'" (Jn. 20:28).

***

Some rumors, like butterflies, lift the soul.

***

"No one ever told me that grief felt so like fear."
C.S. Lewis

Day 290

Searching (AD 55)
Josephus, *The Life of Josephus*, 2

***

When Josephus, a contemporary of St. Paul, was just a teenager, he began a long *search* for his life's purpose. He was born into the most esteemed of the Jewish priests and royal blood through his mother. Royal bloodlines flowed through his veins, and when he turned fourteen, he possessed a deep understanding of the sacred Jewish literature and had a keen memory for details. With these natural gifts, while still in his middle teens, he immersed himself in a study of the Pharisees, the Sadducees, and the Essenes so that he might choose his life's direction.

When he finished these efforts, some of his peers, seeing his potential, told him about a desert dweller named Banus, who lived alone in the wilderness. Banus, perhaps a follower of John the Baptist, pursued the ascetic's life, as did John.

"I found Banus living under extreme desert conditions wearing woven leaves for clothing and foraging for fruit and vegetables. Each day he bathed himself in cold river water. I was so amazed that I imitated him for three years, and when I turned 19, I went back to Jerusalem, joined the Pharisees, and began my life."

***

Searching is part of living. Occasionally, we look for a lost valuable and never stop until we find it. Or perhaps we, like

Josephus, strive for a path to fulfillment. We see this zeal in the woman who lost a valuable coin.

***

"Or what woman, if she has ten silver coins and loses one coin, does not light a lamp and sweep the house and search carefully until she finds it" (Lk. 15:8).

***

Find a quiet place today and search.

***

"Put your ear down close to your soul and listen hard."
Anne Sexton

Day 291

***

Seashells (AD 40)
Suetonius, *Lives of the Caesars*, 4:46

***

Caligula, pretending to be a general, ordered the Roman legions into battle array. Britain glimmered across the English Channel; a glorious prize ripe for the plucking. Though the emperor had never fought in any war battles nor led troops against any enemy, these trivialities did not stop him from rushing to the seashore with his vast Roman siege engines.

The praetorian cohorts dragged the immense war machinery into place along the shoreline at Caligula's command. None of the commanders knew his intentions. No intense midnight strategies had been formed. Soldiers in full combat regalia stood confused but awaiting orders within sight of the turbulent sea.

Suddenly, Caligula gave the order to attack. "Forward, men. Gather *seashells!*" His voice, mingling with sea spray, urged the men to lunge at an invisible enemy. Shouting victoriously, he raced with his men toward the shore, gouging out embedded shells, calling them "plunder from the sea" due to the Capitol and the Palatine Hill of Rome.

Weathered faces used to grueling battles bent to their humiliating task. Calloused war hands gathered in the loot filling the helmets and folds of their robes with these sandy treasures. Caligula commemorated the stunning victory by building a mighty lighthouse patterned after Alexandria.

***

Paul had no time for frivolous *seashell* battles. He summoned his newly minted saints in Ephesus for serious warfare strategy. He began by ordering them all to put on their battle armor.

***

"Put on the full armor of God, so that you will be able to stand firm against the schemes of the devil. For our struggle is not against flesh and blood..." (Eph. 6:11–12).

***

You can't fight the devil with seashells.

***

"That's it. Curtains. Off to the races. Treetops. Seashells and balloons."
Al McGuire

Day 292

Seating (AD 58)
Tacitus, *Annals of Imperial Rome*, 13:54

***

The German ambassadors, Verritus and Malorix, strolled the streets of Rome impatiently, waiting for their appointment with Nero. Stunned by the size of Pompey's Theater, they entered and found the largest theater ever built by the Romans filled to capacity. Four thousand spectators filled the tiered seats, applauding the actors on stage. Noticing that certain areas had seats only for senators and knights, the Germans asked their guide why some foreigners in native garments sat beside the elite senators.

"These men sit with the leading families because of their valor, courage, and loyalty to Rome," replied the guide. The Germans reacted instantly. "There are no greater subjects of Rome than our country!" Then, without asking permission, they boldly strutted down the aisle and claimed the reserved *seats* among the privileged guests.

The audience noticed this affront but smiled, admiring these foreigners' pluck who dared to break with tradition. When Nero heard the news, he declared them Roman citizens, a designation not easily obtained.

***

Self-promotion has its place, I suppose, but I notice James shaking his head. Remembering the humility of Jesus, he seems upset at this precedent. At a recent Christian assembly, he had watched the brethren entering to take their places. The impoverished guests were ushered to the backbench while the men with elegant robes and golden rings sought the prestigious *seats* in front.

***

"Brethren, when you approve this tradition, have you not made distinctions among yourselves, and become judges with evil motives?" (Jas. 2:4).

***

Lay aside privilege. Take the backbench with James.

***

"Those who have the privilege to know have the duty to act." *Albert Einstein*

Day 293

Secrets (AD 10)
Ovid, *Metamorphoses*, 11:177–190

***

The barber suppressed a rising giggle while cutting Midas' hair, struggling not to laugh. Midas' enormous jackass ears, hidden beneath a jungle of shaggy hair, emerged slowly, snip by snip, until the barber, in utter shock, could scarcely believe what he saw.

He did not know of Apollo's curse upon King Midas, who had dared to mock the god's musical abilities. Apollo had just performed before Timolus, the ancient mountain god. He had played a lyre, inlaid with jewels and Indian ivory. His right hand, holding the plectrum, had plucked the sweetest refrains from the charmed instrument, while Midas, listening by accident, scoffed at the melody. Apollo recoiled in anger and turned Midas' ears into shaggy monstrosities.

The barber could scarcely refrain his laughter. When his client finally left the chair, the secret nearly drove the coiffeur mad. Valuing discretion, he ran to a nearby field, dug a hole deep in the ground, and, bending low, whispered his *secret*, with quiet chuckles, into the earth's depths. Then, to bury his voice, he covered the hole and sneaked away silently.

But as the seasons changed, whispering reeds began to grow there, and by summer's end, they rustled in the wind whispering the jubilant words, "Midas has asses' ears!"

***

Even the deepest of black holes will tell all. *Secrets* have their own breath, and they will talk eventually. The only way to tame them is to give them plenty of sunlight. Otherwise, Jesus' predictions will surely come to pass:

***

"But there is nothing covered up that will not be revealed, and hidden that will not be known" (Lk. 12:2).

***

Caution: The field reeds will whisper soon.

***

"The sweetest smiles hold the darkest secrets."
Sara Shepard

Day 294

Serendipity (600 BC)
Herodotus, *The Persian Wars*, 1:23–24

***

Arion, the celebrated Corinthian singer, sensed trouble. As he sailed home from Sicily, he constantly replayed the thrill of winning first prize at the musical concert. His soprano voice, along with skillful strumming on the lyre, set him apart from the other contestants. Now, with his purse filled with gold, he savored the Ionian Sea's salt air and smiled contently at the blue skies.

Suddenly, the shadows of menacing sailors interrupted this pleasant reverie. Surrounding him, they roughed him up and grabbed his gold-filled purse. Dragging the befuddled singer to the edge of the ship's poop, they ordered him to leap overboard.

Terrified, Arion begged to sing one last song on the poop. They agreed, thinking it would be entertaining to hear the world's best singer. Sighing at his unexpected fate, Arion put on his purple robe, cradled his lyre, and sang the "Shrill Strain" a blues melody with lofty notes. Then, when finished, he hurled himself into the sea with his gowns fluttering in the descent. But then, in a *serendipitous* moment, he landed on a dolphin who took him to shore.

***

Something similar happened to Jonah. Sailors tossed him into a raging sea, and a great fish swallowed him and took the bewildered prophet to land. One man stepped upon the back of a dolphin to the squeals of *serendipity* while another nestled in a great whale's gullet.

***

"And the LORD appointed a great fish to swallow Jonah, and Jonah was in the stomach of the fish three days and three nights. Then Jonah prayed to the Lord…" (Jon. 1:17–2:1).

***

Sing to serendipity, but believe in God's mysterious grace.

***

"Serendipity is looking in a haystack for a needle and discovering a farmer's daughter."
Julius H. Comroe Jr.

Day 295

***

Servility (375 BC)
Plato, *Republic*, 2:381

***

Plato didn't think God believed in divine *servility*. Discussing this thought with his brother, Adeimantus, he toyed with the idea that God might humble Himself:

"So, my brother," said Plato, "let me ask you this simple question. Can God change himself into any form?"

Adeimantus thought about it and said, "Sure, I suppose as long as He is doing the changing."

"Okay," responded Plato, "but I have to ask you. If God did decide to alter Himself, would it be for the better or, the worse? I mean, could he go from a beautiful form to an ugly one?"

Adeimantus thought about the question before he answered. Then finally, he muttered, "Well, if He changes at all, it must be for the worse since He is already perfect."

Plato nodded. "That's right, but would God ever want to make Himself less than perfect, you know, humble Himself into a lower form?"

"Impossible!" smirked Adeimantus.

"Well, then, as I see it," said Plato, "God could never change since He would always want to remain in His highest form."

***

I wish Jesus could have pulled up a chair with Plato and his brother during this discussion about humility. That would have been breaking news! These ancient philosophers couldn't grasp that *servility* was a virtue in God's eyes. He demonstrated the world's greatest love story:

***

"and although Jesus existed in the form of God, He did not regard equality with God a thing to be grasped but emptied Himself, taking the form of a bond-servant,... becoming obedient to the point of death, even death on a cross" (Phil. 2:6–8).

***

Let humility shine in you today.

***

"A great man is always willing to be little."
Ralph Aldo Emerson

Day 296

***

Shunning (58 BC)
Caesar, *Gallic Wars*, 6:14

***

In the famous novel *The Scarlet Letter*, a young woman named Hester Prynne was shunned and branded with the scarlet letter "A" on her breast. This dreadful avoidance ruined the life of a vibrant young woman with high aspirations.

Caesar noticed this practice in full force among the ancient British Druids. He wrote this account in his Gallic Wars:

"Their priests ordered everyone to *shun* those who did not submit to Druid authority. This meant they could not participate in the religious life so vital to their society. The highest penalty was to ban them from offering sacrifices or participating in religious observances. Ordinary people turned their faces and stepped to the street's edge when passing these criminals. Nobody could talk to a shunned person without personal repercussions from the priests. Total avoidance was the practice. These religious renegades could never find justice in the courts, and they lost all their dignity in the local towns or villages."

***

The great apostle Paul, after his conversion, felt total exclusion from leading Jews who now *shunned* him after he became a vocal supporter of Jesus (Acts 9:23). He noticed this ugly trend rising in some of his churches. He ordered the members of the Colossian church to be more considerate.

***

"Continue putting up with one another and forgiving one another freely even if anyone has a cause for complaint against another ... clothe yourselves with love, for it is a perfect bond of union" (Col. 3:13–14).

***

Tell the Druids, no! Extend your hands in love.

***

"One day, One hour, and One minute, will not come again in your entire life. Avoid fights, angriness and speak lovely to every person."
Anonymous

Day 297

***

Shushed (AD 54)
Tacitus, *The Annals of Imperial Rome*, 12:66

***

The poison-dipped feather thrust down the throat of Claudius set in motion a tsunami of intrigue and backroom shenanigans. With Emperor Claudius dead, Agrippina rose to conquer her world. As the emperor's attendants wrapped the warm body in blankets and poultices, she quickly gathered Claudius' children, stuffing them into their bedrooms behind bolted doors. No one would get out to the palace before the chessboard was rearranged.

Then, while summoning Nero, her son, she played the role of grieving spouse, shedding stage tears and rushing to embrace the rightful heir, Britannicus, still a lad. She embraced him, cooing softly, whispering tender words to the young man. "You're the spitting image of Claudius," she lamented to the boy while bolting the door to his room.

She likewise detained Britannicus' sisters, Octavia and Antonia, in their rooms like a clever general moving troops beneath a black moon. She ordered the palace soldiers to guard all entrances and exits while simultaneously issuing health snippets about Claudius' improving condition.

With all the pawns *shushed*, she yanked the curtains open at midday and revealed to a breathless world a new emperor. Nero, her son, shuffled out of the palace gates to rule the world.

***

Agrippina gagged the world and got away with it.

Herod Antipas likewise dragged John the Baptist to Machaerus' lofty fortress and locked him away for two years— *shushed* for political gain twenty-two years before Agrippina's crimes.

***

"For when Herod had John arrested, he bound him and put him in prison...." (Matt. 14:3).

***

Never be silenced! Keep a key in your shoe.

***

"A forced silence is a dangerous imposter, painting a canvas of safety while plotting our demise."
Jo Ann Fore

Day 298

***

Signs (1177 BC)
Virgil, *Aeneid*, 8:1–60

***

Aeneas lay on the riverbank, beneath heaven's chilly vault, sleepless. His band of ragtag survivors from Troy's collapse lay scattered in restless night-stirrings along the stream. Hordes of warriors scrambled down from the mountains to defend their ancestral customs and rights against these intruders.

Aeneas, his mind agitated, searched for answers that eluded him. Finally, exhausted at heaven's silence, he closed his eyes and dreamed. Rising from nocturnal mists, he saw a soggy, leaf-draped head emerge from the Tiber's depths. The deity's form rose in the shadows with wet reeds dripping down his spectral brow.

"Aeneas," said Tiberinus with a gravelly voice, "don't lose heart or be frightened by these war threats. The gods have ceased spouting angry threats and now wish you peace."

Tiberinus, sensing disbelief, continued his affirmations with a *sign*. "Aeneas, I see you feel this but a worthless night fiction, but I offer you this confirmation: search the riverbanks beneath the mighty oaks, and you will find a great white sow suckling near the water's edge. This will be proof that you have found your journey's terminus."

***

Long is the season of doubt and worry. We succumb so easily to life's threats and malaise. But God often soothes our night sweats with *signs*, His way of imparting hope on a dreary landscape. So it was with Hezekiah who, after weeping bitterly at his impending death, gained fifteen years:

***

"This shall be the sign to you from the LORD,... Behold, I will cause the shadow on the stairway, which has gone down with the sun on the stairway of Ahaz, to go back ten steps" (Isa. 38:7–8).

***

Stranded on life's dead end? Check heaven's email.

***

"A feather, a robin, a butterfly too, are all signs your angels are standing with you."
Mary Jac

Day 299

Silence (1184 BC)
Homer, *Iliad*, 7:420–430

***

The sun rose like amber poison over Troy's bloody fields. The truce, fresh from morning negotiations, drew both armies together on the rotting plain, as slain warriors sprawled here and there, their bodies locked in rigid hostility. The dead, many gored beyond recognition, drew shocked tears from the hunter-gatherers. These slain warriors were men known for valor in combat, men hardened by fierce winters and the cruel labors of war. One by one, the dead were gathered, washed, and placed on pyres.

Through it all, as tears flowed like mercy, *silence* reigned. Priam, king of Troy, had forbidden his soldiers to weep aloud. A gentle breeze whispered regrets as, one by one, the cleansing fires bolted to life, crackling silent obituaries to the gods above, sentiments unheard by lovers and wives far away in Greek villages dotting Ionian shores.

When the day's drudgery ceased, Greeks returned to their ships while Trojans slipped behind their walled veils in somber moods. Slaughtered oxen, salted with tears, gave hope to the exhausted troops who drank wine from Lemnos and wondered. Locked in mourning, the world slept fitfully, waiting in dread for another day of warfare.

***

There come times of grief when *silence* is the only language. There can be genuine healing in wordless moments when all we do is sigh and breathe and search within. Such was the day when, in the midst of suffering, He stood silently before His oppressors:

***

"he was afflicted, yet he opened not his mouth; like a lamb that is led to the slaughter, and like a sheep that before its shearers is silent, so he opened not his mouth" (Isa. 53:7).

***

Words will find you tomorrow. Silence will heal today.

***

"Silence is the sleep that nourishes wisdom."
Francis Bacon

Day 300

Simulation (AD 62)

Tacitus, *Annals of Imperial Rome*, 15:15

***

The war on the Roman Empire's fringe had not gone well. Parthian aggression had routed the brigades under Roman General Paetus, who tucked tail and ran for his life. His fleeing army streaked westward toward the Euphrates, consuming 40 miles a day, leaving soldiers exhausted and terrified. Paetus' cowardly retreat abandoned wounded veterans discarded on roadsides ditches. Shame was their drumbeat, humiliation their tormentor.

Back in Rome, Nero desperately needed a victory. Ignoring reality, Roman senators ordered celebratory arches erected upon the Capitoline Hill in Rome. Trophy banners flapped beneath the midday sun. Expectations soared as citizens awaited exuberant marching soldiers burdened with Armenian gold and chained slaves dragged behind booty-laden carts.

But, alas, Roman highways moaned in silence when news of defeat crawled across the Tiber River. As the gossip spread, the senators moved quickly to defy reality. Expectant arches were polished, and all roads cleared for imaginary troops led by phantom generals. Reality was brushed aside as fable, while senators praised the shamed army for victories never gained. It was all *simulation*, nothing but appearances.

***

Life seldom soars over majestic mountains and serene valleys. Often, instead, we face uncertainties, turmoil, and devastation. But lying about failures only deepens misery. Honesty and hope need truth to flourish.

Hananiah lied in the temple. He, like Nero, invented a false narrative. "I will defeat Babylon in the next few years, and everything will be like old times at Jerusalem," he said, lying. "You'll see. Just wait."

Jeremiah countered, telling him and the assembled men that it was fantasy. Just thin *dissimulation*.

***

"So Hananiah the prophet died in the same year in the seventh month" (Jer. 28:17).

***

Remove your wonderland glasses. It's time for truth!

***

"All hat, no cattle."
American Proverb

Day 301

***

Singing (1177 BC)
Virgil, *Aeneid*, 8:280–310

***

Twilight settled quietly over Hercules' great altar, the gathering place of King Evander's villagers. Early festivities with sumptuous feasts and dancing had dissolved into silence as the worshippers prepared for the sunset choir and fresh voices to *sing* of Hercules' greatest accomplishments.

Aeneas and his warriors, the king's guests, took their prominent places near the monument as the second banquet began. Delighted by the warm reception Rome had offered, the Trojan prince reflected on his arduous flight from burning Troy. His quest for a home had followed a divine path to this hallowed ground looming over the mighty Tiber.

As tables swayed beneath loaded dishes, meats, and grains of endless variety, all dedicated to the great hero, a quiet signal from the king sparked the singing. With splendid flurry, the Salii, that choir of leaping young men, processed around the altar, their voices entwined with the forest's night melodies. This ensemble of patrician youths moved with somber agility, dressed in red cloaks and bearing the traditional figure-eight shields.

The choral pieces recounted how Hercules killed the monstrous Nemean lion and stalked the River Styx. As the Salii sang, the hills echoed the tunes back, turning the distant mountains into green-robed choirs.

***

Music is soul food, the elixir that feeds our spirit and lifts us heavenward. Without it, we would walk a dull and darkening path to sterile solitude. We must *sing* as Paul made clear to his early followers:

***

"speaking to one another in psalms and hymns and spiritual songs, singing and making melody with your heart to the Lord, always giving thanks for all things in the name of our Lord Jesus Christ..." (Eph. 5:19–20).

***

Gather round God's altar and sing today.

***

"Those who wish to sing always find a song."
Swedish Proverb

Day 302

***

Sinking (590 BC)
Josephus, *Antiquities of the Jews*, 10:7

***

His crime was honesty.

But when truth collides with crusty hearts, truth suffers. And so Jeremiah, weary of endless resistance, decided he would leave Jerusalem and trudge home to Anathoth, his humble village north of Jerusalem. But the king's men, thinking he was deserting to the Babylonian oppressors, arrested the prophet and dragged him to the palace for questioning.

There, before Zedekiah, they smeared the preacher's reputation. "Do what you will with him," said the king, who concealed a secret admiration.

Like jubilant victors in battle, the sinister flock of advisors dragged Jeremiah to a bottomless pit. After tying the traitor with a rope, they lowered him to the quicksand below and strolled away victoriously.

Incrementally, Jeremiah felt his life slipping away as the sand nibbled at his legs. *Sinking* in the darkness, he saw flitting childhood episodes: his mother's smiling face at dinner; his father praising him for a small job well done in the garden.

When the quicksand curled about his neck, the prophet found breathing nearly impossible. Gulping air and preparing for a final breath, he heard the rustle of feet at the rim far above. The cord's splash beside his face sparked a new will to live, and with voices encouraging him, he breathed his thankfulness to God and ascended.

***

Are you *sinking*? Has life lost its allure? It had for a woman in Samaria who had come with a heavy heart to draw water from a well. She looked down into the cistern and saw only life's emptiness until Jesus spoke kind words.

***

"The woman said to Him, 'Sir, I perceive that You are a prophet'" (Jn. 4:19).

***

God is calling. Grab the rope.

***

"Only in the darkness can you see the stars."
Martin Luther King Jr.

Day 303

***

Skeletons (AD 60)
Petronius, *Satyricon*, 5:34

***

Trimalchio's extravagant and outrageous Roman dinner feast paused as Ethiopian slaves hustled away the previous course of peahen eggs. "Oh, so delicious they were," sighed Encolpius, "nicely seasoned with pepper and hiding fat orioles within."

"Soon, two other slaves with curly hair carried little skin bottles and poured wine over our hands. Everyone clapped enthusiastically, and then glass jars, carefully sealed and coated, were set before us.

"Trimalchio, the host, interrupted our wine-label reading and made a surprising announcement:

"This wine is the real stuff, genuine Falerian wine 100 years old, bottled in the consulship of Opimius." He smiled and then chirped, "this expensive elixir will outlast us all, so drink heartily."

"While we were sipping and savoring the elegant wine, a whistling slave brought in a silver *skeleton* fastened so that the joints could be bent in any direction. The servants tossed it upon the table before us and twisted it into several suggestive postures while Trimalchio recited his poem:"

"We're nothing but bones, sad to say,
as Death hustles us off the stage.
We're here today and gone tomorrow,
So live and drink and pay the wage."

***

David said our lives are nothing more than breaths of air that slip into the evening mists with barely a notice. He and Trimalchio, with his wriggling silver *skeleton*, mutter the same truth: we don't have long on this earth.

***

"LORD,... You have made my days as handbreadths, and my lifetime as nothing in Your sight; Surely every man at his best is a mere breath" (Ps 139:4–5).

***

Kiss the skeleton and make today count.

***

"This is a brief life, but in its brevity it offers us some splendid moments, some meaningful adventures."
Rudyard Kipling

Day 304

***

Slavery (1184 BC)
Virgil, *Aeneid*, 3:278–300

***

Andromache, widowed and broken, knelt beside a little unmarked mound of green earth. Her beloved husband, Hector, had been slain in battle beneath the walls of Troy. All that was left on this distant Greek hill was his memory. Here beside a little creek that reminded her of Simois, a mighty Trojan river, she prepared his funeral rites Her long hair, unbound, fluttered to the stream's lapping cadence as she poured wine upon the imagined grave. Hector's tender embraces brought tears to her eyes as she recalled her privileged life in the Trojan palace.

She did her best to blot out reality. Nothing more than a *slave* to a Greek king now, she lived in the shadow of love's joy. Nothing but chattel now, a king's battlefield toy, she lay with Pyrrhus nightly, dreading his touch. The king's contemptuous eyes grated her soul. She did her duty and bore his children, but never once did she forget Hector's smile.

Time passed in slow increments of inner turmoil until one day Pyrrhus, weary with his foreign bride, tossed her like fish bait to another man. These secret funeral memories by the stream brought her a brief respite from a suffocating, manacled life.

***

Life is often unfair; its cruel fingers wrapped tightly about our throats. Perhaps you see no escape. Maybe, you feel forgotten.

Take heart and remember Joseph too caught *slavery's* whip but rose to heights unimagined.

***

"Then some Midianite traders passed by, so they pulled him up and lifted Joseph out of the pit, and sold him to the Ishmaelites for twenty shekels of silver" (Gen. 37:28).

***

Shackled to despair? God has a place for you.

***

"If slavery is not wrong, nothing is wrong."
Abraham Lincoln

Day 305

Sleep (AD 38)
Suetonius, *Lives of the Caesars*, 4:36

***

The auctioneer droned on and on. One by one, the furnishings of a recent theater production hit the public for sale. Caligula, desperate for cash, forced the biddings higher and higher and then demanded selected patrons buy. Bankruptcies and suicides spilled into the Roman streets while the emperor counted his bags of gold with glee.

On one occasion, as the auctioneer gaveled furiously, a Roman senator named Saturninus stopped in to catch a bargain. Sitting near the back, he searched the stage for jewelry he might bring home to his wife. Waiting patiently, the cadence of the auctioneer's voice began to tug at his eyes. Before long, he slumped over, fast *asleep*.

Caligula, ever watchful, noticed this and whispered to the auctioneer to keep an eye on the senator, who kept nodding his head. After clearing the stage of the last item sold, thirteen husky gladiators, manacled with foot irons, shuffled before the crowd.

Saturninus, still waiting for the golden necklace, nodded off again. When the bidding ceased, the crowd congratulated him for purchasing thirteen gladiators for 9 million sesterces, a fortune he did not have.

***

The little congregation, gathered on a back street in Rome, opened the letter. Paul had written again, and everyone was eager to glean his latest thoughts. Some gathered found the candle's glow hypnotic and drifted off to *sleep*. As the divine words fell across the room, Paul issued this warning:

***

"knowing the time, that it is already the hour for you to awaken from sleep; for now salvation is nearer to us than when we believed" (Rom. 13: 11).

***

Sleepy? Wake up! The gladiators are waiting.

***

"Be watchful—the grace of God appears suddenly. It comes without warning to an open heart."
Rumi

Day 306

Slumber (AD 10)
Ovid, *Metamorphoses*, 11:590–620

***

The cavern wound endlessly down beneath a Cimmerian mountain where sunlight never steps. Iris, goddess of the rainbow, was on a secret mission to awaken Sleep, whose palace lay here shrouded in silence. With her thousand-colored mantle fluttering in the breeze, she descended into the foggy deep.

Iris' mission, simple at heart, was to arouse Sleep and urge him to send a dream to grieving Alcyone, whose husband, King Ceyx, had just perished at sea beneath roiling waves. The dream would bear the harsh news and give closure to the grieving widow.

Iris stepped silently over shiny pebbles, wet from a trickling stream that whispered its repeating mantra—Sleep! Absent were the bird's morning cries or a distant dog barking or cackling geese flying south. No human voices bantered at sunset on the long walk home from the fields. Nothing but silence.

Finally, Iris saw the god reclining upon an ebony couch, *slumbering* beneath a black counterpane. Sleep was unaware of Iris or her rainbow mantle, its fringes wet from the stream. Using her hands, Iris parted dreams scattered about as numerous as grains of sand on a shoreline. The god roused with difficulty noting her glittering garment and blinked, his eyes barely half-opened. "Why have you come, Iris?" he mumbled.

***

611

Surely it is a troubling image to see a sleeping god untroubled by humanity's woes. Compare the Psalmist who found a mountain high above the valley's turmoil. There, his eyes settled upon a God always awake, never *slumbering*, always ready to offer help in time of need.

***

"He who keeps you will not slumber. Behold, He who keeps Israel will neither slumber nor sleep" (Ps. 121:3–4).

***

Does your God sleep?

***

"Sleep in peace tonight. God is bigger than anything you will face tomorrow."
Dave Willis

Day 307

Snares (AD 28)
Tacitus, *The Annals of Imperial Rome*, 4:68

***

Sabinus carried a heavy burden. A man of honor, he was the last of the throngs who once fluttered joyfully about Germanicus, the handsome Roman general, and his wife, Agrippina.

Once the darling of Roman society, Agrippina, now a widow after her husband's suspicious death (some say by poison), walked desperately alone through the marketplace. Powerful forces hated her now, casting a long shadow upon her fragile family.

Sabinus became her knight. He strolled with her through city streets, avoiding the tawdry glances and squawking jeers of those who wished them harm. Sabinus bore these burdens silently until Lucanius Latiaris knocked on his door one evening.

Sent by evil forces to *ensnare* the talkative knight, Latiaris befriended the lonely Sabinus. He laid his traps with an almost poetic injustice. Bit by bit, the spy solicited innocent confessions and complaints about the evil forces that surrounded the widow and her courageous knight. Latiaris consoled his new friend, listening and offering soft words of comfort, brushing wings of sympathy against his broken heart.

On several occasions, Sabinus burst into tearful complaints, too willing to share the shackles that bound him to his noble task. These outbursts seemed to cement the camaraderie growing between the two men. Sabinus, a naturally reclusive man, was often seen knocking on Latiaris' door, stepping innocently upon hidden snares.

***

Hidden *snares* surround us in our modern world. We need to develop a sacred suspicion, for danger lurks everywhere. David found a balance of joy while casting wary eyes.

***

"Rescue me, O LORD, from evil men.... The proud have hidden a trap for me..." (Ps 140: 1,5).

***

Walk joyously, but cast an eye for trapdoors.

***

"O thou child of many prayers! Life hath quicksands; life hath snares!"
Henry Wadsworth Longfellow

Day 308

Soliloquy (AD 60)
Petronius, *The Satyricon*, 115

***

Ravaged by the Ionian Sea, the few survivors of the brutal shipwreck dragged themselves upon the beach and wept. A few floating water-soaked provisions bumped the shore, and over a small fire, the sailors cooked a few scraps of galley leftovers. Several bloated bodies floated by in the moonglow eliciting wails from their shivering comrades.

Encolpius, a survivor deep in despair, began to speak softly to the breeze trailing the distant storm's remnants.

"Imagine! This drifting corpse used to be somebody loved, somebody's husband, somebody's father. This is what human hope comes to?"

He paused, gasping. There, caught up in the wavelets on the shore, he saw the ship captain's mangled face. Weeping openly, he beat his breast in a frenzy of grief. "You were once the mighty captain, and look at you now. Fish food. Nothing more."

Shouting over the surf, he continued his futile *soliloquy* facing the wind. "We spend our entire lives dreaming, scrimping, saving gold as if we had a thousand years to live. The great houses we build all crumble into nothingness. The man who has no time to lose tumbles from his chariot and loses time forever. Death is a cruel master!"

***

While this tragic shipwreck desecrated the lives of passengers bound for Italy, the apostle Paul penned a letter to his Corinthian friends who gazed daily across their gulf shores. Death haunted these members as well, who mourned the loss of their loved ones. Summoning Isaiah's comforting words of a heavenly banquet with death vanquished (Isa. 25:6), he offered his *soliloquy*:

***

"O DEATH, WHERE IS YOUR VICTORY? O DEATH, WHERE IS YOUR STING?" (1 Cor. 15:55).

***

Death is only a door to your soliloquy of hope.

***

"The song is ended, but the melody lingers on."
Irving Berlin

Day 309

***

Sorcery (AD 60)
Petronius, *The Satyricon*, 5:51

***

Trimalchio's fantastical banquet rolled on endlessly into the night. At a brief pause between courses, Encolpius told this story:

"I once knew a working stiff who claimed to have a *sorcerer's* glass bottle that would not break. This charlatan managed to gain an audience with the emperor (Tiberius) and, with a magnificent flourish, kneeled and presented it as a gift. The potentate rolled it slowly in his palm, searching for the magical power. Finally, he stretched out his hand to return it. The inventor, ever the fool, pretended to drop it, watching it tumble to the marble floor."

The banquet patrons gasped. "What did he do?" they demanded, imagining the worst.

Encolpius paused for effect and then continued. "Well, he bent down and picked it up unbroken. However, there was a slight bronze dent visible. So, he pulled out a tiny hammer and tapped it back into shape. Instantly, the emperor sensed the ruse and quietly asked the inventor if anyone else knew the secret. The fool blurted out with confidence, 'No!'"

Encolpius paused and took a long drink from a chilled table flask.

"Well, what happened?" shouted the others leaning closer.

"Oh, well, the emperor ordered his head chopped off, noting that if this news got out, the whole trick would be worthless."

***

Magic so easily deceives us. Centuries earlier, the Pharaoh's *sorcerers*, masters of the magical arts, threw their staffs at his feet and watched them become snakes, slithering and hissing until Aaron's vipers consumed them.

***

"But each one threw down his staff and they turned into serpents. But Aaron's staff swallowed up their staffs" (Ex. 7:12).

***

Magic is impotent next to God's grace.

***

"You must dare the impossible. With divine grace, it will be possible."
Lailah Gifty Akita

Day 310

Soul (1178 BC)
Virgil, *Aeneid*, 4:690–705

***

Dido, Carthage's love-stricken queen, lay cradled in Anna's arms, dying. Her sister, angry but overwhelmed, muttered chiding words. "Why didn't you share this secret death with me? Gladly would I have departed this world with you!" But tears were late, so she screamed for water to wash the wounds and quell the spitting gashes.

Thrice the queen tried to raise herself, to utter last syllables, but thrice she collapsed back in Anna's weeping arms. With each attempt, the bejeweled sword scrapped against her chest bone as black blood oozed upon the pyre.

Finally, Iris flew from Mt. Olympus, pity driven, to separate her *soul* still locked in Dido's gasping body. Her limbs, dewy and fading into pale hues of death, clung in whispers to life's final throbs. Then, Iris, Juno's messenger, fluttering in a thousand rainbow's hues, hovered over the gasping widow and spoke these words: "As I was ordered from heaven's throne, I now take this sacred thing, the Death-god's due. I now release you from your body."

With humble flair, Iris snipped a tress from dido's locks. Instantly the warmth left the queen's body, and her soul slipped into the air.

***

We will never know Dido's final words when her soul drifted into the ether. They were locked in graying eyes, speechless to all but her. But John, who lingered heartbroken beneath the cross, caught the Savior's last utterance, drenched in sour wine, that released His *soul* heavenward.

***

"Therefore when Jesus had received the sour wine, He said, 'It is finished!' And He bowed His head and gave up His spirit" (Jn. 19:30).

***

May your last words be a benediction of grace.

***

"Meet me in the middle of your story when the soul is worn but wise."
Angie Weiland-Crosby

Day 311

Sparrows (56 BC)
Catullus, *Poems*, 2–3

***

As Catullus put it, Clodia once loved the little *sparrow* "more than both her eyes." It was his sweetheart's favorite pet. For hours upon end, she would play with it. The bird would hop on her lap and peck her mischievous fingertips. She seemed to court the pain hoping, somehow, that it might offer her some relief from a gloomy, love-stricken heart.

"Oh, little bird," said Catullus moaning, "I wish you would do the same for my daily depressions and gloomy cares."

And then, one unfortunate day, just as dark clouds often sweep across a sunny field, the pretty little sparrow died. Gone were the whimsical battles upon Clodia's lap between darting fingertips and the bird's playful beak. Gone were the idle afternoons when a lover often chokes on loneliness and seeks a frivolous companion.

Catullus mourned as he watched his lady love weeping, her eyes swollen and glazed, as she fumbled through yesterday's fleeting memories. She just couldn't stop sobbing. After all, the sparrow was sweeter than honey to her, and it had never left her lap, singing only for one; its little personal chirps meant only for her ears. And now, suddenly, an everlasting silence took its place.

***

621

When this little bird fell from Clodia's lap, it wasn't just Catullus who noticed. God was watching and caught the hapless *sparrow* in His loving hand. For God notices little moments like this in our lives. And He reassures us all that we are more valuable than sparrows.

***

"Therefore do not fear; you are of more value than many sparrows" (Matt. 10:31).

***

Feeling sad today? Trace the sparrow's shadow nestled in God's palm.

***

"Sorrow looks back. Worry looks around. Faith looks up."
Ralph Waldo Emerson

Day 312

Spectators (AD 14)
Cassius Dio, *Roman History*, 56:34

***

The funeral of Augustus, somber but majestic, left the palace on Palatine Hill in the year AD 14. The emperor's home for over forty years, with its Room of the Masks and pine-festooned frescoes, soon faded from view. *Spectators*, crowding the streets, watched with solemn awe as the procession moved toward the Forum.

The funeral couch that carried Augustus' body breathed of ivory and gold. Richly adorned with purple and golden coverings, it concealed the body hidden in a coffin below the drapery. Visible to the adoring citizenry along the route was the waxen image of Augustus clad in festooned garb.

Behind the funeral bed and chariot came a royal procession of images depicting his many accomplishments. There were representations of all of the nations he had conquered and pictures of prominent leaders.

At the same time, another identical waxen image left the Curia, where senators stood in sorrow, remembering the deliberations of daily business led by this fallen hero. Yet another replica of Augustus rode in a triumphal chariot with prancing stallions toward the Rostrum of Orators.

***

But another procession draws my attention away from the Roman Forum. It, too, boasts celebrity-lined thoroughfares with *spectators* long gone but still visible to spiritual eyes. Lining the parapet of heaven, I see Abel of old and Enoch walking shoulder to shoulder with Noah and Abraham. They all nod to us who live today, lending encouragement for our daily challenges.

***

"Therefore, since we have so great a cloud of witnesses surrounding us ... let us run with endurance the race that is set before us" (Heb. 12:1).

***

Live with purpose knowing Heaven's spectators are watching.

***

"Cycling is a sport of the open road and spectators are lining that road."
Lance Armstrong

Day 313

***

Spurned (37 BC)
Virgil, *Eclogues*, 10

***

Gallus loved a girl, but his love was not returned. Ah, such a painful path to tread. Her name was Lycoris, a moonlight maiden who had already moved on, leaving the *spurned* Gallus tortured with thoughts of what might have been.

War had claimed his soul, forcing him to march into thickets of violence and hostile forces. He still remembered his last glances at her as he trudged off to battle. She was left wandering alone in the frozen Rhine, gazing at crusted snow paths. Finally, love's fickle melody wooed her, and she followed another lover through rough mountain camps.

Now, having returned from the futile battles, she was gone. Gallus wandered daily into the dark forests near his home, calling for Lycoris, her name echoing through sad willow branches—"Lycoris! Lycoris!"

Pausing here and there along leaf-strewn paths, he carved her name into the trunks of lonely trees. His war dagger bit into the bark, planting tearful calling cards throughout the forest. In a mournful soliloquy, he called to Lycoris: "As these trees grow, so will my carved love for you, Lycoris."

***

Perhaps you have tasted the pain Gallus felt. When love *spurns* us, we stumble about disoriented and lost. But there is hope. David, too, felt this same despair. Rising from a deep sorrow, he wrote these touching words; his heart bared before a loving God:

***

"Let the morning bring me word of your unfailing love, for I have put my trust in you. Show me the way I should go, for to you I entrust my life" (Ps. 143:8).

***

Forget Lycoris. God has carved your name upon every tree trunk.

***

"The only love that lasts is unrequited love."
Woody Allen

Day 314

Squeezed (AD 9)
Cassius Dio, *Roman History*, 56:11

***

The Roman general Germanicus studied the lofty Illyricum citadel and sensed an easy victory. Many other regional towns and fortresses along the Adriatic had caved when the Roman legions pressed for battle. "Men," he shouted insolently, staring at the exposed citadel, "this will be an easy one. Form up and wait for my signal to charge."

Suddenly, they noticed the enemy lighting fires to their houses below the fortress heights. The conflagration soon spread throughout the village. Then, the combatants of Raetinum turned and raced to their secure citadel high above.

Germanicus laughed. "It was just too easy," he thought. Ordering his forces to charge, they burst confidently through the burning gate and clambered upward toward the fleeing enemy. A barrage of whistling arrows descended upon them from the fortress peak.

Startled, the Romans turned to flee, only to meet the raging furnace of crumbling houses and burning walls. They could neither charge forward into the raining missiles nor retreat into the blaze behind them. *Squeezed* between two death vices, the Roman soldiers were slaughtered in this tangled death trap.

***

Life often thrusts us into tight places. Only faith knows the exit.

The Israelites stood staring at the Red Sea ahead. Glances behind caught the Pharaoh's dust clouds as he raced to intercept the fleeing slaves. Death *squeezed* them with no hope of escape. Well, not exactly...

***

"But the sons of Israel walked on dry land through the midst of the sea, and the waters were like a wall to them on their right hand and on their left" (Ex. 14:29).

***

Caught in a vice? Faith will lead you forward.

***

"It's not hard to make decisions when you know what your values are."
Roy E. Disney

Day 315

Starting over (546 BC)
Herodotus, *The Persian Wars*, 1:88

***

Sardis, that once majestic mountain city, burned in the distance as Cyrus' men plundered. Croesus, the captured king, pondered it all, standing in chains upon a great pyre. Cyrus, the conquering Persian king, noticed Croesus, once the richest man in the world, considering his plight. In the meditative silence, Croesus uttered three whispered words: "Solon. Solon. Solon."

Cyrus heard but did not understand. As the fire licked the pyre's edges, Cyrus ordered his attendants to find the meaning. Finally, Croesus explained. "Solon, a wise Athenian, came to me once and mocked my wealth. If only I had listened to this insightful man."

By now, the fire raged, and Cyrus regretted the pyre. Ordering it extinguished proved impossible. Croesus prayed to Apollo, who sent a stormy rain that snuffed the fire.

When things quieted, Croesus asked if he could speak freely. "Certainly," replied the Persian king.

"All right then, what are your men doing off in the distance? Everyone is scrambling about frantically. What does this mean?"

"They are plundering your city and carrying off all your possessions," said Cyrus.

Croesus thought about this and then replied, "No. It's not my city any longer, and neither are these my possessions. I'm *starting over* from scratch. It's your wealth they are plundering."

***

Croesus *started over* in an instant, just as Jesus' disciples had to do after the resurrection:

***

"And after He had said these things, He was lifted up while they were looking on, and a cloud received Him out of their sight" (Acts. 1:9).

***

Take Croesus' hand. It's time to start over—today!

***

"There are two mistakes one can make along the road to truth ... not going all the way, and not starting."
Buddha

Day 316

***

Storms (1184 BC)
Virgil, *Aeneid*, 1:50–64

***

Juno, the queen of Heaven, seethed as she paced heaven's corridors alone. Feeling abandoned, her altars void of worshippers, she wanted vengeance. Spotting Aeneas' ship with full sail skimming over the sea, her hatred for Troy blossomed. Dastardly thoughts milled in her fretting heart and pointed her toward the dark caverns where Jove, the Father of Heaven, kept the *storm* winds chained beneath heavy mountains.

Approaching the murmuring cliffs in Aeolus, near Sicily, she listened to the restless, heaving winds bolted in darkness, prohibited from unleashing fury upon helpless humanity. Here, in the dark caves, King Aeolus, aloft on his powerful throne and under orders from Jove, soothed the writhing tempest with his scepter, he disciplined and cooed the impatient winds.

Juno bowed before Aeolus and offered a nefarious petition. "Your majesty, the Trojans, a breed I hate beyond words, sail freely upon the open seas. I beg you to unleash your furious winds and sink that ship. Litter the sea with broken splinters, and I will grant you Deiopea, the fairest of the sea nymphs. She will be yours in eternal marriage, but you must sink that Trojan boat!"

The king, ever suppliant to the gods, jabbed his scepter into the growling storm's flank, releasing it to sweep across the distant seas.

***

Perhaps this very day, the *storm* clouds are rising about you. You feel the wind's intensity as churning waves threaten your inner peace. Just remember. There is one who can still the storm.

***

"And He got up and rebuked the wind and said to the sea, 'Hush, be still.' And the wind died down and it became perfectly calm" (Mk. 4:39).

***

Your storm will meet the Savior today.

***

"There are some things you learn best in calm, and some in storm."
Willa Cather

Day 317

***

Strolling (375 BC)
Plato, *Republic*, 1:327–328

***

A cool spring breeze blew across the Piraeus harbor welcoming travelers for the Bendidean festival. The Thracian festivities delighted the citizens from Athens who hurried from the city toward the port. Socrates, *strolling* carefree beside his friend Glaucon, arrived at the harbor mingling with the throngs of worshippers and Bendis' devotees.

The Thracian goddess, new to Athenians, sparked curiosity among the respectful attendees. As the noonday sun loitered overhead, a magnificent procession began with exuberant singing and music. The goddess's image led the way, dressed in a short chiton that draped her high boots. She was wrapped in animal skins like Artemis, the huntress. Her spear seemed to thrust spiritedly at the crowd as her hooded Thracian mantle, fastened with a gleaming brooch, nodded her approval.

As evening approached, Socrates offered his final prayers to the goddess and headed home. Intercepted by a resident, the men paused for a delightful commentary on the day's events. "Won't you linger till evening?" asked Polemarchus. "My father, Cephalus, would be thrilled to see you again. It's been a long time, you know."

Socrates paused, considering the proposal.

"If you leave now," said Polemarchus, "you'll miss the spectacular midnight torch race on horseback that honors Bendis."

***

Strolling is an ancient melody, an artform easily relegated to the mists of long ago. In the first garden, strolling was the featured pastime, where mingling beneath shaded river branches, the Lord often delighted in Adam's company.

***

"They heard the sound of the LORD God walking in the garden in the cool of the day..." (Gen. 3:8).

***

Find your garden path today. God is waiting.

***

"Deep in the forest I stroll to hear the wisdom of my soul."
Angie Weiland-Crosby

Day 318

***

Substitute (438 BC)
Euripides, *Alcestis*, 1–20

***

A somber gloom smothered the palace overlooking the serene Pagasaean Gulf. Admetus, the Pherean king, embraced his weeping queen, Alcestis, as he glanced tearfully through open palace doors, wondering how this dreadful moment had arrived. She clung to him sobbing silently, stifling her grief in his royal tunic, willing to die for him but dreading the long journey to the underworld.

Words escaped them both. The king, choking on a coward's guilt, sought her forgiveness. It was she alone of all the couple's relatives who had agreed to *substitute* herself for him on this death-determined day. It was his day to tread heavily through the palace doors and into the jaws of Hades. But rather than go willingly, he had begged for reprieve. Only his wife had stepped forward, willing to abandon her palace dreams to dwell forever in the sequestered home of Death's dark recesses.

Dreading parting's fleeting seconds, they tasted love's last kisses, pretending it was all a dream that would end with innocent laughter. But Death's shadow suddenly crossed the threshold, his sword in hand, the very weapon raised to cut her flowing hair, the consecrated gift demanded by the underworld. With glaring eyes, Death growled, ready.

***

Rare the moment in time when one volunteers to die for another. Sacrifice of any type is rare, so when we see it stride forward boldly, we pause in admiration. Such was the tale of the gospel Paul preached to the Romans. Writing a tear-stained letter to his Roman friends, his quill told of another *substitute*:

***

"But God demonstrates His own love toward us, that while we were yet sinners, Christ died for us" (Rom. 5:7–8).

***

Today's sacrifice for another will win's heaven's dividends.

***

"Without sacrifice, true love is incomprehensible."
Toba Beta

Day 319

***

Success (401 BC)
Xenophon, *Anabasis*, 4:7

***

The Greek army's shout ricocheted off the Pontic Mountains and drifted toward the elusive Black Sea thirty miles in the distance. The soldiers, delirious with joy, shouted repeatedly the Greek words, "Thalatta! Thalatta!" (the sea, the sea).

The frigid air, eight thousand feet atop Theches Mountain where they stood, swirled thin clouds that drifted down the steep valley framing a portrait of ultimate victory. They had made it after the perilous eight hundred-mile journey through enemy lands from Baghdad to the coastal town of Trabzon.

Xenophon, following further down the mountain, heard the shouting and galloped forward to see for himself. Soon, all the troops following raced to the peak and began embracing one another with tears in their eyes.

***

This moment when the Ten Thousand first spotted the Black Sea was one of the most haunting scenes to come to us from the ancient world. It was a golden moment of monumental *success* forever etched in time.

For us, each day brings challenges, whether great or small. And in the haze of these ever-present difficulties, we must snatch glorious moments of *success* when they come.

The Israelite's flight from Egypt to the sea, a journey of nearly 500 miles, created a sensation much like that described above.

Here too, there were shouts of "the sea, the sea" by desperate pilgrims in need of miraculous deliverance.

***

"As Pharaoh drew near,... the sons of Israel cried out to the LORD.... Then Moses stretched out his hand over the sea..." (Ex. 14:10/21).

***

Turn your sea into victory. Claim success today!

***

"Success all depends on the second letter."
Harjot

Day 320

Suicide (AD 66)
Tacitus, *The Annals of Imperial Rome*, 16:18

***

Petronius, that famous Roman dilettante, raced for the coast, desperately fleeing Nero's wrath. Known for his lavish dinner parties and exquisite taste among the Roman social elites, Petronius found himself caught in a foul snare. A jealous rival in Nero's inner circle had bribed a slave to lie about the famous voluptuary, accusing him falsely of treason.

Petronius knew the temperament of Nero, who wreaked with nascent cruelty. Flight, now, was his only option. He got as far as Cumae before the cavalry caught him.

Facing imminent *suicide*, Petronius summoned his admirers from Rome's sophisticated families and threw a delightful party. But before guests arrived, he severed his veins and bound them unseen. Circulating among the merry guests, he listened to poetry, sipped champagne, and laughed at jokes while ignoring his fading strength.

In life's final hour, he wrote a tell-all letter naming all of Nero's sex partners and, as his last prank, sent it to the emperor.

***

From the tragic boudoir of a languishing Petronius, I see another distant light fading fast. High atop Mt. Gilboa, soaring over the Jezreel Valley, King Saul lay bleeding, arrow-pierced, and without hope. With his beloved sons lying dead before him, and the enemy pressing, he ordered his attendant to slay him. The servant refused, aghast at such a command. Saul, hearing soldiers clambering up the heights, fell upon his sword, preferring *suicide* to humiliation.

***

"Then Saul said to his armor bearer, 'Draw your sword and pierce me through with it,...' But his armor bearer would not, for he was greatly afraid. So Saul took his sword and fell on it" (1 Sam. 31:4).

***

When panic summons, never heed suicide's subtle whisper.

***

"Suicide is a permanent solution to a temporary problem."
Phil Donahue

Day 321

Superstition (1184 BC)
Homer, *Iliad*, 12: 195–230

***

The eagle soared over the bloody Danaan wall, oblivious to the tumultuous upheaval below. The armies, scattered along the mighty trench, clashed as Trojans stormed forward and fell to gashing wounds. Neither side prevailed. The Greeks held their elevated positions, raining stones upon the clamoring forces.

One gate, however, stared open-eyed at the storming Trojan masses. Far on the wall's extremity, the great bar that crisscrossed the portal was down so pursuing Greek chariots could swiftly race back for cover through this single crack. It was here that valiant Trojans surged, their rage pulsing as they lunged for the possibilities. Warriors along the great stretch of endless trenches and pointed stakes cheered at the breach.

But as the eagle soared above them, holding in its talons a squirming, blood-red snake, they all shuddered. The serpent, twisting with rage, repeatedly lunged at the eagle's breast and face biting mercilessly until the great bird released its prey and flew homeward, tilting in the sky, enfeebled by the poison.

Suddenly, a harmonious gasp settled upon the charging forces as they pointed to the writhing snake that dropped in their midst. This *superstitious* omen unsettled them all, and fighting ceased.

***

Superstitions, those shadowy shackles, can sometimes freeze our faith and send us stumbling backward. Stare at the eyes of the Roman soldiers beneath the Cross. When Jesus breathed his last words, earthquake tremors split rocks and opened tombs. The battel-hardened Romans reacted at once:

***

"Now the centurions, and those who were with him keeping guard over Jesus, when they saw the earthquake and the things that were happening, became very frightened..." (Matt. 27:54).

***

See through the serpent to God's steady hand.

***

"Superstition is the religion of feeble minds."
Edmund Burke

Day 322

Supper (AD 110)
Juvenal, *Satires*, 11:60–80

***

Hurry! Juvenal is inviting us to his humble cottage for *supper*. He assures us it will be a memorable country meal. Not like those glutenous feasts the rich like to spread. No. Come this evening to Juvenal's little place by the river where the willow trees sway.

"Juvenal," I ask, "tell us a little more about the meal."

His eyes twinkled. "Okay. Here's the menu, and by the way, you can't get any of this in those crowded town markets." He waved his hands as if to dismiss the competition.

"I own a little field near Tivoli. I will select the fattest kid in the flock, the tenderest one who has never nibbled on willow twigs or eaten grass. The one I have in mind has more milk in him than blood. You'll see.

"My foreman's wife will go and pick mountain asparagus after she's finished with her weaving. Getting hungry? We'll also have fresh eggs, big ones warm from the nest with straw wisps still stuck to the shells. Oh, and by the way, we'll also cook the hens that laid them.

"I've got grapes, fresh from the vines, and some of those Syrian bergamot pears in the same basket as the scented apples perfectly ripened with Autumn's chill."

***

Wait! I hear a dinner bell ringing near Hebron by the oaks of Mamre. Abraham sits in his tent door's shade on a sweltering day. When three guests appeared, he read the menu and urged them to stay for *supper*.

***

"Abraham also ran to the herd, and took a tender choice calf and gave it to the servant, and he hurried to prepare it" (Gen. 18:7).

***

What's on your supper menu?

***

"What could smell better than supper being cooked by someone else?"
Sue Grafton

Day 323

***

Supplications (AD 110)
Juvenal, *Satires*, 3:9:134–150

***

Naevolus was depressed. His life was in the hands of a few little altar gods, Clotho and Lachesis, who sat spinning his fate in wretched increments. His pitiful career had crumbled away, and all he had now was a shadowy retirement dream, something to keep him slightly amused and out of the breadline.

He sat on his dirty bed, making a list. "First, I need a small, steady check in the mail each month. Not much, just a thousand or so. Then I could buy some silver dishes, nothing too fancy, not engraved or anything. Oh, and maybe a few husky Bulgarian servants. Yes, that would be nice! They could carry me off at my whim to the Circus whenever I wanted some excitement."

He paused as these *supplications* to Clotho danced before his sunken eyes. Then more sugar plums winked. "And wouldn't it be nice to have a painter on call who could whip out some lovely portraits I could send to friends?"

He fell back on the bed, sighing. "What a life I could have!" He stared silently at the hole in the roof and knew it would never happen. "The gods all have wax in their ears when I call," he muttered.

***

Poor Naevolus. He wasn't one of those sitting on the slopes overlooking the Sea when Jesus spoke. He didn't know a God who listens to our *supplications*, a God without wax in His ears.

Can you hear the Savior's voice as it echoes off the mountain slopes?

***

"Ask, and it will be given to you; seek, and you will find; knock, and it will be opened to you" (Matt. 7:7).

***

Hold your prayer list high. God will see it.

***

"Beautify your patience with silence, supplication and tears."
Abdulbary Yahya

Day 324

***

Suppression (AD 55)
Tacitus, *The Annals of Imperial Rome*, 13:16

***

Locusta, Rome's favorite poison master, crushed and mixed away beside a flickering midnight candle. Locked into a small room adjoining Nero's bedroom, she toiled, her life on the line under threats from the emperor. "I want Britannicus dead now!" warned Nero, his steely gaze unflinching.

The sun rose on an exhausted Locusta. Her bomb sizzled in a small bottle, corked and ready. When the evening meal began, the usual royal guests talked merrily around the dinner table. The young nobles sat at their customary place nearby, watched closely by their parents. Britannicus laughed with his friends as food and drink passed before him.

The servant-murderer had discovered a way to circumvent the usual precautions. Britannicus was handed a harmless drink, already tested by a taster but complained it was too hot. Cold water, bubbling with death, was poured into his cup. One sip later, Britannicus convulsed and instantly ceased to breathe.

Shouts of horror erupted. Some rose and fled. Others, understanding, sat stupefied, all eyes upon Nero, who reclined undisturbed. "It's nothing," said Nero calmly. "He has epilepsy, you know."

Octavia, with *suppressed* emotions, sat silently beside her brother. She had learned early to hide all sorrow, affection, and every feeling. After a brief silence, the banquet continued.

***

Poor Octavia. *Suppression* has its necessary moments.

But the Philippian jail was not one of them. There, Paul and Silas huddled in an inner cell with their feet stocked, their backs bleeding. A melancholy silence was their right. But instead, a pugnacious joy reigned.

***

"But about midnight Paul and Silas were praying and singing hymns of praise to God, and the prisoners were listening to them" (Acts 16:25).

***

Celebrate your inner joy today.

***

"It is through suppression that hells are formed in us."
Susan Glaspell

Day 325

Suspended (1184 BC)
Homer, *Iliad*, 15:1–50

***

Zeus awoke from a night of pleasantries atop Mt. Ida. In the distance, far below the mountain peak, he turned his gaze toward the Trojan battle and gasped. His favorite warrior, Hector, lay twitching and vomiting blood. Surrounded by his compatriots, Hector's last moments hovered above his soul.

Leaping up from his bed, Zeus knew it was Hera's doing. With narrowed eyes, he lashed out at his wife. "You lousy trickster! Now I see what you're up to luring me to this hideaway bed. You drugged me with love-making and then took time to slay Hector and rout the Trojan army. But it won't work, my dear."

He paced back and forth; his face flushed with rage. Then turning towards her, he unleashed a flood of verbal threats. "I ought to thrash you for what you've done. Maybe I should do what I did once before. You remember, don't you? I bound your lovely feet with two anvils and tied your hands, painted fingernails and all, in a golden chain that none could break. Then I *suspended* you in mid-air among the clouds. I watched you squirm and struggle, and I laughed at my handiwork. Any soft-hearted gods who tried to rescue you were hurled to the earth."

***

Sometimes, it feels like we stand before two roads diverging in a yellow wood. We're *suspended*, frozen in doubt, dangling in

649

the clouds, anvil bound. Sometimes, though, a suspension can be contemplative, as in Hera's case. She regretted her mischief. Paul, too, faced a complicated suspension:

***

"For to me, to live is Christ and to die is gain ... and I do not know which to choose" (Phil. 1:21–22).

***

Don't fight dilemmas. Light will shine soon.

***

"Somewhere something incredible is waiting to be known."
Carl Sagan

Day 326

***

Suspicion (27 BC)
Tibullus, *Elegies*, 1:7

***

Tibullus' suspicion grew as he caught Delia smiling throughout the day. It wasn't the familiar face he knew so well; her romantic sighs came from beyond the boundaries of his humble cottage. When he confronted her, she spilled a thousand tears, wailing siren-like, an actress on a private stage, her flailing's unconvincing.

"But dearest Tibby, your *suspicions* are false, my love," her confession bathed in tears.

"Ha!" he sputtered. "These histrionic blatherings only heighten all my fears."

But he loved her still. He lived in her shadow, sensing a distance growing. Often a phrase would slip from her tongue about some fashionable young man. He caught it but trembled silently at such provocative thoughts. What if, he mused, some competitor noticed her leaning over a table, wine glass in hand, her bosom heaving.

She had often mentioned that she needed to leave to visit a distant temple on the town's edge. "Why? She's not religious!" And he had noticed a new gem gleaming on her fourth finger. And what about that barely perceptible cough outside the cottage gate?

***

Poor Tibullus. Delia did have another younger lover. Shame. Tibullus loved her so. If only the poet had known about the adultery pledge of Numbers, he could have summoned her to the priest and verified his *suspicion*.

***

"The priest shall then write the curses on a scroll, and he shall wash them off into the water of bitterness. Then he shall make the woman drink the water of bitterness that brings a curse, so that the water which brings a curse will go into her and cause bitterness" (Num. 5:23–24).

***

Suspicion, like hot coals, can sear trust.

***

"Suspicion always haunts the guilty mind."
William Shakespeare

Day 327

***

Sycophant (AD 14)
Tacitus, *The Annals of Imperial Rome*, 1:13

***

Haterius rose regally among the quivering senators. With a theatrical voice, he flung his *sycophantic* question toward Tiberius, heir to Augustus' now empty throne. "Oh, most honorable Caesar, how long will your country wait before you announce yourself, emperor?"

All senate whispering stopped as if it had sucked the oxygen from the room. Every eye followed the narrowing gaze of Tiberius, who despised such slobbering. Wearying of such morning tensions, he flung abuses upon Haterius and then rose, gathered his robe, and stormed from the chamber. Livia, his mother, hurried to catch up. As the couple entered the palace's private hall, Haterius ran to intercept them, intending to apologize. However, as he fell groveling at Tiberius' feet, he caused the emperor to trip, sending him crashing to the marble floor.

The guards drew their swords and meant to kill him, but Haterius crawled to Livy's feet, screeching for his life. Frustrated by the flattering senator, Tiberius let him live only after Livy interceded with fervent pleadings.

***

The *sycophant's* kiss seldom wins genuine adulation. Flattery often merely marks you as a lickspittle. Shadrach and his friends, on the other hand, demonstrated the respect true courage gains when they refused to bow down to King Nebuchadnezzar:

***

"If it be so our God whom we serve is able to deliver us from the furnace of blazing fire; and He will deliver us out of your hand, O king. But even if He does not, let it be known to you, O king, that we are not going to serve your gods or worship the golden image that you have set up" (Dan. 3:17–18).

***

Don't grovel at Livia's feet. Win respect with courage.

***

"I don't like sycophants unless you're a cat."
Primadonna Angela

Day 328

Taunting (1184 BC)
Homer, *Iliad*, 16:725–750

***

Hector, the valiant Trojan warrior, cowered inside the Scaean gates, avoiding the ferocious tumult beyond Troy's walls. Shamed by a restless god's whisperings, he woke from slumbering cowardice and leaped back into his chariot. Ordering Cebriones, his driver, to snap the whips, they lunged again into the fray with renewed purpose. Weaving the horses in and out of the Greek soldiers, he aimed straight at Patroclus, his chief opponent.

All about him, the wild dust flew as arrows whizzed and vulgarities dripped like black paint on a heavy canvas. Patroclus, spotting his adversary ahead bouncing behind the foaming stallions, balanced a spear tightly in his left hand. Gripping a boulder in his right hand, he steadied himself and hurled it at Hector. Missing him, it struck Cebriones, instead, as he held the reins. The stone hit his forehead, crushing his brow and knocking both eyes from his skull. He dropped dead instantly, leaning over the chariot's edge and plummeting like a cliff diver.

Patroclus ran to the twitching body, blood-soaked, and began a fierce mockery, *taunting* the dead driver. "Bless my heart! How beautifully you dived into the dirt. You looked like a deep-sea sailor leaping overboard for oysters. I didn't realize the Trojans had such divers in their army."

***

Taunts thrive on our despair. Flash a slight weakness, and belligerent voices will toss stones, gathering around with mocking eyes. It also happened to our Lord:

***

"And those passing by were hurling abuse at Him, wagging their heads and saying, 'save Yourself! If You are the Son of God, come down from the cross'" (Matt. 27:39–40).

***

Blunt the taunts with Divine forgiveness.

***

"The ego taunts truth with sarcasm."
T.F. Hodge

Day 329

Teamwork (AD 150)
Apuleius, *The Golden Ass*, 6

***

I played basketball in high school, where I learned an elevated truth about life: *teamwork* always wins the day. Slam-dunks garnered the newsreel, but passing the ball to teammates won the game.

Apuleius, the raucous second-century novelist, told of a beautiful young woman named Psyche who made the goddess Venus very jealous. To get her revenge on the girl, Venus searched for endless ways to abuse and humiliate her. She often ripped the girl's clothes into shreds, yanked out her hair, shook the daylights out of her, and belted Psyche's creamy skin until it was a sea of bruises.

One evening, Venus slipped into a frilly silk gown draped like a liquid rainbow and left for a late-night party. Before slamming the door, she poured a pile of seeds on the floor: wheat, barley, mullet, poppy, lentils, and beans. Then with a final wicked glance from the door, she sputtered, "Make sure you put those seeds back into separate piles before I get back from the party!"

Psyche, overwhelmed, sat staring at the seeds, unable to do anything. But amid this paralysis, a tiny ant saw her and had such pity he gathered his friends. Suddenly, a wave of little six-footed angels scurried over the seeds and, before the clock struck midnight, arranged them all in tidy, neat piles.

***

I could have used these ants on my high school team. *Teamwork* is the key to basketball and life. Solomon said this about working together:

***

"Two are better than one; because they have a good reward for their labor" (Eccl. 4:9).

***

Just pass the ball and smile at the sweet victory to come.

***

"Coming together is a beginning, staying together is progress, and working together is success."
Henry Ford

Day 330

***

Tears (BC 1174)
Homer, *Odyssey*, 4:190-235

***

Telemachus, the grieving son of Odysseus, flicked the reins urging the exhausted horses onward. For days he and his friend Pisistratus forced their chariot over steep mountain passes near Pylos and through the lowlands of Pharae where the cornfields blossomed. Nothing would keep him from finding his father, who had vanished beneath the veil of Troy's bloody war. For nearly twenty years he and his mother, Penelope, had cried themselves to sleep lost in twilight's tragedy, hoping against hope that somehow, somewhere Odysseus might be alive.

After darkness had settled over the strange Spartan landscape, Telemachus pulled the trembling horses up to Menelaus' gate, hoping that here they might find news, some lingering traces of faded memories. Surely Menelaus, the king of Sparta, could summon invisible threads of a lost narrative.

After the greetings, a feast was spread in the king's golden palace before these vagabonds of the night. Sorrowful memories tore at their hearts and everyone wept. Helen, the king's wife, joined the weeping guests and smothered by the trauma of painful reminiscing, she pulled from her purse a magic potion given to her by Polydamna, wife of Thon, an Egyptian herbalist. The herbs, when properly mixed with wine, prevented all sorrows, care, along with mournful *tears* from those who drank. She poured it secretly into the bowl and smiled as the evening brightened beneath a waning crescent moon.

***

Come with hallowed hearts and linger beneath flickering candles in the Grotto of the apocalypse. Here on the island of Patmos the aged apostle John who knew the gravitas of Calvary's *tears,* wrote these hopeful words:

***

"and He will wipe away every tear from their eyes..." (Rev. 21:4).

***

Lift your weeping eyes heavenward and smile again.

***

"Lessons are learned once tears have dried."
Sissy Gavrilaki

Day 331

***

Tempest (AD 60)
Petronius, *The Satyricon*, 12:115

***

Like a docile cork, the merchant ship bobbed and twisted violently in the *tempest*. A profound blackness gripped the Aegean Sea as passengers screamed to their gods for assistance, finding little solace in the heavens. Limp lifeboats were flung overboard, and those who could, leaped aboard as the ship splintered apart, leaving only a wooden skeleton left to battle the wind.

Amid this utter chaos, Eumolpus, a lone passenger and poet by calling, sat scribbling verses on a parchment strip. Oblivious to the disaster, all that mattered were the rhymes and cadence of a refrain he was crafting. When his friends found him, they did all they could to drag him to the lowered boat. Eumolpus resisted, shouting about the poem and unrequited love and other mysterious literary themes. Saved against his will, the lifeboat slammed the shoreline spitting the bard and his saviors ashore to live again.

***

Far away on a speck of sea beneath Judean mountains, another *tempest* brewed. Catching the sailors off guard in their tiny fishing boat, all seemed lost. Violent waves billowed, slamming the fragile hull, spreading terror. Spectral images tore at the men who struggled mightily with impotent oars.

In the stern of the small vessel, Jesus lay sleeping, undisturbed by the chaos. Deep in dreamy dialogue with His heavenly father, the Savior rode the waves peacefully until delirious hands begged Him to arise. Leaving the heavenly throne and an unfinished conversation, He stood, irritated, and shamed the storm.

***

"And He got up and rebuked the wind and said to the sea, 'Hush, be still'" (Mk. 4:39).

***

Caught in a tempest? Wake the Savior and find peace.

***

"There are some things you can only learn in a storm."
Joel Osteen

Day 332

***

Temple (AD 10)
Ovid, *Metamorphoses*, 8:689–719

***

Baucis and Philemon, countryside dwellers, lived in sweet balance between poverty and happiness. Their humble thatched cottage had all the essentials: a willow couch, a bare but sturdy table, and views of rolling hills. The elderly couple had married early and remained faithful, their hoary heads symbols of a steady virtue.

One day two divine visitors, Jupiter and his son Mercury, paid a visit. The old couple happily invited them to linger for dinner. Baucis stirred the fire's embers, and before long, a copper kettle boiled with a garden cabbage. Baucis scattered the old table with a handful of green mint and spread warm eggs upon it. Wine, of no particular vintage, filled the beech goblets coated on the inside with yellow wax.

After dinner, the gods urged them hurry to the mountain top. After a struggle up steep slopes, they heard their wicked neighbors screaming as the valley flooded. When the waters receded, all that remained was their cottage, now a gleaming *temple*.

When granted a wish by Jupiter, the couple, after a private discussion, asked for one thing: to serve in the temple their remaining years and to die at the same hour. After years of happiness, they noticed leaves beginning to sprout upon them. They bid the other farewell, and now there stands beside the temple, a linden and an oak, memorials to love.

***

Glancing back in time, my eyes follow the sheep's trail led by a humble country shepherd who, too, loved life's simple pleasures. His one *temple* wish was also granted:

***

"Surely goodness and mercy shall follow me all the days of my life, and I will dwell in the house of the Lord forever" (Ps. 23:6).

***

What will your wish be today?

***

"There's a grain of truth in every fairy tale."
Andrzej Sapkowski

Day 333

***

Temptations (1177 BC)
Homer, *Odyssey*, 12:140–200

***

The boisterous waves ceased their gamboling as the winds died to a whisper. Busy sailors furled their sails and busy oars churned the sea spinning little white caps in their wake. Knowing *temptation* stalked the boat, Odysseus cut a large wax wheel into small portions and molded it into small, pliable ear plugs. Each sailor bowed his head and received the waxen offering from the captain's hands. Then they bound his hands and feet upon a soaring mast, his arms tethered to the cross-piece.

The mellifluous song of the sirens crept innocently over the wave tips summoning the crew to linger awhile. "Come and join us among the purple-tipped flowers at our lovely home ashore" they sang. The maidens, their voluptuous feathered bodies fluttering over the ships bow, painted ethereal images of happiness and peace. "Listen to our melodies born in Zeus's paradise, crafted just for you." And so they sang on, their angelic voices mingling with sea spray, promised wisdom and joy if the ship would but follow the melodies to the valleys of pleasure.

Odysseus, roped tightly to the mast, begged his men to loosen his shackles. But with ears waxed, they quickened their oars and sailed past the snares leaving the sputtering sirens in utter despair.

***

Bathsheba rose like a sea nymph from her bubbling bath overlooking the Tyropoeon Valley. Her long, black hair glistened beneath a *tempting*, waning moon, the shimmering light draping her slender shoulders. If only David's attendants had bound him with flaxen ropes to the temple doors. But, alas, they did not.

***

"Now when evening came David arose from his bed and walked around on the roof of the king's house, and from the roof he saw a woman bathing; and the woman was very beautiful in appearance" (2 Sam. 11:2).

***

There are times when shackles are a man's best friends.

***

"I can resist everything except temptation."
Oscar Wilde

Day 334

Tenderness (195 BC)
Plutarch, *Lives: Marcus Cato*, 5

***

In ancient times, Cato the Elder had a sterling reputation for living frugally and managing his affairs with wisdom. But he had one flaw that Plutarch, the historian, hated. Cato would work his servants and animals until they were old and useless. Then, with a cold wave of his hand, he would sell them off for pennies to avoid feeding them.

When his Spanish campaign was over, he stood at the docks loading his ship to return home. Standing beside his loyal and courageous warhorse, who had carried Cato in scores of brutal battles, he sensed that the cost would be too great to load the horse for retirement on his farm pasture. So, he cruelly abandoned it.

Plutarch, the sensible first-century historian, said this in response:

"When a horse is weary after a life of dedicated service, the animal deserves respect and love. A good man will show a weary old horse kindness. And likewise, it's not enough to dote over little puppies when they are so cute. You must show the same *tenderness* when they are old and feeble. Living creatures aren't like old shoes or broken forks and knives. You can't just throw them out. Instead, we should all cultivate tenderness toward our farm animals because this will teach us to love our neighbors."

***

Paul must have shaken his head in disgust at Cato's harsh philosophy. He, instead, urged his beloved saints to always show *tenderness* to one another.

***

And be kind to one another, tender-hearted, forgiving each other, just as God in Christ also has forgiven you (Eph. 4:32).

***

Hug your old horse and kiss a friend.

***

"There is no charm equal to tenderness of heart."
Jane Austin

Day 335

Thankfulness (1184 BC)
Virgil, *Aeneid*, 1:600–650

***

Dido, the queen of Carthage, addressed the forlorn Trojan survivors of a deadly Libyan sea storm. Violent winds had sent their ships tumbling. Now homeless and lost, they kneeled tearfully before the queen in her palace. She rose and spoke kindly. "I have heard of your valiant Trojan war and King Aeneas, the bravest of warriors. If only he could be here, I would express my admiration for him."

Aeneas, hidden behind a cloak of darkness, rose, cast aside his invisibility, and joyfully declared himself. The queen, shocked by the magnitude of his downfall, expressed her genuine sympathy. "I was once like you are now," she said, her eyes misting. "But I am learning every day how to help the unlucky." With these words, she clapped her hands and ordered an evening of *thankfulness* in the god's temple.

As her enthusiasm grew, she ordered servants to lead a hundred fatted lambs to the beach where the other bedraggled survivors waited. Meanwhile, Dido arrayed her palace with glitter and gold, preparing for a sumptuous thanksgiving banquet. Princely purple hangings, richly embroidered, set an elegant mood hovering over solid silver table plates.

***

In perilous times, nothing lifts us more than a *thankful* friend. When the dawn refuses to shine and you can't shake the shadows, a nostalgic letter from a friend often calms the inner storm. So it was when Jeremiah's letter arrived for the tattered refugees washed ashore in Babylon.

***

"'For I know the plans that I have for you' declared the LORD, 'plans for welfare and not for calamity to give you a future and a hope'" (Jer. 29:12).

***

God's letter to you awaits. Open it and smile.

***

"O Lord that lends me life, lend me a heart replete with thankfulness."
William Shakespeare

Day 336

Tombs (520 BC)
Herodotus, *The Persian Wars*, 1:188

***

Nitocris, the queen of Babylon, placed her *tomb* high above the most used gate of the splendid city. She then engraved a simple but direct message for all to see who passed beneath the lofty entranceway: "If any future king of Babylon ever needs money, let him open my tomb. If not, keep out, or else!"

The offer lay like a silent twinkling star beneath her shroud for centuries. Then one day, Darius, conqueror of Babylon, scoffed and ordered the tomb opened. "I will not walk daily beneath this corpse, nor will I refuse the gold above my head."

When he parted the cobwebs and stared into the darkened tomb, he saw its starkest truth, the crumbling skeleton of a once vibrant queen. On a small tablet beside her sunken eyes, he found this inscription: "Only a greedy fool would have done what you just did!"

***

Every tombstone speaks, and their voices, raspy and distant, remind us of the value of life. Whether it's the cynical voice of an ancient queen or the tears of a Galilean peasant, the lyrics are the same: Time is short!

Jesus confronted a *tomb* once with different results. Standing outside the sealed cylindrical granite stone, Jesus wept. His close friend lay within, dead four days now. Wiping the tears from His eyes, he uttered a simple prayer and then ordered the tomb opened.

***

"The man who had died came forth, bound hand and foot with wrappings, and his face was wrapped around with a cloth. Jesus said to them, 'Unbind him, and let him go'" (Jn. 11:44).

***

Kiss a tomb today, and live with purpose.

***

"That's all, folks."
Mel Blanc

Day 337

***

Tragedy (AD 23)
Tacitus, *The Annals of Imperial Rome*, 4:2

***

Livilla was a *tragedy* in slow motion, a descent of her own making that merely doubled the misfortune. She brought it all on herself. Unattractive as a girl, she had blossomed into a beauty later in life and wed the emperor's son, Drusus. This placed her on a sublime path to glory and fame. But moonlight and forbidden kisses from that sleazy soldier, Sejanus, led her astray down a prickly path to a brutal dead end.

It happened one night when Sejanus, the dashing commander of the Praetorian Guard headquartered in Rome, kissed her hand and then her lips. Faint with a giddy bliss, she plunged headlong into a forbidden romance with this small-town adulterer.

Whispering plans of betrayal and murder in dark palace corridors, the two plotted ways to kill her husband, Drusus. They settled on a silent poison dripped into his meals by a court eunuch. Slowly, Drusus declined until death took him. When the news spilled out into the streets of Rome, the senators wept.

From this cauldron of intrigue, fumes bubbled up to overtake Livilla and Sejanus ending in execution and suicide.

***

Matthew tells us a similar tale of *tragedy*. Judas, too, harboring dark ambitions, slipped unknown to a secret gathering of the high priests. "What will you pay me to betray Jesus?" he asked. Without a word spoken, the treasurer spilled a handful of silver coins on the table before him. And with the tainted melody of tinkling silver in his pocket, Judas betrayed the Lord.

***

"And they weighed out thirty pieces of silver to him" (Matt. 26:15).

***

Guard your steps. Seek the high road in life.

***

"There are seeds of self-destruction in all of us..."
Dorothea Brande

Day 338

Transformations (1184 BC)
Homer, *Iliad*, 5:1–8

***

I love working with chameleons. They're so refreshing since they always put on a fresh face reflecting nature's beauty, a *transformation* that enables them to inspire those around them.

I see something like this in a story Homer told years ago. Once, a great warrior named Diomedes rushed off one day to wage war against the Trojans. A fierce battle unfolded as shields clashed with shields. Death cries rumbled across the fields of blood as Apollo shouted for the Trojan combatants to conquer with courage.

In the middle of this bloodfest, Diomedes suddenly felt a surge of valor within him, placed there by the goddess Athene. She made his shield and helmet glow with the effulgence of the Star of Summer that rose each day from his ocean bath. Instantly he began to reflect the brilliance of the sun. The goddess lit his face with such a starry brilliance no eye could gaze upon him. Covered with this heavenly glory, he strode into the midst of the heated battle brimming with confidence.

***

Moses had a similar experience on the lofty peaks of Mt. Sinai. After speaking with God for many days on the mountain top, he came down brimming with enthusiasm, his face glowing with a divine *transformation*. No one could approach him until he placed a veil over his head.

675

We, too, will one day find our faces glowing. The Bible tells us that:

***

"We all, with unveiled face beholding as in a mirror the glory of the Lord, are being transformed into the same image from glory to glory, just as from the Lord, the Spirit" (2 Cor. 3:18).

***

What does your face say to the world?

***

"Intelligence is the ability to adapt to change."
Stephen Hawking

Day 339

Trapped (1177 BC)
Virgil, *Aeneid*, 9:720–820

***

Pandarus, friend of Aeneas, saw the panic at the open gate. The Latin forces were breaking through in a chaotic struggle at this vulnerable breach along the battlements. Taking swift action, Pandarus lowered his massive shoulders and forced the rusty hinges backward, dragging enemy and foe alike, screaming. With a final effort, the gates shuddered and locked, abandoning some Trojan forces outside the walls.

Unnoticed, however, was the Latin general Turnus who had managed to scramble inside the walls, riding the swinging door inward. With his blood-red helmet plumes quivering, he fought like a cornered lion, slaughtering any foe within reach of his deadly blade. Little by little, however, he gave ground as the enemy *trapped* him against the flowing Tiber.

Turnus, bathed in sweat, his sword arm drooping, stared death down and fought on. The plumes on his crested helmet had vanished, exposing the metal cracks, variegated lines of surrender to enemy rocks. Panting heavily, his mighty shield broken and bent, he grimaced one last time, turned, and plunged into the river. Its yellow tide welcomed him, washing his bloodied body. Bobbing gently, he escaped downriver to rejoin his army.

***

Once, a long time ago, I sat peeling husks from my garden corn. The small, hot parsonage where I daily baked in the southern heat smirked. I was *trapped* in Nowhere Ville, a Turnus with his back to the Tiber.

David, too, had stumbled into a trap at Keilah. When Saul heard the good news, he laughed.

***

"God has delivered him into my hands, for he shut himself in by entering a city with double gates and bars" (1 Sam. 23:7).

***

Trapped? Stay calm and find your river.

***

"Trapped by reality, freed by imagination."
Nicolas Manetta

Day 340

***

Treachery (1184 BC)
Virgil, *Aeneid*, 3:10–68

***

Aeneas and his small fleet of sailing vagabonds lowered their sails near a beautiful Thracian beach. Scrambling through smooth surf, they stepped ashore, breathing air free from Troy's blackened skies. Naming his new city Aenea, he set up an altar. Searching the forest's edge for garlands to festoon the altar, he pulled up some foliage and gasped. Black blood dripped upon his hands. "What does this mean?" he wondered. "Have the gods turned upon us so early in our quest for a homeland?"

His hair on end, he pulled another clump of greenery, and it, too, dripped black blood. Frozen with terror, Aeneas heard a moaning buried beneath the sand. "My friend, you are tearing me. I am buried here. Please, no more! I am Polydorus, a friend of your father, Priam, who ruled Troy. He sent me here to hide the golden treasures of Troy's palace until the war ended. But the *treacherous* king here betrayed me. He stole the gold and buried me here."

Shaken, Aeneas cursed the wicked potentate who loved gold more than honor. Summoning the ship's pilgrims, they buried anew their betrayed friend as the women stood round the tomb, their hair unbound as the rites required.

***

Gold and its allurements often ravage our best intentions. Who can hold the higher cause above money's hungry reach? Moses' *treacherous* comrades, desert vagabonds, joined the Thracian king above in his debauchery:

***

"Then all the people tore off the gold rings which were in their ears and brought them to Aaron. He took this from their hand, and fashioned it with a graving tool and made it into a molten calf..." (Ex. 32:3–4).

***

Treachery summons today. Will you be true?

***

"There is no knife that cuts so sharply and with such poisoned blade as treachery."
Ouida

Day 341

Treason (AD 14)
Cassius Dio, *Roman History*, 56:31

***

The aged Augustus strolled lovingly through his father's gardens in the town of Nola, not far from Rome. The small cottage where his father had died 72 years earlier served as a respite from his duties as emperor. Now 75, he moved slowly, his faltering steps weaving in and out of the fig trees he loved, the ones his father had planted.

The morning Aegean mists blew softly across the old homeplace as Augustus made a selection of figs for breakfast. Cradling his morning catch, he handed them to Livia, his wife of 50 years, kissing her softly, bidding her to prepare the quaint feast.

Livia lovingly smeared poison on the figs he had selected and set the table, smiling *treasonously* as her husband savored the sun-ripened fruit. By noon, Augustus, sweating and feverish, called for his closest associates, sensing his end was near. After telling them his wishes, he uttered a final summation of his long life: "Rome was just dirt when I found her; I leave behind a city of marble." On this August 19, when the evening sun cooed softly over the shadowed fig-trees, he died.

***

Loving *treason* bears the deepest crimson stains. So it was with Livia; so it was with Delilah. Samson loved her, but she loved the 1100 pieces of silver offered to her more. With treasure embedded in her soul, she coaxed the secret of his strength, killing the mighty giant softly, whispering love words while he slept upon her knees.

***

"She made him sleep on her knees, and called for a man and had him shave off the seven locks of his hair" (Judg. 16:19).

***

Purge your life of poisonous intent. Live with innocence.

***

"Ready tears are a sign of treachery, not of grief."
Publilius Syrus

Day 342

***

Treasure (53 BC)
Caesar, *The Gallic War*, 6:17

***

As Caesar traveled through the land of the Gauls, he noticed an unusual custom observed by these warrior peoples. After battles, the Gauls gathered the spoils of war into the local village and piled them publicly in sacred heaps. As the inhabitants went about their regular duties, they often passed by the glittering mounds of gold and silver objects with no thought of pilfering them secretly.

Day after day, the morning sun reflected off the treasures reminding citizens of battle victories, fanning a pride in accomplishment. And in the evening's moon glow, as people returned from the fields, these spoils of war ushered them home, breeding quiet confidence in the army's power.

Should anyone break these rules and steal from the *treasure* pile secretly, woe to them. If discovered, they were dragged from their home and tortured grievously for the offense.

***

Achan could have profited from this custom of honesty. It was Achan who stole from his town's sacred pile of war *treasure*, dreaming night after night of a beautiful mantel from Shinar. Pausing one night at the war pile, he took the Shinar mantle and stole 200 shekels of silver and a heavy bar of gold. Then he hurried home and buried them beneath his family tent. When

Joshua discovered this breach of trust, the retaliation was brutal and swift (Josh. 7).

Jesus offers valuable spiritual advice about treasure:

***

"But store up for yourselves treasures in heaven, where neither moth nor rust destroys, and where thieves do not break in or steal; for where your treasure is, there your heart will be also" (Matt. 6:20–21).

***

Earthly treasures fade. Heavenly treasures glitter forever.

***

"Memories are timeless treasures of the heart."
Anonymous

Day 343

Trinity (AD 60)
Petronius, *The Satyricon*, 5:60

***

Three slave boys burst through the kitchen doors into the banquet hall. Their snowy garments flowed with a heavenly trail behind them as they carried three little statues with graceful dignity. Trimalchio's endless banquet paused to consider the divine implications unfolding before the guests' eyes.

Each figurine, a personal god of the host, wore a golden medallion in honor of Trimalchio. The sated revelers put down their wine goblets and with hazy eyes, felt themselves being dragged into church. No one dared refuse. Each watched warily as one of the angelic servants carried around a bowl of wine and solemnly intoned a prayer for blessings on the guests and the home.

Trimalchio tapped his wine glass with a dainty spoon and called everyone to order. "Let me introduce my homeboys." Strolling to the side of the first statue, he caressed its long golden hair. "This one," he announced," is called 'Fat Profit.'" Then with a slight wave, he averted everyone's eyes toward the second idol. "And this little deity is 'Good Luck.'" Everyone chuckled beneath their hands. "And finally, this last fella is 'Large Income.'"

A ghostly confusion bemused the guests. Nobody had met this *trinity* in the temples of Rome.

***

Trimalchio's gods formed a silly *trinity* of muckrakers, spirits of the working stiffs who labored daily for wealth and the pursuit of gold. But in the same year, across the Ionian Sea, Paul closed a personal letter with the names of a different trinity:

***

"The grace of the Lord Jesus Christ, and the love of God, and the fellowship of the Holy Spirit, be with you all" (2 Cor. 13:14).

***

Choose your trinity, and bow to them today.

***

"Isn't it a comfort to worship a God we cannot exaggerate?"
Francis Chan

Day 344

***

Triumph (46 BC)
Suetonius, *Lives of the Caesars*, 1:37

***

On the morning of September 21, 46 BC, the city of Rome witnessed two weeks of spectacle, an extravaganza unsurpassed on its streets. Julius Caesar celebrated four *triumphs*, an accomplishment never before achieved by any Roman general.

Passing through the Porta Triumphalis, past the Field of Mars, and then along the Sacred Way, Caesar rode in a chariot of honor led by four horses. He held an ivory scepter in his left hand and a laurel branch in his right. Behind him in the chariot stood a slave grasping Caesar's golden crown and continually whispering in the general's ear: "Remember. You're just a man. Nothing more."

Every few days, Caesar unveiled a new spectacle, a triumph celebrating one of his four recent battlefield conquests. On the day he rode into the city with frightened Pontic captives parading before him, he had inscribed these words on one of the wagons: "I came. I saw. I conquered!" The phrase he coined emphasized how quickly he had vanquished Pharnaces II in Zela. Torch-bearing elephants paraded before this wagon as Roman youths led a sacrificial ox to the temple. Chained men, women, and children stared blankly at the splendor of the Forum.

***

Caesar shared a throne with no one. He came, saw, conquered the known world, and reigned in solitary glory before a stunned republic. But John saw a more sublime theme. We all can *triumph* and share God's throne:

***

"He who conquers, I will grant to him to sit down with Me on My throne, as I also conquered and sat down with My Father on His throne" (Rev. 3:21).

***

Celebrate your triumph today with God's help!

***

"Always seek out the seed of triumph in every adversity."
Og Mandino

Day 345

Troublemakers (1184 BC)
Homer, *Iliad*, 2:211–270

***

Thersites was a brute with a bald, pointed head. Achilles and Odysseus couldn't stand him because he always spun lies, stirring up trouble with his shrill, squeaky voice. Worse yet, this bow-legged *troublemaker* zigzagged up and down the Trojan shore, his rounded shoulders hunched over a sunken chest, mocking truth and nobility.

Thersites hated anybody in authority, especially King Agamemnon, who was often the theme of his seditious rants. All he wanted was a laugh as he railed before weary soldiers on the front lines.

As morning spilled over the Aegean Sea, the Greek fighters gathered in mass by their boats, stumbling about in confusion. Some had heard the war was over. Many homesick veterans shouted deliriously, racing to ready their ships for departure. As thousands sprinted for the boats, dust balls spun heavenward beneath feet that longed to touch abandoned thresholds.

But as Achilles, ever wary, hurried to block this mass exodus, demanding them to hold their battle stations, Thersites countered with raucous jeers, mocking the call to arms, even challenging the king. "He's a spoiled brat," he said, his stubby arms beating the shore air as stunned Greeks guffawed. "Your king already has all the gold and women. Why should we linger another minute for this guy?"

***

Clowns often have a dark side. Mockery can bruise the conscious and dampen duty. Achilles, fed up with the pest, humiliated Thersites until he fell weeping on the beach. God, too, finds little humor in *troublemakers*:

***

"The six things doth the LORD hate: yea, seven are an abomination unto him: A lying tongue ... and he that soweth discord among brethren" (Prov. 6:16–19).

***

Greet Thersites' raucous humor with disgust.

***

"From a certain point of view our real enemy, the true troublemaker, is inside."
Dalai Lama

Day 346

Turmoil (AD 60)
Petronius, *The Satyricon*, 5:63

***

Trimalchio blew out the banquet candles. "I'm gonna tell you all a ghost story," he said in a gravelly voice. The guests shivered mockingly.

"My best friend and I used to be little slave pets of our master. One day, my friend died unexpectantly. At the funeral, as everybody wept quietly, a bunch of witches began to howl, screaming furiously like a pack of hounds after a hare."

Trimalchio paused for effect, watching as the guests squirmed. "Now there was another huge slave from Cappadocia, a giant who could have picked up a mad bull with his right hand. This guy grabbed his sword, ran out to the witch pack, and stabbed one of the demons through her gut."

The banqueters shuddered; the silence palpable.

"As soon as the brute had stabbed the witch, he came stumbling back inside the house and collapsed on his bed, groaning. That night, when his mother came in to give the big fella a night hug, she found nothing but straw. Those damn witches must have made off with the brute and left this bundle of hay."

Trimalchio took a deep breath and closed with this casual remark. "It just goes to show you that witches and ghouls are constantly stirring up *turmoil*, turning the whole world upside down."

***

But wait. I've heard that phrase about *turmoil* before. Follow me to a gathering mob in the marketplace of old Thessalonica. The local officials are dragging Jason, Paul's friend, to court, shouting this charge to the judges:

***

"These men who have turned the world upside down have come here also" (Acts 17:6).

***

Today it's your turn to shake things up for God.

***

"The world is upside down, it's going to take a lot hands to turn it right side up."
Leymah Gbowee

Day 347

Urgency (401 BC)
Xenophon, *Anabasis*, 3:1

***

A dreadful *urgency* befell Xenophon as he tossed fitfully beneath Babylonian stars, unable to sleep. He and his fellow Greek soldiers were trapped in a strange land at the mercy of the Persian king. Their only hope was to bolt for the Black Sea, eight hundred miles away, a perilous journey across impassable rivers. Barbarians and hostile tribes hid in mountain valleys with murderous intent should anyone challenge them.

The Greek army, dispirited and homesick, huddled idly beneath night's drapery, mourning the slaughter of their generals. No one had a plan. Only a few managed to kindle a fire against the cold, and few Greek soldiers bothered to eat. Lying aimlessly on the Babylonian plain, they almost seemed to accept their fate, dreaming of their wives and children at home.

Xenophon, fearful and restless, dreamed that Zeus sent a lightning bolt that burnt his home. He awoke trembling and knew this was a sign to awaken his slumbering heart and find a way out of Babylon.

"Why am I just lying here in the dark? The night is nearly over, and when daybreak comes, the enemy will probably be upon us all. When this happens, the Persians will torture us to death, humiliating the Greek people. Nobody is coming to rescue us, and I'm not getting any younger. I've got to do something now!"

***

Fifteen hundred miles due west of Xenophon's crisis, on the fringe of western Turkey, Paul, too, slept fitfully until an *urgent* God-sent dream propelled him across rugged terrain.

***

"When he had seen the vision, immediately we sought to go into Macedonia..." (Acts 16:10).

***

Dream tonight and rise with urgency.

***

"The trouble is, you think you have time."
Buddha

Day 348

Valor (AD 100)
Juvenal, *Satires*, 1

***

Some mornings it takes courage just to get out of bed knowing what you face at work. Juvenal, a Nero contemporary, observed firsthand courage's risks and rewards. He was just a teenager when the deranged emperor, Nero, bolted to a servant's house outside Rome, running for his life. He hid in a slave's dirty bed beneath the covers, a fool lacking courage.

Juvenal longed for the days when integrity and truth reigned, and people lived without submission to evil. Laying his satirist's pen down, he reveled in the *valor* of Mucius, who had volunteered for a dangerous mission to kill King Porsena, an enemy of Rome. When caught, Mucius held his arm in a fire to show his disdain for death. But Juvenal, though he admired the young soldier's courage, mocked him anyway since such altruism no longer existed in modern corrupt Rome.

"Who cares about Mucius? Try that today and see what happens? You'll be one of Nero's living torches dangling from a stake with your tunic flaming as you struggle and choke to death. Then your corpse will fall to the arena ground, where you'll make a disgusting charcoal furrow in the bloody sand. And what about that fat fellow riding high in his cushioned coach. He poisoned three uncles to get rich. But you better not say a word."

***

When I read the New Testament, I hear chilling words of men and women who took *valor* seriously:

***

"and others were tortured, not accepting their release, so that they might obtain a better resurrection; and others experienced mockings and scourgings, yes, also chains and imprisonment" (Heb. 11:35–36).

***

Make your life count. Live with courage.

***

"Fear is a reaction. Courage is a decision."
Sir Winston Churchill

Day 349

Veil (1184 BC)
Homer, *Iliad*, 5:120–130

***

Diomed stared in disbelief at Pandarus' arrow lodged near his shoulder. He yanked the reins and ceased his Trojan assault. The arrow tip had pierced the metal armor, and blood poured over his cuirass, dripping to the chariot floor. The enemy warriors roared triumphantly as they watched this Greek champion slink off the battlefield.

But Diomed refused death. Fighting delirium, he managed a faint call to a nearby soldier. "Sthenelus, please pull the arrow from my shoulder. I can't die here!"

Sthenelus guided his horses to the dying comrade and, leaping from his chariot, delicately tugged at the arrow, sending blood spurting from the fresh cut.

In a gasping whisper, Diomed prayed: "Please, Athene, help me. Don't let me die here, humiliated on Trojan plains."

The goddess heard the summons and scurried to his side. She touched his hands and feet, imparting life and strength. Her heart broken, she leaned down and offered encouragement. "Dear friend, I am removing the *veil* from your eyes that limit humans. Now, as you race across the battlefield, you can distinguish gods from mortals. This way, you can avoid the deities who meddle in men's affairs."

***

It's rare to see an unveiled face today. Masks are the rage in a world that fears transparency. We seem to live in a Mardi Gras holiday, moving freely from home to work in disguise. I am reminded of Moses, who descended *veiled* from the mountain, only truly revealing himself unveiled before God. I think Paul said it best:

***

"But whenever a person turns to the Lord, the veil is taken away" (2 Cor. 3:16).

***

Today will be your unveiling!

***

"Lift the veil that obscures the heart, and there you will find what you are looking for."
Kabir

Day 350

Vice (AD 120)
Juvenal, *Satire*, 1:70–80

***

They say that crime pays. Ask any godfather gangster, and he'll shake his mangy head in the affirmative. Juvenal, a citizen of Rome, knew this all too well. Everywhere he looked, it seemed as if the racketeers of the capital city were living large. Here's how he put it in one of his stinging satires.

"Virtue around this town is just talk; it shivers in the streets. If you want to be in the limousine crowd, you have to have the guts to think big, commit crimes that will hit the evening news, roll the weighted dice, and cash in big. Everywhere I look in Rome, I see how *vice* pays: nobodies living in palaces, dining on tables with silver goblets embossed with goats, sashaying through lavish gardens that roll on forever down toward the Tiber."

***

Juvenal claimed that the wages of sin are wealth; Paul said the wages of sin was death. I wonder if Paul ever passed Juvenal on the byways of Rome. Their lives did overlap a little. In a way, Paul agreed with the Roman poet. He, too, saw the power of *vice* in the lives of everyday people.

He reminded the Roman saints that there was a time when they had been slaves of sin. But everything changed when Christ joined them on the streets. Now we are slaves to God, he noted with a smile. And the payoff wasn't palaces or embossed silver goblets; instead, believers gain God's gift.

***

"For the wages of sin is death, but the free gift of God is eternal life in Christ Jesus our Lord eternal life in Christ Jesus our Lord" (Rom. 6:23).

***

Get rid of your gangster hat. Exchange *vice* for victory in Jesus.

***

"Monsters are real, and ghosts are real too. They live inside us, and sometimes, they win."
Stephen King

Day 351

Vomit (AD 54)

Tacitus, *The Annals of Imperial Rome*, 12:67

***

Narcissus, Claudius' protector and confidant, had to get out of Rome. He couldn't take the suffocating pressure of endless palace intrigues. Agrippina stifled a smile as the emperor's guardian left.

She made a hasty stop at Locusta's home, the poison wizard, who handed Agrippina the finished product. "Just sprinkle a little on his evening meal," she said, her voice cackling before a flickering flame. "It will work slowly so no one will suspect."

Claudius ate sumptuously that evening, noticing the succulent mushrooms near his plate. Drunk and satiated, he nibbled on a few with no one suspecting. Before long, his stomach bubbling, attendants led him to the bathroom, where the quick evacuation of his bowels seemed to save him.

Agrippina was horrified. With a quick look across the crowded banquet room, she summoned the doctor, Xenophon, who was in on the scheme. "I'll handle it," he whispered darkly. "Don't worry." He rushed to the emperor's side, lying sprawled on the floor, weak and flushed in the face. "You must *vomit*, Claudius. Let me help." He took a poison-tipped feather and tickled the victim's throat. Before the banquet ended, Claudius lay sprawled in vomit, dead.

***

The stench of that backroom disgusts me. The queen's virulent betrayal lingers in the hot air, and even now, the feather haunts me. But I don't have to wander far before a similar *vomit* scene opens before me. The wealthy Laodicean saints clothed in lukewarm spirituality irritated God, who was quick to react.

***

"So because you are lukewarm and neither hot nor cold, I will vomit you out of My mouth" (Rev. 3:16).

***

Are you tempting God's feather? Live honorably.

***

"Each betrayal begins with trust."
Martin Luther

Day 352

***

Voting (432 BC)
Thucydides, *History of the Peloponnesian War*, 1:87

***

The tension in the room was palpable, the stakes high. Archidamus, the Spartan king, spoke with urgent eloquence against war with Athens. "We're not ready!" he shouted bluntly. "They're stronger than you think." His long impassioned monologue finished, he sat down to murmurs and rustling in the seats.

The prime minister, Sthenelaidas, strode impatiently to the podium and called for silence before the *vote*. "What are we stalling for?" he asked, avoiding the king's eyes. "Athens is out of control. I say let's vote for war! All in favor say *war*." A roar of support erupted from the audience. The prime minister quieted the room with difficulty. "All in favor of delay and more negotiations with Athens say *No War*." Again, a loud contingent screamed their response.

Sthenelaidas faltered. Both responses were heated.

"Gentlemen, I want everyone who is for war to stand up and go to that wall. Those opposed to war stand and go to the other wall." As the seas parted in the heated room, the war hawks fluttered loquaciously on the right, far outnumbering the doves. Finally, the moderator swung his gavel like a death bell, and the men exited, rushing for their weapons.

***

Jesus raised His hands, requesting silence. Then with the Sea of Galilee as his backdrop, He stood quietly, aware of the political tensions. The Romans choked the life out of them, and many wanted to rebel. So, choosing His words carefully, He *voted* for Peace.

***

"The gentle people will inherit the earth. What we need now more than anything are peacemakers, for they shall see God" (Matt. 5:5/9).

***

In the sweltering heat of political divide, vote for Peace.

***

"Lord, make me an instrument of thy peace. Where there is hatred, let me sow love."
St. Francis of Assisi

Day 353

Vows (1177 BC)
Virgil, *Aeneid*, 11:1–15

***

Aeneas rose at dawn as Aurora ascended from the ocean mists. Anxious to march against King Latinus, he paused to honor his *vow* to the War-god for the victory just won at the Roman battlements. Tearfully remembering his slain friends, their laughter gone forever, he made time for a proper memorial.

Selecting a giant oak, he lopped off the branches and set the trunk upon a mound. Then, solemnly, he dressed the stripped tree with Mezentius' gleaming armor, that wicked-hearted general slaughtered in hand-to-hand combat. The blood-spattered plumes mingled with broken spears; spindly trophies now silenced forever. The enemy's breastplate, dented and pierced in twelve places, was propped against the other trophies as Aeneas rebuilt the hulk of the man. He set Mezentius' bronze shield, no longer needed, with the accouterments and then hung from the trunk's neck the general's ivory scabbard.

Stepping back, he glowered at the foe as if he still breathed. Anger mingled with sorrow for war's tragedies as he summoned his commanders to gather round. Then he made a rousing speech. "Here lie the spoils of war from this insolent king, Mezentius. He's here before us in these arms I won beneath the ramparts and vowed to present to Ares. Now we must prepare for the final battle against Latinus."

***

Vows, those fox-hole God-pledges we make on bended knee, must be honored. Better to lock lips and keep silent than pledge a frivolous vow. This truth Ananias learned the hard way:

***

"But Peter said, 'Ananias, why has Satan filled your heart to lie to the Holy Spirit and to keep back some of the price of the land?'" (Acts 5:3).

***

Make your vows with Divine solemnity.

***

"This is what we are made for: promises, pledges, and sworn oaths of obedience."
Lauren Oliver

Day 354

***

Vulnerabilities (200 BC)
Plautus, *The Two Bacchises*, Act 2, Scene 3

***

Plautus, the famous comedian playwright of old, wrote about life's everyday risks. Even innocent surprises can catch us off-guard, leaving us *vulnerable* to the unexpected. He demonstrated this with a quaint description familiar to travelers in the ancient world. Disembarking in a strange seaport often had its challenges.

There was an old custom in harbor towns like Epidamnus. The harlots that lived there were constantly squinting at the coast, looking for the arrival of foreign ships. When they spotted one, they scurried around, ordering their servants to check out the tourists.

"These ladies of the night were smart," he wrote. "They trained their servants to look for vulnerable passengers, the ones that looked disoriented. The servants asked a million questions as soon as passengers disembarked, latching on to a gullible one. Then, they would entice the confused businessman into their harlot's web, work him over a bit and spit him out a ruined man. I swear those harlots were worse than pirates with their endless looting and pillaging."

***

I can almost see the apostle Paul stepping off the ship at another old port, Corinth, a classic ancient harbor town teeming with vice and pirates. He was supremely *vulnerable* and probably knew quite a few pesky miscreants. But he never forgot his purpose in life nor allowed himself to wander into the devil's snare.

***

"I came to you in weakness and fear, and with much trembling and my speech and my message were not in plausible words of wisdom.... But he said to me, 'My grace is sufficient for you, for my power is made perfect in weakness'" (1 Cor. 2:3–4).

***

Know your vulnerabilities, but trust in God's protection.

***

"What makes you vulnerable makes you beautiful."
Brene Brown

Day 355

***

Walls (479 BC)
Thucydides, *History of the Peloponnesian War*, 1:90

***

It was a 007 ruse from top to bottom with Themistocles wearing the James Bond mask. His mission was simple: secretly build a wall about Athens before the Spartans caught on to the ruse. His tactics were crude but efficient: stall, stall, stall until the wall was up. While Themistocles visited the Spartan capital to discuss politics, he urged the Athenians to rebuild the *walls* at breakneck speed.

No one was exempt. The women set aside their domestic chores and raced to gather rocks. Children, abandoning their toys, scrambled up and down the rising structure. High-born men, farmers, aristocrats, and servants all labored with one intent—erect the defensive wall before the Spartans could react.

No building was spared, with noblemen conceding their marble estates. Majestic temples that once adorned the classic city streets heeded the call. All fell that the wall might rise. Within one year, the city wall, crammed with odd stones and leftover spoils, stood like a spent sea hag, bent but proud.

***

Look across a distant horizon a mere thirty-five years or so later and see another wall rising in the east. Nobody thought it possible. The *walls* of Jerusalem were nothing but rubble. Listen carefully, and you will hear the voices of men, women, and children singing. Watch as they erect the ancient city's burnt defenses from the northern Sheep Gate to the Valley Gate in the south.

***

"Then they said, 'Let us arise and build.' So they put their hands to the good work.... So the wall was completed on the twenty-fifth of the month Elul, in fifty-two days" (Neh. 2:18).

***

Today you will conquer the impossible task.

***

"Sometimes I've believed as many as six impossible things before breakfast."
Lewis Carroll

Day 356

Warnings (1184 BC)
Virgil, *Aeneid*, 2:40–50

***

High on a hill beneath Troy's citadel, a wooden horse sat, its pinewood ribs breathing silently, waiting. Far off in the watery mists, the ghosts of exhausted Greek soldiers sailed away, weary of war, wanting nothing more than home and hearth.

The Trojans cheered, assuming victory. Opening their heavy gates, Troy's citizens spilled out into the expanse that led to the enemy's shore, where Greek soldiers had once supped and scribbled war plans in the sand.

Flocks of Trojans gathered around the horse, gaping at the colossal trophy. Thymoetes, an elder, urged that the gift be dragged through the city gates and placed triumphantly in the citadel. Others demanded this booby-trap be set afire and tossed into the sea. As the arguments unraveled, Apollo's priest, Laocoon, came tumbling down from Troy's metropolis shouting warnings. "It's a trap. Can't you see, or have you all gone stark mad? There's either a tangle of Greek soldiers inside or some mechanism to take down our walls. Destroy it now!"

Before the echoing words could settle, he spun his great spear at the monster's flank, watching it puncture the steed's belly, the shaft quivering. The horse seemed to grunt at the concussion, the hollow womb quivering as everyone weighed the *warning*.

***

Ignoring *warnings* in our lives can often be fatal. We pretend the whispering angels know nothing, preferring to skip down endless dead ends. Jeremiah warned his recalcitrant people repeatedly to accept Babylon's role in the world.

***

"So do not listen to the words of the prophets who speak to you, saying, 'You will not serve the king of Babylon,' for they prophesy a lie to you" (Jer. 27:14).

***

Humble yourself, today, and welcome the warning.

***

"Everything we know and love is at risk if we continue to ignore the warnings."
Laurie David

Day 357

Weaknesses (AD 8)
Ovid, *Metamorphoses*, 12:120–145

***

Cygnus smirked as Achilles' gleaming spear, cast with skill, merely bounced off his breastplate. "Nothing can hurt me." he boasted. "I have no *weaknesses*. I wear a golden crested helmet and hold a hollow shield on my left arm, but I don't need them. As the son of Neptune, I am invulnerable to any weapon!" Cygnus, to prove his point, tossed his armor down on the battlefield taunting his opponent.

Achilles, enraged, reined in his chariot's stallions and, with full force, hurled another spear that crumbled before the brilliant warrior. Befuddled, Achilles questioned himself for a moment. "Are my spears defective? Has my strength waned?" But each inquiry met logic, and he knew it was none of these things. Still, his enemy stood before him untouched, gloating.

Refusing to yield to the braggart, Achilles leaped from his lofty chariot and lunged at Cygnus in mortal, hand-to-hand combat. He attacked the one vulnerability he saw—the temples. With shield and sword hilt, he hammered his foe's face without rest, pressing relentlessly for the kill.

Cygnus stumbled backward under the assault. His head caved beneath the barrage as dark shadows danced before his eyes. Falling back, he collapsed, bleeding, upon a boulder.

***

Save yourself from endless battlefield humiliations and admit your *weaknesses* now. We all have them. Paul, unlike Cygnus, knew his vulnerable points. He prayed daily about them and even learned to exalt them:

***

"And he has said to me, 'My grace is sufficient for you, for power is perfected in weakness.' Most gladly, therefore I will rather boast about my weaknesses, so that the power of Christ may dwell in me" (2 Cor. 12:9).

***

Affirm your weaknesses and live with confidence.

***

"What makes you vulnerable makes you beautiful."
Brene Brown

Day 358

Wealth (AD 120)
Juvenal, *Satires*, 3:211–220

***

The news spread as fast as the fire. Asturicus' mansion had burnt to the ground a little after midnight, Roman time. A Persian rags to riches story, Asturicus had made it big in a city that rewards ingenuity and shady dealings. Aghast at the fire's dark wrath, Asturicus stood forlorn amid the smoke and wondered who would replace his burnt statue by Euphranor or all those impeccable bronzes sacred to Asian gods.

As morning's fingers stretched silently across the Tiber River, citizens woke to the smell of disaster. Criers ran through the seven hills shouting frenzied tales of the night's tragedy. Rome instantly convulsed with mothers disheveling themselves and many august leaders dressing in black. All city courts adjourned for the day as a heavy sorrow shrouded the streets. Asturicus, the *wealthiest* man in the neighborhood, had lost it all!

But then, amid communal tears, the miraculous happened. One by one, friends and strangers alike began to bring treasures to the smoldering site. A cart laden with pristine marble arrived with cherished artworks and pledges of a building fund. A bushel of silver coins lay at the feet of a newly arrived bust of Minerva.

***

Wealth and status saved this esteemed Persian magnate. But just across town, where the slums had tumbled beneath the fire's breath, no one stirred or cared. I can't help but think about the wealthy young man whom Jesus loved.

***

"Just give away your fortune and follow me," He urged him. "But at these words, he was saddened, and he went away grieving, for he was one who owned much property" (Mk. 10: 22).

***

Let the mansion burn. Discipleship summons.

***

"He who wishes to be rich in a day will be hanged in a year." *Leonardo Da Vinci*

Day 359

***

Weariness (401 BC)
Xenophon, *Anabasis*, 5:8

***

A fierce, wintery wind whipped the beaten soldiers as they trudged through the Pontic Mountains toward the Black Sea. Artaxerxes had chased them for weeks, exhausting the Greek army. One by one, the Greeks fell, frostbitten and defeated by winter's merciless breath.

Xenophon, the general, saw one man unable to go on. He ordered a fellow soldier to carry him. Begrudgingly, the private obeyed, lifting the dying warrior to his shoulder. Later in the day, Xenophon came back and loomed over a grave, freshly dug by this very private. At first, the general commended him for the act of decency. But then the corpse moved, lifting his frostbitten leg. "He's still alive!" shouted Xenophon. "You were going to bury the man alive!"

"He will die anyway," said the soldier. "I'm *weary*, and I'm not carrying him anymore. Let this grave take him. It's inevitable."

When the general heard this, he leaped down from his horse and struck the private with his fist. "We're all going to die, so are you going to bury us too?" shouted the general in disgust.

***

In 1941, the founder of Boys Town, Father Flanagan, saw a drawing of a *weary* boy carrying a younger disabled boy on his back. The caption beneath the picture said this: "He ain't heavy,

Mr., he's my brother." The priest commissioned a drawing and placed it on the Boys Town campus.

Paul said it best:

***

"Bear one another's burdens, and thereby fulfill the law of Christ.... And let us not be weary in well doing: for in due season we shall reap, if we faint not" (Gal. 6:2/9).

***

Put the shovel down! Don't let weariness win.

***

"I know not age, nor weariness, nor defeat."
Rose Kennedy

Day 360

***

Wishes (AD 10)
Ovid, *Metamorphoses*, 12:189–210

***

Caenis was the loveliest girl in Thessaly. Heads turned when she waltzed through the local villages beneath Mt. Olympus. Suitors across the Thessalian Valley came calling, hoping for a chance. Caenis, however, was not interested in marriage, preferring to stroll the lonely shores of the Aegean where the soft waves soothed her and stirred quiet dreams.

Unaware that Neptune watched these daily excursions, she walked contentedly by the sea, selecting shells and whispering to the warm winds. One day, however, Neptune stalked her as she studied the hues of a starfish washed ashore. Tossing his flashing trident aside, he lunged, dragging her down upon the white sand, stealing Caenis' innocence and ripping her soul apart.

When the sirens subsided, and Neptune sat breathing heavily, he smiled. Caenis, disheveled and weeping softly, gathered her torn robe, wondering. As she stared blankly at sea, Neptune, pleased with the transaction, offered a consolation. "Ask me for anything. Whatever you *wish*, I shall grant it."

She studied his flushed face with disgust and then replied. "I never want to be hurt like this again. Make me strong and invincible."

Neptune agreed, promising that she would never again fall prey to violence.

***

Wishes come rarely to us who travel life's difficult paths. When we do stumble upon them, great care must be taken. Salome was granted a rare request, and she abused its power:

***

"and when the daughter of Herodias herself came in and danced, she pleased Herod and his dinner guests; and the king said to the girl, 'Ask me for whatever you want and I will give it to you...And she said, 'The head of John the Baptist'"(Mk. 6:22/24).

***

Make a joyful wish today. Change your life forever.

***

"Where there is great love, there are always wishes."
Willa Cather

Day 361

Wonder (15 BC)
Josephus, *Antiquities of the Jews*, 15.9.6

***

Josephus, a first-century contemporary of the apostle Paul, felt
wonder when he wrote about the spectacular city of Caesarea:

"Herod discovered a beautiful seaside place that he thought
well-suited for a city dedicated to Caesar. He put his whole heart
into the project, using white stone and other valuable materials
to adorn the city with an exquisite palace and a spectacular
harbor as big as Athens. He built dwellings of polished stone
in a circle around the harbor and then constructed a temple of
Caesar that merchants could see from great distances as their
ships approached. South of the port, he placed a theater of stone
and then farther back, an amphitheater with a view of the sea."

***

The harbor lingers today beneath the crystal water just off the
current shoreline in Israel. Stand quietly by the lapping sea,
and you can still hear the heartbeats of Cornelius' family as
they listened to Peter's gospel message. Breaking with Jewish
tradition, Peter entered Caesarea, passing the 4000-seat arena
and the hippodrome where crazed crowds screamed for their
chariot heroes.

When evening's glow had settled in over the boisterous city,
Cornelius, standing at his door, greeted Peter and his associates,
who came in obedience to a heavenly vision. Off at the harbor's
edge, Herod's magnificent lighthouse spread hope for mariners

searching for the harbor's entrance. Within Cornelius' home, another light flickered with the joyful news of resurrection, redemption, and *wonder*.

***

"While Peter was still speaking these words, the Holy Spirit fell upon all who those who were listening to the message" (Acts 10:44).

***

Step outside your house this morning, stare up at the sky— and wonder!

***

"Wonder is the first of all the passions."
Rene Descartes

Day 362

***

Words (664 BC)
Herodotus, *The Persian Wars*, 2:2

***

The king of Egypt summoned the little kids to court. Raised as orphans by a kind shepherd, the two children had never spoken a word or heard a word from anyone. They were like sheep raised in the flock who wandered the fields daily.

One day the shepherd heard the twins saying a *word* formed first among the flock of sheep grazing on a mountain slope. "Bekos," they said playfully to the animals who knew them best. The shepherd heard this first oracle and raced to the king with the news.

"Bring them to me at once," he commanded.

The shepherd obliged, and when the children stepped upon the polished palace floor and ambled toward the great throne, they repeated the word heard only by the ewes, "bekos."

The king called for his linguists. "What are the children saying, and what language is this that they instinctively speak?"

"It is a Phrygian word, my lord."

"What does it mean" pressed the king.

"It means *bread*," they replied.

***

What will your first *words* be today? Will they be pleasing to the king? Will they be sounds of inner joy and peace or a phrase tinged with bitterness?

Herodotus told his readers that he had heard this story from priests of Hephaestus' temple in Memphis, Egypt. It reminds us that first words are powerful, as another king knew. It was David who said,

***

"Let the words of my mouth and the meditation of my heart be acceptable in Your sight, O LORD, my rock and my Redeemer" (Ps. 19:14).

***

The King is waiting. What will you say today?

***

"Quiet the mind, and the soul will speak."
Ma Jaya Sati Bhagavati

Day 363

Worry (AD 120)
Juvenal, *Satires*, 3:260–266

***

The man, dead since morning, sat huddled and shivering on the banks of the Styx. Charon, the ferryman, fought the river's murky turbulence as he steered his boat shoreward. An ugly wind howled, yanking at the ferryman's pole. Charon held it firmly and toiled onward, anxious to fill the craft with his next load of terrified passengers.

The dead man in our tale longed for his home, its cozy images fading fast. He could still see his boys' fleeting movements, who rushed around the kitchen as if nothing was amiss. Several servants washed dishes following the wake while others puffed a fading fire. He could hear the house's clatter faintly as his wife directed servants to gather spent towels and flasks of oil used earlier to anoint her husband's body.

Now, cowered in the river's spray with only a few streaks of moonlight to guide his eyes riverward, he searched for the ferry. Suddenly, a dreadful *worry* horrified him: he could not find the coin! Where was the copper for the boat's captain? Had his wife forgotten? His weary fingers scrambled, searching desperately among his shredded tunic as the ferry slid through a muddy whirlpool toward the shore.

***

Worry comes in various shades of black, taunting us often on our daily trek through life: a confession, a regret, a failure, and its hollow wake. All too often, we sit with the terrified character above, fearful of the unknown, dreading the ferry.

But wait! Another boat approaches, its captain smiling, His arms outstretched. He calls your name. "Come to Me," he cries.

***

"Come to Me, all who are weary and heavy-laden, and I will give you rest" (Matt. 11:28).

***

Sigh, and be happy today. Jesus' boat has landed.

***

"Fear God, dread nought."
Sir Winston Churchill

Day 364

Worship (AD 40)
Suetonius, *Lives of the Caesars*, 4:22

Caligula smiled demurely as Rome's visitors to the Temple of Castor and Pollux slipped past him on the entrance steps. Standing between the Twins, he greeted each guest with a divine glare that demanded obsequious submission. His see-through robe made of the sheerest Koan silk, tinged in evocative purple, floated upon his figure like gossamer feathers. His eyes were painted with dark, alluring mascara accentuating his blond wig, flinging curls over his thin shoulders.

Caligula mastered these sartorial skills from his mother, Agrippina. She had often gathered her children and followed Germanicus off to distant battlefields. There, his mother would dress him in Roman military garb sewn specially for her little soldier. As emperor of Rome, he preferred the effeminate silks from Cos as he stood in the temple each morning demanding *worship*.

Beside him, a golden statue of himself, dressed riotously in the exact silken robes, forced submissive glances. Drifting about the temple's entranceway were exotic flamingos, peacocks, black grouse, guinea hens, and pheasant, all destined for slaughter upon the altar to Caligula, Rome's living god.

Perhaps you smile at this flamboyant ego fluttering in history's breeze. But many today strut modern paths with distorted personal assessments. It wasn't that long ago that Nebuchadnezzar made a statue of gold and dared his people to ignore it. The fiery furnace burned daily for Daniel and anyone else who mocked the call to *worship* the king:

***

"when you hear the sound of the horn, pipe, lyre, trigon, harp, bagpipe, and every kind of music, you are to fall down and worship the golden image that King Nebuchadnezzar has set up" (Dan. 3:5).

***

Worship wisely. God is watching.

***

"Worship is an act of war against the enemy of our hearts."
Holley Gerth

Day 365

Wounded (55 BC)
Catullus, *Poems*, 30

***

Catullus, the young sensitive poet of the classical age, can tell you about wounds. One of his lawyer friends, Alfenus, humiliated him. It was raw betrayal darkly shaded with callousness.

Searching his former friend's once loyal eyes he found them empty, distant.

Don't you care anymore?" he pleaded. I was one of your intimate friends, a bosom buddy.

"How can you look past me as if I don't matter anymore?"

Alfenus merely shrugged in disinterested silence as if he was plotting another court case, his mind far away. When he did manage to drizzle out a few platitudes, they seemed like a hot desert wind.

Catullus tried to push back, but to no avail. "Alfenus, you lied about me to win a little prestige from your stupid associates. You're such a loser. You won't get away with it. Heaven doesn't like cheaters like you."

But try as he might Catullus couldn't seem to get over it. He twitched with emotional agony:

"Damn! Now I can't trust anybody. You had all my respect, and look how you *wounded* me!"

Catullus stood to go but hurled one last warning at his former confidant: "Maybe you can walk away, forget our friendship, but the gods won't forget. Never!"

***

Paul, too, was *wounded* when one of his closest friends deserted him as he languished in a Roman jail. Catullus seethed with disillusionment, while Paul was quick to forgive as he said with a quivering pen:

***

"For Demas, having loved this present world, has deserted me... At my first defense no one supported me, but all deserted me.... May it not be counted against them" (2 Tim. 4:9/16).

***

Sprinkle some forgiveness on your wounds. Move on.

***

"Hearts live by being wounded."
Oscar Wilde

Day 366

Wrestling (AD 10)
Ovid, *Metamorphoses*, 9:1–126

***

Hercules was tired of talking; he wasn't much with words. He would *wrestle* for the woman. Winner takes all. Achelous, the river god, agreed.

The two circled, warily staring. Hercules stooped and grabbed a fistful of dirt. Flinging it upon his opponent so he could grip him better, he likewise sprinkled it upon his own bulging muscles.

Hercules lunged first, gripping Achelous by the neck, his feet shifting here and there. But the river god was heavy and held like a sea wall before heavy storms. The tangled hold loosened, and they circled again. Both gripped simultaneously as their foreheads touched, each sweating angrily. Three times Hercules tried to throw his challenger to the ground. Wearying quickly, Achelous could hold no longer as Hercules swung him wildly in the air. Leaping upon the god's back, he forced Achelous' face into the dirt.

Utterly exhausted, Achelous played his last hand. Changing into a snake and then a bull, he danced and darted before his enemy, all to no avail. Hercules only scoffed. Slamming Achelous to the ground, he yanked the horn from his head and flung it to the Naiads, who filled it with fruit and flowers. Achelous, bloodied and beaten, slinked away beneath the waves, conceding defeat, embarrassed, but without shame.

***

Wrestling is not an option. Circling about you daily are rulers of darkness, wicked principalities whose sole task is to pin your soul to the mat, to force surrender squeals.

***

"For we wrestle not against flesh and blood, but against principalities, against powers, against the rulers of the darkness of this world, against spiritual wickedness in high place" (Eph. 6:12).

***

Be ready. You will wrestle today.

***

"Once you've wrestled, everything else in life is easy."
Dan Gable

References

All classical texts cited in this work come from the *Loeb Classical Library*, Cambridge, Mass. Harvard University Press.

Index of Authors

Aeschylus, (525–456 BC), known as the father of tragedy was born in Eleusis, northwest of Athens. In 490 BC he fought against Darius I of Persia at the Battle of Marathon. He wrote nearly ninety plays, but only seven have survived intact including *Seven Against Thebes*.

Appian, (AD 95–165), was a Greek historian, born in Alexandria who gained Roman citizenship and flourished during the reigns of Trajan Hadrian, and Antoninus Pius. He served as an advocate in the province of Aegyptus and pleaded cases in Rome as well. His *Roman History* covers Rome's civil wars.

Apuleius, (AD 124–170), whose full name was Lucius Apuleius Madaurensis, lived in the Roman province of Numidia (Algeria). He wrote the only surviving Latin novel, the *Metamorphoses*, also known as *The Golden Ass*. He was an initiate in several cults and supposedly used magic to gain the attention and fortune of a wealthy widow.

Aristophanes, (446–386 BC), was a comic Athenian playwright, whose power of ridicule was feared by influential people of his day. Eleven of his forty plays are extant such as *Wasps, Peace, Clouds*, and the *Acharnians*.

Avianus, date uncertain but possibly in the age of the Antonines (AD 96–192) or as late as the sixth century AD. He wrote fables that soon became popular as a school-book.

Babrius, (AD 200 or earlier), wrote Greek fables much in the form of Aesop's fables.

Caesar, (100–44 BC), was a Roman general and statesman. He fought valiantly in the *Gallic Wars* and eventually became dictator of Rome.

Cassius Dio, (AD 155–235), was a Roman historian and senator. He wrote a *Roman History* in 80 books over a twenty-two-year period. Although he was a Roman citizen, he wrote his histories in Greek.

Catullus, (84–54 BC), was a Latin poet in the late Roman Republic. He focused his writing on personal life rather than classical heroes. He fell passionately in love with a married woman named Clodia Metelli whom he calls "Lesbia" in his poems.

Euripides, (480–406 BC), was a tragedian of classical Athens. He wrote over ninety plays but only eighteen have survived such as *Alcestis, Medea, Hippolytus, Heracleidae* and *Alcestis*. He wrote some of his plays in a cave on Salamis.

Herodotus, (484–425 BC), was an ancient Greek historian and geographer who was born in Halicarnassus. Cicero called him "The Father of History," (Cicero, *De Legibus*, 1:5). One of his works is titled *The Persian Wars*.

Homer, (eighth century BC), is the reputed author of the *Iliad* and the *Odyssey* which form the foundation of ancient Greek literature. The Iliad covers the final year of the Trojan War.

Horace, (65–8 BC), lived in the time of Augustus and was the leading Roman lyric poet of his day. His writings, such as the *Satires* and the *Odes*, were full of charm and wit and had a way of plucking on one's heartstrings. He told the world much about himself, his character and his way of life.

Josephus, (AD 35–100), was a Jewish historian and military leader born in Jerusalem. His mother claimed royal ancestry and his father descended from a priestly line. He wrote the *Jewish War* and *Jewish Antiquities*. Freed by Vespasian after the conflict, he assumed the emperor's family name of Flavius.

Juvenal, (AD 55–127) He is the author of several *Satires* many critical of ancient Rome. He may have been the adopted son of a nobleman and perhaps practiced rhetoric for legal purposes and amusement.

Livy, (59 BC–AD 17), was a Roman historian who wrote a history of Rome titled *From the Founding of the City*, (*Ab Urbe Condita*). He was born in northern Italy in what is now Padua. He had a mild temperament, opposed to violence. He spent a lot of time in Rome devoted much of his life to the writing of history.

Lucretius, (99–55 BC), was a Roman poet and philosopher. He wrote *On the Nature of Things*, (De Rerum Natura), a book promoting epicureanism. Jerome suggests that Lucretius maybe had bouts of insanity and was driven mad by a love potion and took his life at the age of 44.

Ovid, (43 BC–AD 17), was a Roman poet who wrote during the reign of Augustus. Although very popular as a writer, he was banished to the Black Sea area where he remained for a decade until his death. He wrote a 15-book mythological narrative called *Metamorphoses*.

Pausanias, (AD 110–180), was a Greek traveler famous for his *Description of Ancient Greece*. His simple writing style was full of many pleasurable digressions.

Petronius, (AD 27–66), was a playboy of types in Nero's court. Many believe him to the be the writer of the *Satyricon*, a satirical novel set in Nero's day.

Phaedrus, (15 BC–AD 50 or 60), was the first writer to translate *Aesop's Fables* into Latin.

Plato, (428–348 BC), was a Greek philosopher from Athens who established an Academy on the outskirts of Athens when he was about forty years old. He wrote *Republic* around 375 BC in which he discussed the order and character of the just city-state.

Plautus, (254–184 BC), was a Roman playwright who favored comedies. Originally a stage-carpenter, he learned to love the theater and began writing his own plays which became very popular.

Plutarch, (AD 46–119), was a priest at the temple of Apollo in Delphi. He wrote *Parallel Lives*, a series of biographies comparing illustrious Greeks with Romans.

Propertius, (50–15 BC), was a Latin elegiac poet who had Maecenas as a patron. He wrote four books of *Elegies*. His early love poems were dedicated to an older woman named Cynthia.

Seneca, (4 BC–AD 65), was a Roman writer and philosopher who served as Nero's advisor. Falsely accused in a conspiracy against Nero, he took his own life in stoical fashion. He wrote several plays such *Phaedra* and *Medea*.

Sophocles, (497–406 BC), was one of the three Greek tragedians. Only seven of his 120 plays have survived such as *Oedipus Tyrannus, Antigone, Oedipus at Colonus*. He competed in thirty competitions at Athens and won twenty-four.

Suetonius, (AD 69–122), was a Roman historian during the early Imperial era of the Roman Empire. He wrote biographies of 12 successive Roman rulers from Julius Caesar to Domitian titled *The Lives of the Caesars* (De Vita Caesarum).

Tacitus, (AD 56–120), was widely regarded as the greatest of the Roman historians. His two major works, the *Annals* and the *Histories* describe the emperors of the first century.

Thucydides, (460–400 BC), was an Athenian historian and general. He is famous for his *History of the Peloponnesian War* in which he relates the struggle between Sparta and Athens. One ancient anecdote claims that as a young boy he wept when hearing Herodotus speak about historical observations.

Tibullus, (55–19 BC), was a writer of Latin *elegies* of which several are extant. He lost his considerable estate during the confiscations of Mark Antony and Octavian in 41 BC. Tibullus died almost immediately after Virgil leaving a deep impression on Rome.

Virgil, (70–19 BC), was a poet of the Augustan period. His is known for his epic *Aeneid* and he is ranked as one of Rome's greatest poets. Considered shy and aloof during childhood, he lived much of his life as an invalid.

Xenophon, (430–355), was a Greek military leader and historian born in Athens. His historical work, *Anabasis*, tells of his adventures with the 10,000 after Cyrus the Younger's death in Persia.

Bible Index

***

Old Testament

***

***

***

Leviticus 19:32, Elderly

***

Numbers 5:23–24, Suspicion

***

Joshua 1:9, Panic
Joshua 3:1, Crossings
Joshua 7:25, Guilt
Joshua 24:14–16, Decisions
Joshua 24:15, Choices

***

Judges 7:4, Cowardice
Judges 14:14, Riddles
Judges 16:19, Treason

***

Ruth 3:8, Dreams

***

1 Samuel 9:2, Admiration
1 Samuel 12:12, Dissatisfied
1 Samuel 17:32, Fearless
1 Samuel 17:40, Bravado
1 Samuel 17:49, Braggadocious

1Samuel 20:16–17, Alliances
1 Samuel 20:41, Partings
1 Samuel 21:13, Disguises
1 Samuel 23:7, Trapped
1 Samuel 31:5, Suicide
1 Samuel 31:8–10, Repercussions

***

2 Samuel 6:14–16, Inhibitions
2 Samuel 6:15, Procession
2 Samuel 11:4, Mistakes
2 Samuel 12:16–17, Loss
2 Samuel 12:7, Revelations
2 Samuel 15:23, Homeless
2 Samuel 16:11, Humiliation
2 Samuel 16:13, Nuisance

***

I Kings 3:34, Heartless
1 Kings 18:27, Bluffing
1 Kings 18:37, Intractable
1 Kings 21:8, Letters

***

2 Kings 5:14, Baptism
2 Kings 6:22-23, Enemies
2 Kings 20:6, Rejuvenation
2 Kings 22:11, News

***

Daniel 1:5, School
Daniel 3:17–18, Sycophant
Daniel 3:5, Worship

***

Jonah 1:15, Overboard
Jonah 1:17, Serendipity

New Testament

***

Matthew 24:7–8, Birth
Matthew 26:15, Tragedy
Matthew 26–27, Chalice
Matthew 26:35, Loyalty
Matthew 26:39, Pleading
Matthew 26:45–46, Rousing
Matthew 26:48, Kiss
Matthew 26:52, Revenge
Matthew 26:74, Oaths
Matthew 27:23, Charade
Matthew 27:24, Indifference
Matthew 28:20, Promises

**

Mark 2:16, Frustration
Mark 4:39, Tempest
Mark 4:39, Storms
Mark 5:2, Descents
Mark 6:22, Wishes
Mark 6:22, Dancing
Mark 9:34, Greatness
Mark 10:22, Wealth
Mark 10:22, Sacrifice
Mark 10:49, Mercy
Mark 12:43, Destitute
Mark 13:28–29, Deterrents
Mark 14:55, Instigator

**

Luke 1:37, Impossible
Luke 4:29, Hostility
Luke 4:39, Healing

Luke 7:13, Pity
Luke 10:32, Empathy
Luke 10:33, Compassion
Luke 10:40, Impatience
Luke 10:41, Pleasures
Luke 11:39, Rituals
Luke 12:2, Secrets
Luke 12:41, Oblivious
Luke 15:20, Embraces
Luke 15:28, Bitterness
Luke 15:8, Searching
Luke 15:8, Reunion
Luke 18:13, Invocation
Luke 19:35, Privilege
Luke 19:41, Concern,
Luke 22:19, Remembrances
Luke 22:44, Garden
Luke 22:60–62, Betrayal

***

John 1:47, Integrity
John 3:29–30, Humblebrag
John 4:15, Mirage
John 4:19, Sinking
John 8:6, Alphabet
John 8:12, Illumination
John 11:35–36, Affliction
John 11:35–36, Grief
John 11:44, Tombs
John 12:3, Perfume
John 12:5–6, Deception
John 14:1–2, Mansions
John 14:2, Death

John 14:3, Absence
John 14:2–5, Departures
John 14:27, Peace
John 15:13, Friendship
John 18:10–11, Restraint
John 18:25, Lies
John 19:18, Portrait
John 19:30, Soul
John 19:34, Blood
John 20:19, Invisible
John 20:28, Scuttlebutt

***

Acts 1:8, Ascensions
Acts 1:9-12, Starting
Acts 5:3, Vows
Acts 5:39, Fighting
Acts 7:59–60, Petition
Acts 7:60, Execution
Acts 9:18, Breakthrough
Acts 9:25, Rescued,
Acts 9:25–26, Escape
Acts 9:8, Beginnings
Acts 10:44, Wonder
Acts 14:28, Resilience
Acts 16:15, Consequences
Acts 16:7–8, Barriers
Acts 16:9–10, Urgency
Acts 17:23, Atheist
Acts 17:6, Turmoil
Acts 18:24, Eloquence
Acts 19:19, Magic
Acts 20:10, Accidents

***

***

***

***

James 2:4, Seating
James 3:8, Poison
James 4:2, Feuds
James 4:13–14, Reaper

***

1 Peter 2:5, Community
1 Peter 2:9, Chosen
1 Peter 2:21, Imitation
1 Peter 3:3, Adornment
1 Peter 3:3–4, Grasshoppers
1 Peter 3:5:4, Recognition

***

1 John 1:9, Reprisals
1 John 2:19, Desertion

***

Revelation 1:16–17, Paralysis
Revelation 3:16, Vomit
Revelation 3:21, Triumphs
Revelation 7:17, Heaven
Revelation 9:2, Bottomless
Revelation 20:12, Books
Revelation 21:2, City
Revelation 21:2, Bride
Revelation 21:3, Jerusalem
Revelation 21:4, Exits

MANTRA
BOOKS

EASTERN RELIGION & PHILOSOPHY
We publish books on Eastern religions and philosophies. Books
that aim to inform and explore the various traditions that
began in the East and have migrated West.
If you have enjoyed this book, why not tell other readers by
posting a review on your preferred book site.

The Less Dust the More Trust
Participating in The Shamatha Project, Meditation and Science
Adeline van Waning, MD PhD
The inside-story of a woman participating in frontline
meditation research, exploring the interfaces of mind-practice,
science and psychology.
Paperback: 978-1-78099-948-7 ebook: 978-1-78279-657-2

I Know How To Live, I Know How To Die
The Teachings of Dadi Janki: A warm, radical, and life-
affirming view of who we are, where we come from, and what
time is calling us to do
Neville Hodgkinson
Life and death are explored in the context of frontier science
and deep soul awareness.
Paperback: 978-1-78535-013-9 ebook: 978-1-78535-014-6

Living Jainism
An Ethical Science
Aidan Rankin, Kanti V. Mardia
A radical new perspective on science rooted in intuitive
awareness and deductive reasoning.
Paperback: 978-1-78099-912-8 ebook: 978-1-78099-911-1

Ordinary Women, Extraordinary Wisdom
The Feminine Face of Awakening
Rita Marie Robinson
A collection of intimate conversations with female spiritual
teachers who live like ordinary women, but are engaged
with their true natures.
Paperback: 978-1-84694-068-2 ebook: 978-1-78099-908-1

The Way of Nothing
Nothing in the Way
Paramananda Ishaya
A fresh and light-hearted exploration of the amazing reality of
nothingness.
Paperback: 978-1-78279-307-6 ebook: 978-1-78099-840-4

Readers of ebooks can buy or view any of these bestsellers by
clicking on the live link in the title. Most titles are published
in paperback and as an ebook. Paperbacks are available in
traditional bookshops. Both print and ebook formats are
available online.

Find more titles and sign up to our readers' newslett er at
http://www.johnhuntpublishing.com/mind-body-spirit. Follow
us on Facebook at https://www.facebook.com/OBooks and
Twitter at https://twitter.com/obooks.